MAKING HISTORY

COMPLETE JUNIOR CYCLE HISTORY

Dermot Lucey

Gill Education
Hume Avenue
Park West
Dublin 12
www.gilleducation.ie

Gill Education in an imprint of M.H. Gill & Co.

ISBN: 978 07171 79756

Design: Design Image
Illustrations: Jeremy Bays, Andriy Yankovskyy and Oxford Designers & Illustrators
Picture research: Claire O'Rourke

At the time of going to press, all web addresses were active and contained information relevant to the topics in this book. Gill Education does not, however, accept responsibility for the content or views contained on these websites. Content, views and addresses may change beyond the publisher or author's control. Students should always be supervised when reviewing websites.

The paper used in this book is made from the wood pulp of managed forests. For every tree felled, at least one tree is planted, thereby renewing natural resources.

Contents

01

HOW DO HISTORIANS AND ARCHAEOLOGISTS FIND OUT ABOUT THE PAST?

LO 1.1, 1.2, 1.4, 1.5, 1.6, 1.7, 1.8

HISTORICAL ENQUIRY

Who shot Michael Collins?

ARCHAEOLOGICAL INVESTIGATION

Who was Ötzi the Iceman?

What you will learn ...

- ⊘ Explain the meaning of 'history'
- ⊘ Research the job of the historian
- ⊘ Distinguish between historical sources
- ⊘ List where historians find sources
- ⊘ Consider controversial issues in history
- ⊘ Develop a sense of historical empathy
- ⊘ Appreciate the contribution of archaeology and new technology to historical enquiry
- ⊘ Investigate a repository of historical evidence

🗝 KEY WORDS

- History
- Primary
- Bias
- Timeline
- Libraries
- Prehistory
- Tree-ring dating
- Radiocarbon dating

- Sources
- Secondary
- Interpretations
- Museums
- Archaeology
- Excavate
- Dendrochronology
- Pollen analysis

- Evidence
- Viewpoint
- Chronology
- Archives
- Artefact
- Stratigraphy

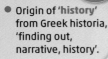

- Explain the meaning of 'history'
- Explain how historians group sources
- Identify where historians get their sources
- Explore how sources can present problems for historians

How do Historians Find Out about the Past?

What is history?

History is the **story of the past** based on **evidence**.

The evidence is provided by **sources**.

Sources come in many different forms or types.

KEY WORD

- Origin of **'history'** from Greek historia, 'finding out, narrative, history'.

Written
Documents
Newspapers
Texts
Emails

Visual
Photographs
Videos
Paintings

Aural
Sounds of
the past

Oral
Interviews
Recordings

Tactile (by touch or feel)
Artefacts (objects)
Buildings
Monuments
Models

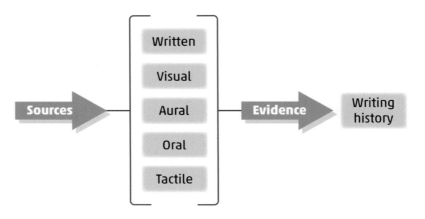

How are sources grouped together?

Sources are divided into **primary** and **secondary sources**.

Primary sources are sources which come **from the time that is being studied**. They are **first-hand accounts** of what happened.

These can be original documents, photographs, newspaper reports, diaries, emails, texts, tweets, videos, statistics, songs and so on.

Secondary sources are sources which come **from after the time which is being studied**. They are **based** on primary sources or other secondary sources.

This textbook is an example of a secondary source. Why?

Primary or Secondary source?

Go onto YouTube and look up 'Miss Stout's History Class Primary or Secondary Source?'

Primary Source	Secondary Source
Anne Frank, *The Diary of a Young Girl* (Penguin, London, 2011)	Melissa Müller, *Anne Frank, The Biography* (Bloomsbury Publishing, London, 2013)

Q

Which of the following are primary sources and which are secondary sources? Explain your answers.

1. A Roman general, who wrote an account of his life when he was old.
2. The clothes you are wearing.
3. The desk you are sitting at.
4. Your teacher tells you a story about his/her grandparents' childhood.
5. A news story on Twitter, Facebook or Snapchat.
6. A video of a concert, shot on a smartphone.
7. An old person, living in the last century, who was interviewed about memories of his/her childhood.
8. An Irish person, who lived in Ireland all his/her life, tells the story about the sinking of the Titanic.

Look at the pictures below. Which of these are primary sources and which are secondary?

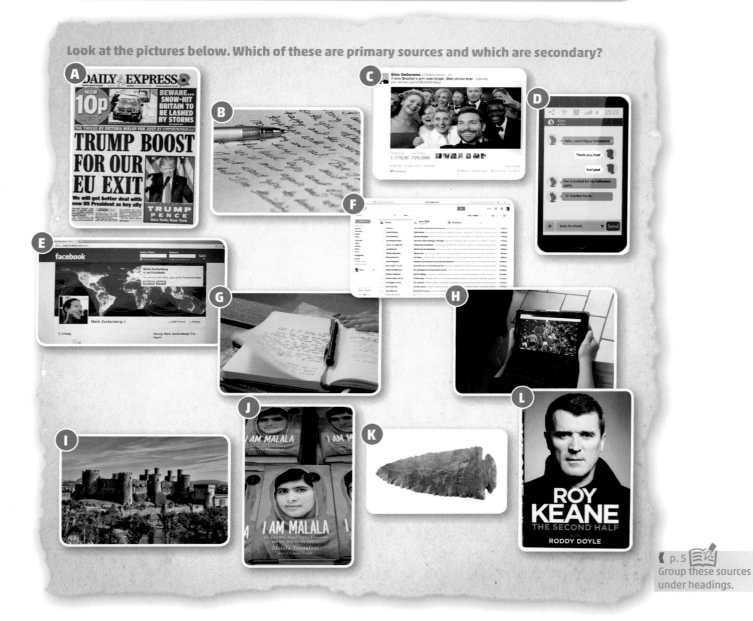

p. 5
Group these sources under headings.

How do historians use sources?

Historians use information (**evidence**) from sources to tell the story of the past.
Historians must distinguish between **fact** (what happened) and **opinion** (what people think about what happened).

Historians can tell **different stories** (different **interpretations**) about the same events because their sources may be different. Historians may also tell different stories because of their own **viewpoint** (opinion).

Their **viewpoint** can be based on **facts** so it can be **objective** (*not* based on personal feeling or opinion). Historians try to be objective. In some cases though, a historian's viewpoint can be **biased** (based on personal opinion or prejudice).

Sources, too, can be **biased** or **one-sided accounts** of what happened. They can **favour** one group or person over another, or they can be **prejudiced** against one group or another.

Some sources are deliberately written or created to persuade people to support a cause or a person. This is called **propaganda**.

Sources can also have problems with the **accuracy** of the information in them. **Eyewitnesses** or **participants** can **exaggerate** or **mistakenly report** what happened.

Q

Are all of these examples of bias?

1. You give an account of a match that only favours your team.
2. You read a newspaper article that only gives one side of a story.
3. You 'Like' something on Facebook.
4. You retweet a tweet.
5. You write the life story of a person and only included the good points.

Can you think of more examples of bias?

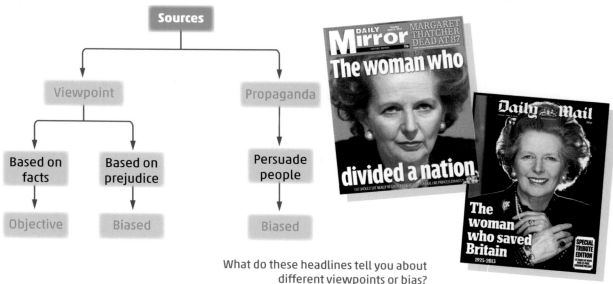

What do these headlines tell you about different viewpoints or bias?

RELIABLE

How can you judge if a source is reliable (if you can trust it)?

- Who is the author of the source?
- Is the person who made the source a witness?
- When did they make the source – at the time or later?
- Does the author have a point of view?
- Is the author biased (one-sided)?
- How does the source compare with what you know already or with other sources?

USEFUL

How can you judge if a source is useful?

A source is useful if it tells you information about the topic you are researching.

Where do historians get their sources?

Museums – places where **objects** are cared for, studied and displayed.

Archives – places where historical documents, maps, photographs, recordings and films are stored and studied.

Libraries – places where reference books, and also documents, are stored and studied.

Interviews – meetings with people involved in historic events to obtain information.

Websites – used by museums, archives and libraries to make available **digital versions** of the sources – documents, newspapers and photographs – that they hold.

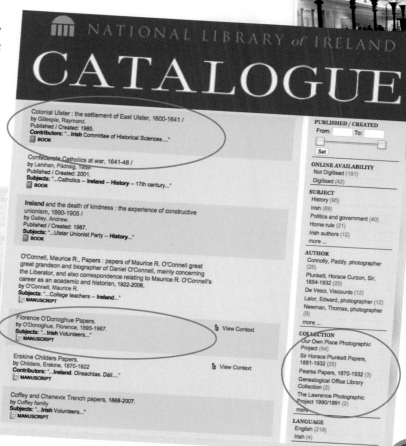

Where are the nearest museums, libraries and archives to you? Do they have websites?

Primary or secondary sources?

This is a screen shot of the National Library of Ireland catalogue. Which of the sources circled here are primary sources and which are secondary sources? Look back at the explanations for primary and secondary sources before you examine these.

Historians and time – Chronology

Time is very important to historians. It helps historians put their stories in the order in which events happened. This order can explain **how** and **why** events happened.

To put events in the right order, historians use the **dates** of the calendar. This study of time and dates is called **chronology** (Greek for 'knowledge of time'). By putting events in chronological order, historians are putting them in the order of the time they happened.

KEY WORD

- **Chronology** is the order in time in which events happened.

BC and AD

In the Western world, the birth of Jesus Christ is an important dividing line in counting time. We call the years and centuries before Christ was born **BC**. For example, the year 244 BC is in the third century BC, which began with the year 299 BC and ended with the year 200 BC.

The years and centuries after Christ was born are called **AD**, Latin for 'the year of Our Lord'). For example, the year 1589 AD is in the sixteenth century, which began with the year 1500 AD and ended with the year 1599 AD.

Stone age

Bronze age

Iron Age
Ancient Rome

Early Modern
Period

Modern Period

6000 BC | 4000 BC | 2000 BC | 0 | 1000 AD | 2000 AD

Middle Ages

CHRONOLOGICAL AWARE NESS

THE 'BIG PICTURE'

Q

1. Which is earlier: 96 BC or 90 AD?
2. Which is earlier: 200 BC or 299 BC?

Q

Which years are at the beginning and end of the following centuries?
(i) First century
(ii) Sixteenth century
(iii) Twenty-first century

Which centuries do the following years belong to?
(i) 200–299
(ii) 1300–1399
(iii) 1492
(iv) 1914

Divisions of time

Decade = 10 years
299–290, 520–529, 1670–1679, 2010–2019
Century = 100 years
299–200, 500–599, 1800–1899, 2000–2099

Which century? 5 Anno Domini (AD), 1066 AD, 1921 AD, 500 before Christ (BC)

Cover the last 2 numbers and add 1 to give the century.

5 >0+1 = 1st century AD; 1066 >10+1 = 11th century AD; 1921 >19+1 = 20th century AD; 500 >5+1 = 6th century BC

Age/Era = A number of decades or centuries marked by a distinctive feature: Stone Age, Middle Ages, Age of Exploration, Computer Age, Roman era, etc.

INVESTIGATE A REPOSITORY OF HISTORICAL EVIDENCE

- The National Library, www.nli.ie/
- The National Archives, www.nationalarchives.ie/
- Your local archives

p. 11
Web Resources and Reading

We will look at other aspects of the job of the historian in later chapters.

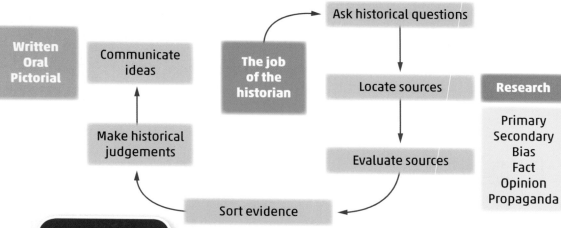

Written
Oral
Pictorial

Communicate ideas

The job of the historian

Ask historical questions

Locate sources

Research

Primary
Secondary
Bias
Fact
Opinion
Propaganda

Make historical judgements

Evaluate sources

Sort evidence

Focus Task

Using the internet, access **two conflicting stories** about a major recent event.

> What are the differences in the stories?
> Why do the stories differ, do you think?
> Did you learn about bias from the stories?
> Explain your answers using information from both newspaper reports.

Analysing Sources

Who shot Michael Collins? – Problems with Sources

JOB OF THE HISTORIAN

CONTROVERSIAL ISSUES

HISTORICAL EMPATHY

Michael Collins, one of the founders of the Irish Free State, was shot in an ambush at Béal na Bláth, Co. Cork on 22 August 1922, during the Irish Civil War. He was returning to Cork city after visiting West Cork that day. There has been controversy since then about who actually shot him.

Here you will see some of the **difficulties historians face** as they look for and examine sources.

Source 1

Gen. Collins, who had been lying firing from a position six feet from me, now stood erect, and after firing several rounds, fell on the roadside, with a gaping wound near the left ear lobe extending to the upper section of the skull; there was also a tear in the front of the forehead, and a hole nipped in the front of his cap close to the badge.

(Michael Corry's account of Collins' assassination; he was co-driver of Collins' car [interview])

Source 2

We accidentally ran into the Ballinablath [sic] thing, Tom Hales and myself. We heard about the party going through in the morning. They took a wrong turning, and went into Newcestown. We went down to look at the position in Ballinblath [sic]. We took up a position there, and held it till late in the evening.

(Sworn statement made by Denis [Sonny] O'Neill on 16 May 1935 to Advisory Committee on Military Service Pensions)

Using the word 'sic' in brackets means you are quoting the source directly, and that errors, such as spelling mistakes, appeared in the original.

Source 3

Denis O'Neill, O/c 3rd Southern Div .... height 5'8", of very stout build .... A very downcast appearance, hardly ever smiles .... he is a first-class shot and a strict disciplinarian.

(Intelligence report on Denis [Sonny] O'Neill, 9 April 1924)

Source 4

Republicans who participated in the engagement told the author that they took an oath of secrecy at the time not to reveal who was there or what happened. There were good reasons for their silence – the fear of retaliatory [revengeful] action by Government forces.

(Michael Collins, His Life and Times, Collins 22 Society, www.generalmichaelcollins.com/)

Source 5

[The] Government issued a directive [order] that documents relating to three classes of incident were to be destroyed, those dealing with courts martial, executions and – the death of Collins.

(Tim Pat Coogan, Michael Collins: A Biography [1990])

Source 6

The weapon that killed him, consistent with the evidence, was a Lee Enfield .303 and used by the man I believe shot Collins ... He was 32-year-old, Denis O'Neill (nicknamed Sonny O'Neill), an ex-British army marksman ... who had joined the IRA. According to this letter [shown on screen], he came to Dublin and gave a graphic description of his shooting of Collins to the IRA's then Chief Intelligence Officer, Comdt. General Sean Dowling.
(Colm Connolly, *The Shadow of Béal na Bláth* [RTÉ documentary, 1989])

Source 7

The remarkable thing was you had four British officers guarding him [Collins] ... 'Tis hard to understand that from my point of view ... And I believe one of the four said we'll get him before we'll come back and they got him ... One of the four shot him, I believe ... The IRA did not shoot him.
(Comdt. General Tom Kelleher, involved in the organisation of the ambush [interview])

Source 8

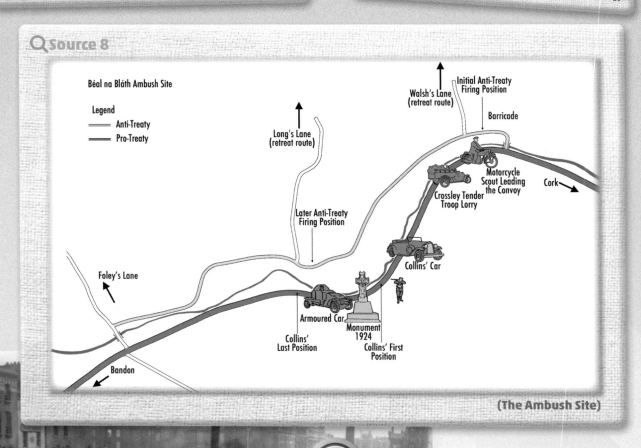

(The Ambush Site)

> Which of these sources are **primary** sources and which are **secondary** sources?
> Which sources provide **conflicting** information?
> Which sources do you think are more **reliable** (dependable, trustworthy) than the others?
> What **other information** would you need to decide who shot Michael Collins?
> Explain your answers in each case.

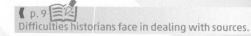

p. 9
Difficulties historians face in dealing with sources.

How do Archaeologists Find Out about the Past?

What is archaeology?

Archaeology is the story of the past from **material remains**.

Material remains are mainly **artefacts** and **buildings**. **Artefacts** are **objects made by people**, such as axes, spears, coins, phones, clothes and watches. What other objects (or artefacts) can you name that you use?

What is the contribution of archaeology to historical enquiry?

Historians depend mostly on **written** or **visual** sources for their information. However, when examining time periods before writing was invented, artefacts and buildings are the only sources available to study. Their study depends mostly on **archaeology**. This time before the invention of writing is sometimes called **prehistory**.

Archaeologists also study artefacts and buildings **after** the invention of writing, up to the present day. This is where historians and archaeologists **work together**. Historians depend on all sources – written and unwritten – for their evidence. Archaeologists study mostly material remains, but they use other sources – written and visual – to find those remains or for further investigation.

How do archaeologists find sites for excavation?

Archaeologists depend on getting evidence **above** and **below** the ground. Once they have identified a site for investigation, they will **excavate** (dig) that site to gather the evidence. Sites **above the ground**, such as **castles** or **monasteries**, are easily found. But many different methods are used to find sites **below the ground**.

⊘ Explain what is archaeology
⊘ Explain what archaeologists contribute to historical inquiry
⊘ Identify how archaeologists find sites for excavation
⊘ Explore how archaeological investigations produce historical information

How do Archaeologists Find Sites below the Ground?

1. **Chance discoveries** – by accident
2. **Stories from History** – from legends and old documents
3. **Maps** – particularly, old maps
4. **Geophysical Survey** – using scientific instruments to find archaeological features under the surface of the ground
5. **Aerial photography** – from drones, helicopters or airplanes

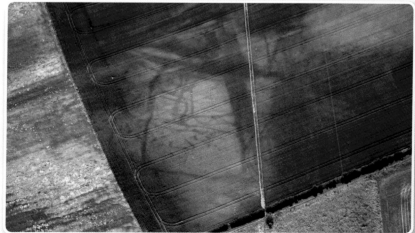
Aerial photographs show up crop marks in fields where crops grow taller over ditches and shorter over walls

NEW TECHNOLOGY

6. **Satellites** – using radar which penetrates the ground

7. **Rescue or salvage archaeology** – in cities or new road projects before development goes ahead

8. **Underwater survey** – in seas, lakes and inland waterways

Can you match the explanations above (1–8) with each of the explanations or pictures below?

Find out more about the new technology archaeologists use to find sites.

For an example of a geophysical survey, go onto YouTube and look up 'Geophysical Survey Kerry County Museum'.

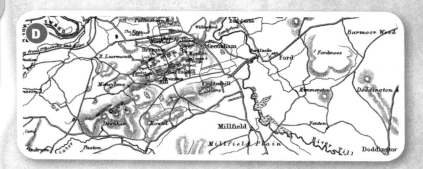

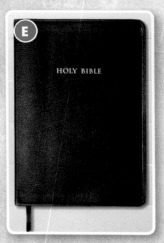

 p. 9

Finding Sites for Excavation

F
The Iliad is an epic poem by the ancient Greek poet, Homer, which tells the story of events in the Trojan War and the Greek siege of the city of Troy. It was written nearly 3,000 years ago.

G
The Terracotta Army was discovered in March 1974 in China by farmers digging a well.

H
The Ardagh Chalice was found in the 19th century by a young man digging for potatoes near Ardagh, Co. Limerick.

We will investigate how archaeologists excavate sites in Chapter 2.

Which of the major responsibilities listed in this advertisement tell you how archaeologists find out about the past?

ARCHAEOLOGIST: JOB DESCRIPTION

Archaeologists study human history by examining artefacts, which range from prehistoric tools and buildings to animal bones and tiny organisms.

What does an archaeologist do? Typical employers | Qualifications and training | Key skills

Archaeologists study past human activity by excavating, dating and interpreting objects and sites of historical interest. They implement excavation projects at historical sites and collect data that informs their understanding of the past.

Main job responsibilities include:

- using geophysical surveys and aerial photographs to locate suitable excavation sites
- planning surveys and excavations
- examining, documenting and preserving artefacts
- producing, compiling and maintaining written, photographic and drawn records and electronic databases
- supervising and guiding staff
- collecting, analysing and interpreting data
- writing reports, papers and other articles for publication
- dating and interpreting finds
- mathematical, statistical and computational modelling
- assessing planning applications for building developers
- creating virtual simulations of how sites or artefacts would have looked.

Visit ...
The History Hunters Experience in Dublinia or Kerry County Museum in Tralee for a display on the work of the archaeologist.

How do archaeologists test the evidence they find in excavations?

Dating

One of the most important tasks of archaeologists is to **date the objects** they find in excavations. This is done in a variety of ways.

Stratigraphy

The basic idea of **stratigraphy** is that the oldest layers and finds are at the bottom, and the latest/youngest are at the top.

Tree-ring dating or dendrochronology

Each year, trees grow a **ring** of new wood. These rings can be seen in cross-sections of the tree trunk. They vary in thickness depending on conditions. It is possible to work out when a tree was growing and when it was cut down by studying the rings. This is called **tree-ring dating** or **dendrochronology**.

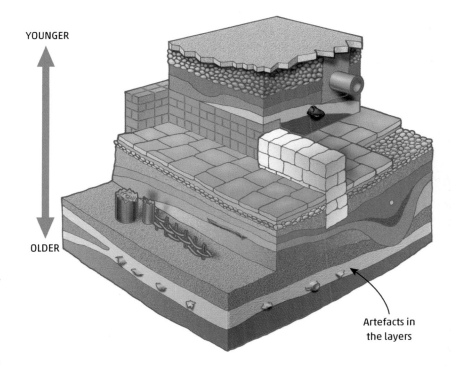

YOUNGER

OLDER

Artefacts in the layers

Each of the layers was laid down or deposited on top of the other. The underlying layer was deposited first and is therefore earlier/older than the layer above it.

To use this method, archaeologists have built up a continuous record of tree-ring growth going back thousands of years. In **Ireland**, this record was compiled in Queen's University, Belfast. It records tree-ring growth in our country back to 5300 BC.

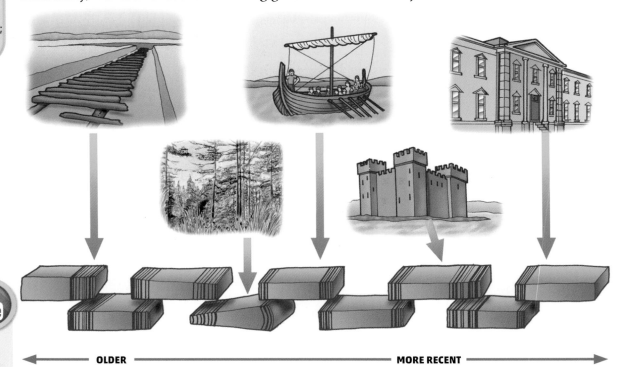

◄ **OLDER** ——————————————— **MORE RECENT** ►

Dendrochronology: New pieces of wood found in ruins or buildings in different parts of Ireland are compared with the record of tree-ring growth to date when the timber was grown and when it was used

Dendrochronology
Go onto YouTube and look up 'Why Do Trees Have Rings? – James May's Q&A'

Radiocarbon Dating

Plants and animals take in **carbon-14** when they are alive. When they die, carbon-14 begins to **decay**. Samples such as charcoal, wood, seeds and human and animal bone can be investigated when they are found. The **age** of the plant, person or animal can be worked out by measuring the amount of radiocarbon left in the sample or piece.

Coins have a date or head of a ruler stamped on them. Objects found with them will be from the same time.

Other evidence used by archaeologists

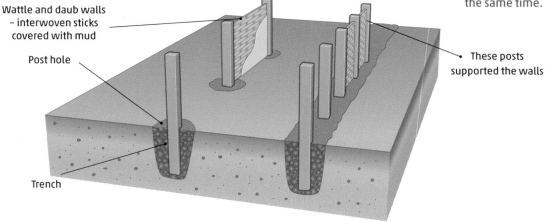

Wattle and daub walls – interwoven sticks covered with mud

Post hole

Trench

These posts supported the walls

Post holes – darkened soil patches where posts have rotted away – show the shape and size of buildings

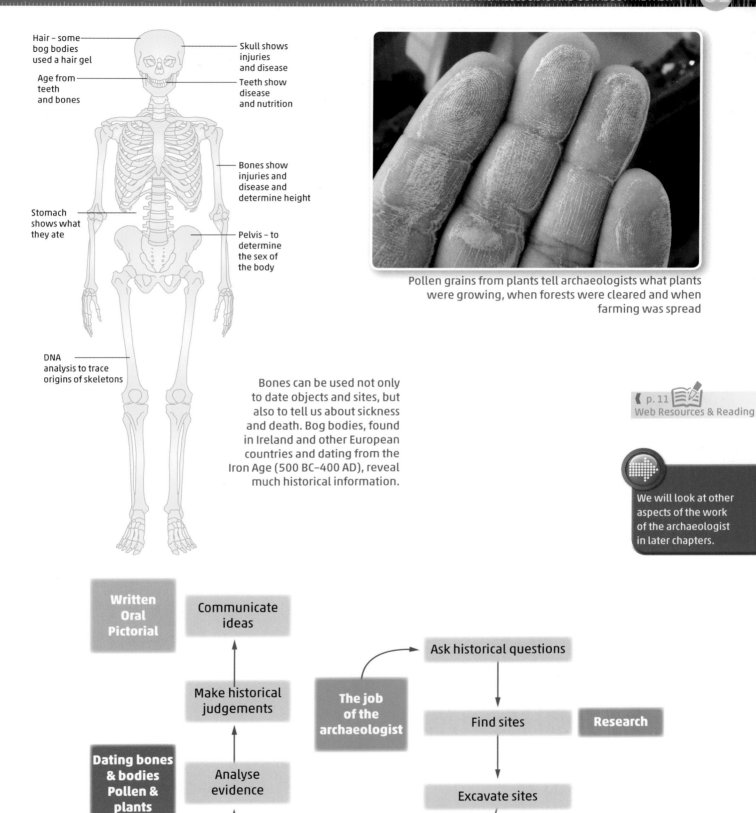

Hair – some bog bodies used a hair gel

Skull shows injuries and disease

Age from teeth and bones

Teeth show disease and nutrition

Bones show injuries and disease and determine height

Stomach shows what they ate

Pelvis – to determine the sex of the body

DNA analysis to trace origins of skeletons

Pollen grains from plants tell archaeologists what plants were growing, when forests were cleared and when farming was spread

Bones can be used not only to date objects and sites, but also to tell us about sickness and death. Bog bodies, found in Ireland and other European countries and dating from the Iron Age (500 BC–400 AD), reveal much historical information.

p. 11
Web Resources & Reading

We will look at other aspects of the work of the archaeologist in later chapters.

Written
Oral
Pictorial

Communicate ideas

Make historical judgements

The job of the archaeologist

Ask historical questions

Research

Find sites

Dating bones & bodies
Pollen & plants

Analyse evidence

Excavate sites

Collect evidence (artefacts)

Analysing Sources

Who was Ötzi the Iceman? – An Archaeological Investigation

In 1991, two mountain walkers discovered **the frozen body of a man** in the Ötztal Alps on the border between Austria and Italy. The body was found at a height of over 3,000 metres in a melting glacier.

Since then, his body, his clothes and weapons have been **investigated** by x-rays, CT scans, high definition cameras and laboratory analysis.

Here are some of the findings. What do they tell you about the life and death of **Ötzi the Iceman**, who lived about 5,300 years ago? They will also tell you about some of the **work of the archaeologist**.

Q What did he work at?
> Was he a copper miner?
> Did he work as a shepherd?
> Did he hunt?
> Did he trade?

Q How did he die?
> Did he fall into the glacier?
> Was he killed?
> Was he sacrificed?

Q What else do you know about him?

 p. 11 〉

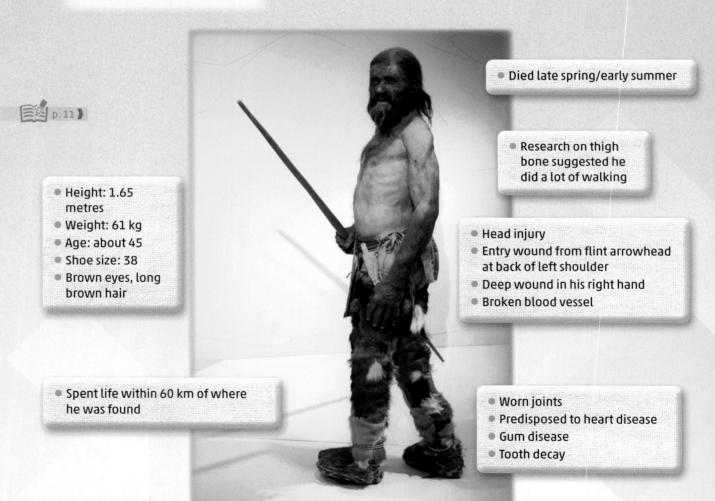

- Died late spring/early summer

- Research on thigh bone suggested he did a lot of walking

- Head injury
- Entry wound from flint arrowhead at back of left shoulder
- Deep wound in his right hand
- Broken blood vessel

- Height: 1.65 metres
- Weight: 61 kg
- Age: about 45
- Shoe size: 38
- Brown eyes, long brown hair

- Spent life within 60 km of where he was found

- Worn joints
- Predisposed to heart disease
- Gum disease
- Tooth decay

CONTRIBUTION OF ARCHAEOLOGY

NEW TECHNOLOGY

HISTORICAL EMPATHY

- Copper axe with a yew handle
- Flint blade knife
- Quiver with 14 arrows
- Longbow

Ötzi's clothes on display at the Museum of Archaeology, Bolzano, Italy: Top left: A shoe with grass inside (left) and leather outside (right); Top right: the leather coat (reassembled by the museum); Bottom left: leather loincloth; grass coat; fur hat; and leather leggings

- Different types of pollen were found in his stomach and on his clothes

❮ p. 12
What does Ötzi's story tell you about the work of the archaeologist?

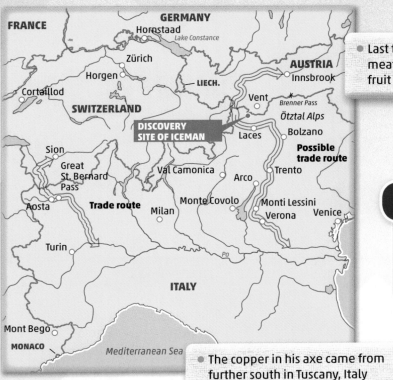

- Last two meals, goat and deer meat, wheat/bread, roots and fruit

- The copper in his axe came from further south in Tuscany, Italy

Focus Task

> Undertake further research on Ötzi the Iceman.
> What role did **new technology** play in investigating his life (see pp. 9–13)? Why was he so well preserved when he was found? How is he preserved today?

Who will be the experts on Ötzi the Iceman?

EUROPEAN HISTORY

02

LIFE IN ANCIENT ROME

L.O. 3.1; 3.14
The Nature of History: 1.1,
1.3, 1.4, 1.5, 1.6, 1.7, 1.8,
1.9, 1.10, 1.11
CBA2

You will learn to ...

⊘ Investigate the lives of people in Ancient Rome

⊘ Explain how their actions contributed to the history of Europe and/or the wider world

⊘ Explain how their achievements contributed to the history of Europe and/or the wider world

⊘ Illustrate patterns of change in Crime and Punishment or Health and Medicine

⊘ Explore the Nature of History

CHRONOLOGICAL AWARENESS

4000 BC .... New Stone Age

3000 BC — Bronze Age

2000 BC

1000 BC

Ancient Greece

0 — Iron Age Ancient Rome

What do these pictures tell you about life in Ancient Rome?

KEY WORDS

- Excavation
- Aqueduct
- Villa
- Plebian
- Dole
- Source
- Secondary
- Survey
- Patrician
- Toga
- Insulae
- Dictator
- Evidence
- Museum
- Domus
- Stola
- Orator
- Slave
- Primary

1000 AD

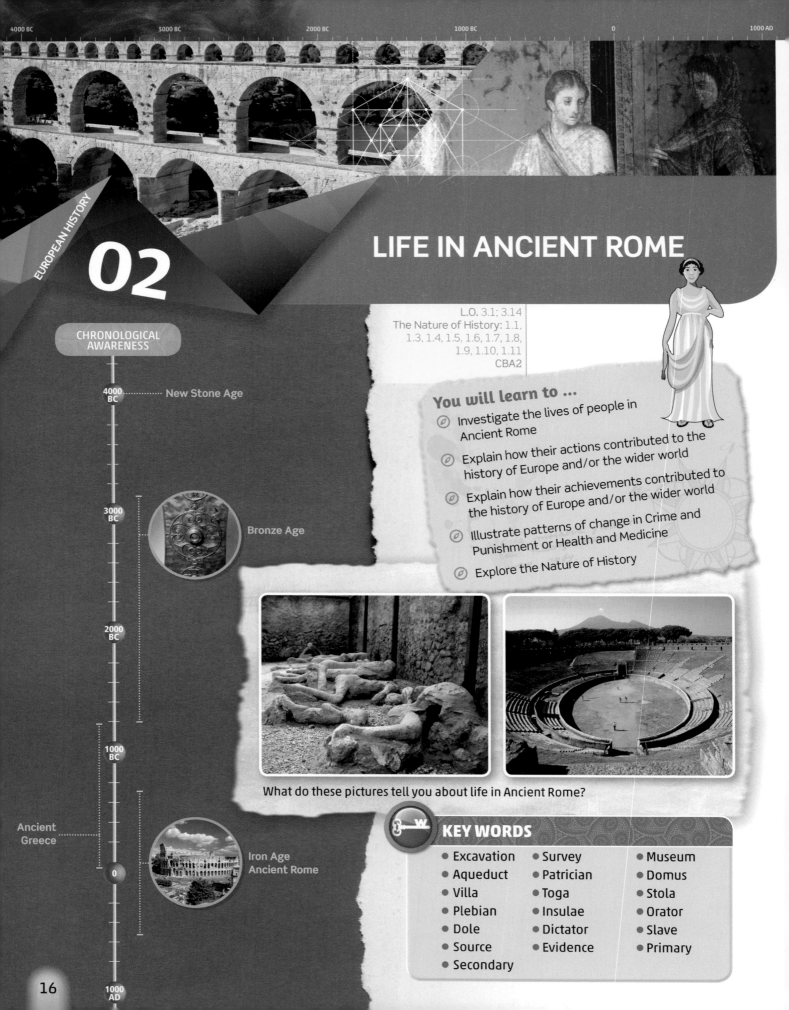

Life in Ancient Rome

The story of Rome

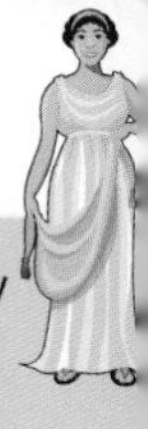

- Describe the Story of Ancient Rome
- Identify the map of Ancient Rome
- Place events in Ancient Rome in chronological order

p. 13 The myth of Romulus and Remus

The story of Rome began in the eighth century BC (799–700), when **villages** grew on **seven hills** along the banks of the River Tiber. The villages joined together to form the city of Rome in 753 BC.

Rome expanded, and conquered all of Italy by 250 BC. The city then conquered all the lands around the Mediterranean Sea. Eventually the Roman Empire stretched from **Hadrian's Wall** (built between Scotland and England), along the Rhine and the Danube to **Turkey**. The Empire also controlled all the lands of North Africa. For the next 600 years, the Roman Empire dominated these lands, until its final collapse in **476 AD**.

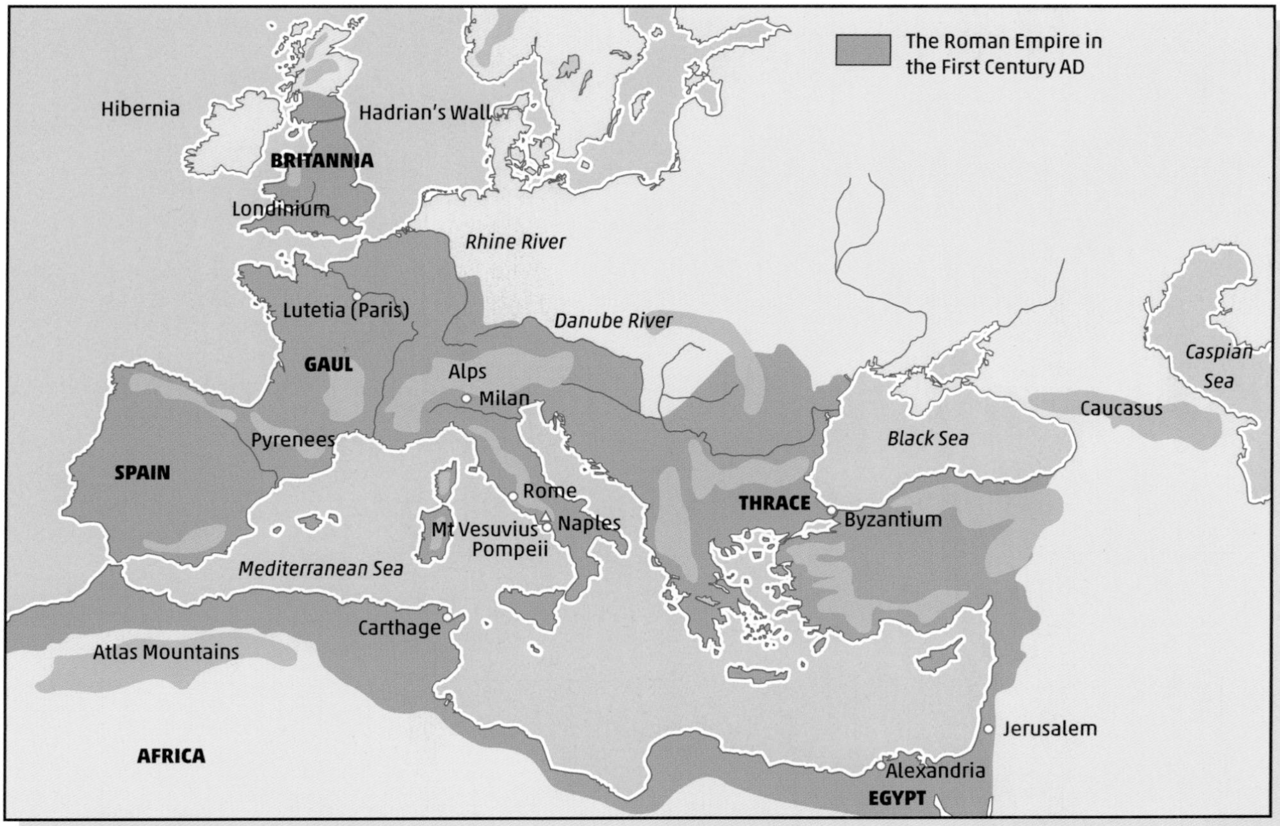
The Roman Empire in the First Century AD
Hibernia
Hadrian's Wall
BRITANNIA
Londinium
Rhine River
Lutetia (Paris)
Danube River
GAUL
Alps
Milan
Pyrenees
SPAIN
Rome
Mt Vesuvius
Naples
Pompeii
Mediterranean Sea
Carthage
Atlas Mountains
AFRICA
THRACE
Byzantium
Black Sea
Caucasus
Caspian Sea
Jerusalem
Alexandria
EGYPT

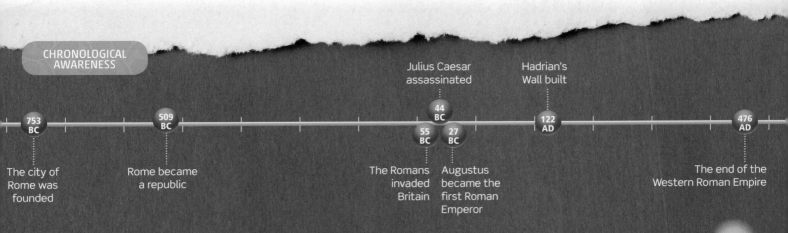

CHRONOLOGICAL AWARENESS

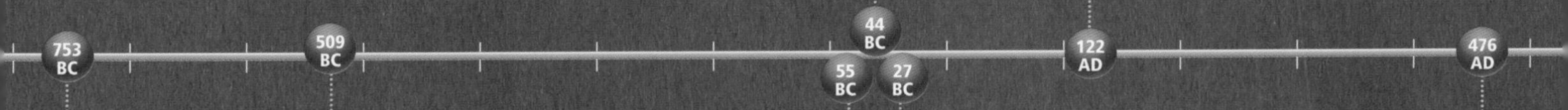
753 BC
The city of Rome was founded
509 BC
Rome became a republic
55 BC
The Romans invaded Britain
44 BC
Julius Caesar assassinated
27 BC
Augustus became the first Roman Emperor
122 AD
Hadrian's Wall built
476 AD
The end of the Western Roman Empire

How do Archaeologists Excavate Sites?

We know a great deal about the life of Ancient Rome from **documents** of the time, and also from the **work of archaeologists**.

Archaeologists have **excavated** (dug) many sites connected to Ancient Rome. Their findings are housed in **museums** in Italy, Britain and in other countries that formed part of the Roman Empire.

ARCHAEOLOGICAL INVESTIGATION

KEY WORD

- **Excavations** show human activities at a **particular time** and **changes over time**. But because excavations **destroy** much of the evidence, everything has to be **recorded**.

The Excavation Process: How We Excavate

Go onto YouTube and look up 'The Excavation Process: How We Excavate'.

Who will be the expert on excavations?

Recording on a laptop

Sorting finds

Surveying the site

Drawing frame to record position of objects (artefacts)

Layers (stratigraphy)   Sketching

Investigating a skeleton

Archaeological tools

1. The site is **surveyed** and an accurate plan is drawn up
2. Mechanical **diggers** take away topsoil, if necessary
3. A grid of **squares** is laid out to record the location of finds accurately
4. Archaeologists dig the ground carefully, using **shovels** and **trowels**
5. Archaeologists use **brushes** to clear around objects
6. **Sieves** are used to recover small artefacts (objects)
7. All artefacts, bones and plants are **numbered** and **stored** in separate bags
8. All finds are **catalogued** in a site book or field computer
9. **Photographs** and **drawings** record the site
10. Finds are investigated in a **laboratory**
11. Finds are stored in **museums** (for example, The British Museum, www.britishmuseum.org)

What do we know about Roman Life from the Excavations of Pompeii and Herculaneum?

What happened at Pompeii and Herculaneum?

Pompeii and Herculaneum were situated on the Bay of Naples, just short distances from **Mount Vesuvius**. In 79 AD, both towns were buried under volcanic ash and lava from the **eruption** of Mount Vesuvius. Over time, the locations of the towns were **forgotten** but letters by **Pliny the Younger** described what had happened when the volcano erupted.

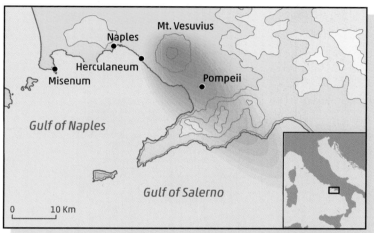

The spread of ash clouds from Mount Vesuvius

Pliny the Younger witnessed the eruption of Mount Vesuvius from across the Bay of Naples, at Micenum. He described how his uncle, Pliny the Elder, was killed by the volcano. This is the only written primary source available on the volcanic eruption.

How does this help the work of archaeologists?

Since both towns and some of their people were covered by layers of ash and lava, the towns were 'frozen in time'. The layers protected all the evidence from 79 AD underneath, ready to be discovered by archaeologists.

How were Pompeii and Herculaneum rediscovered?

Both towns were rediscovered **by accident**. Pompeii was discovered when men were digging a water channel, while Herculaneum was discovered when men were sinking a well shaft.

How were they excavated?

The first excavations began in the 18th century. The finds were not recorded and mosaics, statues, coins and vases were taken into private collections. The artefacts were seen more as **art objects** rather than used for **analysing** the history of the towns.

Soon, however, archaeologists wanted to study the site to find out about life in Pompeii before the eruption. More organised methods were used and **artefacts**, as well as their location, were recorded. It wasn't until the middle of the 19th century that **systematic archaeological methods** were being used.

In the 20th century, so much of the town had been excavated that **conservation** of the ruins became a problem. Today, **photography** and **computer reconstruction** with 3D models are providing evidence of the lives of the people of Pompeii and Herculaneum.

What is left to excavate?

About one-third of Pompeii has yet to be excavated but much more of Herculaneum is still covered. The volcanic layer over Pompeii is softer and thinner than Herculaneum. Also, a town has been built over the site of Herculaneum so it is more difficult to excavate.

What have the excavations shown?

Timeline of Pompeii and Herculaneum

c. 700 BC	First traces of continuous settlement of Pompeii
c. 300 BC	Earliest traces of settlement at Herculaneum
62–63 AD	Earthquake caused major damage to Pompeii and Herculaneum
79 AD	Eruption of Vesuvius
1592 AD	Some artefacts discovered when digging a water channel in Pompeii
1709–10	The theatre in Herculaneum was discovered during work to sink a well shaft
1738	The King of Naples ordered Herculaneum to be excavated by tunnelling
1748	The first formal excavations of Pompeii
1860	Systematic excavations begin at Pompeii
1943	Allied bombing of site during World War II

Source 1

There is an old archaeological joke that Pompeii has died twice: first, the sudden death caused by the [volcanic] eruption; second the slow death that the city has suffered since it began to be uncovered in the mid-eighteenth century. Despite the heroic efforts of the Pompeiian archaeological service, the city is disintegrating (decaying). It is a gradual process of dilapidation (ruin), aggravated (worsened) by earthquakes and mass tourism, and given an extra helping hand by the rough methods of the early excavators; by allied bombing campaigns in 1943; and by thieves and vandals, for whom the archaeological site, large and hard to police, is an enticing target.

(Edited extract from Mary Beard, *Pompeii: The Life of a Roman Town* [2008])

Source 2

Though our tools today – the trowels, shovels, buckets, and brushes – are nearly identical to [those used in past excavations], many advances have been made in archaeological method and methodology over the course of the past 70+ years. We are now able to reexamine [the work done by archaeologists in the past].

('What Happened in Pompeii', www.interactive. archaeology.org/pompeii/history.html)

HISTORICAL EVIDENCE

Answer these questions from the text and sources

1. Which was the older settlement, Pompeii or Herculaneum?
2. How were the sites at Pompeii and Herculaneum **found**?
3. What **advantages** did archaeologists have when they were excavating Pompeii and Herculaneum?
4. What **problems** did they face?
5. When were the first excavations done in Pompeii and Herculaneum?
6. Why are these two sites so **important** for the story of life in the Roman Empire?
7. Are the **artefacts** that they dug up primary or secondary sources?
8. What is the main point of Source 1? What is the main point of Source 2?
9. Which of the two archaeologists in the sources is the **more optimistic** about the excavations?

Explain your answers.

Excavations in Pompeii
Go onto YouTube and look up 'Pompeii, Italy: Window on Ancient Rome'.

Roman Lives – The Patrician

Wealthy and powerful Romans were called **patricians**. The patricians controlled the Roman Senate, which made the laws for Rome. Patricians lived in private houses in the city, called a **domus**. They also had **country villas**, with a farm run by a manager and worked by slaves.

The domus looked plain from the outside, with blank walls facing the street. **Shops** often occupied the front of the house.

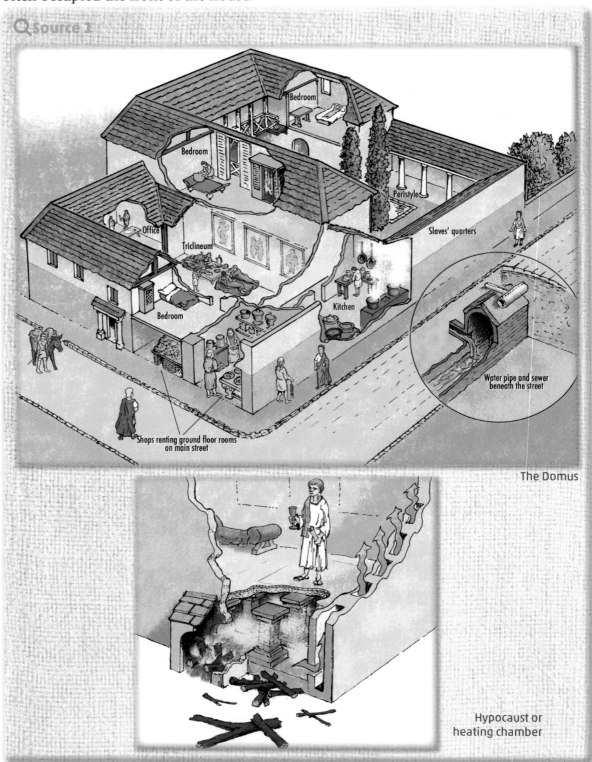

Q Source 1

Bedroom

Bedroom

Peristyle

Office

Triclineum

Slaves' quarters

Bedroom

Kitchen

Water pipe and sewer beneath the street

Shops renting ground floor rooms on main street

The Domus

Hypocaust or heating chamber

Investigate the lives of people in Ancient Rome

Appreciate the contribution of archaeology to historical enquiry

22

Patrician families

In patrician families, the **family group** was large, including husband, wife and children, but also other relations. The **father** was fully in charge and the children were expected to obey their father, even after they had grown up.

The main job of the **mother** was to run the household. She gave orders to the slaves, who did the work.

Marriages were often arranged to increase a family's wealth and influence. Girls were allowed to marry at twelve years of age and boys at fourteen.

Men and women wore short-sleeved, knee-length **tunics**, tied at the waist. Wealthy Romans wore a **toga** over the tunic. Wealthy women wore a **stola** (a long tunic) over the undertunic.

Toga   Stola   Tunic

Source 2

Richer families had two simple **meals** for breakfast and lunch, and waited until the evening for the main meal of the day. This was after a visit to the **baths**.
The main meal, called the **cena**, had three courses. The men and women lay on couches around a central table. **Slaves** served the food and musicians entertained during the meal. Sometimes people ate so much that they deliberately got sick so that they could begin again.

Source 3

About the privileged – the haves – of the Roman world we know a great deal. All over the empire the rich paraded their wealth in large and expensive accommodations, measured not by floor area but by the number of tiles on the roof. And they indulged in the many pleasures that money could buy, from silks to oriental spices, skilled slaves to pricey antiques.

Source 4

For the most part ancient cities were not zoned as modern cities are. Rich and poor lived side by side, large houses with many tiles sharing the same streets and districts as tiny hovels. The same diseases, and much the same dirt, killed the children of rich and poor alike.

Edited extracts from Mary Beard, *SPQR: A History of Ancient Rome* (2015)

HISTORICAL JUDGEMENTS

Answer these questions using the sources and text
1. How did the patricians show off their wealth?
2. How did patricians organise their families?
3. What common experiences did rich and poor have?
4. Why, do you think, 'we know a great deal' about the haves? Explain your answers.

p. 14 Evidence from a Roman Rubbish Pit

Entertainment

Most Romans had very little free time, but Rome was well known for its **public entertainment**. This was often paid for by the government to keep the people happy.

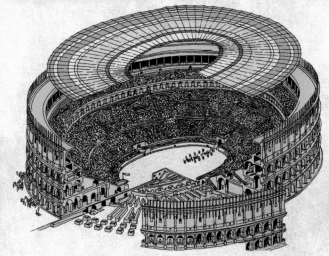

The Colosseum could hold 50,000 spectators to see gladiator contests

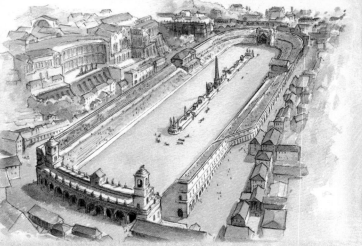

The Circus Maximus, for chariot-racing

Gladiators fighting with nets, trident, shields, swords and helmets

Roman baths with warm room, hot room and cold room

A Roman theatre

p. 15 ❯
Entertainment
in Ancient Rome

What role did each of these play in entertaining the people of Ancient Rome?

Roman Lives – The Plebeian

In the city, most Romans were called **plebeians**. Plebians included those who produced and sold anything such as bread, footwear or clothes down to the very poor.

Plebeians lived in **insulae**, apartment blocks which were five or six storeys tall. The rooms at street level were rented as **shops**. Better-off families rented a number of well-furnished rooms on the lower floors. Poorer families lived in the upper-floors. They had bare rooms and lived in bad conditions.

Usually, there were no toilets in the insulae, so tenants had to use **public toilets**. There was no **water supply** either, so people had to draw water from the **public fountains** which were supplied through **aqueducts** (channel for water). Rubbish was thrown out the windows onto the street. Wood-burning stoves provided heat, but there was a great danger of **fire**.

DID YOU KNOW?
The streets had **thermopolia** – take-away shops which sold hot food.

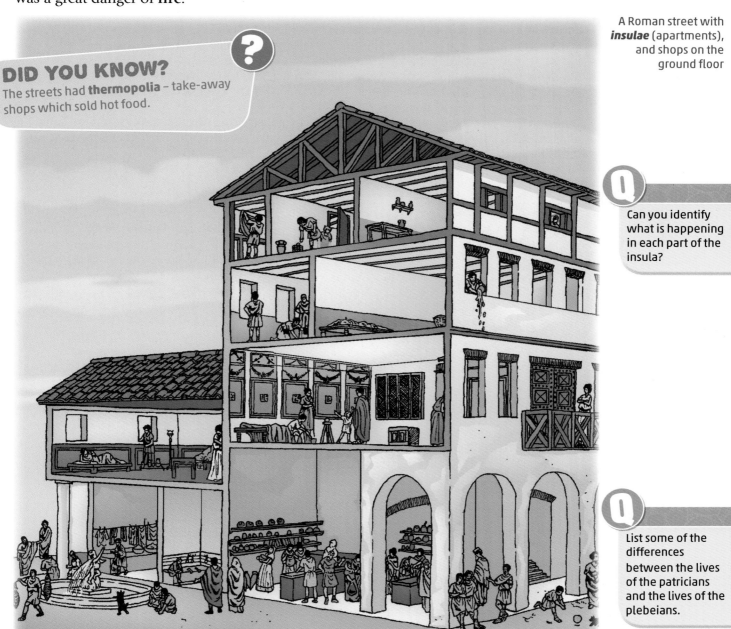

A Roman street with *insulae* (apartments), and shops on the ground floor

Q Can you identify what is happening in each part of the insula?

Q List some of the differences between the lives of the patricians and the lives of the plebeians.

25

Poorer families depended on bread or wheat biscuits for their breakfast and lunch. They also ate a kind of **porridge** made from wheat and barley. They could not cook in their apartment blocks (**insulae**), so their evening meals were either cold or bought from inns or take-away shops.

Poverty was so great in the city of Rome that emperors gave a free supply of grain to 200,000 people every month to keep them happy. This was called the **dole**.

CONTRIBUTION OF ARCHAEOLOGY

Sacks of Human Waste Reveal Secrets of Ancient Rome

You might turn your nose up at sifting through hundreds of sacks of human excrement, but researchers are doing just that in Italy – and happily.

Ten tons of the stuff has been excavated from a cesspit (a pit for holding sewage) beneath the ancient town of Herculaneum, near Naples.

Flushed down sewers from apartment blocks and shops, the deposit – the largest collection of ancient Roman garbage and human waste ever found, researchers say – dates to about AD 79.

Coming from a one-time district of shopkeepers and artisans, the organic material has revealed just what your run-of-the-mill Roman might have eaten in this coastal town. Seeds, bones, shell fragments, and other remains suggest Herculaneum residents had a diverse (varied) diet, which included chicken, mutton, fish, fig, fennel, olive, sea urchins and mollusk. 'This is absolutely standard diet for ordinary people in the town.'

The waste was excavated and put through a series of graded sieves. The first sieving captured larger objects such as pottery and bone. The second caught smaller objects, including nuts and seeds. 'It's in these progressive stages that, bit by bit, you capture more and more information.'

Future microscopic analysis of bits of the ancient Roman stool could reveal evidence of disease, such as bacterial or parasitic infections.

(www.news. nationalgeographic.com/ news/2011/06/110623- ancient-rome-human-waste- herculaneum-science-diet- excrement-italy/)

A public toilet in Pompeii

1. Why, do you think, researchers are happy going through hundreds of sacks of excrement?
2. Who are 'run-of-the-mill Romans'?
3. Was the standard diet of the people in Herculaneum good?
4. How was the waste tested?
5. What did you learn about the work of the archaeologist from this source?
6. What did you learn about the contribution of archaeology to historical enquiry? Explain your answers.

Roman Lives – Roman Women

In Roman society, a **woman's place** was in the home. She was under the control of her husband. Her job was to have **children** who, amongst the rich, would inherit the property of the family.

The ideal Roman woman was **hard-working** and **obedient** to her husband. The role of the mother was to pass on the same ideas to her daughters and younger women.

The main job of the mother was to run the **household**. In **richer families**, she gave orders to the slaves who did the work; the only traditional work that richer women did was spinning or weaving. **Poorer women** worked in the markets, the shops and the baths.

Daughters of richer families went to **primary school** where they learned to read and write using **wooden tablets** coated with wax. Their education ended at primary school, in contrast to the boys who went to secondary school. Instead, the girls stayed at home to prepare for **marriage**.

Girls were allowed to marry at **twelve years of age**. They provided a **dowry** for their new husbands. The dowry could be money or property. Since the dowry had to be returned in the case of a divorce, this gave women some influence over their husbands. Roman women were encouraged to have **large families** because many children died at birth or at a young age. Childbirth was also dangerous for mothers, and many died in their thirties.

Sources On Roman Women

HISTORICAL JUDGEMENTS

Source 1

A woman's whole role is to care for children, for her husband, and for her home ... For human activity is divided into two spheres, one pertaining (relating) to life outside the home, and one to life within it: as we might say, 'public', and 'private'. God assigned a role to each sex; women have the care of the home, men of public affairs, business, legal and military activities – indeed, all of life outside the home.

(John Chrysostom, *The Kind of Women Who Ought to be Taken as Wives* [4th century])

Source 2

Pompullius Antiochus, her husband, set up this gravestone to Caecilia Festiva, his dearest, sweet wife, hard-working and well-deserving, who lived with me for 21 years without a contrary word. She was a wife most virtuous and chaste, incomparable among women. Farewell.

(A gravestone inscription)

Source 3

Visitor, I have something to say to you; stop and give a read. This is a common tomb for an uncommon woman. Her parents gave her the name, Claudia. She loved her husband with all her heart. She brought forth two children. One she left above the earth, the other below. Her conversation was lovely, her walk was graceful. She managed the household. She wove in wool. I have spoken. Go on your way.

(A gravestone inscription)

Source 4

[Mother to daughter] greetings. If you are well, it would be as I pray to the gods to see you well. I received the letter from you in which you inform me that you have given birth. I prayed to the gods daily on your behalf. Now that you have escaped [from danger], I shall pass my time in the greatest joy. I have sent you a flask of oil and dried figs.

(A letter)

Source 5
Frescoes of Roman women

1. What is the **message** of John Chrysostom in Source 1?
2. What do the gravestone inscriptions (Sources 2 and 3) say about the **relationship** between men and women?
3. Do the gravestone inscriptions support the views of John Chrysostom?
4. What does the **letter** (Source 4) say about the relationship between mothers and daughters?
5. What do the **frescoes** (Source 5) show you about the lives of women?
6. Are the extracts (Sources 1 to 4) **primary** or **secondary** sources?
7. Are the frescoes primary or secondary sources?
8. Are any of the sources biased?
9. Select **one fact** and **one opinion** from the sources.

Explain your answers.

Roman Lives – The Army Commander, Julius Caesar

Julius Caesar was born in 100 BC into an influential Roman family. He joined the army and proved to be an able soldier and officer in operations in Turkey. He returned to Rome and showed his gifts as an **orator**. The great Roman orator, Cicero, said of him,

'Do you know of a man who... can speak better than Caesar? Or anyone who makes so many witty remarks?'

Life and conquests

He was **married** three times into other influential families and this helped his rise to power. He also created **alliances** with other Roman leaders such as Pompey, a general, and Crassus, the wealthiest man in Rome.

He then went to **Spain** as governor, subdued warring tribes, and brought peace to the area. On returning to Rome, he, **Pompey** and **Crassus** jointly ruled the city. Caesar brought in **popular reforms** such as redistributing land to the poor.

Caesar then spent eight years as governor in **Gaul** (France), subduing the tribes as he had done in Spain, conquering modern Belgium and invading Britain. He added these lands to the Roman Empire. He built up his reputation by writing his account of the wars in Gaul in *De Bello Gallico* (The Gallic Wars).

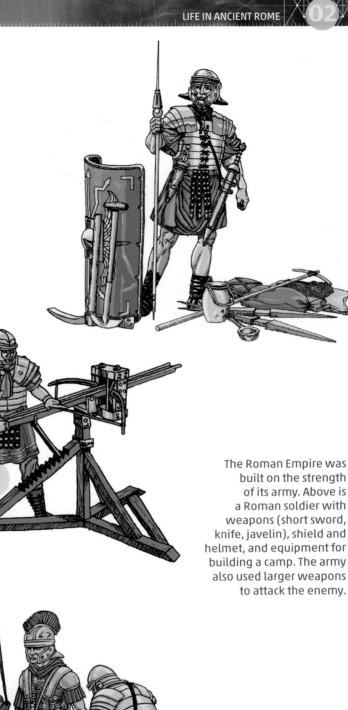

The Roman Empire was built on the strength of its army. Above is a Roman soldier with weapons (short sword, knife, javelin), shield and helmet, and equipment for building a camp. The army also used larger weapons to attack the enemy.

Timeline of Julius Caesar's Military Career

80 BC	Military service in Turkey
78 BC	Caesar kidnapped by pirates, released with ransom paid
	Caesar hunted down the pirates and killed them
61 BC	Campaign in Spain
58–50 BC	Conquest of Gaul – The Gallic Wars
	Invasion of Britain
	Battle of Alesia – Gauls defeated
49 BC	Crossing the Rubicon, Civil War began
48 BC	Defeated Pompey at Battle of Pharsalus
	Caesar dictator of Rome
47 BC	Victory in the Battle of the Nile
45 BC	Caesar dictator for life
44 BC	Assassination of Julius Caesar

Q

1. Was Caesar born into a well-off family?
2. What helped his rise to power?
3. What is the meaning of the phrase, 'Crossing the Rubicon'?
4. Investigate where the comment of Caesar's, 'Veni, Vidi, Vici' was used in more modern times.

Civil War

However, his alliance with Pompey collapsed with the death of Crassus, and Caesar was ordered to return to Rome without his army. Caesar disobeyed the order and instead crossed the **Rubicon River** and marched on Rome in 49 BC. Pompey fled to Egypt where he was assassinated. Caesar made himself consul and **dictator** of Rome.

> Caesar's comment after winning a battle in Asia
> *Veni, Vidi, Vici*
> I came, I saw, I conquered.

He brought in more *popular reforms*, including reforming the **calendar**. He changed the year from 355 to 365 days and added the month of July (after his name). He ruled without consulting the Senate so some senators feared that it would be abolished. They planned and carried out his **assassination** on 15 March, 44 BC – the Ides of March. He was stabbed twenty-three times.

His death led to civil war between two of Caesar's followers, **Mark Antony** and **Gaius Octavian**, adopted heir of Caesar's. Octavian had Caesar *deified* (made as a god), and established himself as **Augustus Caesar**, Emperor. He ended the Roman Republic and replaced it with the **Roman Empire**.

Sources on Julius Caesar

Q Source 1

The military campaigns of Julius Caesar

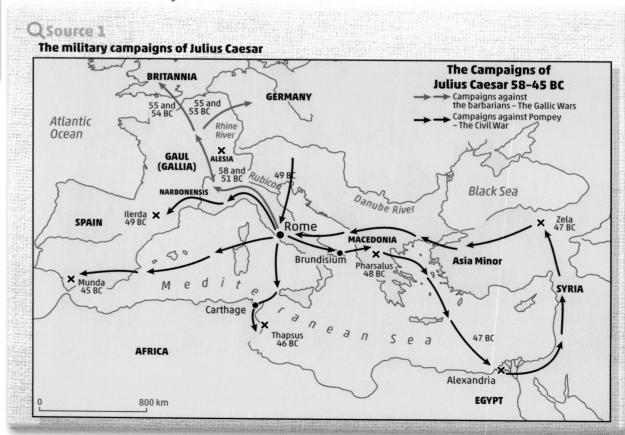

Q Source 2
Caesar was a most skillful swordsman and horseman, and showed surprising powers of endurance. He always led his army, more often on foot than in the saddle, went bareheaded in sun and rain alike, and could travel for long distances at incredible speed... If Caesar's troops gave ground he would often rally them in person, catching individual fugitives (deserters) by the throat and forcing them round to face the enemy again... He always addressed his soldiers not with 'My men', but with 'Comrades' ... which put them into a better humour. He fixed the daily pay of the regular soldiers at double what it had been and occasionally gave each man a slave.
(Suetonius, *Life of Julius Caesar* [c.110 AD])

Q Source 3
Caesar saw that his clemency (mercy) was so well known that no one would think him a cruel man if for once he took severe measures. So he decided to deter all others by making an example of the defenders of Uxellodunum (a hill fort in France). All who had borne arms had their hands cut off and were then let go, so that everyone might see what punishment was meted (given) out to evildoers.
(Hirtius, one of Caesar's generals in the Gallic Wars [c. 42 BC])

Q Source 4
What made Caesar hated was his passion to be king.
(Plutarch, *Julius Caesar* [c. 110 AD])

Q Source 5
When his friends advised him to have a guard, and several offered their services, he would not hear of it; but said it was better to suffer death once than always to live in fear of it.
(Plutarch, *Julius Caesar* [c. 110 AD])

Q Source 6
He fought 50 pitched battles and was the only one to beat Marcus Marcellus who fought 39 – for I would not count it to his glory that, in addition to victories over fellow citizens [in the Civil War], he killed 1,192,000 people in his battles, a huge, if unavoidable, injury to the human race.
(Pliny's *Natural History* [c. 77 AD])

1. Are these sources **primary** or **secondary**?
2. What can you learn about Caesar's wars from Source 1?
3. Which sources are **favourable** to Caesar and which are not? Are they biased?
4. Which **sources** help you understand more about Caesar's rise to power?
5. How did his **military career** help his rise to power?
6. How do the sources help you **understand** why he was assassinated?
7. What would you consider were Caesar's **achievements**?
8. What did you learn about **life in Ancient Rome** from the story of Julius Caesar?
Explain your answers.

Extracts from Spartacus Educational, www.spartacus-educational.com

The assassination scene in Shakespeare's play, *Julius Caesar*.

Roman Lives – The Slave, Spartacus

Slaves in Ancient Rome

It was estimated that there were between 1.5 and 2 million slaves in Italy, which was about **20 per cent** of the population. Slaves were workers who were **owned** by Roman citizens or by the government. Many ordinary Romans did not have any slaves. Slaves could be bought and sold at **markets**. Many were brought back from foreign wars. Some were born as slaves to slave women.

Slaves did most of the work on farms and in the towns. The government used slaves to maintain public buildings and to work in the public baths.

The **treatment** of slaves varied from owner to owner. The owners had the power of 'life and death' over the slaves. Many were treated very harshly; some got their freedom.

Slaves **rebelled** many times against their harsh treatment. **Spartacus** led one of those rebellions.

Spartacus' rebellion

Spartacus was born in Thrace, near Macedonia. Very little is known about how he became a slave but, because of his size and strength, he was sent to a **gladiatorial school** near Naples. He and others rebelled against the conditions there in 73 BC and headed for Mount Vesuvius. Thousands joined him, and soon he led an army of up to 90,000.

He **defeated two armies** sent against him. Then he headed for northern Italy in 72 BC.

> *By this time Spartacus had grown to be a great and formidable power, but he showed no signs of losing his head. He could not expect to prove superior to the whole power of Rome, and so he began to lead his army towards the Alps. His view was that they should cross the mountains and then disperse to their own homes, some to Thrace and some to Gaul. His men, however, would not listen to him. They were strong in numbers and full of confidence, and they went south through Italy ravaging everything in their way.*
>
> *(Plutarch)*

This alarmed the **Roman Senate**, but Spartacus defeated two more armies sent against him. Then in 71 BC the Senate appointed Marcus Licinius **Crassus** to lead an army against him. After much manoeuvering and fighting in the south of Italy, Crassus eventually defeated Spartacus.

> *… pushing his way towards Crassus himself through many flying weapons and wounded men, [Spartacus] did not indeed reach him, but slew two centurions (officers) who fell upon him together. Finally, after his companions had taken to flight, he stood alone, surrounded by his foes, and was still defending himself when he was cut down.*
>
> *(Plutarch's Life of Crassus)*

Over 6,000 rebels were captured and crucified; their bodies were displayed along the **Appian Way** into Rome.

The Thrilling Adventure that Electrified the World!

KIRK DOUGLAS · LAURENCE OLIVIER · JEAN SIMMONS
CHARLES LAUGHTON · PETER USTINOV · JOHN GAVIN
AND TONY CURTIS AS ANTONINUS

SPARTACUS

TECHNICOLOR PANAVISION®

Directed by STANLEY KUBRICK · Music Composed and Conducted by ALEX NORTH · Screenplay by DALTON TRUMBO
Produced by EDWARD LEWIS · Executive Producer KIRK DOUGLAS
A BRYNA PRODUCTION · A UNIVERSAL RELEASE

Q

1. How important were slaves to the **economy** of the Roman Empire?
2. How did Spartacus' life as a slave **differ** to most other slaves?
3. Why, do you think, the captured rebels were **crucified**?
4. Does Plutarch **admire** Spartacus?
5. Do you think Plutarch's account is **reliable**?

Explain your answers.

? Based on this image from *Spartacus* (film, 1960), how do you think Spartacus is viewed today? Would Ancient Romans like this poster?

Verus the Gladiator

DID YOU KNOW?

Revolutionaries and politicians used the story of Spartacus as an inspiration in the 19th and 20th centuries. *The Spartacist League* was a revolutionary socialist group in Germany which led a failed uprising in 1919.

Crime and Punishment

Crime and Punishment in Ancient Rome

Illustrate patterns of change in crime and punishment

Crime and punishment in Ancient Rome – Who made the law?

The Romans had a written code of law, called the **Twelve Tables**. The laws were made by the emperors and by the Senate. The laws laid down what Romans could do legally, so that everybody was treated fairly under the law.
The courts ruled on guilt or innocence.

p. 262

If a crime was committed, Romans had to catch the criminal and bring them for trial. Victims of crimes collected their evidence and brought the accused to court. In serious crimes, people were entitled to a trial by jury; less serious crimes were tried before a magistrate.

Who enforced the law?

Ancient Rome did not have a police force. Instead, they used **soldiers** who had the job of keeping order. These soldiers did not patrol the streets, but were called on when needed. At night, the **vigiles** patrolled the streets to watch out for fires, and to prevent crimes.

The Romans believed that punishments for crime should be severe so that they would act as a **deterrent** to committing future crimes.

What were the crimes?

Rome was a very crowded city, and there were great divisions between rich and poor. This resulted in causing some crimes, particularly robbery and burglary. Other crimes included fraud in trade, such as cheating about goods which were sold. More serious crimes included arson and murder. Since there were so many slaves in Rome, not surprisingly, slaves running away was regarded as a crime.

What were the punishments?

Punishments often depended on **your position** in society. Nobles were treated better than ordinary Romans, citizens of Rome were treated better than non-citizens, and slaves were treated worst of all.

Whip

Ordinary citizens got whipped or were fined for small crimes. They were executed by hanging or beheading for more serious ones, such as murder. **Nobles** were unlikely to commit small crimes since they were rich. However, for more serious crimes they would be executed or sent into exile to some other part of the empire. **Slaves** were treated harshly – they could be crucified or forced to fight in combat.

There were also harsh punishments in the **army** to impose discipline. Every tenth soldier could be taken out for execution. This was called **decimation**.

Crucifixions

Health and Medicine

p. 255

⊘ Illustrate patterns of change in Health and Medicine

An 18th century engraving of Galen, a Roman doctor. Galen wrote many books which influenced medicine up to the Renaissance in the 15th and 16th centuries, and beyond.

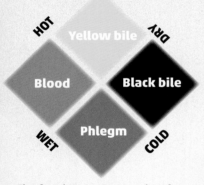

HOT — Yellow bile — DRY
Blood — Black bile
WET — Phlegm — COLD

The four humours passed on from Greek to Roman medicine to explain the causes of diseases. These ideas influenced medicine up to the 17th century.

The symbol of the World Health Organisation uses the staff of Aesculapius (the Greek and Roman god of medicine), which links Roman medicine to the modern world

Health and Medicine in Ancient Rome

What were the four humours?

The Romans learnt about health and medicine from the Greeks, and they added some of their own ideas.

The most famous doctor in Ancient Rome was **Galen**. He was born in Turkey to Greek parents, but he came to live in Rome.

He followed the Greek ideas about the **four humours**. The four humours were four body fluids – yellow bile, black bile, blood and phlegm. Galen thought that if they were in the correct proportions in the body, a person would be healthy. But if there was too much or too little of any of the four, then this caused sickness.

How did the Romans cure diseases?

Galen believed in the **theory of opposites** to cure the sickness he diagnosed. He used hot pepper to cure a cold, for example. Others believed in getting rid of the excess fluid – to restore balance in the fluids – if that caused the sickness. An example of this was **bloodletting**, where blood was taken from the patient.

The Romans also had other cures. They had various **herbal remedies**, some of which, such as the use of garlic, were effective. One of the Roman doctors compiled a list of these remedies, which was used in Europe for a thousand years after. People with very serious diseases prayed to the **gods** to cure them.

The Romans would not allow the dissection of humans, so Roman doctors had to learn from dissecting animals. Galen **dissected different animals** so he made mistakes because he thought other animals were like humans.

Roman Cures	
Sickness	**Cure**
Sore eyes	Boiled liver
Epilepsy	Drink the blood of a slain gladiator
Dysentery (diarrhoea)	Egg yolk mixed with poppy juice and wine
Skin infections	Broccoli
Swelling, bruises	Apply unwashed wool
Acne	Apply dried slab of crocodile meat
Warts	Burnt cow dung
Fatigue	Tarragon, a herb

Rome – The Achievements

Concrete

The Romans mixed lime with volcanic ash and rocks to create an early form of **concrete**. This is the reason why some of their biggest buildings, such as the **Colosseum** and the **Pantheon**, are still standing.

Architecture

Roman architecture became the model for later architecture. It used **pillars**, **domes** and **rounded arches**.

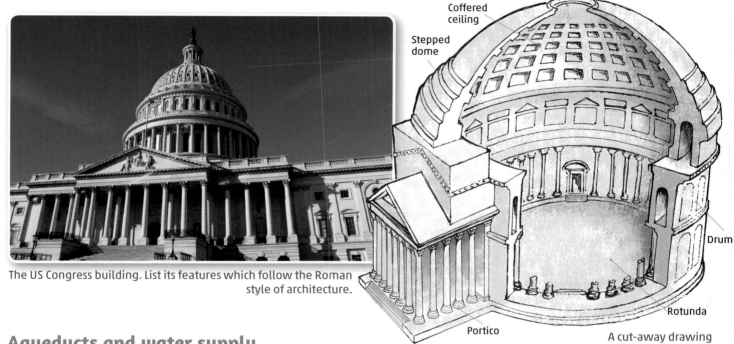

The US Congress building. List its features which follow the Roman style of architecture.

Oculus

Coffered ceiling

Stepped dome

Portico

Rotunda

Drum

A cut-away drawing of the Pantheon in Rome showing the features of Roman architecture

⊘ Explain how the achievements of Ancient Rome influenced the history of Europe and/or the wider world

SIGNIFICANT CONNECTIONS

Aqueducts and water supply

Romans discovered that **rounded arches** could support a great weight. Arches were used in the building of **aqueducts** so that water could be supplied to the towns and cities. **Public fountains** were built so that people could access fresh water.

Towns and cities

The Romans founded many modern cities and towns.

Cities founded by the Romans:
Paris, London, Lyons and Cologne

Aqueducts were used to transport water across valleys, bringing water to towns and cities

Romans planned their **new towns** in a **grid pattern**. This was followed by some modern cities, such as **Washington** and **New York**.

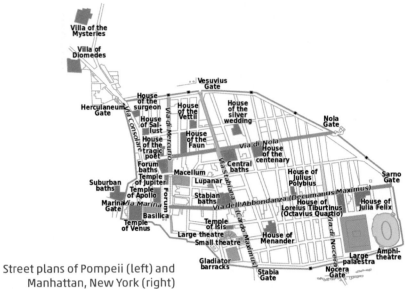

Street plans of Pompeii (left) and Manhattan, New York (right)

What are the advantages of a grid pattern in the layout of a city or town?

Language

The Romans spread their language, **Latin**, wherever they went. Many **modern European languages** – French, Italian, Portuguese and Spanish – are based on Latin. The **English** language is not, but it contains many words that are derived from Latin. Scientists use Latin for naming plants, animals and insects.

Roman Words	English Words
Aqua (water)	Aquarium
Semi (half)	Semi-final
Sub (under, below)	Submarine
Super (above)	Superior
Trans (across)	Transport

Politics

What is meant by 'checks and balances' in the American Constitution?

Ancient Rome was not a democracy. However, writers in the 18th and 19th centuries used the ideas of the Roman Republic to promote **democratic ideas**. The leaders of the **American Revolution** in the 18th century borrowed their ideas for a mixed constitution with **checks and balances** from Cicero's description of politics in the Roman republic.

Religion

In its early years, **Christianity** was persecuted (badly treated) by the Roman Empire. But once it was legalised by Emperor **Constantine** (313 AD), it spread rapidly throughout the Empire. The **Bishop of Rome** became the leader of the Roman Catholic Church, or Pope. **Latin** was the language of church ceremonies until the 1960s.

Saint Peter's Basilica, Rome

Art – Frescoes and sculpture

Roman sculptures, such as the Laocoön, were studied by sculptors of the Renaissance in the 14th to 16th centuries to create the great sculptors of their time (see Ch. 5)

A fresco from Pompeii. Romans painted frescoes, paintings done on wet plaster, and this style of painting continued through the Middle Ages and the Renaissance

What did the Romans ever do for us?

Go onto YouTube and look up *'What Have The Romans... – Monty Python's Life of Brian'*.

Next, look up 'What the Romans Did For Us – 01/06'.

What were the greatest achievements of the Romans?

p. 20 Characteristics of Ancient Rome

Calendar

The modern calendar is based on the calendar introduced by **Julius Caesar** in 46 BC. This divided the year into 365 days over 12 months. The **Julian calendar** was replaced by the **Gregorian calendar** in the 16th century when the Julian calendar was too much out of line with the movements of the sun.

Who are the experts on life in Ancient Rome?

》 Preparing for CBA2

A project on the life and experience of a person of historical interest

PERSONS OF INTEREST FROM ANCIENT ROME

- Julius Caesar
- Spartacus
- Trajan
- Augustus
- Cicero
- Lucilla
- Livia Drusilla
- Virgil
- Hannibal
- Nero
- Constantine
- Helena

p. 14 Web Resources and Reading

03

EARLY CHRISTIAN IRELAND

CHRONOLOGICAL AWARENESS

L.O. 2.6
The Nature of History: 1.1, 1.3, 1.4, 1.5, 1.6, 1.7, 1.8, 1.9, 1.10, 1.11
CBA1
CBA2

You will learn to ...

⊘ Consider the historical significance of Christianity

⊘ Consider the contribution of Christianity to culture and society in Early Christian Ireland

⊘ Explore the Nature of History

Old Stone Age
No evidence of people living in Ireland

8000 BC

Milddle Stone Age (Mesolithic)
First people in Ireland

6000 BC

4000 BC

New Stone Age (Neolithic)
First farmers in Ireland

Skellig Michael

Clonmacnoise

What do these pictures tell you about Early Christian Ireland?

2000 BC

Bronze Age
First use of metal

KEY WORDS

- Excavations
- Evidence
- Stratigraphy
- Round Tower
- Tonsure
- Crozier
- Manuscripts
- Radiocarbon dating
- Monastery
- High Cross
- Scriptorium
- Filigree
- Sources
- Dendrochronology
- Beehive hut
- Scribe
- Chalice

Iron Age
Iron replaced bronze; arrival of Celts

0

Early Christian Ireland
Arrival of Cristianity

Early Christian Ireland

Pre-Christian Ireland

Before the coming of Christianity to Ireland, the country was dominated by **Celtic culture**. The Celtic way of life had come to Ireland about 900 years before. It coincided with the development of the **Iron Age**, when iron replaced **bronze** as the main metal for weapons and tools.

Unlike Britain, the **Romans** had not conquered Ireland. The Celtic language, laws and religion were spoken and practised here. The **druids**, or priests, controlled the Celtic religion. It was a **pagan religion** which believed in **many gods**.

The coming of Christianity to Ireland

There were Christians in Ireland by the early **fifth century** (400–499 AD). Some came from **Roman Britain**, where they had been captured in raids by Irish warriors, while others were Irish people who had been converted during contact with Christians in Britain.

The pope sent a number of **missionaries** to visit the Irish Christians. The first of these was **Palladius**, who was sent in 431 AD as a bishop to 'the Irish who believe in Christ'. But the most famous of the missionaries was **St Patrick**, who told his story in his *Confession*.

St Patrick

St Patrick was born in **Roman Britain**, but at the age of **sixteen** he was captured by Irish raiders. He was kept as a **slave** for six years, tending sheep on mountains in the West of Ireland. Then he escaped and eventually returned to his family in Britain. Some time later, he became a priest and bishop and returned to Ireland as a **missionary**.

Through the work of St Patrick and other missionaries, Ireland was largely a Christian country by the early sixth century. The coming of Christianity made **significant changes** to Irish culture and society. It replaced the pagan religion and many Celtic festivals became Christian festivals instead. For the rest of this chapter, we will consider other **significant changes**.

What is St Patrick's *Confession*?

The *Confession* is an account written by St Patrick. It gives brief details of his life. It explains why he did certain things and it defends his good name against any attack on his character. The Book of Armagh, housed in Trinity College, Dublin contains the earliest copy of Saint Patrick's *Confession* known to exist.

- ⊘ Describe the story of the coming of Christianity to Ireland
- ⊘ Consider the meaning of 'historically significant'
- ⊘ Outline some of the work of the early Irish monasteries
- ⊘ Investigate how historians and archaeologists know about Clonmacnoise

You Tube

Celtic Ireland
Go onto YouTube and look up 'Miss Stout's History Class The Celts'

WHAT DOES 'HISTORICALLY SIGNIFICANT' MEAN?

Definition: The **significance** of something is the importance that it has, usually because it will have an effect on a situation or shows something about a situation. **(Collins English Dictionary)**

Historically significant events include those that resulted in **great change** over long periods of time for large numbers of people.

In relation to **Early Christian Ireland**, you will be asked to judge
- How did the events cause change?
- What impact/effect did the events have on their own time?
- What impact/effect do the events have on us today?

Q Extracts from St Patrick's *Confession*

1.

My name is Patrick. I am a sinner, a simple country person, and the least of all believers. I am looked down upon by many. My father was Calpornius. He was a deacon; his father was Potitus, a priest, who lived at Bannavem Taburniae. His home was near there, and that is where I was taken prisoner. I was about sixteen at the time. At that time, I did not know the true God. I was taken into captivity in Ireland, along with thousands of others. We deserved this, because we had gone away from God, and did not keep his commandments.

2.

It was there [in Ireland] one night in my sleep that I heard a voice saying to me: 'You have fasted well. Very soon you will return to your native country.' Again after a short while, I heard someone saying to me: 'Look – your ship is ready.' It was not nearby, but a good two hundred miles away. I had never been to the place, nor did I know anyone there. So I ran away then, and left the man with whom I had been for six years.

3.

It was while I was there [back home in Britain] that I saw, in a vision in the night, a man whose name was Victoricus coming as it were from Ireland with so many letters they could not be counted. He gave me one of these, and I read the beginning of the letter, the voice of the Irish people. While I was reading out the beginning of the letter, I thought I heard at that moment the voice of those who were beside the wood of Voclut, near the western sea. They called out as it were with one voice: 'We beg you, holy boy, to come and walk again among us.' This touched my heart deeply, and I could not read any further; I woke up then. Thanks be to God, after many years the Lord granted them what they were calling for.

4.

How has this happened in Ireland? Never before did they know of God except to serve idols and unclean things. But now, they have become the people of the Lord, and are called children of God. The sons and daughters of the leaders of the Irish are seen to be monks and virgins of Christ!

(Source: www.confessio.ie/etexts/confessio_english#01)

Q

1. What does Patrick say about himself when he was young?
2. Why did he write the *Confession*?
3. Why did he go back to Britain?
4. Why did he return to Ireland?
5. Is the *Confession* a primary or a secondary source for the life of St Patrick?
6. What information is not included that you would like to know?

Timeline of St Patrick

Patrick provides no dates in his *Confession*. Later writers provide some of the dates but they may be wrong.

?387 AD	Birth of Patrick
403	Captured as a slave
409	Escaped and returned to Britain
??	Trained as a priest and bishop
432	St Patrick came back to Ireland as missionary
?461	Death of St Patrick

Early Irish monasteries

In the sixth century (500–599 AD) and after, many monasteries were built in Ireland. Holy men who wanted places to pray and honour God founded most of the monasteries. However, women, such as, **St Íta** and **St Brigid**, also founded some. Men such as **St Enda** in the Aran Islands, **St Finian of Clonard**, **St Ciarán of Clonmacnoise** and **St Brendan of Clonfert** built monasteries, which became centres of learning and culture:

- The **Bible** was studied
- **Manuscripts** (hand written books) were studied

- **Metal-working** and **stone-carving** produced great works of art
- **Visitors** were welcomed

However, the monks lived simple lives:

- They followed **strict rules**, with an **abbott** in charge
- They produced their own food
- They wore **long tunics** with woollen cloaks, and shoes or sandals

Christian missions to Ireland in the fifth century

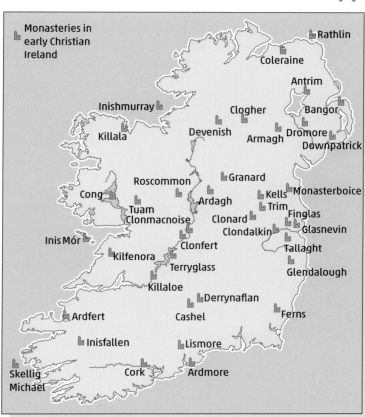

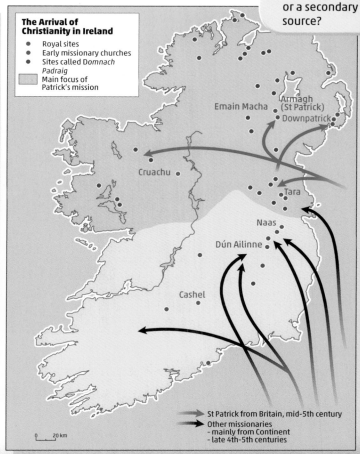

TIME AND SPACE

Q

1. What does this map tell you about how Ireland was converted to Christianity?
2. Is this a primary or a secondary source?

CHRONOLOGICAL AWARENESS

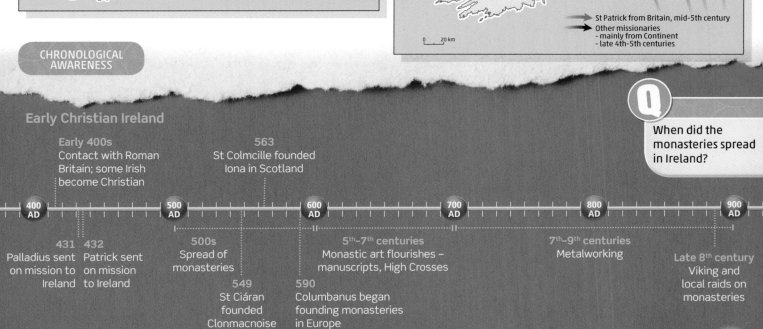

Q

When did the monasteries spread in Ireland?

Early Christian Ireland

Early 400s Contact with Roman Britain; some Irish become Christian

563 St Colmcille founded Iona in Scotland

400 AD — 500 AD — 600 AD — 700 AD — 800 AD — 900 AD

431 Palladius sent on mission to Ireland

432 Patrick sent on mission to Ireland

500s Spread of monasteries

549 St Ciáran founded Clonmacnoise

590 Columbanus began founding monasteries in Europe

5th–7th centuries Monastic art flourishes – manuscripts, High Crosses

7th–9th centuries Metalworking

Late 8th century Viking and local raids on monasteries

How do Historians and Archaeologists know about Clonmacnoise?

Historians and archaeologists often begin their investigations with **questions**. They research **sources** to provide the **evidence** which will answer the questions. **Clonmacnoise**, on the banks of the River Shannon, just south of present-day Athlone, was one of the greatest monasteries in Early Christian Ireland.

HISTORICAL EVIDENCE

ARCHAEOLOGICAL INVESTIGATION

What questions did historians and archaeologists ask about Clonmacnoise and where did they find some of the answers?

1. How old is Clonmacnoise and who founded it?

2. Did many people live here?

3. What did they work at?

4. What connection did the monastery have with the river?

5. Why was this location chosen for the monastery?

6. Was there only one wall around it?

7. What use was made of the buildings?

 p. 24 ❭

e there any other questions ou would like to add to the questions above about Clonmacnoise?

How does new technology help in the investigatng and understanding what life was like in Clonmacnoise?

Go onto YouTube and look up 'The Lost City of Clonmacnoise – Secret of the Stones Excerpt'. Next, look up 'The Lost City of Clonmacnoise 3D App'.

Visit ...
Clonmacnoise, Co Offaly

Geophysical survey

Touch screen and virtual reality (VR)

Underwater archaeology

Some monks developed great skills in **writing** and **illuminating** (illustrating) the religious books.

These monks were called **scribes**. They practised their skills on wax tablets. The scribes copied the manuscripts in the **scriptorium** on **vellum** (calfskin) or **parchment** (sheepskin). The monks used **reeds** or **quills** – the tail feathers of geese or swans – to write. The **ink** was produced from minerals, plants and leaves.

Examples of manuscripts

- The **Annals of Tigernach**, **Chronicon Scotorum** and the **Annals of Clonmacnoise** were written in Clonmacnoise. The Annals of Tighernach and Chronicon Scotorum still survive, but the original manuscripts of the Annals of Clonmacnoise are lost. Instead, there is a copy done in the 17th century.

- The **Cathach** is a copy of the psalms in **Latin** on **vellum**. It is one of the oldest existing manuscripts in Ireland and is now in the Royal Irish Academy in Dublin.

- The **Book of Durrow** is a copy of the Gospels of Matthew, Mark, Luke and John in **Latin**. It is copied on vellum and is housed in Trinity College, Dublin.

- The **Book of Kells** is a copy of the four Gospels in Latin. It is copied on vellum and preserved in Trinity College, Dublin.

- **Lebor na hUidre** or the **Book of the Dun Cow** is a vellum manuscript with stories and legends from Ancient Ireland, written in **Clonmacnoise**. It is the oldest manuscript written in **Irish**, and it is held in the Royal Irish Academy, Dublin.

The monk is copying a manuscript. His head has been shaved in a tonsure. Can you describe his clothes, his appearance and the work he is doing?

It contains the four Gospels ... with almost as many drawings as pages, and all of them in marvelous colours ... If you take your time to look at them closely you will notice such intricacies (details), so delicate and subtle, so fresh still in their colourings that you will not hesitate to declare that all these things must have been the result of the work not of men but of angels.
(Gerald of Wales described seeing a manuscript in Kildare [1185 AD])

Q According to Gerald of Wales what was 'the result of the work not of men but of angels'?

You Tube
The Book of Kells
Go onto YouTube and look up 'RTE – The Book of Kells'

p. 27 Manuscripts

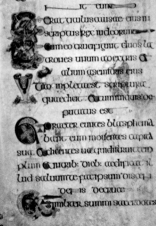

The Book of Durrow

The Book of Kells

The Cathach

High crosses

The monks also carved **high stone crosses**. The first stone crosses were simple in design, but later crosses had details of scenes from the Bible, as well as figures of saints. These carvings were used to **teach** people about Christianity.

The Cross of the Scriptures, Clonmacnoise

The Ardagh Chalice
Go onto YouTube and look up 'Deirdre Morgan Ardagh Chalice'.
Tara Brooch
Next look up 'Deirdre Morgan Tara Brooch'.

Metalworking

Monks also produced fine silver **chalices**, **croziers** and **brooches** decorated with gold, amber and enamel. The intricate gold wiring was called **filigree**. The influence of Celtic designs – the La Tène style – can be seen clearly in their work.

A crozier

Who are the experts on Early Irish Christian art?

The Ardagh Chalice

Derrynaflan Hoard

To Europe

Some Irish monks went abroad to found monasteries. **St Colmcille** went to Scotland to found the monastery of Iona. **St Columbanus** and his followers travelled to the Continent and **founded** many monasteries in France, Switzerland and Italy. The Irish monks produced **manuscripts** in the Irish style and **converted** non-Christian tribes to Christianity. Historians look on this time as a **'Golden Age'** in Irish learning.

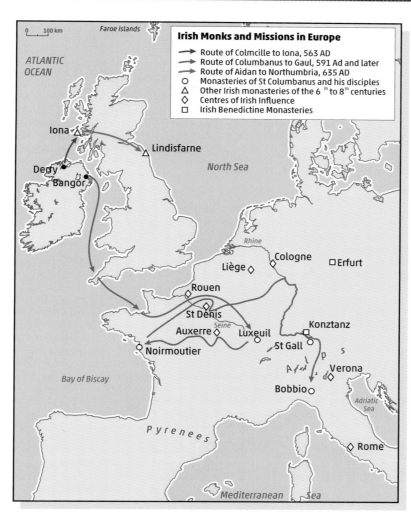

How widespread was the influence of Irish missionaries in Europe?

TIME AND SPACE

St Patrick's Day

St Patrick's Day on 17th March is a **national holiday**. Irish people in Ireland and abroad celebrate this day. St Patrick and stories associated with him have become part of Irish **national identity**. The national holiday is now a **major tourist attraction**, as cities and towns in Ireland hold parades to celebrate St Patrick. Abroad, in cities such as New York, it brings the **Irish Diaspora** together.

A St Patrick's Day parade

CHANGE AND CONTINUITY

- What was Christianity's contribution to society and culture in Early Christian Ireland?

Christianity's most important contributions.

📖 **p. 29** ❯
What did Christianity contribute to culture and society in Early Christian Ireland?

'Since the historian depends mainly on written documents for his knowledge of the past, Irish history properly speaking must begin with St Patrick, the author of the earliest documents known to have been written in Ireland.'
(Ó Fiaich)

Irish people were converted to a **new religion**, Christianity. The Celtic religion was gone. 'A pagan Ireland in which the **druids** held a central position was transformed (changed) into a Christian Ireland in which the Church had taken their central place.'
(Charles-Edwards)

Irish missionaries took their learning to the **Continent** and founded many monasteries there; 'helped to make [the Continent] ready for the flowering of learning which was to follow in ninth-century Gaul (France).'
(Hughes)

What was Christianity's contribution to society and culture in Early Christian Ireland?

By the eighth century the Church had become a **great patron of art**.

Christianity influenced new laws for society.

By the twentieth century, St Patrick and the coming of Christianity became part of **Irish national identity**.

Ireland became **literate** – reading and writing came to Ireland.
Irish monks became great **Latin scholars**.
Irish monks produced **great works** of art in manuscripts, stone crosses and religious ornaments.

Other aspects of Celtic Ireland, such as how people lived and worked, changed – only **slowly**.

📖 **p. 30** ❯
Characteristics of Early Christian Ireland

INVESTIGATING A REPOSITORY OF HISTORICAL EVIDENCE FOR EARLY CHRISTIAN IRELAND

The National Museum,
www.museum.ie/Archaeology/Exhibitions/Current-Exhibitions/The-Treasury
The Ulster Museum,
https://nmni.com/um/Collections/Archaeology/Early-Medieval-Ireland
The Irish National Heritage Park, Wexford
www.irishheritage.ie/early-christian-ireland-400-800ad-2/
Clonmacnoise Visitor Centre and site,
www.heritageireland.ie/en/midlands-eastcoast/clonmacnoise/
Glendalough Visitor Centre and site,
www.heritageireland.ie/en/midlands-eastcoast/glendaloughvisitorcentre/

❯ Preparing for CBA1

Your locality can include your county

A project related to an aspect of the history of your locality or place (or personal/family history)

LOCAL PROJECTS FROM EARLY CHRISTIAN IRELAND

- A monastery in my locality
- Early Christian art from my locality
- The life of a local monk or saint

❯ Preparing for CBA2

A project on the life and experiences of a person of historical interest

PERSONS OF INTEREST FROM EARLY CHRISTIAN IRELAND

- St Patrick
- St Brigid
- St Colmcille
- St Columbanus
- St Ciarán
- St Íte
- Brendan the Navigator

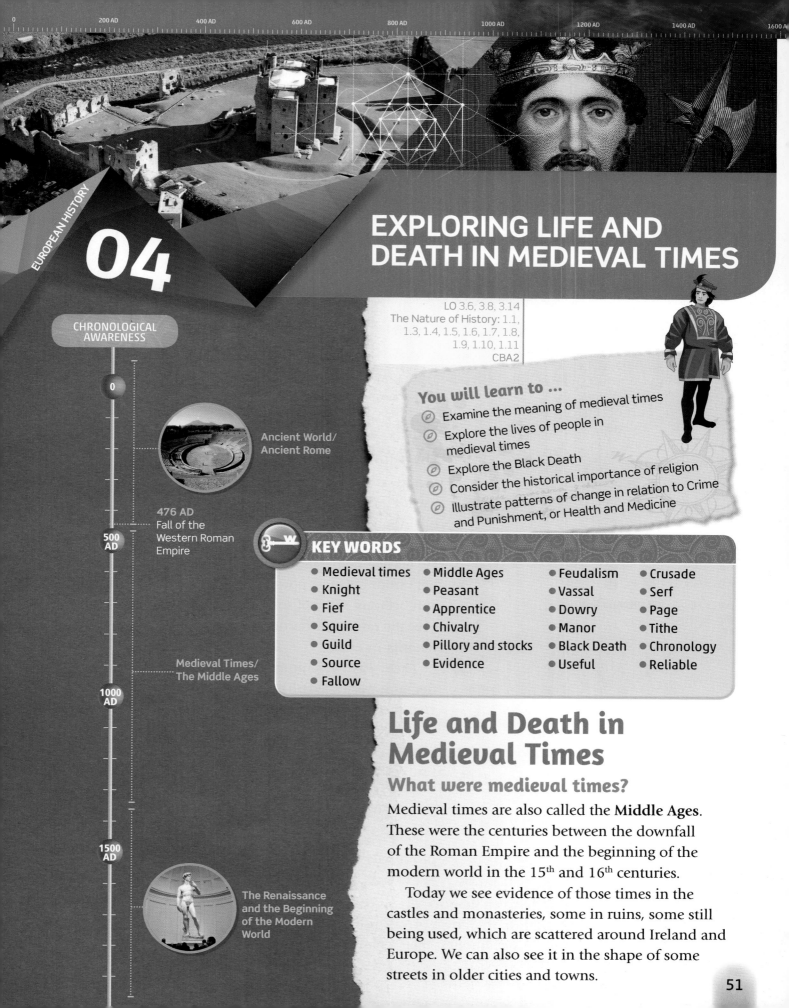

04

EXPLORING LIFE AND DEATH IN MEDIEVAL TIMES

CHRONOLOGICAL AWARENESS

LO 3.6, 3.8, 3.14
The Nature of History: 1.1,
1.3, 1.4, 1.5, 1.6, 1.7, 1.8,
1.9, 1.10, 1.11
CBA2

You will learn to ...

⊘ Examine the meaning of medieval times

⊘ Explore the lives of people in medieval times

⊘ Explore the Black Death

⊘ Consider the historical importance of religion

⊘ Illustrate patterns of change in relation to Crime and Punishment, or Health and Medicine

0

Ancient World/
Ancient Rome

500 AD

476 AD
Fall of the
Western Roman
Empire

KEY WORDS

- Medieval times
- Middle Ages
- Feudalism
- Crusade
- Knight
- Peasant
- Vassal
- Serf
- Fief
- Apprentice
- Dowry
- Page
- Squire
- Chivalry
- Manor
- Tithe
- Guild
- Pillory and stocks
- Black Death
- Chronology
- Source
- Evidence
- Useful
- Reliable
- Fallow

Medieval Times/
The Middle Ages

1000 AD

Life and Death in Medieval Times

What were medieval times?

Medieval times are also called the **Middle Ages**. These were the centuries between the downfall of the Roman Empire and the beginning of the modern world in the 15th and 16th centuries.

Today we see evidence of those times in the castles and monasteries, some in ruins, some still being used, which are scattered around Ireland and Europe. We can also see it in the shape of some streets in older cities and towns.

1500 AD

The Renaissance
and the Beginning
of the Modern
World

51

⊘ Explore the meaning of medieval times
⊘ Explore the lives of medieval people

Medieval people

Medieval writers divided people into **three groups**:

- Those who **fought**
- Those who **worked** and
- Those who **prayed**

Identify the medieval people. Who fought? Who worked? Who prayed?

King   Lord   Lady   Child   Knight   Peasant   Merchant   Craftsman   Labourer   Child   Bishop   Monk   Nun   Beggar

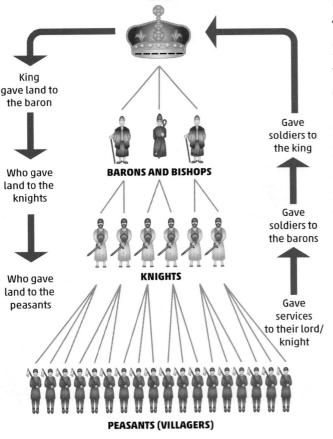

The feudal system

Medieval society

The feudal system

Land was very important in the Middle Ages, as it meant wealth and power. The ownership and control of land was organised through **feudalism** or the feudal system.

In medieval times, all the land was owned by the **king**. He needed help controlling and defending it. He got the help from his most powerful subjects – **barons** (lords) and bishops. He kept some land for his own use and gave the rest to the barons and **bishops** – who were his **tenants-in-chief**.

There was a ceremony for handing over the land (or **fief**, as it was called). The lord who was receiving the land knelt before the king and placed his hands in the hands of the king. He swore an oath to become a **vassal** of the king.

'I will be your man from this day onwards. I shall be true and faithful to you for the lands I hold from you.'

The lord also promised:

- To fight for the king and provide him with knights

The barons and bishops gave land to the **knights** who promised:

- To fight for their lords and obey them

The knights were given **manors**, that is, villages with land around them. Knights kept some of the land for their own private use – this land was called the **demesne**. They divided the rest amongst their tenants, who were called peasants or farmers.

Analysing Sources

How historians investigate sources – the Bayeux Tapestry

The Bayeux Tapestry or Embroidery tells the story of the invasion of England in 1066 by **William the Conqueror** from Normandy, France. He defeated King Harold of England at the **Battle of Hastings**. He brought the **feudal system** to England.

The tapestry is about 70 m long and 50 cm wide, and dates from about from the 1070s–1090s. It is believed to have been commissioned (ordered) by Odo, the Bishop of Bayeux, a half-brother of William the Conqueror. It has 50 main scenes, which were embroidered onto a woven linen background.

Norman knights attack Harold's soldiers

William's army being transported to England

The death of King Harold

Questions to ask about the usefulness of a source

> Is the source relevant (related) to what you are researching?

> Does it give you information that you need?

> Is the information reliable (trustworthy)?

> Is the Bayeux Tapestry a **primary** or a **secondary** source?

> What **story** does it tell?

> Is it a **reliable** source?

> What **evidence** (information) does it provide for historians about medieval warfare?

> Is the source written, visual, aural, oral or tactile?

Explain your answers.

Analysing Sources

How historians investigate sources – the Domesday Book

HISTORICAL JUDGEMENT

The Domesday Book was a 'great survey' of England and parts of Wales ordered by **William the Conqueror** after his conquest of England. It was completed in 1086 and it is written in **Latin**. It records who held the land and how it was used. It also includes information on how the land ownership had changed since William conquered England and Wales in 1066. It lists mostly landholders so it is not a census of population.

Why did he need to know this?

How did they travel?

Source 1

After this the king had a large meeting with his council about this land; how it was occupied, and by what sort of men. Then he sent his men over all England into each shire (county); commissioning (requiring) them to find out 'How many hundreds of hides (animal skin) were in the shire, what land the king himself had, and what stock upon the land; or, what dues (taxes) he ought to have by the year from the shire.'

(From The Anglo-Saxon Chronicles)

Getting answers

Detailed information

Extract from Domesday Book, 1086, showing original entry for Knebworth, England

Land holder

Written in Latin

Place names

Shorthand

Old place names

Source 2

Eudo FitzHubert holds Chenepeworde (Knebworth) and Humphrey holds it from him. There is enough land for 12 ploughlands (a measure of land). The lord has enough land in demesne for four ploughlands and 24 villagers have enough for eight plough teams between them. There is 1 mill and woodland for 1,000 pigs. Eskil, a lord of King Edward, held this manor.

(Edited extract from *Domesday Book*, 1086, for Knebworth, England)

What is a 'ploughland'?

Who is the tenant-in-chief?

Who was the previous lord?

Value of the land

Q

> Is the Domesday Book a **primary** or a **secondary** source?

> Using the information in this page, explain the difference between 'evidence' and 'source'.

> Noting the labels, what useful information does the Domesday Book provide for historians?

> Is the Domesday Book a **reliable** source for historians?

> How would you **compare** the Bayeux Tapestry and the Domesday Book as sources for historians of the Middle Ages?

Explain your answers.

Medieval People – Those Who Fought
The Lord and Lady of the Castle

The lord of the castle

The king divided up his land amongst the main lords. Each of those lords built castles and ruled their area.

The lord organised the business of the castle, kept his territory under control and carried out the wishes of the king. He had to fight for the king and help him rule the country. He had to go to the king's court when called. Since he was lord of his own area, he had to hold court and settle disputes. The lord passed on his land to his eldest son when he died.

The lady of the castle

Noblewomen were married off by their parents. Marriage was not a love match. Instead it forged links between important families. The bride's father provided gifts to take to her new family. This was her **dowry**.

Once she was married, she became the lady of the castle and had to ensure the daily running of the castle went smoothly. She was in charge of the stores, the baking, the brewing and the cellar. She gave directions to the servants, including the **pages** who came to the castle about seven years old. She spun flax and wool for thread with other ladies. She was also responsible for her daughters' education.

Building castles

Some of the first castles were built as **motte and bailey castles**. Later castles were built of **stone** and were much larger.

Motte and bailey castle

A motte and bailey castle being attacked from the Bayeux Tapestry

Building a motte and bailey castle

It is the custom of the nobles who spend much of their time fighting and slaughtering their enemies, in order to be safer from their opponents and to overcome them, to make a mound of earth as high as they can, and encircle it with a ditch as broad and as deep as possible. They enclose the upper edge of this mound with a stockade of logs firmly fixed together, strengthened at intervals with towers, according to their means. Within this enclosure they build their house, a central tower which commands the whole place. The entrance may only be reached across a bridge.

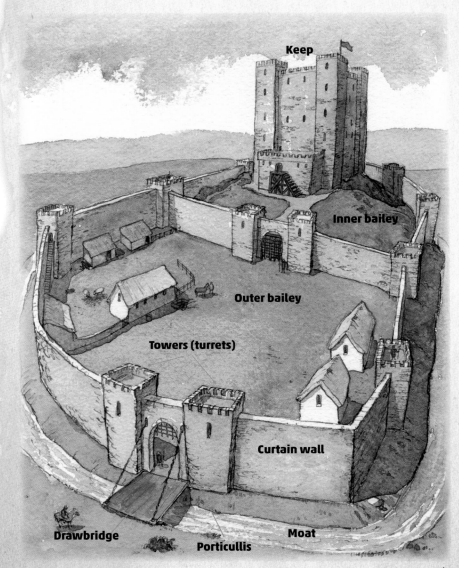

A stone castle

1. Why were castles built?
2. Why, do you think, the first castles were motte and bailey castles?
3. Why is there very little evidence of these in the countryside today?
4. What were the advantages of stone castles?
5. Identify different parts of the castle.

Life in the castle

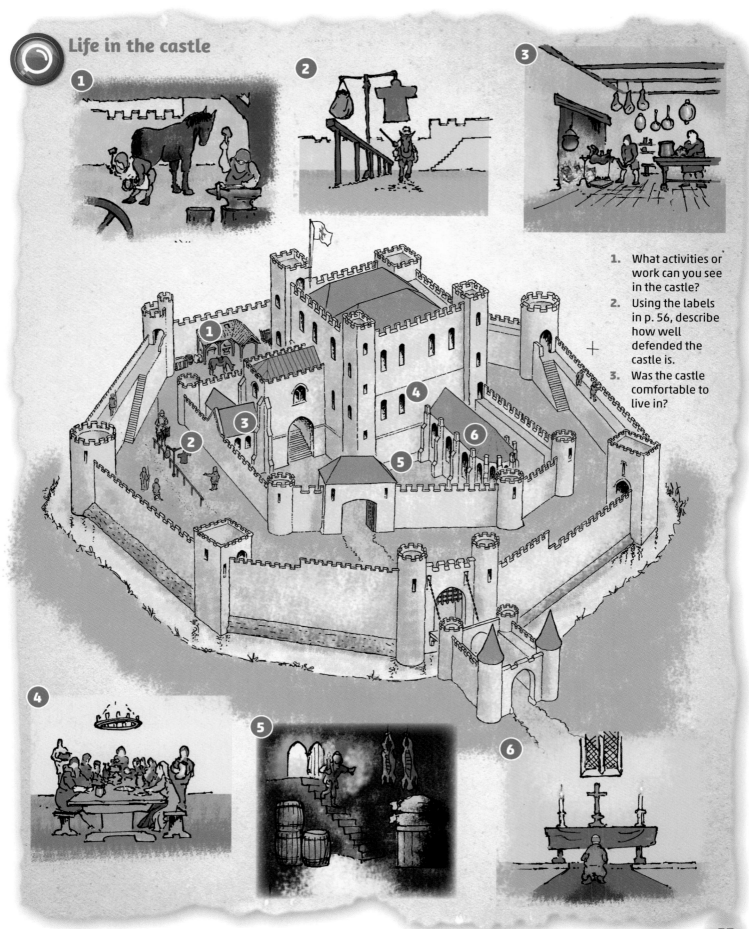

1. What activities or work can you see in the castle?
2. Using the labels in p. 56, describe how well defended the castle is.
3. Was the castle comfortable to live in?

Attacking and defending a castle

Attacking a castle:

Can you identify each of the methods of attack? How would each of the methods here be used to attack the castle?

Which of these methods would be the most effective method for attacking a castle?

Defending a castle

Trim Castle, Co. Meath

1. How are each of the features labelled here used to defend the castle?
2. Why was it so difficult to capture castles?

 p. 36

Pastimes of lords and ladies of the castle

1. Which of the following medieval pastimes of lords and ladies are featured in these pictures?
   - Hunting
   - Tournaments
   - Hawking
   - Hunting Dogs
   - Embroidery
   - Feasting
   - Drinking
   - Chess
   - Story Telling
   - Dancing
   - Spinning
   - Jousting
2. Are some pastimes mainly male and some mainly female?

 p. 38

Go onto YouTube and look up 'Miss Stout's History Class Life in a Medieval Castle'.

Medieval People – The Knight

The lord provided soldiers for his king. He got these soldiers from his sub-tenants or under-tenants who were knights.

Knights were **specially trained fighters** in the Middle Ages. They were usually the sons of lords or other knights. They were the backbone of the medieval army. They went through three stages of training:

At seven, they became **pages**, and were fostered by another lord and went to live in his castle. There they learned good manners, music, dancing, horse riding and helped the lady of the castle.

At 14, they became **squires**. They helped the lord dress for **jousts** (combats between two knights) and battles. They practised with lances, swords and shields, and bows.

At 21, they were **dubbed knights** by their lord. As they knelt before their lord, he struck them on the shoulder with the flat of the sword and said, 'Arise, Sir'...

The knight followed the code of **chivalry**. He promised:

- To be truthful, generous and loyal
- To be courteous to the poor
- To protect women and children

Explore what life was like for knights in medieval times

Q What does this source from the Middle Ages tell you about those who wanted to be knights?

Q Gerald of Wales, concerning the instruction of a prince (c. 1190)
The Count of Flanders caused a quintain (target) to be set up in the market place. This quintain was a strong shield firmly hung to a post. On it, those who wanted to be knights and strong young men might practice warlike sports. They rode at it at full gallop, and tried their strength, either by breaking their lances, or by piercing through the shield.
(Spartacus Educational, www.spartacus-educational.com)

Crest
Helmet
Valet is holding the Knight's Lance
Armour
Sword
Shield

Go onto YouTube and look up 'How to Joust like a Medieval Knight'

Jousting

Q Use the labels from the picture of the knight to say what is happening in this joust.

Medieval People – Those Who Worked

A medieval peasant

The lords and knights divided their land into manors. A **manor** was a village and the land around it.

A knight kept some of the land for his own use (the **demesne**) and rented the rest to **peasants**. The knights used **bailiffs** or **stewards** to run the manors.

The peasants lived in a village, in small houses with a plot of ground for growing vegetables or vines.

⊘ Explore what life was like for peasants in medieval times

The walls were made of **wattle and daub** – interwoven sticks covered with mud

The peasants were either freemen or **serfs**. Freemen paid a money rent and could move away whenever they wanted to. Serfs were not free. They needed the permission of the lord to travel to the nearest town.

What are the main features of a peasants house in medieval times?

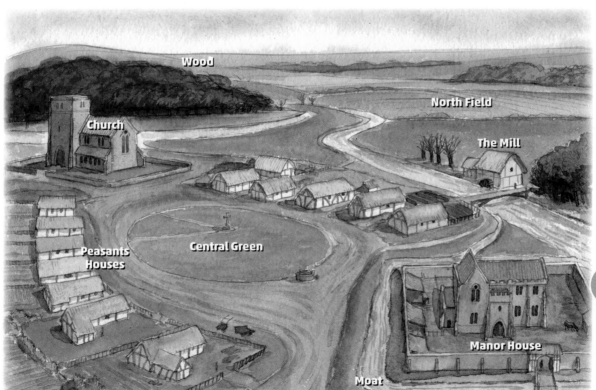

Wood

North Field

Church

The Mill

Peasants Houses

Central Green

Manor House

Moat

A medieval manor

All peasants had to work on the lord's demesne (private estate) at certain times. They also had to pay a **tithe** (one-tenth of their produce) to the parish priest. They had to grind their corn in the lord's mill.

Explain how the Open Field System below was applied to this village.

Fallow: land allowed to lay idle for a year so that it can recover

Crop rotation – the Open Field System

	Field 1	**Field 2**	**Field 3**
Year 1	Wheat	Oats/barley	Fallow
Year 2	Oats/barley	Fallow	Wheat
Year 3	Fallow	Wheat	Oats/barley

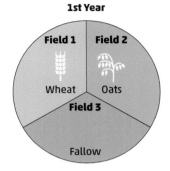
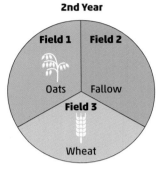
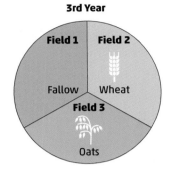

What work did the peasants do?

HISTORICAL EMPATHY

Peasants at work

1. Can you identify the peasant's work – ploughing, digging and sowing, reaping, threshing and winnowing?

2. Using the information in the pictures and the extract from Aelfric's Colloquy, would you say the work of the peasants was difficult? Use the evidence from the sources to support your answer.

Go onto YouTube and look up 'Life in the Middle Ages The Serf'.

Teacher: Can you tell us, ploughman, how you do your work?

Ploughman: Master, I have to work so very hard. I go out at the crack of dawn to drive the oxen to the field and yoke them to the plough. For not even in the bitter winter would I dare to stay at home for fear of my lord; but, when I have yoked up the oxen and fastened the plough and the ploughshare to the plough, then I must plough a whole field or more for the whole day. I have much work to do.

Shepherd: As soon as it is light, I drive the ewes (female sheep) to the pastures and guard them with dogs through heat and cold, so that the wolves do not devour them. I drive them to the folds, where I milk them twice a day. I move their folds and I make butter and cheese as well, and I am faithful to my lord.

(Aelfric's Colloquy, translated from the Latin by Ann E. Watkins, www.kentarchaeology.ac/authors/016.pdf

Medieval People – The Merchant and the Craftsman

Towns and cities grew rapidly in the Middle Ages. Towns were given **royal charters** by the king, which gave them permission to have a town government or corporation, fairs and markets and their own courts. They also collected **tolls** (taxes) to pay for repairing the walls.

The two main groups of people in the towns were **merchants** or **traders** and **craftsmen**.

⊘ Explore what life was like for merchants and craftsmen in medieval times

Merchants and traders

The merchants bought and sold goods. Some traded far distances. They attended fairs and markets.

Craftsmen

The craftsmen made and sold goods. They had **workshops** on the ground floor where they made and sold their goods. A sign over the door with a symbol such as a boot for a shoemaker showed the occupation of the workshop. Their living quarters were over the shops.

The workshop was run by a **master craftsman** who trained apprentices in the trade. **Apprentices** began at 14, lived with the master's family and slept in the workshop.

At the end of seven years, the apprentice made a **masterpiece** to prove his skill. Then he became a journeyman who travelled around working wherever he could, and getting paid by the day (journée = day).

Each of the trades formed their own **guild** to control the business of the trade or craft. The guilds controlled the standard of craftsmanship and decided who could be a craftsman. They also took care of their members when they fell on hard times, for example, by looking after those who got sick. Each guild had its own hall and its own coat of arms. In larger towns, guilds combined to build a guildhall.

ZUNFTWAPPEN. II.

1. Maurer. 2. Dachdecker. 3. Schornsteinfeger. 4. Glaser. 5. Töpfer. 6. Zimmerleute. 7. Stellmacher. 8. Böttcher. 9. Tischler. 10. Drechsler. 11. Grobschmiede. 12. Schlosser. 13. Nagelschmiede. 14. Messerschmiede. 15. Kupferschmiede. 16. Zinngiesser. 17. Goldschmiede. 18. Uhrmacher. 19. Schiffer. 20. Bergleute.

Medieval craft signs

What are the stages in becoming a master craftsman?

Street and family names

In larger towns and cities also, craftsmen of the same trade worked in the same street. For this reason, streets were given names such as Winetavern Street, Baker Street, Cook Street, Brogue Street, Dyer Street, Saddler Street, Carpenter Street and Miller Street.

Some family names also came from medieval trades, such as:

- Smith, Potter, Cooper, Mason, Tailor or Taylor, Spinner, Sawyer, Turner, Roper, Mercer, Farmer, Chapman.

Investigate what each of these trades did.

Guild rules

Poor workmanship will be punished by a fine and having all goods confiscated.

(Shoemakers' Guild, Chester)

No one shall make or sell hats within the city unless he is a burgess (a freeman) of the city.

(Hatmakers' Guild, London)

If by chance any member of the guild shall become poor through old age, accident or sickness, then he shall have 7 pence from the guild every week.

(Leatherworkers' Guild, London)

How did the guilds ensure a good standard of work?

Markets and fairs

Markets were held at least once a week. People from outside the town came to sell their produce – eggs, vegetables, milk. They bought from the traders who sold clothes, shoes, knives, pots and pans.

Fairs were much bigger, and they lasted much longer. They were held only once or twice a year. They were usually held outside the town walls, in a **fair green**, and merchants and traders came from far and near.

Crime and Punishment

The king organised **judges** to travel around the country to try certain crimes. This was in an effort to get rid of **trials by combat** and **trials by ordeal**. In the trial by combat, the winner was proved right. In the trial by ordeal, the innocent would survive the pain.

Night-time was dangerous in towns because there was no public lighting. A watchman was paid to patrol the streets, but no one was allowed out after curfew.

Crimes were punished severely by the town governments. Thieves could have their hands cut off, and executions were in public. Some were put in **pillorys** or **stocks**, and some were ducked into water.

1. Were trials by combat and by ordeal fair ways of deciding if a person was guilty?

2. Can you identify the different forms of punishment that you see in the pictures on the next page?

Trial by combat

Trial by ordeal

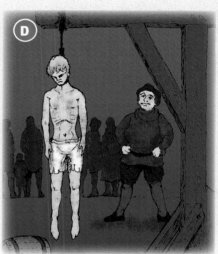

Is justice served?

SOURCES AND
EVIDENCE

p. 263

Source 1

Emma wife of Walter of Elsfield says that Roger Mock on the Thursday after Epiphany [8 January] 1238 came to her in her house and hit her with a pair of tongs in the eye so that she lost her right eye. And that he did this wickedly against the king's peace she offers to prove. Roger comes and denies everything, and since it is demonstrated (shown) that she made no appeal against him until now and this happened 3 years ago, it is adjudged that the appeal is null (invalid), and let an enquiry be made by jury. The jurors say that Roger is not guilty, so he is acquitted (found not guilty), but they say that Walter of Elsfield, Emma's husband, hit her so that she lost her eye, so he is committed to gaol.

(Oxfordshire Records Society vol. LVI, 1047, www.nationalarchives.gov.uk/)

Source 2

John Scot lodged at the house of John Wenge in Ekynton, rose by night wishing to do away with John Wenge, who seeing this, raised the hue (shout, noise). John Scot fled at once. Richard, former groom of Hugh de Cantilupo, hearing the hue, joined in and together they pursued John Scot whom they beheaded as a thief in flight.

(1281 Derbyshire Eyre, Case 454, www.nationalarchives.gov.uk/)

Q Do you agree with the result or outcome in each case here?

How violent were the Middle Ages?

Now that you have studied the sources above about trials and punishments in medieval times, are you surprised at the figures (statistics) about the number of murders? Explain your answer.

To decide whether the amount of violent crime is great or small, the number of murders is measured against the number of people. Thus the number of murders per 100,000 people in 1995–7 was:

For London – 2.1

For Washington DC – 69.3

For Moscow – 18.1

And, by one historian's estimate, for 14th century England – 12.0

www.nationalarchives.gov.uk/

- Consider the historical importance of religion
- Evaluate what life was like for monks and nuns in medieval times

The Catholic Church played a very significant role in the Middle Ages.

What do these sources tell you about its significance or importance in those centuries?

Medieval People – Those Who Prayed
The role of the Catholic Church

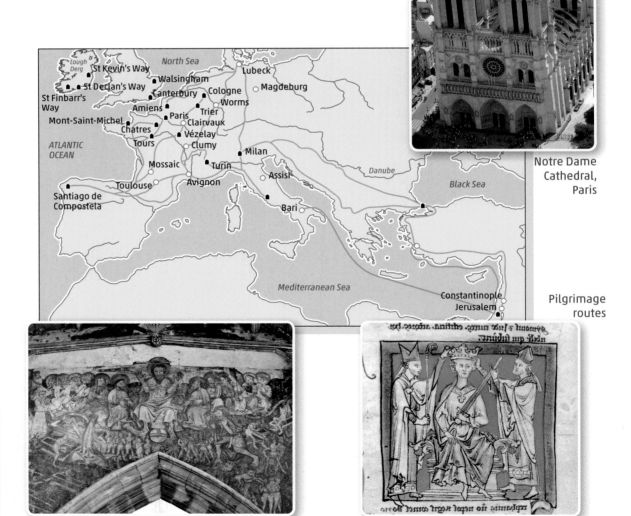

Notre Dame Cathedral, Paris

Pilgrimage routes

A 'doom' painting of the Last Judgement

An archbishop crowning a king

Visit …
Dublinia – Viking and Medieval Dublin, the Medieval Experience, Kerry County Museum, Tralee, and Medieval Museum Waterford to learn more about the Middle Ages

What were the consequences of the Black Death?

Overall estimates for the **numbers of people killed** in Europe by the Black Death vary from about 30% to 60% of the population of Europe.

The Black Death had a huge effect on the **economy** of Europe. It took almost 150 years before the population of Europe was back to the levels before the Black Death. Some villages were wiped out. As the plague killed so many labourers, those who survived demanded **higher wages** and tenants got **lower rents**.

In some places, where Jews were blamed for causing the plague, there was a rise in **anti-Semitism** (hatred of the Jews).

The plague returned at various times over the next few centuries.

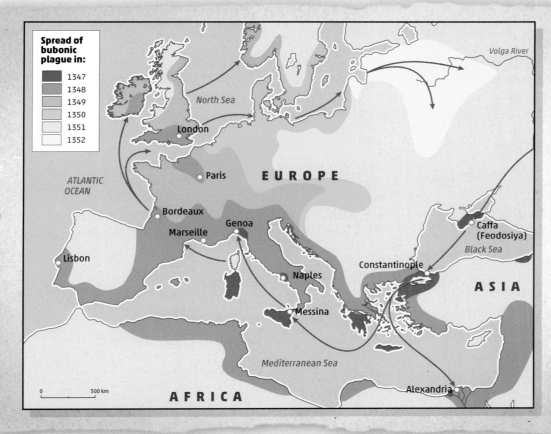

Spread of bubonic plague in:
- 1347
- 1348
- 1349
- 1350
- 1351
- 1352

1. Describe how the Black Death spread around Europe.
2. Why, do you think, the Black Death spread so quickly around the countries off the Mediterranean Sea?
3. Why did some parts of Europe escape the worst effects of the Black Death?
4. According to the map, how did the Black Death reach Ireland?

Franciscans treat people who have the plague

(p. 256

Analysing Sources

What did people think caused the plague?

CAUSE AND CONSEQUENCE

p. 42

Flagellants who came together in various parts of Europe believed that by flogging themselves they would atone (make up) for their sins and save themselves from the plague.

A plague doctor with herbs in the mask to overcome the vapours (fumes, smells).

Q

1. Which of these sources is primary and which is secondary?
2. Are these sources useful for studying the Black Death?
3. What did people think caused the plague?

Q Source 1

And all generally agree ... that the plague derives from corrupt and poisonous air ... From this I conclude that the most secure remedy against the disease is to flee as early as possible to a place with healthy air and leave behind the corrupt and infected air.

(Adapted from a medieval manuscript)

Q Source 2

For many the disease was caused by the vapours (fumes) coming from lakes and bogs ... The wrath (anger) of God at the sins of Mankind often provided the main force, followed by the influence of the coming together of the planets, especially Mars and Saturn. Some said the corrupt air was released from below the surface by earthquakes, along with snakes and frogs.

(Adapted from a modern history book)

Q Source 4

Deaths and Burials

The data is sufficiently widespread and numerous to make it likely that the Black Death swept away around 60 per cent of Europe's population. It is generally assumed that the size of Europe's population at the time was around 80 million. This implies that around 50 million people died in the Black Death.

(Ole J Benedictow, The Black Death: The Greatest Catastrophe Ever, History Today, Volume 55 Issue 3 March 2005)

Q Source 3

Blaming the Jews

In the matter of this plague the Jews throughout the world were reviled (hated) and accused in all lands of having caused it through the poison which they are said to have put into the water and the wells – that is what they were accused of – and for this reason the Jews were burnt all the way from the Mediterranean into Germany, but not in Avignon, for the pope protected them there.

Nevertheless they tortured a number of Jews in Berne and Zofingen [Switzerland] who then admitted that they had put poison into many wells, and they also found the poison in the wells. Thereupon they burnt the Jews in many towns and wrote of this affair to Strasbourg, Freiburg, and Basel in order that they too should burn their Jews ... On Saturday – that was St Valentine's Day – they burnt the Jews on a wooden platform in their cemetery. There were about two thousand people of them.

(The Cremation of Strasbourg Jewry St Valentine's Day, 14 February 1349 – About The Great Plague And The Burning Of The Jews, www.sourcebooks.fordham.edu)

Q Source 5

Deaths and Burials

All the citizens did little else except to carry dead bodies to be buried [...] At every church they dug deep pits down to the water-table; and thus those who were poor who died during the night were bundled up quickly and thrown into the pit. In the morning when a large number of bodies were found in the pit, they took some earth and shovelled it down on top of them.

(An account from Florence)

Experience Medieval Times in Ireland

The Normans brought the medieval life to Ireland. Led by Strongbow, they invaded the country in 1169–70. Sources and evidence of Ireland in the Middle Ages can be found in many parts of the country.

Life in medieval Ireland can be used as the basis for a project for **CBA1** – an aspect of the history of your locality or place:

- A local medieval church or town
- A Norman family in my locality
- The Black Death in my locality

CULTURAL INHERITANCE

INVESTIGATING A REPOSITORY OF HISTORICAL EVIDENCE FOR MEDIEVAL TIMES

Dublinia,
www.dublinia.ie
Kerry County Museum,
www.kerrymuseum.ie
Waterford Treasures Medieval Museum,
www.waterfordtreasures.com

Map of Ireland showing: Derry/Londonderry, Carrickfergus, Carlingford, Drogheda, Trim Castle, Co. Meath, Trim, St. Patrick's Cathedral, Dublin, Dublin Castle, Dublin, Rindoon/Lecarrow, Galway, Athenry, Bunratty Castle, Co. Clare, Athy, Castledermot, Holy Cross Abbey, Co. Tipperary, St. John's Castle, Limerick, Limerick, Kilkenny, Cashel, Fethard, Kilmallock, Clonmel, New Ross, Buttevant, Cahir Castle, Co. Tipperary, Waterford, Wexford, Ross Castle, Killarney, Cork, Youghal, Bandon. Scale 0 20 km

❯ Preparing for CBA2

A project on the life and experiences of a person of historical interest.

PERSONS OF INTEREST FROM THE MIDDLE AGES

- Charlemagne
- Eleanor of Aquitaine
- Christine de Pizan
- Marco Polo
- William the Conqueror
- Richard the Lionheart
- Joan of Arc
- Hildegard of Bingen
- Dante
- Richard de Clare, Strongbow

Visit:
Irish Walled Towns,
www.irishwalledtownsnetwork.ie

Focus Task

❯ Use Google Earth, Google Maps and/or Apple Maps (including street view and photographs) to examine evidence for medieval towns in Athenry, Co. Galway; Kilmallock, Co. Limerick and/or Fethard, Co. Tipperary (or other towns in Ireland with medieval remains). Insert the information in short-note form in a box in your copybook.

	Evidence
Street names	
Religious buildings	
Defence	
Location	
Evidence of marketplace	
Other medieval features	
Evidence of modern development of the town	

p. 44
Web Resources and Reading

HISTORICAL INVESTIGATION

Go onto YouTube and look up 'Miss Stout's History Class First Year History Key Words and Terms Part 1'.

Next, look up 'Miss Stout's History Class First Year History Key Words and Terms Part 2'.

Writing Historically 1

Express my ideas through sentences

In history, it is important to clearly organise your writing to get across **your ideas** and **viewpoint** on any historical event or person. This makes it easier for your reader (it could be yourself, your classmates, your teacher or an examiner) to understand your **point of view**.

In your study of history, you should be able to develop single points in a **sentence or two**, and write a **paragraph** to further develop your viewpoint.

You can first begin with **well-structured sentences**. These sentences will state clearly what you mean.

STATEMENT AND DEVELOPMENT

In a sentence, you should make a **statement about history**. Then **expand** or **develop** the information in that statement. To take an example from Ancient Rome (p. 31):

> Slaves could be bought and sold in markets.

We need to **expand** what we mean by adding on **further historical information**.

> Many were brought back from foreign wars. Some were born as slaves to slave women.

We have now made our statement, and developed it. You should **practise** that with all writing about history. You will be able to take these statements and develop them.

PRACTISE

> In Roman society, a woman's place was in the home. ...
>
> In the city, most Romans were called plebeians. ...

Sometimes, you do not have to add a second sentence, just expand the first sentence. For example:

> St. Patrick was born in Roman Britain.

This is a statement about where St. Patrick came from (p. 39). It can be expanded in the following way:

> St. Patrick was born in Roman Britain, but at the age of sixteen, Irish raiders captured him.
>
> He was kept as a slave for six years, tending sheep on mountains in the West of Ireland.

Another example is:

> The first reading and writing was done in Latin, which was the language of the Catholic Church.

TWO OR MORE SENTENCES

Sometimes sentences can be **too long** and they will need to be broken into two or more sentences.

> Julius Caesar went as governor to Spain, where he subdued warring tribes and brought peace to the area and then he returned to Rome where he, Pompey, and Crassus jointly ruled the city and he brought in popular reforms such as redistributing land to the poor.

Try breaking down that sentence before you look at one possible result on p. 29.

You can now look for **examples** of all the above sentences as you are reading this textbook. You can **practise** when you are writing answers by making statements and developing or expanding them.

We can now move onto **paragraphs**.

74

Historically significant events include those that resulted in **great change** over long periods of time for large numbers of people.

In relation to the **Renaissance**, you will be asked to judge:

● How did the events cause change?

● What impact/effect did the events have on their own time?

● What impact/effect do the events have on us today?

What Significant Changes Occurred in Painting?

See p. 80

⊘ Explain the changes in the Arts brought about by the Renaissance

The **Arts** include painting, sculpture, and architecture. What else is included in the Arts?

Medieval painting

Cimabue's *Madonna Enthroned*

Renaissance painting

Raphael's *The Marriage of the Virgin*

Renaissance artists made significant improvements in painting compared to medieval artists. You will be able to see these differences by studying these two paintings.

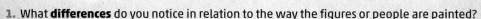

1. What **differences** do you notice in relation to the way the figures or people are painted?
2. Which painting is more **realistic**?
3. What do you notice about the **colours**?
4. Is there a difference in relation to the **topic** or **theme** of the paintings?
5. What difference do you notice about the **depth** of the paintings?
6. Do both paintings make use of **light** and **shade**?
7. Are the paintings **primary** or **secondary** sources?

Massacio's *The Trinity* (1427–28)

What is the illusion here? How did the artist create this illusion?

What is perspective?

The use of **perspective** creates an **illusion**. It makes you think that there is **depth** in the painting. It gives a feeling of 3-dimensions (height, width and depth) even though it is painted on a 2-dimensional (height, width) surface. The use of perspective was one of the most important developments in Renaissance art.

What other changes did the Renaissance bring about in painting?

Paints

In the Middle Ages, pictures were usually painted using **egg yolk** mixed with **coloured pigments**. This was called **tempera**. This dried quickly so changes could not be made to the painting.

In the Renaissance, **oil** was mixed with **coloured pigments**. This dried more slowly so changes could be made, and shading could be used.

How do you think the coloured pigments were created?

Wooden panels and canvas

In the **Middle Ages**, pictures were painted on **wooden panels** and on **walls**.

In the **Renaissance**, pictures were also painted on wooden panels and walls. But paintings were also done on **canvas**.

Frescos

A **fresco** was a painting done on **wet or damp plaster**. The paint soaked into the plaster and became part of it. Frescos were painted in ancient Egypt, Greece and Rome, and also in the Middle Ages. Some of the most important paintings of the Renaissance were frescos.

What changes occurred in Sculpture?

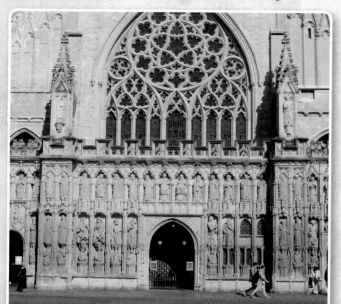

A section of the west front of Exeter Cathedral. The figures here were originally painted in bright colours.

The *Fountain of Neptune* in Florence by Bartolomeo Ammannati (1563–65)

What differences can you see between the medieval sculpture and the Renaissance sculpture?

How apprentices learned to paint and sculpt

Apprentices were trained by Masters.

Apprentice mixing paints

Apprentice learning to draw

Apprentice learning to sculpt

Apprentice painting minor parts of master's work

CULTURAL INHERITANCE

What significant changes occurred in Architecture?

These are **features** of medieval (Gothic) and Classical architecture. Match each of these labels to one of the pictures below:

KEY WORD

- **Architecture** is the art of planning, designing, and constructing buildings.

- Dome
- Pointed window
- Rounded window

- Buttress and flying buttress
- Rose window
- Pointed door

- Pointed arches
- Classical columns
- Pediment
- Spire

Medieval architecture

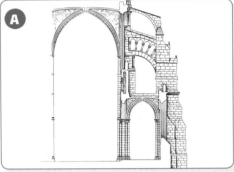

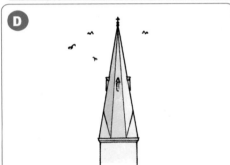

Renaissance architecture

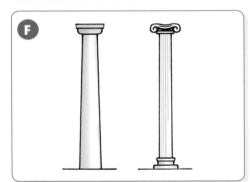

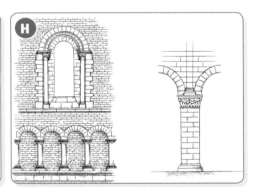

Leonardo's notebooks

Leonardo was interested in many different subjects – biology, botany, engineering, geology and mathematics. He wrote thousands of pages of **notebooks** in which he kept his ideas. He wrote **left-handed backwards** so it was difficult to read what he wrote. Here are some of his drawings of people and body parts.

Q

1. Leonardo dissected dead bodies. How would that help him in drawing these?
2. How would these drawings help him when he was painting?

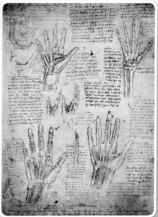
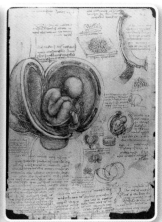
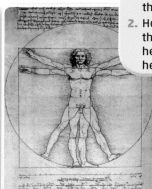

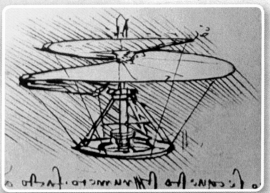

Helicopter

Parachute

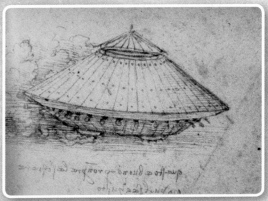

Tank

Wing detail

Go onto YouTube and look up 'Miss Stout's History Class Leonardo da Vinci'.

Who will be the expert on Leonardo da Vinci?

How do these show that Leonardo was well ahead of his time?

Michelangelo – The Greatest Artist?

- 1475 Born near Florence
- Apprentice to Master Ghirlandaio in Florence
- Studied sculpture in Medici's sculpture garden
- Carved *Pieta* in Rome
- Carved *David* in Florence
- Painted ceiling of Sistine Chapel in Rome
- Designed dome of St Peter's Basilica in Rome
- 1564 Died in Rome

Michelangelo

Michelangelo was born near Florence in 1475. He was apprenticed to Master **Ghirlandaio**. Later he trained at the sculpture school set up by **Lorenzo de Medici**, ruler of Florence and **patron** of the Arts. Michelangelo was invited to Rome to carve the *Pieta*. For the rest of his life he worked between Florence and Rome. He died in Rome in 1564.

How was Michelangelo historically significant?

Q

What do these figures tell you about Leonardo and Michelangelo?

Works of Art		
	Leonardo	**Michelangelo**
Paintings	15–25	9
Sculptures	None	42
Architecture	None	5

How good was Michelangelo as a sculptor?

Pieta

What is Carrara marble?

Michelangelo's first great work of art was the *Pieta*, which is in **St Peter's Basilica** in Rome. Michelangelo carved the *Pieta* from a block of **Carrara marble**. Michelangelo carved the idealised (perfect) human form in the head of Mary. He said she could not age because she was so pure. His sculpture of the dead Christ was very realistic. He was helped by his **study** of ancient Greek and Roman sculptures, and by dissecting dead bodies.

The **Pieta** in St Peter's Church, Rome. Why is the **Pieta** considered a great work of art? Do you agree? Michelangelo was very religious. How does this show in his works?

DID YOU KNOW?

Pieta is the only work of art signed by Michelangelo. Michelangelo overheard two strangers naming an artist from Milan as the sculptor. 'Michelangelo remained silent, but it seemed strange to him that his labours should be attributed to another. And one night he shut himself into the place with a light and cut his name upon it.'

David

Michelangelo sculptured *David* from a block of marble in Florence which had been damaged by another sculptor. David faced and killed the giant, Goliath, in the Old Testament.

Go onto YouTube and look up 'A Renaissance sculptor; Michelangelo 1475–1564'.

How good was Michelangelo as a painter?

The ceiling of the Sistine Chapel

Pope Julius II asked Michelangelo to paint the ceiling of the Sistine Chapel. He painted **four main scenes** and many smaller scenes from the Old Testament. It took Michelangelo four years to finish this **fresco** painting (see Analysing Sources p. 91).

 KEY WORD

- **Frescoes** are paintings done on damp or wet plaster.

A section of Michelangelo's poem on painting the ceiling of the Sistine Chapel

> My beard doth point to heaven, my scalp its place
> Upon my shoulder finds; my chest, you'll say
> A harpy's* is; my paintbrush all the day
> Doth rain a rich mosaic on my face …
> In front to utmost length is stretched my skin
> And wrinkled up in folds behind, while I
> Am bent as bowmen bend a bow in Spain
> No longer true or sane.

Michelangelo Buonarroti, Sonnet V (to Giovanni da Pistoia)(c. 1509), transl. S. Elizabeth Hall, *The Sonnets of Michelangelo Buonarroti*, (1903)

Harpy – half human, half-bird-like monster

89

What does the poem tell you about Michelangelo's attitude to painting the ceiling of the Sistine Chapel?

1. What is a fresco painting? (see p. 80 if you are not sure)

2. Can you find the **four main scenes** on the ceiling – the Creation of the World, the Creation of Adam, the Fall in the Garden of Eden, and the Flood? What do these tell you about Michelangelo's view of humans?

3. Michelangelo said, 'the nearer painting approaches sculpture the better it is … sculpture is worse the nearer it approaches painting.' Can you see the **influence of sculpture** in his painting of the figures on the ceiling of the chapel?

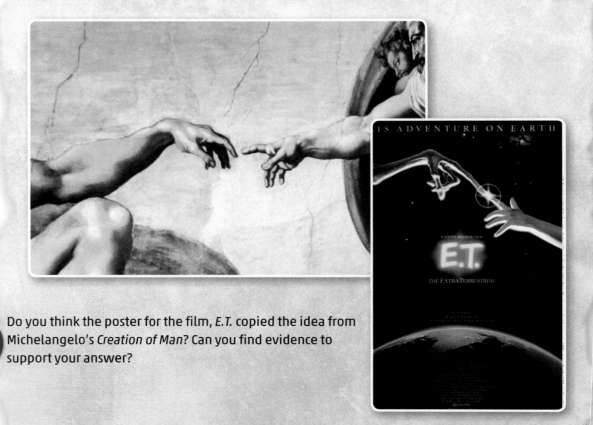

Do you think the poster for the film, *E.T.* copied the idea from Michelangelo's *Creation of Man*? Can you find evidence to support your answer?

What difficulties did Michelangelo face in painting the ceiling of the Sistine Chapel?

Analysing Sources

Vasari's *Lives of the Artists*, published 1550, 2nd ed., 1568

Source 1

From the hour when the Lord God, by His outstanding kindness, made me worthy not just of the presence, but of the love, of the conversation, and of the close intimacy of Michelangelo Buonarroti, the unique sculptor and painter, I gave myself all possible attention and study to assembling (putting together) not only the precepts (principles) he taught me about the art of design, but also his sayings, deeds, and habits. I also intended to write about it at some future time. This was as much to show him gratitude for my infinite obligations (duty) towards him, as to give others the benefit of the advice and example of this great man.

(Vasari's introduction to his account of Michelangelo's life)

Source 2

Giorgio Vasari (30 July 1511–27 June 1574) was an Italian painter, architect, writer, and historian, most famous today for his *Lives of the Most Excellent Painters, Sculptors, and Architects*.

(Wikipedia)

Source 4

Considered the first art historian and often referred to as the 'father of art history', Vasari's contribution was to create a critical, i.e., evaluative (appraisal, assessment) history of artistic style, although he was far from unbiased.

(Dictionary of Art Historians, *https://dictionaryofarthistorians.org/vasarig.htm*)

Source 3

In 1550 a little known Italian artist, Giorgio Vasari, published a revolutionary book. For the first time, Vasari set out to record artists' oddities and faults as well as their artistic triumphs. In more recent decades, Vasari has been criticised for not allowing factual accuracy to get in the way of a good story. Nonetheless, his work has formed and defined the way we think about Renaissance art to this day and some credit him with being the founder of the discipline of the history of art.

(BBC Radio, In Our Time,*www.bbc.co.uk/programmes/b00sg2y4*)

Q **What do you know about the source?**

> Based on Source 1, do you think Vasari was **biased**?
> Do the other sources **praise** Vasari's *Lives*?
> Do the other sources **criticise** Vasari's *Lives*?
> What do the sources tell you about how well qualified Vasari was to write a biography of Michelangelo?
> Is Vasari's book a **primary** or a **secondary** source?

Explain your answers by using evidence from the sources.

WHAT CAN YOU LEARN FROM THE SOURCE? **Q**

> Who persuaded the Pope to ask Michelangelo to paint the ceiling of the Sistine Chapel? Why did he persuade the Pope?
> What 'discomfort' did Michelangelo suffer while painting?
> How did the Pope react on seeing the painting?
> Write out **one fact** and **one opinion** from the document.
> How would you prove your selection of 'fact' is correct?

Source 5

An edited extract from Vasari's *Lives of the Artists* on the painting of the ceiling of the Sistine Chapel

When the Pope was returned to Rome, Bramante (a friend of Raphael, and therefore little a friend to Michelangelo) persuaded him that on Michelangelo's return he should set him to paint the ceiling of the chapel in the palace. For Bramante and Michelangelo's other rivals thought to draw him away from sculpture, in which they saw he was perfect, and make him produce less worthy works, knowing he had had no experience in painting in *fresco*. ... Michelangelo prepared to do the whole work himself. The work was done in great discomfort from constantly looking up ... The work has been, indeed, a light of our art, illuminating (lighting up) the world which had been so many centuries in darkness. When it was uncovered every one from every part ran to see it, and gazed in silent astonishment; and the Pope, inspired by it and encouraged to greater undertakings, rewarded him liberally with money and rich gifts.

The Last Judgement

Pope Julius II asked Michelangelo to paint a **fresco** of *The Last Judgement* on the wall of the Sistine Chapel. Michelangelo portrayed God in the centre raising the dead to Heaven, as the damned fall to Hell. He included the story from **Ancient Rome** of Charon, the boatman, ferrying the people across the River Styx.

DID YOU KNOW?
Michelangelo included a self-portrait in *The Last Judgement* as the flayed skin held by Saint Bartholomew, below and to the right of Christ.

Q
1. Why do you think this is considered a great painting?
2. How would you compare it with the painting of the ceiling?

The Last Judgement was painted behind the altar in the Sistine Chapel

How good was Michelangelo as an architect?

Michelangelo was given the job of redesigning the Capitoline Hill, one of the seven hills of Ancient Rome. He created a **square** (piazza) with three palaces around it and steps leading up to it. The buildings followed **Classical** (or Roman) designs.

Q
What features of Classical architecture can you see in the Campidoglio?

The Campidoglio, a square on the Capitoline Hill in Rome, designed by Michelangelo

The dome of St Peter's Basilica, Rome

Michelangelo was asked by the pope to design the **dome** of the new St Peter's Basilica in Rome. It was his **last great project**. He did not live to see its completion because he died in 1564 at the age of eighty nine.

St Peter's Basilica, Rome

Q

1. What other domes could Michelangelo study before he designed the dome for St Peter's Basilica?
2. What other features of Classical architecture can you see in St Peter's Basilica?

Close up of dome

Who will be the expert on Michelangelo?

Analysing Sources

What was significant in the lives of Renaissance women?

- Explore the role of Renaissance women
- Investigate the life of Sofonisba Anguissola – a Renaissance artist

The role of Renaissance women

The women of the Renaissance were **second-class citizens**. They were denied political rights and, if they married, they were legally subject to their husbands. They were expected to perform the duties of a housewife.

Women as wives and mothers

Source 1

Women should follow these rules: the first is that they should bring up their children in the fear of God; and the second is that they should keep quiet in church, and I would add, stop talking in other places as well, for they cause much mischief thereby.

(V. da Bisticci, *Lives of Illustrious Men of the 15th century* [1475])

Source 2

Tomorrow morning send back the small jar of dried raisins and the bread. And send the barrel of vinegar … remember to wash the mules' feet with hot water down to her hoofs. And have my stockings made and soled. Give some millet to the nag … sell the two barrels of wine quickly.

(A letter from a merchant to his wife)

Women as slaves

Source 3

If there is sweeping to be done? Then make your slave sweep. Are there pots to be scoured? Then make them scour them. Make her look after the children and everything else. If you don't get her used to doing all work, she will become a lazy little lump of flesh.

(Fra Bernadino, a preacher from Siena)

DID YOU KNOW?

Male and female slaves from Africa and Asia were common in the city-states of Italy during the Renaissance. They were mainly used as domestic servants by the wealthy.

Source 4

Cosimo de Medici, who became ruler of Florence in 1434, lived in Rome away from his family for two years. There Maddelena, a slave girl he had bought in Venice, looked after him. She bore him a son, Carlo. Carlo and his mother came to live in Cosimo's palace in Florence where Carlo was educated with Cosimo's other children.

(Various secondary sources)

Women as Patrons of the arts

Source 5

Women as Patrons of the Arts: Isabella d'Este, Duchess of Mantua, had a large collection of paintings and supported many artists. She is sketched here by Leonardo da Vinci for a portrait which was never painted.

Source 6

An historian's view

In Renaissance Italy, most women from the upper classes had only two options in life: marriage or the cloister (convent). Women of the upper classes were not expected, or even allowed, to work outside the home. Women in the growing middle class sometimes worked in shops, though this was more common in Northern Europe than in Italy. Poorer women had a hard lot in life, working in the fields or in cities as servants.

(Women in the Renaissance, www.vam.ac.uk)

- What do Sources 1 and 2 tell you about the **attitude to women** in Renaissance Italy?
- How were slave women treated according to Sources 2 and 3?
- Do the sources support the historian's view in Source 6?
- Which of the sources are **primary** and which are **secondary**?
- **Summarise** the role of women in the Renaissance.

Women as artists

Sofonisba Anguissola – a Renaissance artist

Sofonisba Anguissola was born in Cremona, in Northern Italy in 1532, the daughter of a nobleman. Her parents encouraged her to paint. She was apprenticed to a **local master** for three years, and later helped her sisters who were also artists. She painted many **self-portraits** and also paintings of her family. Due to her fame, the **King of Spain** invited her to become a court painter. She later married twice, and continued to paint until her eyesight faded. She died in 1625.

Q Source 1

Self-Portrait at the Easel, 1556

Q Source 2

The Chess Game, 1555 includes depictions of Sofonisba Anguissola's sisters

Q Source 3

Sofonisba of Cremona has laboured at the difficulties of design with greater study and better grace than any other woman of our time, and she has not only succeeded in drawing, colouring, and copying from nature, and in making excellent copies of works by other hands, but has also executed by herself alone some very choice and beautiful works of painting.

(Vasari's *Lives of the Artists*)

Q Source 5

Sofonisba painted with something of that tepid rose-tinted sentimentality proper to the woman-painter, then as now.

(Claude Philips, art critic, 1913)

Q Source 4

While I was making her portrait she alerted me to various things: not to hold the light too high so the shadows aren't too deep in the lines of an old person's face, for instance; and she told me many good things about her life, too. It was clear that she was a born painter and a wonderful one, and it pains her greatly not to be able to paint anymore because of her vision. Her hand was steady, without the slightest tremor.

(Anthony van Dyck, a great 17th century portrait painter, on meeting Sofonisba)

Q Source 6

Sofonisba Anguissola is a remarkable figure from both an artistic and historical perspective (viewpoint). Not only was she the first woman painter ever to achieve international renown (fame), but she was also the first female painter of achievement who was not the daughter of an artist.

(Sharlee Mullins Glenn, 1990)

Q

> What **features** of the paintings do you like in Sources 1 and 2? How would you consider them to be Renaissance paintings?
> Do Vasari and van Dyck **admire** Sofonisba as an artist, according to Sources 3 and 4?
> What is the significance of Sofonisba Anguissola, according to Source 5?
> **Investigate** the 'List of paintings by Sofonisba Anguissola' in *Wikipedia*.
> **Summarise** the life and work of Sofonisba Anguissola.

Explain your answers using evidence from the sources.

> What are **your favourite Renaissance works of art** from the ones you have studied here and why?

⊘ Describe how views about the universe changed

⊘ Explain why Galileo is called the 'Father of Modern Science'

KEY WORD

- **Astronomy** is the study of the universe, including the planets and stars.

How Significant were Developments in Renaissance Science?

Astronomy from Ancient Greece

During the Middle Ages many learned people were influenced by the ideas of **Ptolemy**, a Greek scientist and mathematician, based in Egypt in the second century BC. He believed that the Earth was the **centre** of the universe and that the sun and other planets revolved around it.

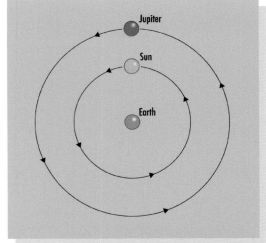

Why did the Catholic Church support this view of the Earth-centred universe?

How did the views about the universe change during the Renaissance?

Nicholas Copernicus

Johannes Kepler

Nicholas **Copernicus** was a Polish-born monk who studied mathematics, astronomy and medicine in Italy. He studied the sky and concluded that the sun was the **centre** of the universe and that the Earth and other planets revolved in **circles** around it. He published his views in *On The Revolutions of the Heavenly Spheres* the year he died.

Johannes Kepler was a German astronomer. He used **mathematics** to work out how the planets moved. He proved that Copernicus was right about the sun being the centre of the universe. But he said Copernicus was wrong to say that the planets moved around the sun in **circles**. Instead, Kepler said their orbits were **elliptical** (oval). This was one of his **three laws** of planetary motion. These laws led to Isaac Newtons' **law of gravity** later in the 17th century.

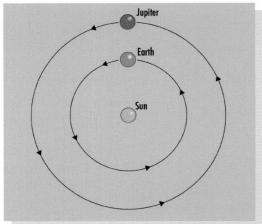

This is Copernicus' view of the universe

CHRONOLOGICAL AWARENESS

Q

1. Why, do you think, Copernicus was afraid to publish his views about the sun being at the centre of the universe?

2. What was the main difference between Copernicus' system and Kepler's?

RENAISSANCE SCIENCE

1610
Galileo published *The Starry Messenger* about the surface of the moon and about moons around Jupiter

1633
Galileo charged with heresy by Catholic Church

1550   1600   1650

1543
Copernicus' *On the Revolution of Heavenly Spheres* published

1596
Kepler defended Copernicus' system of the sun-centred universe

1609
Kepler published the *New Astronomy*
Galileo's Law of Falling Bodies
Galileo's telescope

1614
Kepler completed the astronomical table begun by Brahe

1632
Galileo published *Dialogue Concerning Two Chief World Systems*

96

What significant contributions did Galileo make to Renaissance Science?

Galileo was born in Pisa, Italy in 1564. He studied mathematics and physics. He became **Professor of Mathematics** in the University of **Pisa** in 1589. Three years later he became Professor of Mathematics in **Padua**.

Scientific method

Galileo said that scientists must base their results on **experiments** and **evidence**. *'Measure what is measurable, and make measurable what is not so.'*

He said physics must be based on **mathematics**.

'The grand book of the universe is written in the language of mathematics, and its characters are triangles, circles, and other geometrical figures.'

Einstein, one of the greatest 20th-century scientists, said of Galileo, *'Because Galileo saw that ideas need to be tested, and particularly because he drummed it into the scientific world, he is the father of modern physics – indeed of modern science altogether.'*

Q What does your **science teacher** say about the law of falling bodies and the pendulum clock?

The Law of Falling Bodies

Most people followed **Aristotle**, the Greek philosopher, who said heavier objects fall **more quickly** to the ground when dropped from a height. Galileo disproved this – instead he said all objects fell to the ground at the **same speed**.

The pendulum clock

Aristotle also claimed that when a pendulum swung, a long swing would take longer than a short swing. Galileo proved through experiments that longer swings took the same amount of time as shorter swings. His discovery led to the development of **pendulum clocks**.

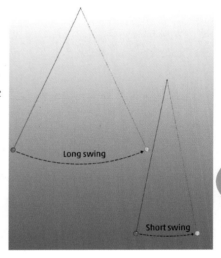

Long swing

Short swing

Q What did Galileo add to our knowledge of the universe?

The telescope

Galileo heard about a **telescope** developed in Flanders. He then invented his own. He used the telescope to study the **surface** of the moon. He also discovered the **rings** around Saturn but he did not realise what they were. He also discovered **four moons** around Jupiter.

Go onto YouTube and look up 'Galileo Galilei – in a nutshell'.

Astronomy

Galileo used his study of the planets to **support Copernicus' views** about the universe. He published his views in *Dialogue Concerning the Two Chief World Systems*. This got him into trouble with the Catholic Church. Galileo was brought before the **Inquisition**, a Church court, and forced to say publicly that the sun was not the centre of the universe. He was also sentenced to **house arrest** for the rest of his life. The Catholic Church banned his book, and this ban was not lifted for over 200 years.

Who will be the expert on Renaissance Science?

Health and Medicine

Illustrate patterns of change in Health and Medicine

How Significant were Developments in Renaissance Medicine?

Medicine in the Middle Ages – What do these sources tell you about ideas on medicine in the Middle Ages? (See p. 69)

 p. 258

> **Source 1**
>
> Many of the ideas on medicine in the Middle Ages were based on the teachings of **Galen**, a doctor in Ancient Rome.
> - Galen accepted the Greek theory of the four humours or bodily fluids as the cause of diseases.
> - He thought that muscles attach to the bone in the same way in humans and in dogs.
> - He thought that blood was created in the liver.
> - He thought the human jaw-bone was made up of two bones, like a dog's.
>
> **(Adapted from Medieval Medical Knowledge, www.bbc.co.uk/schools)**

> **Source 2**
>
>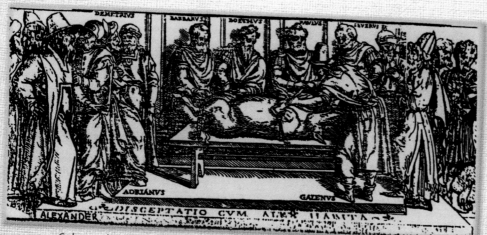
>
> Galen, a doctor in Ancient Rome, dissecting a pig, taken from his *Collected Works* published in the 16th century

> **Source 3**
>
> The most deadly plague arrived, either because of the movements of the planets, or because our sinful deeds had made God so angry he decided to punish us.
>
> **(A 14th century Florentine writer)**

Why was the work of Vesalius significant?

KEY WORD

- **Anatomy** is the study of the human body

Vesalius was a Belgian-born doctor. He was **Professor of Anatomy** in the University of Padua. Even though the Catholic Church was opposed to dissecting human bodies because they were regarded as sacred (holy), Vesalius got permission from his university to **dissect** the bodies of executed criminals. He published his findings in *On The Fabric of the Human Body* in 1543. Here he used evidence from dissections to prove Galen was wrong. In this way Vesalius made a significant contribution to Renaissance medicine.

Renaissance Literature – Shakespeare

William Shakespeare was born in **Stratford-on-Avon** in 1564. In his twenties, Shakespeare became an actor and writer of plays for the **King's Men**, a theatre company in London.

Shakespeare is considered the **greatest playwright** in the English language. His plays had a huge **influence** on the English language and theatre. He contributed greatly to the use of the language of the people (**vernacular**). He drew on stories from Ancient Greece and Rome, and from English history. His characters were very **realistic**, and they displayed a wide range of **emotions**.

Appreciate the importance of Shakespeare

Shakespeare wrote:
- 38 plays
- 154 sonnets
- Two narrative poems

Some of Shakespeare's Plays	
Tragedies	Hamlet, Romeo & Juliet, Macbeth, King Lear
Comedies	The Merchant of Venice, A Midsummer Night's Dream
Histories	Henry V, Richard II, Julius Caesar

Shakespeare's plays were performed in the Globe Theatre, which was an open-air theatre. They were performed in daylight.

How were plays performed in Shakespeare's time?

Source 1

No playwright before him could appeal to the masses quite like Shakespeare. Theatre up until his time had been uniquely reserved for the wealthy and the educated. With the emergence of Shakespeare's writing came tales that appealed to the masses.

(*William Shakespeare's Impact on Theatre,* https://www.octaneseating.com/the-impact-of-william-shakespeare-on-theater

Source 2

If you've ever been 'in a pickle', waited 'with bated breath', or gone on 'a wild goose chase', you've been quoting from *The Tempest, The Merchant of Venice* and *Romeo and Juliet* respectively.

(*How Shakespeare influences the way we speak,* www.bbc.com/culture/story/20140527-say-what-shakespeares-words)

Source 3

Shakespeare's writings greatly influenced the entire English language. Prior to and during Shakespeare's time, the grammar and rules of English were not standardised (regular). But once Shakespeare's plays became popular in the late seventeenth and eighteenth century, they helped contribute to the standardisation of the English language.

(*Shakespeare's influence,* www.wikipedia.org)

Q

Make a list of the ways Shakespeare is historically significant, based on these sources.

How was the Renaissance Historically Significant?

Look back to p. 79 on 'historically significant'

CONSEQUENCES

Age of Exploration

The discovery of Ptolemy's *Geographia*, which was a compilation (collection) of the geographical knowledge of Ancient Greece and Rome, led to interest in rounding Africa to reach the East. The new learning of the Renaissance led to new methods of navigation and of calculating latitude.

Astronomy

Renaissance scientists made many discoveries which influenced 20th century space exploration, such as the Galileo spacecraft investigation of Jupiter.

New Learning

'*For now we see the languages restored, and not only the deeds and writings of the ancients brought back to light, but also many fine things **newly discovered**. In this period, grammar, poetry, history, oratory and discussions have been illuminated (lit up) by displays and innumerable translations. Never has mathematics been so well known, nor astrology, cosmography (study of universe) and navigation … physics and medicine … arms and military instruments … painting, sculpture, modeling and architecture … law and eloquence, even politics … and theology. Printing has greatly aided this work and made easier its development.*' **(Louis le Roy, On Science and Progress [1575])**

The Reformation

The building of **St Peter's Church in Rome** was being paid for by money collected around Europe. **Martin Luther**, who began the Reformation in Germany, objected to this: '*Why doesn't the Pope build the basilica of St Peter out of his own money?*' The Renaissance also let to questioning of the teachings of the Catholic Church.

Education

There was new knowledge to be taught in schools and universities, and new methods of research. The printing press spread **education** and **literacy**. Vernacular languages (the language of the people) were more widely used.

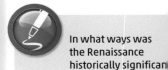

In what ways was the Renaissance historically significant

Painting and sculpture: there were new developments in painting and sculpture – perspective, sfumato, oil painting, realism, new themes.

Tourism: The Sistine Chapel has 6 million visitors a year, up from 1.8 million in 1980.

Architecture: many public buildings, such as the White House, are influenced by Classical Renaissance architecture.

104

INVESTIGATING A REPOSITORY OF HISTORICAL EVIDENCE FOR THE RENAISSANCE

Italian Renaissance Learning resources,
www.italianrenaissanceresources.com
Italian Renaissance, Painting,
www.louvre.fr/en/routes/italian-renaissance
Italian Renaissance Art,
www.italian-renaissance-art.com

》 Preparing for CBA2

A project on the life and experience of a person of historical interest

PERSONS OF INTEREST FROM THE RENAISSANCE

- Cosimo de Medici
- Michelangelo
- Sandro Botticelli
- Titian
- Galileo Galilei
- Nicolaus Copernicus
- Levina Teerlinc

- Lorenzo de Medici
- Raphael
- Filippo Brunelleschi
- Jan van Eyck
- Andreas Vesalius
- Ambroise Paré
- Lavinia Fontana

- Leonardo da Vinci
- Donatello
- Giorgio Vasari
- Albrecht Dürer
- William Harvey
- Sofonisba Anguissola

Focus Task

Historical Debate

> Draw up a table in a page of your copybook with the following headings: Renaissance Learning – changes in the arts and sciences: Painting; Sculpture; Architecture; Science; Medicine; Literature. Use your textbook and the internet and fill in information in short note/ bullet point form under each of the headings.

RENAISSANCE LEARNING – HANGES IN THE ARTS AND SCIENCES				
Painting	**Sculpture**	**Architecture**	**Medicine**	**Lierature**

EUROPEAN HISTORY

06

EVALUATING THE IMPACT OF CONQUEST AND COLONISATION
– The Portuguese and Spanish Explorations

L.O. 3.2, 3.10
The Nature of History:
1.1, 1.2, 1.4, 1.5, 1.6, 1.7,
1.8, 1.9, 1.10, 1.11
CBA2

CHRONOLOGICAL AWARENESS

1420 AD
c. 1420
Prince Henry the Navigator of Portugal began organised voyages down the coast of Africa

1434
The Portuguese rounded Cape Bojador in Africa

1489
Diaz (Portugal) rounded the Cape of Good Hope

1440 AD

1444
African slaves brought to Portugal

1460 AD

1492
Columbus's first voyage, he explored islands off the coast of America

1480 AD

1494
Treaty of Tordesillas

1519
Magellan's voyage around the world began
Cortés begins conquest of Aztec Empire in Mexico

1497–98
John Cabot, an Italian, explored the coast of North America on behalf of England

1498
Da Gama (Portugal) reached India

1500 AD

1502
First shipment of African slaves to Cuba and the New World

1520 AD

1521
Aztec capital, Tenochtitlan, destroyed; Mexico city built in its place

1532
Pizarro conquers the Inca Empire in Peru

1542
New Laws passed in Spain to protect Indians on encomiendas of New World

1540 AD

1545
Silver discovered in Potosi (in modern Bolivia)

1560 AD
c. 1550
Beginning of yearly shipment of silver to Spain from New World
African slave trade to Brazil

You will learn to …

- Explore the contribution of technology to historical change.
- Evaluate the impact of Portuguese and Spanish conquest and colonisation
- Examine the significance of genocide
- Explore the Nature of History

KEY WORDS

- Conquest
- Colonisation
- Genocide
- Exploration
- Empire
- Impact

What was the Age of Exploration?

In the 15th and 16th centuries, Europeans began to explore other parts of the world. The Portuguese and the Spanish led these explorations. Later, other countries, such as France and England, explored and conquered different parts of the world.

Technology and Historical Change

Technology and Historical Change in the Age of Exploration

There were many causes of the Age of Exploration.

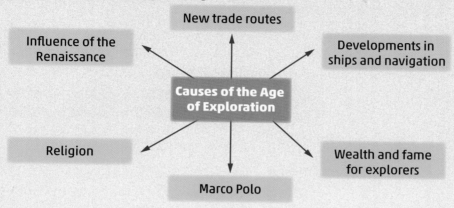

One of the most important causes was **developments in ships and navigation**.

New technology in ships and navigation

We know why the explorers wanted to find new sea routes. But they could not have gone on voyages of exploration without improvements in ships and methods of navigation. This new technology influenced historical change in the Age of Exploration.

 p. 249

Ships

New ships called **caravels** were built. These ships brought together the best qualities of ships that sailed in the Atlantic Ocean and the Mediterranean Sea. Without this **new technology**, the long voyages of exploration from Europe could not have been undertaken.

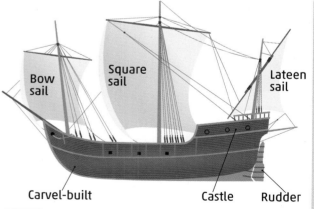

A caravel

- They were **carvel-built**. The boards on the side of the ship (hull) were fitted edge-to-edge. Carvel-built ships could be made longer than clinker-built ships (with overlapping boards), and carry more masts.
- They used both **square** sails and **lateen** (triangular) **sails**. Square sails were used to sail faster with the wind following behind. Lateen sails were used to sail **against the wind**. They were also useful for exploring bays and river mouths.
- The caravels were steered by **rudders**. This gave more control over the steering.
- They had **castles** (raised structures) on the decks at the front and back. From the castles, sailors could sight enemy ships more easily and take defensive action.

A larger ship, the **carrack** or **nao**, was later developed to undertake longer voyages along the coast of Africa and across the Atlantic Ocean.

New technology in navigation

Compasses

Compasses were used to tell sailors which direction they were sailing in. But the compasses were often unreliable because iron objects on the ship affected them.

Compass

Latitude and Longitude

Sailors could work out the latitude of the ship, that is, how many degrees north or south of the Equator it was. They used **astrolabes**, **quadrants** and **cross-staffs** to do this. But **longitude** – degrees east and west – could not be worked out, because explorers did not have an accurate clock, called a **chronometer**, until the 18th century.

Maps

The earliest maps used by sailors were called **portolan charts**. They showed places along the coasts joined by straight lines. These lines gave the course or direction, which the sailors followed by compass.

Soon mapmakers had to develop **new ways of drawing maps** that included the whole world. They developed maps to show true direction, correct area and the shape of land masses, which helped later discoveries.

Speed

Speed was measured using a **log and line** and a **sand-glass**. The line, with a log tied to the end of it, was thrown out of the ship. The line was marked by **knots**, with an equal distance between each knot. The speed of the ship was calculated (worked out) by measuring the time it took the knots on the line to pass through a sailor's hand. Today, a ship's speed is given in '**knots**' (nautical miles).

Quadrants were pointed at the sun or the North Star to tell the latitude

Astrolabes were pointed to the North Star to tell the latitude

The cross-staff was used to work out latitude

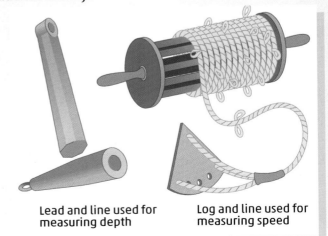

Lead and line used for measuring depth

Log and line used for measuring speed

Log and line used for measuring speed

New technology in ships and navigation

- **Direction**   Compass
- **Latitude**   Quadrant, astrolabe, cross-staff
- **Speed**   Log and line
- **Ships**   Caravels, carracks (naos), carvel-built
- **Sails**   Lateen, square
- **Steering**   Rudder
- **Time**   Sand-glass/hour-glass

Hour-glass

The Portuguese explorations

Prince Henry the Navigator, the third son of the King of Portugal, led the Portuguese explorations. Under Henry's leadership, the Portuguese explored along the coast of Africa, hoping to find a route to the **riches of Asia and the Spice Islands**. After Henry died, the Portuguese continued exploring. Two great voyages resulted in the Portuguese reaching India. First, **Bartholomew Diaz** rounded the Cape of Good Hope in the southern tip of Africa (1489).

Cabral (centre-left, pointing) sights the Brazilian mainland for the first time on 22 April 1500. A painting by Aurélio de Figueiredo.

Define the Age of Exploration

Then, **Vasco da Gama** sailed as far as India (1498). A year later, in 1500, Pedro Cabral reached the coast of Brazil. Very soon, the Portuguese **controlled** the sea trade between Europe and Africa and Asia.

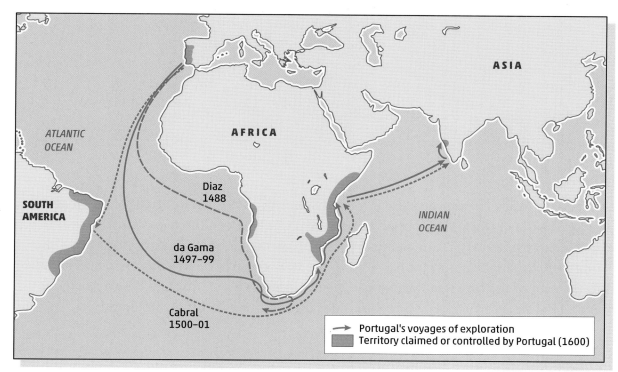

ATLANTIC OCEAN

AFRICA

ASIA

SOUTH AMERICA

Diaz 1488

da Gama 1497–99

INDIAN OCEAN

Cabral 1500–01

→ Portugal's voyages of exploration
  Territory claimed or controlled by Portugal (1600)

The Spanish explorations

The Spanish explorations were inspired by the great voyages of **Christopher Columbus**. Although he was born in Genoa (Italy), Columbus got help from the King and Queen of Spain, **Ferdinand** and **Isabella**. They had just conquered the last stronghold of the Moors (or Muslims) in Granada, and united their country.

Columbus sailed with three ships westwards because he knew the world was round and he wanted to prove it by reaching Asia and the Spice Islands from this side. However, instead of reaching Asia, he discovered islands off a **new continent**, the Americas, which became known as the **New World** (1492). Columbus made three other voyages which explored the main continent even though he still thought he was off the coast of Asia.

Christopher Columbus

Columbus was followed by **conquistadors** (conquerors), such as **Hernan Cortés** and **Francisco Pizarro**, who explored and conquered the mainland. Cortés conquered the great **Aztec Empire** in Mexico, while **Pizarro** conquered the empire of the **Incas** in Peru.

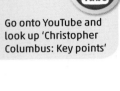

Go onto YouTube and look up 'Christopher Columbus: Key points'

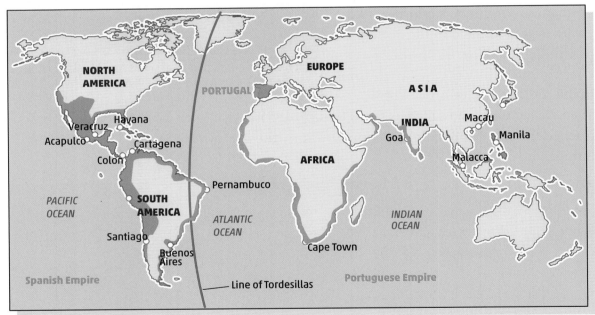

Treaty of Tordesillas

After Columbus' first voyage, the pope got Spain and Portugal to agree to the **Treaty of Tordesillas** (1494). He wanted to prevent a war between the two countries over the newly discovered lands. The treaty drew a **line** on the globe from north to south – the line of Tordesillas. All land discovered to the **west** of this line was **Spanish**, and all land to the **east** of the line was **Portuguese**. As the line ran down through South America, **Brazil** became Portuguese while the rest of the continent belonged to Spain.

Spain and Portugal created **their own empires** out of the lands they conquered. Most of the Spanish and Portuguese empires collapsed in the early 19th century when South American countries got their independence.

Conquest – The Decline of the Native People

How did the conquest of the New World by Spain and Portugal impact on the native people?

According to the **Treaty of Tordesillas**, all of the land of the new continent, except Brazil, belonged to Spain. Spanish adventurers – known as **conquistadors** (conquerors) – began the conquest of these lands. They were seeking gold and silver.

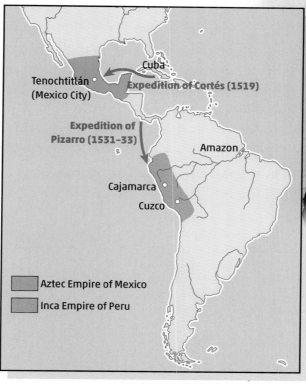

Cortés and the Aztecs

Hernando Cortés was responsible for the defeat of the great empire of the **Aztecs**, based in Mexico.

Cortés was in charge of an expedition of 11 ships and 500 men which sailed to Mexico in 1519. As he marched inland, native tribes who had been conquered by the Aztecs helped him. They did not like the **heavy taxes** and **slavery** imposed on them by the Aztecs. Many were also **sacrificed** to the Aztec gods.

The Aztec emperor, **Montezuma**, came to greet Cortés as he approached the Aztec capital, **Tenochtitlan**. The Spaniards were allowed into the city, but soon trouble broke out between them and the Aztecs. Cortés and his men had to escape.

Cortés got help from neighbouring tribes and led 100,000 men against the Aztecs. He destroyed their city, and the Aztecs were forced to work as **slaves** in mines or in the fields. Cortés later rebuilt Tenochtitlan as **Mexico city**.

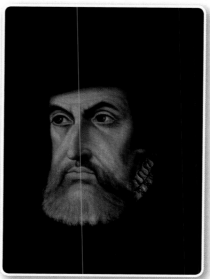

Cortés, conqueror of the Aztecs

Timeline of Independence

1625 Dutch began taking over Portuguese trade in Asia

1809 Independence movements began in South America which led to countries becoming independent of Spain

1822 Brazil declared independent of Portugal

1875 Slavery banned in Portuguese empire

1898 Spain sold Philippine Islands to USA for $20 million

1970s Portuguese-controlled countries in Africa gained independence

Evaluate the impact of Spanish and Portuguese conquest in the New World

Soon, the Spaniards brought cattle, plants, ploughs and hundreds of priests to establish a colony in the Aztec lands, and renamed them **New Spain**.

Pizarro and the Incas

Pizarro, conqueror of the Incas

Pizarro set out to conquer the **Inca empire** in Peru. He captured and killed the Inca emperor, **Atahualpa**. Pizarro and his men then captured the Inca capital, **Cuzco**, in the Andes Mountains. They seized the Inca treasures and melted them down for gold. But the Spaniards also fought amongst themselves, and Pizarro was killed by his own soldiers.

The Spaniards later discovered **gold and silver mines**. For the next 100 years, gold and silver was mined by Incas, who died in their thousands. Peru and Bolivia supplied about 65% of the gold and silver sent to Spain in the 16th century. As a result, Spain became very **wealthy**. Spanish ships, sailing between the New World and Spain, were attacked by English ships, eventually leading to **war** between the two countries.

The Spaniards also conquered the **south-west of North America**, around present-day New Mexico and California. Some place names there still bear **Spanish names**: Los Angeles, San Francisco in California and Las Vegas in Nevada, for example.

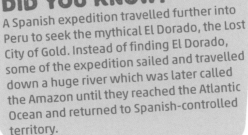

DID YOU KNOW?

A Spanish expedition travelled further into Peru to seek the mythical El Dorado, the Lost City of Gold. Instead of finding El Dorado, some of the expedition sailed and travelled down a huge river which was later called the Amazon until they reached the Atlantic Ocean and returned to Spanish-controlled territory.

Impact on the New World

- Destroyed kingdoms of New World
- Gold and silver sent to Europe
- Opened up the Americas to other European countries
- Brutal treatment of native people
- Brought European diseases to New World
- Brought new animals and plants to New World
- New farming methods
- New languages and cultures
- New religion

Analysing Sources

Decline of Native People of the New World

⟨ p. 60

Source 1

Native Population of New Spain (approx. modern-day Mexico)

1492	25 million
1532	17 million
1548	6.3 million
1568	3.0 million
1580	1.9 million
c. 1600	1.25 million

Source 2

'Though the conquistadores were brutal, the major killers were the new diseases they brought – measles, influenza, pneumonia, tuberculosis, diphtheria, pleurisy and, in 1518, smallpox.'

(Ben Kiernan, *Blood and Soil, A World History of Genocide* [2007])

Source 3

As for the vast mainland, which is ten times larger than all Spain, we are sure that our Spaniards, with their cruel and abominable (dreadful) acts, have devastated (destroyed) the land and exterminated (killed) the people who fully inhabited it. We can estimate very surely and truthfully that in the forty years that have passed, with the infernal (wicked) actions of the Christians, there have been unjustly slain more than twelve million men, women, and children. In truth, I believe without trying to deceive myself that the number of the slain is more like fifteen million. The common ways mainly employed by the Spaniards is by unjustly waging cruel and bloody wars. Then, when they have slain all those who fought for their lives, they enslave any survivors. With these infernal methods of tyranny (oppression) they debase (humiliate) and weaken countless numbers of those pitiful Indian nations.

(Bartolomé de Las Casas, *A Brief Account of the Devastation of the Indies* [1542]; de Las Casas was a Spaniard Dominican priest who settled in the New World.)

Source 4

The Spanish have a perfect right to rule these barbarians (savages, uncivilised) of the New World. Those are called barbarians who can't think due to their upbringing or due to some evil habit by which men become brutes. Races of this sort should obey those who are more civilised so that they may be governed by better customs and practices.

The barbarians who approve of the public murder of innocent people who are sacrificed and who adore false gods are breaking the laws of nature, which is the most serious of sins.

(Juan Ginés de Sepúlveda, *Concerning the Just Causes of War against the Indians* [1547]: de Sepúlveda was a Spanish theologian who did not visit the New World.)

Drawing of an Aztec sacrificial massacre from the *Mendoza Codex* (an Aztec manuscript). The drawing shows the advanced architecture of the Aztecs along with their brutal killing. Many people, often from captured tribes, were sacrificed in Aztec religious ceremonies. On one occasion, up to 20,000 captured people were slaughtered by the Aztecs. The Spanish stopped these massacres.

KEY WORD

What is genocide?
- The **deliberate killing** of a large group of people, especially those of a particular nation or ethnic group. (*oxforddictionaries.com*)

1. What was the fall of the native population of New Spain between 1492 and 1600?
2. Why did this population decline, according to historian Ben Kiernan in Source 2?
3. How does de Las Casas' account in Source 3 **differ** from de Sepúlveda's in Source 4?
4. Why do you think they differ?
5. Do de Las Casas' account and the account of the historian Ben Kiernan, in Source 2, **agree**?
6. Select **one sentence which is a fact** and **one sentence which is an opinion** from any of the sources.
7. Examine the meaning of 'genocide'. Did the Spanish conquest show evidence of genocide?
8. Did the Aztecs show evidence of genocide? Explain your answers using evidence from the sources.

Colonisation – What was its Impact?

How did colonisation impact on the people of the Americas and Spain and Portugal?

⊙ Evaluate the impact of Spanish and Portuguese colonisation on the Americas and on Spain and Portugal

The slave trade

Shortages of native people to work on the estates of the Europeans in the **New World** led to slaves being brought from Africa. These worked on cotton and sugar **plantations** (or estates), in mines or as domestic servants, in Central, South and later North America. The slave trade continued for 300 years.

Portugal controlled the **Atlantic slave trade** for many years. The Portuguese first brought African slaves to sugar plantations in Madeira, an island off the coast of Africa, in the first half of the 15th century. Then they had the contract to supply slaves to Spanish plantations in the New World. They also shipped slaves to their own plantations in Brazil. It is estimated that **12.5 million slaves** were shipped from Africa to North and South America between the 16th and 19th centuries. About 1.8 million of these died on the way – in what was called the **Middle Passage** – as conditions on board the slave ships were very cruel. The slaves were packed close together, men and women were separated, and men were chained for most of the voyage.

Q Source 1
Distribution of slaves in the New World, 1519–1867

- Dutch West Indies 2.0%
- Danish West Indies 0.3%
- French Americas 13.6%
- Portuguese America 38.5%
- British territories in Americas 28.1%
- Spanish Empire 17.5%

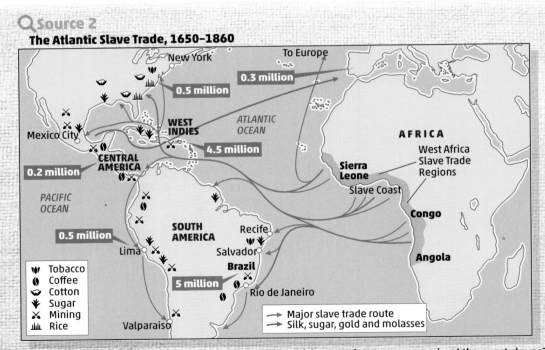

Q Source 2
The Atlantic Slave Trade, 1650–1860

New York · To Europe · 0.3 million · 0.5 million · WEST INDIES · ATLANTIC OCEAN · Mexico City · 4.5 million · CENTRAL AMERICA · 0.2 million · PACIFIC OCEAN · SOUTH AMERICA · Recife · 0.5 million · Lima · Salvador · Brazil · 5 million · Rio de Janeiro · Valparaiso · AFRICA · West Africa Slave Trade Regions · Sierra Leone · Slave Coast · Congo · Angola

Legend:
- ♣ Tobacco
- ♦ Coffee
- ⌣ Cotton
- ♥ Sugar
- ✕ Mining
- ⅲ Rice

→ Major slave trade route
→ Silk, sugar, gold and molasses

1. Why did the Atlantic slave trade begin?
2. What is the connection between the beginning of the slave trade and the impact of the 'Conquest – the decline of the native people' (p. 111)?
3. How many slaves were shipped to: **(a)** Brazil **(b)** the West Indies?
4. Which countries or areas received the most slaves?
5. Why did those countries receive the most slaves?
6. From which countries in Africa were most of the slaves shipped?

Plantations

Plantations in the West Indies were much larger than those in North America. As a result, West Indian plantations held more slaves on average, with many having over 150 slaves. The death rate was high and the birth rate was low amongst Caribbean slaves so there was a constant flow of slaves from Africa to these islands.

Spanish system

The Spanish developed their land using *haciendas*, which were great estates bought from or granted to them by the king. In those *haciendas*, the landowners used the *encomienda* system to work their land. This entitled them to use free native Indian labour and in return the landowners gave the natives protection and a Christian education.

This system created a small rich ruling class in control of the majority of the poorer population.

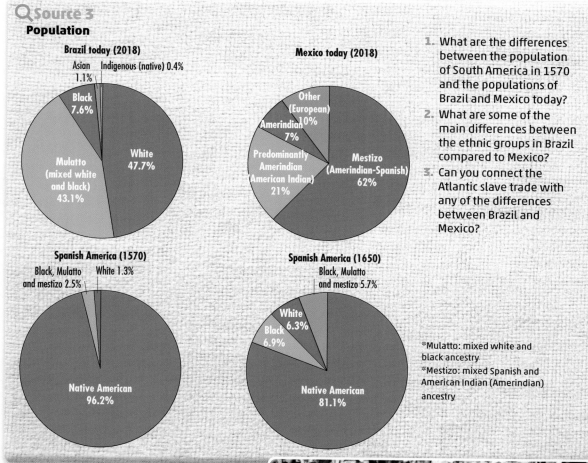

Q Source 3

Population

Brazil today (2018)
- Asian 1.1%
- Indigenous (native) 0.4%
- Black 7.6%
- Mulatto (mixed white and black) 43.1%
- White 47.7%

Mexico today (2018)
- Other (European) 10%
- Amerindian 7%
- Predominantly Amerindian (American Indian) 21%
- Mestizo (Amerindian-Spanish) 62%

Spanish America (1570)
- Black, Mulatto and mestizo 2.5%
- White 1.3%
- Native American 96.2%

Spanish America (1650)
- Black, Mulatto and mestizo 5.7%
- White 6.3%
- Black 6.9%
- Native American 81.1%

*Mulatto: mixed white and black ancestry
*Mestizo: mixed Spanish and American Indian (Amerindian) ancestry

NUMERACY

1. What are the differences between the population of South America in 1570 and the populations of Brazil and Mexico today?
2. What are some of the main differences between the ethnic groups in Brazil compared to Mexico?
3. Can you connect the Atlantic slave trade with any of the differences between Brazil and Mexico?

Brazil won the World Cup in 1970 (and on four other occasions). This was a mixed race team. It included Pelé, whose real name is Edson Arantes do Nascimento, one of the greatest footballers of all time. He is of African-Brazilian descent. His family name, Nascimento, is Portuguese for 'birth'.

Q

1. What can you learn about Brazil from the information on Pelé?
2. Where does he fit into the pie chart on ethnic groups in Brazil?

Source 4
Religion and Language

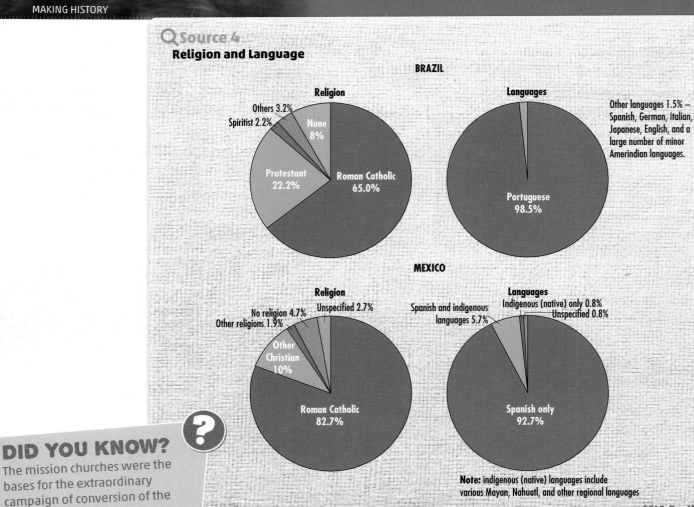

BRAZIL

Religion

- Others 3.2%
- Spiritist 2.2%
- None 8%
- Protestant 22.2%
- Roman Catholic 65.0%

Languages

Other languages 1.5% — Spanish, German, Italian, Japanese, English, and a large number of minor Amerindian languages.

- Portuguese 98.5%

MEXICO

Religion

- Unspecified 2.7%
- No religion 4.7%
- Other religions 1.9%
- Other Christian 10%
- Roman Catholic 82.7%

Languages

- Spanish and indigenous languages 5.7%
- Indigenous (native) only 0.8%
- Unspecified 0.8%
- Spanish only 92.7%

Note: indigenous (native) languages include various Mayan, Nahuatl, and other regional languages

(CIA Factbook)

DID YOU KNOW?
The mission churches were the bases for the extraordinary campaign of conversion of the native people. Priests were known to baptise 1,500 people in a single day.

Source 5
Economy
The Spaniards brought a new **diversity** into the economy of New Spain and caused a major revolution in the use of land. Much of the land was divided into *haciendas*, large estates. This created a small rich ruling class, with a great deal of poverty amongst the rest of the people.

The Spanish brought horses to the New World and horses had a large impact on the economy and society there

Change in clothing
Woollen capes or blankets soon began to displace the traditional *manta* woven from cotton or other vegetable fibre. Other styles of clothing changed.

Source 6
Architecture

Cathedral Metropolitana in Mexico City, which is built in the European Baroque style

1. What impact did colonisation have on religion and language in (a) Brazil and (b) Mexico?
2. What impact did colonisation have on (a) the native economy, (b) clothing and (c) architecture?

116

Impact on Spain

Every year from the middle of the 16th century to the end of the 18th century, a **Spanish silver fleet or treasure fleet** sailed as a convoy with silver for Spain. This made Spain the richest country in Europe by the end of the 18th century with a huge empire.

As a result of the conquest of the Americas, Spain controlled a huge new empire which was available for **settlement**, **investment** and **exploitation**. It made Spain wealthier and more powerful, and it increased the pride and confidence in the kingdom.

The flow of silver into Spain also caused **inflation** (rising prices), which spread to other European countries. Spanish landowners benefitted as the value of their land increased but the standard of living of other Spaniards got worse.

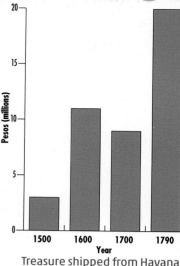

Treasure shipped from Havana (Cuba) to Spain

Impact on Portugal

Portugal also **prospered** from its empire. Many fine buildings were erected in the country. However, much of the power and wealth in Portugal was in the hands of a **small ruling class**.

Thousands of Portuguese were attracted to settle in Brazil, and **Portuguese emigration** to Brazil continued until a few decades ago.

Source 7
Export of Raw Sugar from Brazil 1580–1820
Portuguese imports from Brazil

Turkey
Pepper
Pineapple
Maize
Tea
Sugar
Tomatoes
Potatoes
Coffee
Chocolate

New foods brought to Europe from America in the Age of Exploration. These varied the diet of Europeans.

❰ p. 62
Evaluating the Impact of Conquest and Colonisation

❱ Preparing for CBA2

A project on the life and experience of a person of historical interest

PERSONS OF INTEREST IN THE AGE OF EXPLORATION

- Henry the Navigator
- Ferdinand Magellan
- Bartolomé de Las Casas
- John Cabot
- Samuel de Champlain

- Vasco da Gama
- Hernan Cortés
- Giovanni da Verrazano
- Francis Drake
- Henry Hudson

- Columbus
- Francisco Pizarro
- Walter Raleigh
- Jacques Cartier
- Queen Isabella

❰ p. 64
Web Resources and Reading

EUROPEAN HISTORY

07

MARTIN LUTHER AND THE REFORMATION
– The Historical Importance of Religion

LO: 3.8
The Nature of History:
1.1, 1.2, 1.3, 1.4, 1.5, 1.6,
1.7, 1.8, 1.9, 1.10, 1.11
CBA2

CHRONOLOGICAL AWARENESS

1510 AD

1517
Luther's 95 Theses

1519
Charles V
became
Holy Roman
Emperor

1520 AD

1521
Luther excommunicated
Diet of Worms
Edict of Worms

1530 AD

1534
Henry VIII's Act of Supremacy

1536
Calvin's
*Institute
of the
Christian
Religion*
published

1540 AD

1540
Society of Jesus (Jesuits)
approved by the pope

1546
Luther's
death

1545
Council of Trent began

1550 AD

1555
The Peace of Augsburg

1560 AD

1564
Calvin's death

1568
French religious wars between
Catholics and French
Protestants (Huguenots) began

1570 AD

You will learn to ...

- ⊘ Consider the historical importance of religion
- ⊘ Evaluate the historical importance of the Reformation
- ⊘ Explore the role of one reformer, Martin Luther
- ⊘ Explore the Nature of History

KEY WORDS

- Lutheran
- Jesuits
- Calvinist or Presbyterian
- Inquisition
- Protestant
- Indulgences
- Theses
- Heresy

Christianity in Europe in 1500

In 1500, Christianity in Europe was divided between the Catholic religion and the Orthodox religion. The **Orthodox religion** was found mainly in Greece and Russia, while the **Catholic religion** was more important everywhere else. In Catholic countries, the **pope** in Rome was the head of the Church, and Catholic cardinals and bishops had great power in their countries.

Religion played a very important part in people's lives. People explained happenings according to God's will. They also believed that the Church provided all the answers to life and that it was only through the Catholic Church that **salvation** (a place in heaven) could be achieved.

What does this procession in St Mark's Square in Venice tell you about the importance of religion in the 16th century?

But there were many problems with the Catholic Church. These problems led to the Reformation in the 16th century.

What was the Reformation?

The Reformation began in **Germany** in the 16th century as a protest against the abuses in the Catholic Church. It began as an attempt to improve the Catholic Church. But less than 100 years later, most of the people of northern Europe were Protestants, who rejected the pope and his teachings. The Reformation brought about this **change**.

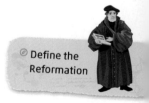

⊘ Define the Reformation

Who was Martin Luther?

Martin Luther was born in Eisleben in Germany in 1483. He joined the Augustinian Order to become a monk and a priest. He later became Professor of **Theology** (study of God) at Wittenberg University in Saxony.

Going to heaven

Luther was a holy man who worried about going to **heaven** (salvation). He was worried that God would not forgive sinners like himself. He found his answer in the **Bible**. He read that *'the just man shall live by faith alone'*; good deeds or works such as praying to the saints or gaining **indulgences** (pardons for sins) would not help. Only **faith in God** would allow a person to go to heaven – this was called **justification by faith**.

⊘ Consider the causes of Luther's Reformation

119

Sale of Indulgences

In 1517, a Dominican friar, Johann **Tetzel**, came to Wittenberg to preach and sell indulgences. Tetzel said that anyone could buy an indulgence to get into heaven. Half the money collected was to go for the building of **St Peter's Basilica** in Rome. The other half was to go to the **Archbishop of Mainz** to pay back money he had borrowed to buy bishoprics.

Tetzel frightened people into buying indulgences:

Can't you hear the voices of your dead parents and other relatives crying out, 'Have mercy on us for we suffer great punishment and pain. Why do you leave us to suffer in the flames when it takes only a little to save us?'

(Johann Tetzel preaching indulgences)

Q

What is Tetzel's message to his listeners?

Buying indulgences in a market place

1. What is your opinion of this scene?
2. What is its message about buying indulgences?
3. Is it a primary or a secondary source?
4. Is it biased?

A German woodcut from Luther's time

Luther's 95 Theses

Luther objected to Tetzel's preaching. He wrote **95 Theses** (arguments) against the sale of indulgences. He wrote them in **Latin**, the language of scholars, because he wanted to discuss his views with others. He did not set out to begin a rebellion against the Catholic Church.

Luther wrote to the **Archbishop of Mainz** complaining about the false impressions which the people had about indulgences; *'the unhappy souls believe that if they have purchased letters of indulgence they are sure of their salvation.'* He included a copy of his **95 Theses** with his letter.

One of the most popular stories about the Reformation is the story of Luther nailing the 95 Theses on the church door at Wittenberg.

But did this really happen? Historians must have evidence to prove this. What is your conclusion?

CHRONOLOGICAL AWARENESS

Timeline of Luther's life

1483	Martin Luther born
1505	Luther joined the priesthood
1511	Luther began lecturing at Wittenberg University
1517	The 95 Theses published
1518	Luther before Cardinal Cajetan in Augsburg
1519	Luther before John Eck in Leipzig
1521	Luther excommunicated by Pope Leo X The Diet of Worms Luther to Wartburg Castle
1525	Luther married Katherine von Bora
1530	The Confession of Augsburg
1546	Luther died
1555	The Peace of Augsburg

Why did he publish his 95 Theses?

Luther began his 95 Theses with this statement.

> *Out of love for the truth and from desire to elucidate (explain) it, the Reverend Father Martin Luther, Master of Arts and Sacred Theology, and ordinary lecturer at Wittenberg, intends to defend the following statements and to dispute on them in that place. Therefore he asks that those who cannot be present, and dispute with him orally, shall do so in their absence by letter. In the name of our Lord Jesus Christ, Amen.*

These are some of his 95 Theses. What is he objecting to? Summarise what he is saying here:

5. The pope has no power to forgive penalties due to sin.
21. Indulgences do not save people from all punishment.
43. It is better to give to the poor than to buy pardon.
86. Some may go against the pope saying, 'Why doesn't the pope, whose riches are enormous, build the Basilica of St Peter with his own money instead of taking it from poor believers?'

Wealth of the Church

Influence of the Renaissance

Long-term causes of the Reformation

The printing press

Abuses in the Catholic Church

The power of kings and princes

Why did people support Luther?

The 95 Theses were translated into German and were then printed, so that Luther's views were spread all over Germany very quickly.

- **What evidence can you get from the sources on the next page which would explain why some people in Germany supported Luther?**
- **Do these sources explain all the causes of the Reformation?**

p. 67

Analysing Sources
What Were the Causes of the Reformation?

Source 1
The arrival of the printing press to cities of the Holy Roman Empire

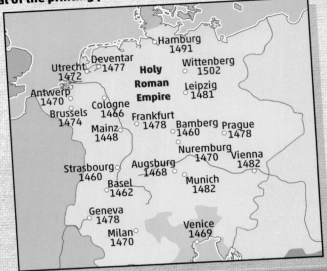

Hamburg 1491
Deventar 1477
Utrecht 1472
Wittenberg 1502
Holy Roman Empire
Leipzig 1481
Antwerp 1470
Cologne 1466
Brussels 1474
Frankfurt 1478
Mainz 1448
Bamberg 1460
Prague 1478
Nuremburg 1470
Vienna 1482
Strasbourg 1460
Augsburg 1468
Munich 1482
Basel 1462
Geneva 1478
Venice 1469
Milan 1470

Source 2
We see there is no gold or silver in our German land. What little there is left is taken by the Church in Rome. Would you know, dear Germans, what they do with our money? It does not lie idle! (Pope) Leo X gives part to his relatives, cardinals and officials. They build marble homes. They are clothed in purple and fine linen. They live in luxury.

(A follower of Luther)

Source 4
It was widely recognised that Alexander owed his position as pope to the widespread **bribery** of the College of Cardinals. Although Alexander started brightly by restoring order in Rome and challenging the authority of the Italian princes, he soon held a string of mistresses and fathered a number of illegitimate children, most of whom were looked after with clerical titles and income. In total, Alexander appointed 47 cardinals, including his teenage son, Cesare. Alexander enjoyed a great deal of **luxury**, and he was an important patron of the arts – he commissioned Michelangelo to draw up plans for the rebuilding of St Peter's Basilica in Rome.

(Robert Scribner, *The German Reformation*, 1986)

Source 3
The **bishops** have no belief in God, and jeer at the mysteries of our faith! O Lord! Arise and come deliver Thy Church from the hands of the devils, from the hands of tyrants, the hands of bad bishops.

(Girolamo Savonarola, an Italian critic of the Catholic Church)

How did Rome respond to Luther?

The pope took action against Luther. Luther was ordered to meet **Cardinal Cajetan**. They met but Luther refused to change his ideas.

Luther had a **public debate** with John Eck, a theologian. In the debate, Luther questioned the authority of the pope.

The pope sent a **special letter** called a **papal bull** excommunicating Luther (disallowing him from receiving the sacraments). Luther burned the papal letter in **public**.

Source 5
Luther, relying on [Frederick] the Duke of Saxony's protection, wrote and published new attacks on the Catholic faith. The pope launched a most severe bull against Luther and his supporters. Then Luther publicly burned all books on Church law he could find in Wittenberg.

The report of these events, spread throughout all Germany, stirred up the Germans against Rome. I fear that this evil will spread so widely as to be incurable.

(Alfonso de Valdés, an official of the Emperor, Charles V, who attended the Diet of Worms)

Q Why does the writer 'fear this evil will spread so widely'?

What Happened at the Diet of Worms?

Charles V became Holy Roman Emperor in 1519. He ruled over many lands, including Germany. The pope asked him to intervene because Luther was becoming more popular. Charles called Luther to the **Diet** (parliament) **of Worms**, near Mainz in Germany in 1521. Here Luther appeared before the Emperor and German princes.

Luther spoke before the Diet and **refused to withdraw** his teachings.

At Worms, the emperor said this man's foolishness should be put down by the Empire at once, to stop others from becoming his followers. In reply Luther said he would withdraw nothing written in his books, unless it were proved by the Bible that he was mistaken.

Some imagine this to be the end of the tragedy, but I am convinced this is not the end, but the start of it. The minds of the Germans are against Rome. Luther's books are sold freely at every street corner and marketplace. The Germans do not seem to attach much importance to the emperor's edicts (orders).

(Alfonso de Valdés, official of the Emperor, Charles V, who attended the Diet of Worms [1521])

⊘ Examine how the Lutheran religion spread quickly

Q Is this a **primary** or a **secondary** source? Why does the author think Lutheranism will spread?

What happened at Wartburg Castle?

After Luther left the Diet, the emperor issued the **Edict** (Order) **of Worms**: *'If you have sufficient force, you shall take Luther prisoner and deliver him to us.'*

On Luther's way home, he was 'captured' by the soldiers of **Frederick the Wise**, Elector of Saxony, who was a supporter of Luther.

The soldiers took him to **Wartburg Castle** so that he would be safe. Luther spent a year there disguised as 'Knight George'. During the year, he translated the **New Testament** into German. Later, he translated the **Old Testament** into German. Now ordinary Germans could read the Bible themselves.

Lutheranism spreads

Divisions between Catholic and Protestant princes grew in Germany. Most of Luther's support came from princes in northern Germany. The emperor Charles V rejected the **Augsburg Confession**, which was a statement of Lutheran beliefs. Lutherans took over Catholic churches and built some of their own. **Luther died** in 1546 before war broke out between the two sides.

Luther in 1520 and 1522

Why has he changed his appearance so much?

The Peace of Augsburg, 1555

A **civil and religious war** broke out in Germany and lasted nine years. Even though the Catholic princes won some battles, Lutheranism was too strong in Germany to be defeated.

The **Peace of Augsburg** (1555) brought the war to an end. This treaty stated that each ruler was free to decide the religion of his or her state. Catholics living in Lutheran states had to leave, as did Lutherans living in Catholic states.

Go onto YouTube and look up 'Miss Stout's History Class Martin Luther'

Analysing Sources

The importance of Propaganda during the Reformation

⊙ Evaluate the importance of propaganda in the Reformation

Luther as a propagandist – What was the importance of the printing press for getting Luther's message across?

Source 1

There were many printing presses in Germany during the Reformation (see map p. 122)

Source 2

Printings and re-printings of Luther's Works, excluding editions of the Bible, 1516–26

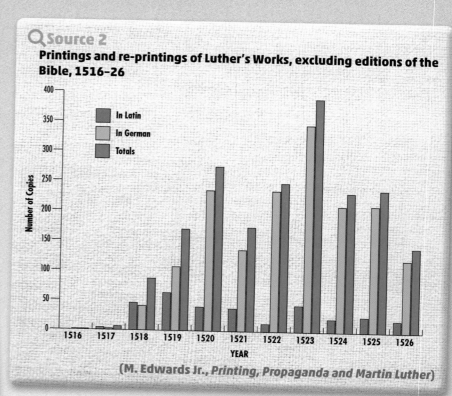

- In Latin
- In German
- Totals

(M. Edwards Jr., *Printing, Propaganda and Martin Luther*)

Source 3

Now we drive out the pope
from Christ's church and God's house.
Therein he has reigned (ruled) in a deadly fashion
and has seduced (enticed) unaccountably many souls (people).
Now move along, you damned son,
you Whore (prostitute) of Babylon*.
You are the abomination (hated) and the Antichrist,
full of lies, death and cunning.

*a place of luxury and corruption

(A verse of the ballad, *Now We Drive Out the Pope*, attributed to Luther [c. 1523])

Q

Study the sources 1–3. What conclusions would you come to about Luther's use of propaganda? Explain your answer with evidence from the sources.

Source 4

Luther as the German Hercules (a Greek hero with great strength), killing churchmen. (c. 1519)

Source 5

A *caricature** of the pope (c. 1520), showing the papal flag and the pope portrayed as a donkey. The devil is also visible.

*Caricature: An exaggerated drawing or description of a person or an animal.

Source 6

Lucas Cranach the Younger and Pancratius Kempff, *Difference Between the True Religion of Christ and the False Idolatrous* (false gods) *Teaching of the Antichrist in its Principal Features* (1546)

[© bpk / Kupferstichkabinett, Staatliche Museen zu Berlin / Jörg P. Anders]

Q What do each of the sources 4–6 tell you about propaganda used by Luther's followers? Explain your answers with evidence from each of the sources.

125

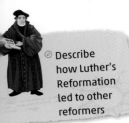

Other Reformers

Luther's opposition to the Catholic Church encouraged **other reformers** in Europe. They challenged the Catholic Church and, in some cases, they set up their own churches.

John Calvin

Calvin began his Reformation in **Geneva**. He founded the Calvinist or **Presbyterian Church** which spread to many countries. Followers of Calvin included **Huguenots** in France, **Puritans** in England and **Presbyterians** in Scotland.

John Calvin

Ulrich Zwingli

Zwingli preached his views in Switzerland. He believed, like Luther, in the authority of the Bible. He did not set up a church or movement.

Henry VIII and the Reformation in England

Henry VIII began the Reformation in England. He made himself **Supreme Head** of the Church of England and he closed the monasteries. His daughter, **Elizabeth I**, completed the English Reformation.

The English kings and queens introduced the same religious changes into **Ireland**. However, they **failed to convert the vast majority of Irish people to Protestantism.** It was mainly through the Plantations that the Protestant population grew in Ireland (Ch. 8).

Ulrich Zwingli

Elizabeth I

Henry VIII

Consequences of the Reformation – Was the Reformation Historically Important?

The Catholic Counter-Reformation

As Protestantism spread, the Catholic Church was faced with a **crisis**. It had to control the spread of Protestant faiths, or else it would continue to lose followers. The reform of the Catholic Church was an **important result** or **consequence** of the Protestant Reformation.

The Council of Trent

Pope Paul III called the cardinals and bishops together in the Council of Trent. Between 1545 and 1563, they ruled on matters of **faith** (what Catholics should believe) and **discipline** (how the Church should be organised).

As a result of the Council of Trent, the Catholic religion remained the **most important religion** in Europe. The **authority and control of the pope** over the Catholic Church was strengthened. There were **greater divisions** between Catholics and Protestants.

A painting of the Council of Trent, held to reform the Catholic Church

Religious orders – the Jesuits

The pope encouraged the foundation of religious orders to promote the Catholic religion. The most important of these was the **Jesuits**, founded by **Ignatius of Loyola**. The Jesuits spread the Catholic faith through public preaching, spiritual exercises, deeds of charity and education. The Jesuits also became **missionaries** in different parts of the world, including Ireland. One of the most famous of these was **Francis Xavier**, who travelled to India and Japan.

The Inquisition

The Court of Inquisition was a court of the Catholic Church which was mainly active in **Spain** and **Italy**. It tried people accused of **heresy** (beliefs contrary to the Catholic Church). As a result of the Inquisition, Protestantism was crushed in Spain and Italy, and those countries remained Catholic.

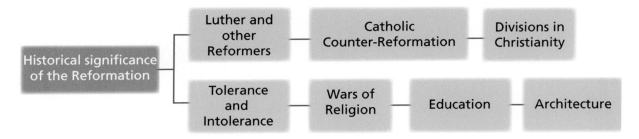

Historical significance of the Reformation — Luther and other Reformers — Catholic Counter-Reformation — Divisions in Christianity

Tolerance and Intolerance — Wars of Religion — Education — Architecture

127

Divisions in Christianity

p. 71 ❯

What conclusions can you draw from this map and the figures below about divisions in Christianity after the Reformation?

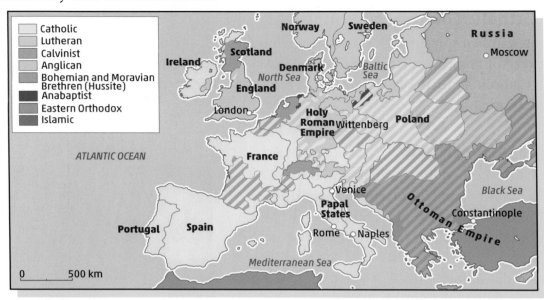

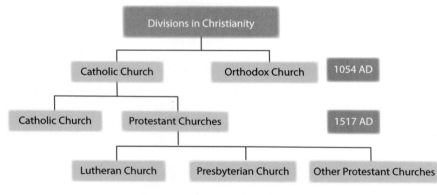

Christianity in the world today	
Roman Catholic Church	50%
Protestant religions	37%
Orthodox Christians	12%
Other Christians	1%
Total = 2.2 billion	2.2 billion

Churches and architecture

What were the **main differences** between Catholic and Lutheran churches, according to the extract and the picture below?

Source 1

Lutheran Church

[The Lutheran church] looks like a great college hall. There are no images, organs or crosses. The wall is leaded with lots of writings in German and passages from the Bible. There are two pulpits, one for the minister to preach from and another below for the man who leads the singing of the psalms. At certain prayers the people rose and clasped their hands, and at the name of Jesus Christ made a low bow.

(Michael de Montaigne, a famous French writer who visited Augsburg in Germany in the 16th century)

Source 2

Baroque Style

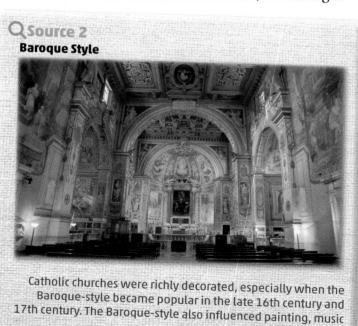

Catholic churches were richly decorated, especially when the Baroque-style became popular in the late 16th century and 17th century. The Baroque-style also influenced painting, music and sculpture.

Tolerance and intolerance

What examples of tolerance and intolerance can you find in the extract and the picture? Is there any information in the other results which would suggest that intolerance won out? How does that information compare with today's world?

Source 3

In the Catholic ones, which are in greater number, the service was well done. There are six Lutheran churches and sixteen ministers; two of the six are former Catholic churches, the other four they have built. There was much more of a crowd this morning in this church alone than in two or three of the Catholic churches together. Marriages between Catholics and Lutherans are common, and the more eager party submits to the laws of the other. There are a thousand such marriages.

(Michael de Montaigne, a famous French writer who visited Augsburg in Germany in the 16th century)

Source 4

The St Bartholomew's Day Massacre in France in 1572, when Catholics attacked French Protestants, called Huguenots. Painting by François Dubois.

Calvinists destroying a Catholic Church in the 16th Century.

Education

Why did the rise of Protestantism play an important part in spreading education? See source 5.

Religious Wars

Some of the Wars in which religion played a part in the causes

- The Peasants Revolt in Germany, 1524–25
- The French Wars of Religion or Civil Wars (1562–98)
- The Spanish Armada, 1588
- The English Civil War (1642–51)
- The Thirty Years War (1618–48)

Source 5

Every kirk (church) shall have a schoolmaster appointed, such a one at least as is able to teach grammar and Latin. The rich and powerful must be compelled to educate their sons at their own expense. The children of the poor must be supported by the kirk (church).

(John Knox, Scottish Presbyterian leader)

⊚ Examine the importance of Luther today

Luther Today

Germany celebrated the 500th anniversary of the Reformation in 2017 with a programme of events and speeches.

According to these sources, is Luther historically important today?

Q Source 1

Catholics are now able to hear Luther's challenge for the Church of today, recognising him as a 'witness to the gospel'. And so after centuries of mutual condemnations and vilification, in 2017 Lutheran and Catholic Christians will for the first time commemorate together the beginning of the Reformation.

(Jointly prepared and published by The Pontifical Council for Promoting Christian Unity [Catholic Church] and The Commission on Faith and Order of the World Council of Churches [Protestant churches])

Q Source 2

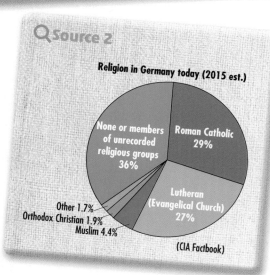

Religion in Germany today (2015 est.)

None or members of unrecorded religious groups 36%

Roman Catholic 29%

Lutheran (Evangelical Church) 27%

Other 1.7%
Orthodox Christian 1.9%
Muslim 4.4%

(CIA Factbook)

Q Source 3

'US President Barack Obama's participation ... on a joint stage with the Chancellor [of Germany], Angela Merkel, ... underscores how internationally we are celebrating 500 years of the Reformation.'

》 Preparing for CBA2

A project on the life and experience of a person of historical interest

PERSONS OF INTEREST IN THE REFORMATION

- Martin Luther
- John Calvin
- Ulrich Zwingli
- Pope Paul III
- Henry VIII
- Thomas Cromwell
- Elizabeth I
- Ignatius of Loyola
- Francis Xavier

p. 73 》
Web Resources
and Reading

Focus Task 1

Research

> Research 'A mighty fortress is our God', a hymn written and composed by Martin Luther.

> What role did music play in the Protestant Reformation and the Catholic Counter-Reformation?

Focus Task 2

Historical Debate

> 'Martin Luther was right'.
Use your textbook and the internet to present the case, for and against, this motion.

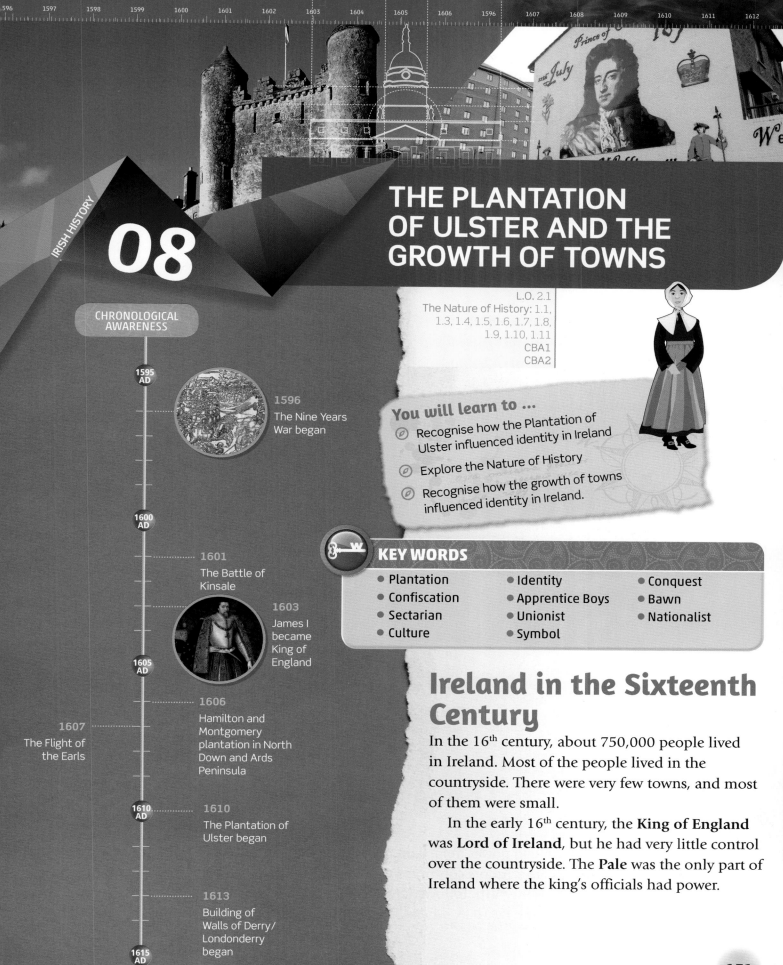

08

THE PLANTATION OF ULSTER AND THE GROWTH OF TOWNS

L.O. 2.1
The Nature of History: 1.1,
1.3, 1.4, 1.5, 1.6, 1.7, 1.8,
1.9, 1.10, 1.11
CBA1
CBA2

CHRONOLOGICAL AWARENESS

1595 AD

1596
The Nine Years War began

1600 AD

1601
The Battle of Kinsale

1603
James I became King of England

1605 AD

1606
Hamilton and Montgomery plantation in North Down and Ards Peninsula

1607
The Flight of the Earls

1610 AD

1610
The Plantation of Ulster began

1613
Building of Walls of Derry/ Londonderry began

1615 AD

You will learn to ...

◎ Recognise how the Plantation of Ulster influenced identity in Ireland

◎ Explore the Nature of History

◎ Recognise how the growth of towns influenced identity in Ireland.

KEY WORDS

- Plantation
- Confiscation
- Sectarian
- Culture
- Identity
- Apprentice Boys
- Unionist
- Symbol
- Conquest
- Bawn
- Nationalist

Ireland in the Sixteenth Century

In the 16th century, about 750,000 people lived in Ireland. Most of the people lived in the countryside. There were very few towns, and most of them were small.

In the early 16th century, the **King of England** was **Lord of Ireland**, but he had very little control over the countryside. The **Pale** was the only part of Ireland where the king's officials had power.

131

◎ Describe Ireland in the 16th century

The Pale was a small area to the north and south of Dublin. Here people followed **English law** ('common law') and **customs**, and spoke the **English language**.

Outside the Pale, the **Anglo-Irish lordships** controlled large areas of land. These lords were the descendants of the Anglo-Normans who had invaded Ireland in the 12th century. They followed English common law, but sometimes they used Gaelic **Brehon law**.

The **Gaelic Irish lordships** were controlled by native Irish lords. These followed **Brehon law**. They did not recognise the English king as lord of Ireland. Instead, each kingdom (or **tuath**) had its own king or chief.

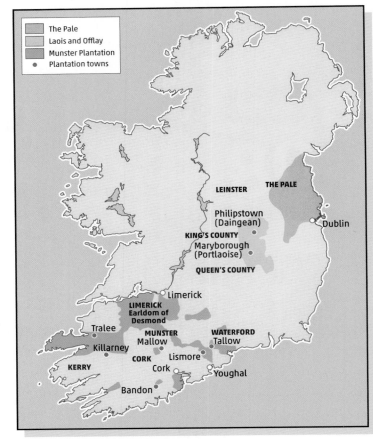

Gaelic family from the 15th century, with the child holding bagpipes

◎ Consider the reasons for the policy of plantation

Differences between Gaelic Brehon law and English common law	
Brehon law	**English common law**
The chief (or Taoiseach) was elected from the *derbhfine* (or royal family).	The eldest son became the new lord.
The land was owned by the clan (or tribe).	The lord owned the land.

Efforts to Conquer Ireland: Why the Land Changed Hands

Henry VII came to power in England in 1485. This was the beginning of the reign of the **Tudor** family. The Tudors continued to rule there until 1603. The descendants of Henry VII – his son, Henry VIII, followed by Edward VI, Mary I and Elizabeth I – took a close interest in Ireland. By 1603, when Elizabeth died, the **English Crown had conquered Ireland**.

Tudors and Stuarts

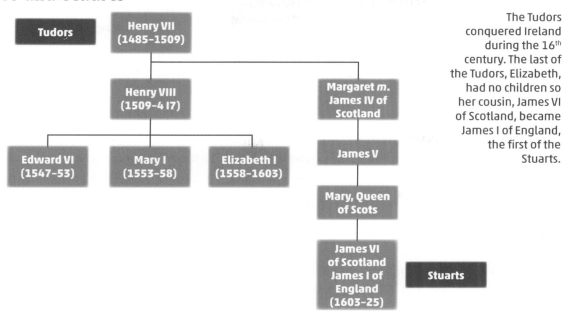

The Tudors conquered Ireland during the 16th century. The last of the Tudors, Elizabeth, had no children so her cousin, James VI of Scotland, became James I of England, the first of the Stuarts.

Military conquest

During the 16th century, the Tudors extended their power beyond the Pale. In a series of **wars**, they reduced the power and influence of the great Anglo-Irish lords, such as the Fitzgeralds of Kildare and the Fitzgeralds of Desmond (Munster).

However, even though their use of the army was very successful, it was also very **expensive**. Along with that, families could **rise up again** in later years, so military conquest had its **weaknesses**.

A new policy: plantations

The English government decided to use another policy to conquer Ireland. This was called **plantation**. This was how it worked:

- After rebellious chiefs or lords were **defeated**, their lands were **confiscated** (taken over)
- The land was given to **loyal settlers**, or 'planters'
- The planters would use **English law, language and customs**
- The planters would **defend** their new land.

Where was the plantation policy tried?

The new plantation policy was first tried in **two main areas**:

- **Laois-Offaly**

  The Plantation of Laois-Offaly was very **limited** and it was **unsuccessful**.

- **Munster**

  The Plantation of Munster was **more extensive**. Settlers or planters came from England, new towns were established, and new farming methods were introduced. A **wealthy Protestant minority** who controlled large estates was established, but fewer planters came than expected so overall, the plantation was a failure.

KEY WORD

Identity
- The characteristics determining who or what a person is.
- The qualities of a person or group that make them different from others.
- The characteristics that make one group of people different from another.

Timeline of the Plantations

1556	Plantation of Laois-Offaly (Queen Mary I)
1586	Plantation of Munster (Queen Elizabeth I)
1610	Plantation of Ulster (King James I)
1652	Cromwellian Plantation (Oliver Cromwell)

The Plantation of Ulster

Background and causes

Gaelic society dominated Ulster. Gaelic chiefs and clans were the main rulers of Ulster. The most powerful of these were the **O'Neills of Tyrone** and the **O'Donnells of Donegal**.

In 1594, the **Nine Years War** began when the **Ulster chiefs** rebelled against efforts by the English government to impose English law and the Protestant religion on the province. The Ulster chiefs, led by **Hugh O'Neill**, Earl of Tyrone, won a number of battles, including the **Battle of the Yellow Ford**. This encouraged other parts of the country, including Munster, to rise in **rebellion**.

Spanish help

Philip II of Spain sent ships with 4,000 soldiers to help the rebellion. These ships landed at Kinsale, Co. Cork but were surrounded by an English fleet and an English army. When O'Neill and O'Donnell came to help, they were defeated at the **Battle of Kinsale** in 1601.

Even though O'Neill made peace with the English government in the **Treaty of Mellifont** (1603), the English government still harassed the Ulster chiefs and wanted to force English law and control over them.

Flight of the Earls, 1607

In 1607, O'Neill and other Ulster chiefs fled Ireland to the continent. This event was later called the **Flight of the Earls**. The English government under **King James I** declared the leaders traitors and **confiscated** their land. He now intended to introduce **loyal planters** to the area.

Reasons for the plantation

King James I wanted the plantation for a **number of reasons**:
- He wanted to create a **loyal and Protestant population.**
  - He wanted to **protect England**. He did not want other countries, such as Spain and France, using Ireland as a base from which to attack England.
  - He wanted to **spread the Protestant religion** in Ireland because he thought Catholics would be disloyal to the Crown.
- He thought that **English culture** was **superior** to **Irish Gaelic culture**.
- He wanted to gain **money** for the Crown for rents and to **pay** soldiers and officials who fought in the Nine Years War and organised the plantation.

The plan of plantation
Survey

Lands were confiscated in **six counties** – Derry, Donegal, Cavan, Tyrone, Fermanagh and Armagh. A **Commission of Inquiry** visited the confiscated counties and investigated the ownership of the land. A team of **surveyors**, protected by soldiers, travelled with them. The Commission divided the land into two parts – **crown land** (belonging to the king) and **church land** (belonging to the Protestant clergy). All church land was given to the Church of Ireland and Trinity College, Dublin. The crown land was used for **plantation** and for **towns** and **schools**.

> ## DID YOU KNOW?
> **Montgomery** and **Hamilton** planted North Down and the Ards Peninsula as part of a private plantation. This plantation was begun in 1606, prior to the government-organised Ulster Plantation. The success of the private plantation was due to the introduction of lowland Scottish tenant farmers and their families – people who were used to a similar damp climate and living off subsistence farming. The **MacDonnells in Antrim** were allowed bring in more Scottish settlers there.

The Plantation in action

The land was divided into estates of **1,000**, **1,500** and **2,000 acres**. It was given to three different groups under the **Articles of Plantation, 1610**.

Conditions of Plantation		
PLANTERS	**WHO WERE THEY?**	**CONDITIONS**
Undertakers	English and Scottish planters	Not allowed to have Gaelic tenants Rent: £5.33 (€5.97) per 1,000 acres
Servitors	English soldiers and officials who were owed money after the Nine Years War and later	Could take some Gaelic tenants Rent: £8 (€8.96) per 1,000 acres
Loyal Irish	Irish of 'good merit': Gaelic Irish who had not taken part in the rebellion	Could take Gaelic tenants Rent: £10.46 (€11.71) per 1,000 acres

Defence

All three groups had to fulfil certain conditions for defence.

(i) Those with 1,000 acres had to build a **bawn** (a stone wall around an enclosure).

(ii) Those with 1,500 acres had to build a **bawn** and a **stone house**.

(iii) Those with 2,000 acres had to build a **bawn** and a **defensive tower**.

The Plantation of Londonderry

King James I asked the guilds of London merchants to help with the Plantation of Derry. The merchants agreed. **Twelve companies of merchants** formed the **Irish Society**. They brought settlers to

The Plantation of Londonderry

Co. Derry, which they now renamed Londonderry. Two hundred workmen were sent to build the new towns of **Coleraine** and **Londonderry**.

Thomas Raven's map of the county of Londonderry, 1622, showing how the land in the Plantation of Co. Londonderry was divided

1. Is this a **primary** or a **secondary** source?
2. **Compare** this map to a current map of Co. Derry and Northern Ireland. What is the name of The Maine Sea today? How accurate is the map?
3. VINTNERS is the name of one of the London companies asked to take over Co Londonderry. Name three more of the London companies marked on the map.
4. How many forts and castles are shown on the map? Why do you think there were so many forts and castles?
5. How **useful** is this map for studying the plantation of Co Londonderry?
6. How does it help with explaining how the Ulster Plantation influenced **identity**?

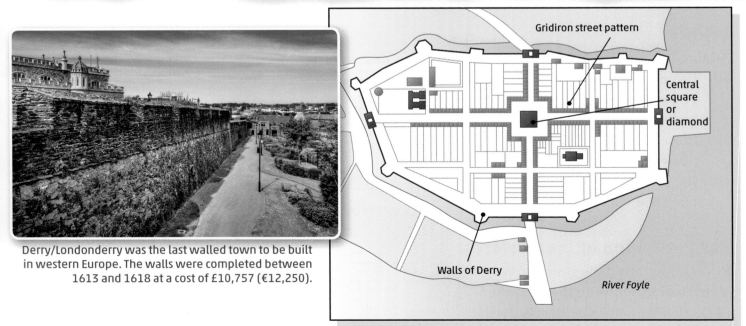

Derry/Londonderry was the last walled town to be built in western Europe. The walls were completed between 1613 and 1618 at a cost of £10,757 (€12,250).

The planned town of Londonderry: note the street pattern, central square and walls

How successful was the Plantation?

From the point of view of the English government, the Ulster Plantation was more successful than the plantations of Laois-Offaly or Munster.

(i) It increased the **influence** of English law, the English language and English farming methods in Ulster

(ii) It ensured a **loyal population**

(iii) It spread the **Protestant religion**.

An English View of Plantation

'The lands of the Irish in Ulster were the most rude and unreformed part of Ireland, and the centre of the last great rebellion. They are now better organised and established than any of the lands in the other provinces... The organisation of those lands happened with the special providence of God, who cast out those wicked and ungrateful traitors, the enemies of the Reformation in Ireland...

His Majesty did not utterly exclude the natives out of this plantation ... but made a mixed plantation of British and Irish, that they might grow up together in one nation. The Irish were in some places transplanted from the woods and mountains into the plains and open countries, that being removed (like wild fruit trees) they might grow the milder, and bear the better and sweeter fruit. When this plantation hath taken root, and been fixed and settled but a few years, with the favour and blessing of God . . . it will secure the peace of Ireland, assure it to the Crown of England for ever; and finally, make it a civil and a rich, a mighty, and a flourishing Kingdom.'

(Extract from Sir John Davies, 'A Discovery of True Causes why Ireland was entirely subdued', written in 1612. Davies was an English nobleman who gained from the Plantation of Ulster. [The British Library])

1. Is this a **primary** or a **secondary** source?
2. Is the writer **biased** or **objective**?
3. Select **one fact** and **one opinion** from the source.
4. What are the **consequences** (results) of the plantation, according to this writer?
5. What does he hope will happen when the plantation 'hath taken root'?
6. What, do you think, the native Gaelic Chiefs of Ulster would think of the opinions of Sir John Davies?
   Explain your answers using evidence from the source.

How did the Plantation of Ulster influence identity?

The New Population

The planters came from **Scotland** and **England**. They were either **Presbyterians** (Calvinists) or **Church of England** (Anglican). They brought their own clergy, took over Catholic churches and also built their own. By 1641, there were about 40,000 Scottish and English settlers (planters) in Ulster.

In later years, large numbers of Scottish migrants continued the tradition of Scottish settlement in Ulster; between 1690 and 1698, 80,000 Scottish people came to Ulster due to famine in their own country.

Source 1

English names	Scottish names
Babingtons	Adams
Blennerhassets	Armstrongs
Bartons	Beattys
Flowerdews	Crawfords
Parkes	Cunninghams
	Elliotts
	Grahams
	Humes
	Hamiltons
	Johnstons
	Stewarts

Source 2

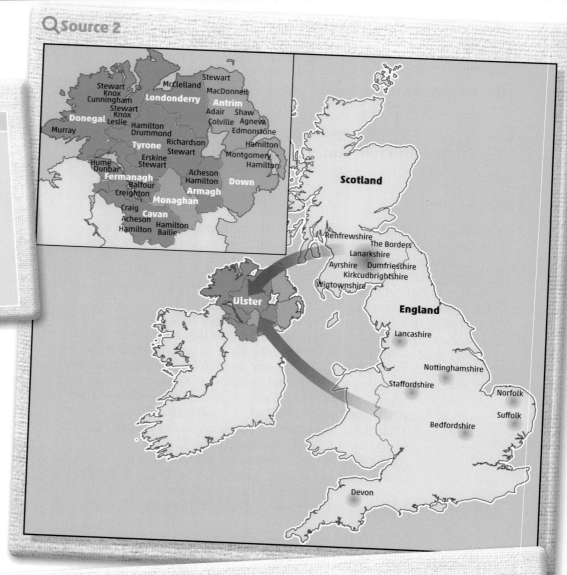

Q

1. Examine Source 1 and Source 2. Do you have **family names** in your class matching names listed in these sources?

2. Select **one name** of English origin and **one name** of Scottish origin, and research the **origin** of the name in each case.

3. Examine Source 2 and Source 3. In which **counties** are the Ulster-Scots dialects to be found?

4. Which of those counties were included in the Plantation of Ulster?

5. Which of those counties was included in the Hamilton and Montgomery plantation?

6. How **useful** are maps as sources for historians?

7. Are the maps in Sources 2 and 3 **primary** or **secondary** sources?

8. How do these sources explain how the Plantation of Ulster influenced **identity**?

Source 3

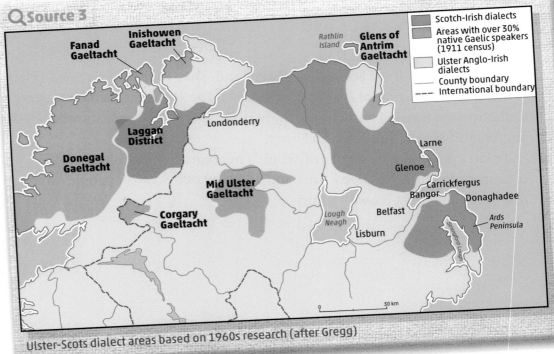

Ulster-Scots dialect areas based on 1960s research (after Gregg)

Source 2
Unionist symbols

Source 3
Nationalist symbols

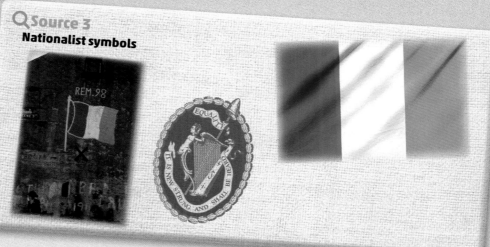

Source 4
Symbols common to both identities, but used differently

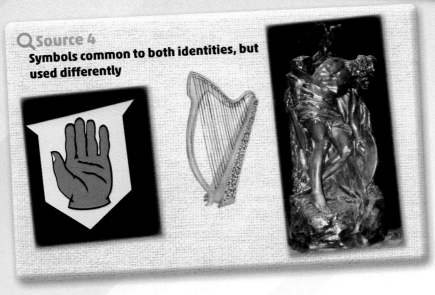

Q DIVIDED IDENTITIES AND LOYALTIES

1. Construct a pie chart based on the views of Protestants in Northern Ireland on their **Britishness** according to Source 1.
2. What **conclusions** can you draw from the information about **identity** in Source 1?
3. Select **one** of the symbols associated with **unionists** in Source 2, and investigate its **meaning**.
4. Select **one** of the symbols associated with **nationalists** in Source 3, and investigate its meaning.
5. Select **one** of the symbols in Source 4, and investigate how unionists and nationalists use that symbol.
6. What is the importance of **symbols** for **identity**?
7. How do you react to the symbols shown in these sources?

Analysing Sources

Historians' Views of the Impact of the Plantation

HISTORICAL JUDGEMENT

Source 1

What happened after the plantation

I think in some ways it's what happens after the Plantation which is much more important for the enduring legacy. It's the fears of the Irish which are created in 1641, the fear of massacre, the fear of attack, that somehow or other accommodations (arrangements) which had been made before were no longer possible after that because the Irish were quite simply, as John Temple put it in his history of the rebellion, 'untrustworthy'.

(Dr. Raymond Gillepsie)

Source 2

Less dense Protestant settlement further west

The significant thing is that the further you go west, the less dense Protestant settlement was and, to some extent, at the time of partition (of Ireland in 1920), this is reflected in the fact that Donegal was a planted county – but it became part of ultimately the Irish Free State: there weren't sufficient numbers of Protestants in Donegal and similarly in Cavan. The Plantation hadn't taken root there as much as it had in other counties.

(Dr. John McCavitt)

Source 3

Segregation (separation) built into the Plantation

The other interesting aspect, as far as the legacy of the Plantation is concerned, is that segregation (separation) was built into the Plantation at the start: we have this modern problem where you know segregated or divided societies. It's just not a product of what has happened today; to a large extent, it actually reflects the fact that the Plantation itself enshrined (preserved) the doctrine of segregation. In the lands allocated to British undertakers, whether they be English or Scots, the intention was to clear all native Irish Catholics off those lands.

(Dr. John McCavitt)

Source 4

What makes the Ulster Plantation different

The Plantation happened in many parts of Ireland other than in Ulster. The principal ingredient that makes Ulster different is that the Plantation in Ulster was followed at the end of the 17th century, in the 1690s, and again continuing into the early years of the 18th century, by a significant further influx of Scottish people. So that it was at this juncture (point) that the population balance in Ulster moves ... significantly towards Protestantism rather than Catholicism, and towards Scots rather than English.

(Professor Nicholas Canny)

Who are the experts on the Plantation of Ulster?

Q

1. According to Source 1, 'what happens after the plantation which is much more important for the enduring **legacy**'?
2. In Source 2, what happens 'the further you go west'?
3. What **explanation** is given for Donegal being included in the Irish Free State rather than Northern Ireland after partition?
4. How is the **experience** of Donegal and Cavan the same?
5. In Source 3, how was **segregation** built into the plantation?
6. According to Source 4, what made the Ulster Plantation **different** to the other plantations?
7. How do any of these sources help you understand more about how the Plantation of Ulster influenced **identity**?
8. Why would these sources be considered **secondary** sources?
9. What **advantage** does a secondary source have over a primary source?
   Explain your answers using evidence from the sources.

Washington Crossing the Delaware, painted by Emanuel Leutze (1818-68) about 1850. The crossing took place on the night of 25-26 December 1776. What emotions are depicted (shown) in the painting? How is Washington highlighted? Is the painting a primary or a secondary source? Is the painting propaganda? Investigate the historical accuracy of the painting.

1777 – A turning point in the war

The year 1777 was an important **turning point** in the war. The American general, Horatio Gates, forced a large British army to surrender at the **Battle of Saratoga**. This victory encouraged **France**, and later **Spain** and **Holland**, to join the war on the American side. These three allies provided money, men and ships for America. The American cause also encouraged volunteers, such as the **Marquis de Lafayette**, a French general, to fight for America.

Winter in Valley Forge

Washington failed to prevent the British capturing **Philadelphia**, which was regarded as the capital of the 13 colonies. Washington retreated for the winter to **Valley Forge**, 20 miles from Philadelphia. Here half of his army deserted and a couple of thousand died from disease. But the small army that remained was well trained by a German officer, **Von Steuben**. Washington himself became a **hero** to his army for staying with them.

Victory at Yorktown

The war continued from 1778 to 1781, with each side winning some battles. In 1781, the war ended suddenly. **Cornwallis**, the British commander, camped his army in the **Yorktown** peninsula in Virginia. He was surrounded by Washington's forces by land, and by a French fleet at sea. Cornwallis was forced to **surrender**. It was the end of the war, even though some fighting continued.

Go onto YouTube and look up 'Miss Stout's History Class George Washington'

In 1783, in the **Treaty of Paris**, the British government finally recognised the independence of the United States of America. The Treaty gave America the land between the Atlantic Ocean and the Mississippi river.

The Consequences of the American Revolution

1. **The United States of America was founded**. The new state expanded as far as the Mississippi river and this encouraged people to migrate westwards. This resulted in **clashes** with the Native Americans who lived there.

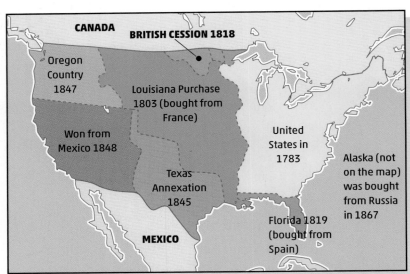

The US began as 13 states but later expanded during the 19th century. It is now 50 states, and the most powerful country in the world.

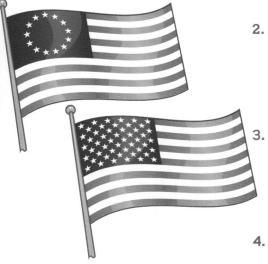

US Flags – the Stars and Stripes: the revolutionary flag (top) of 13 states; the present-day flag (bottom) of 50 states

2. The **American Constitution** was drawn up in 1787. This created a **federal government structure** with a central government in the capital, Washington, sharing power with the states. George Washington became the **first President**. He became known as the **Father of the United States**.

3. The Declaration of Independence said **'all men are created equal'** but slaves, Native Americans and women still did not have equal rights. However, the Declaration inspired these groups to campaign over the next two centuries to improve their status (position) in society.

4. **More independence**: The United States set an example for other countries seeking independence from larger empires. People in other countries followed the ideas of the Declaration of Independence. A new form of government, a **republican government**, based on the consent of the people and without a monarch (king or queen) was set up in America.

5. The victory of the Americans **inspired** French people to challenge their king. The war cost France a great deal of money which resulted in increased taxes on the people. This led to the **French Revolution** in 1789.

6. In **Ireland**, a Volunteer movement grew up which won greater independence for the Irish parliament from the British government. Some in Ireland, such as **Wolfe Tone and the United Irishmen**, took their inspiration from the American Revolution and the French Revolution. They wanted **full independence** from Britain.

Was the American Revolution really a revolution?

With whom do you agree?

A. *'One might be forgiven for concluding, as [Edmund] Burke [Irish writer and Member of Parliament, London] did at the time, that there was no real revolution in America, but simply a successful war of independence which ended British rule but otherwise left things pretty much as they had been.'* (M. A. Jones, *The Limits of Liberty: American History, 1607–1922* (1995))

B. *I see a new nation ready to take its place in the world. Not an empire, but a republic. And a republic of laws, not men. Gentlemen, we are in the very midst of revolution. The most complete unexpected and remarkable of any in the history of the world.* (John Adams, 1776, later second President of America)

KEY WORD

- **Revolution** A sudden, radical, or complete change; a fundamental change in political organisation (ww.merriam-webster.com)

For and against?

- The creation of an entirely new country
- The adoption of democracy by the country
- 'All men are created equal'
- Government by 'consent of the governed'
- Slavery continued
- Some states banned slavery
- Native Americans, women and slaves inspired by Declaration of Independence
- Women were involved in campaigns to boycott British goods
- It created a federal government structure
- Women were not allowed to vote

Q

Which of the arguments in A and B do each of these points (For and against?) favour?

Which do you agree with?

INVESTIGATE A REPOSITORY OF HISTORICAL EVIDENCE

Investigate the Museum of the American Revolution, Philadelphia,
www.amrevmuseum.org
George Washington's Mount Vernon,
www.mountvernon.org

》 Preparing for CBA2

A project on the life and experiences of a person of historical interest

PERSONS OF INTEREST FROM THE AMERICAN REVOLUTION

John Adams	Samuel Adams	Abigail Adams
Andrew Jackson	George Washington	Alexander Hamilton
Molly Pitcher	Thomas Jefferson	Benedict Arnold
Benjamin Franklin	Marquis de Lafayette	George III

《 p. 90
Web Resources and Reading

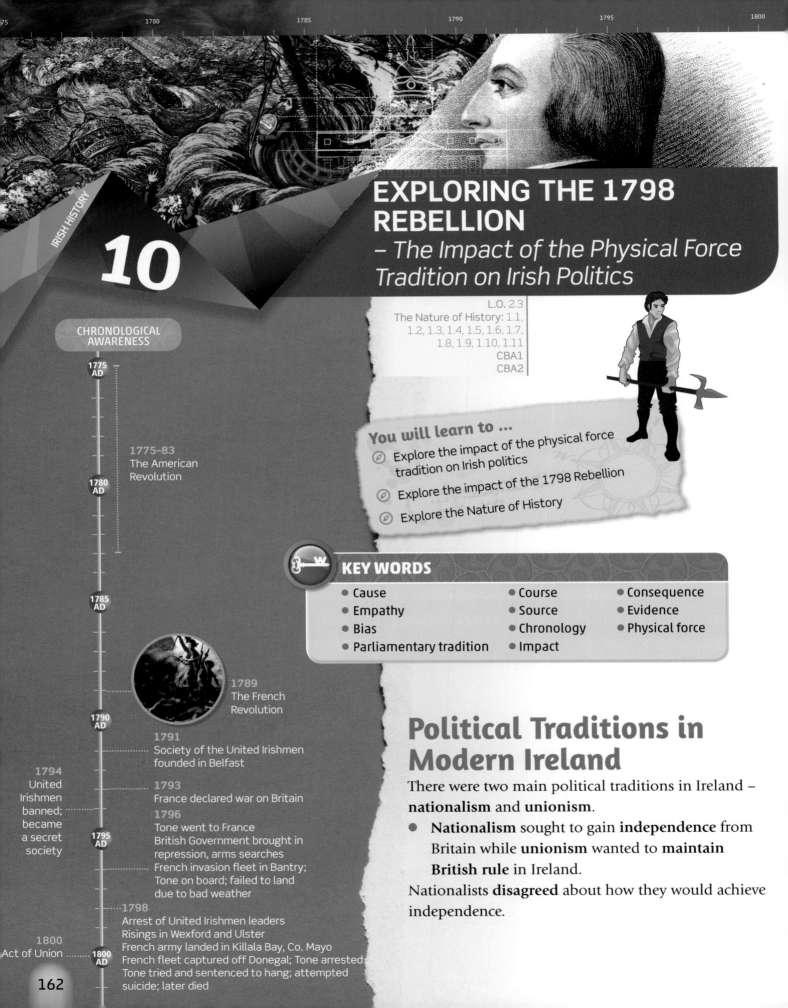

10

EXPLORING THE 1798 REBELLION
– The Impact of the Physical Force Tradition on Irish Politics

L.O. 2.3
The Nature of History: 1.1, 1.2, 1.3, 1.4, 1.5, 1.6, 1.7, 1.8, 1.9, 1.10, 1.11
CBA1
CBA2

CHRONOLOGICAL AWARENESS

1775 AD

1775–83
The American Revolution

1780 AD

1785 AD

1789
The French Revolution

1790 AD

1791
Society of the United Irishmen founded in Belfast

1793
France declared war on Britain

1794
United Irishmen banned; became a secret society

1796
Tone went to France
British Government brought in repression, arms searches
French invasion fleet in Bantry; Tone on board; failed to land due to bad weather

1795 AD

1798
Arrest of United Irishmen leaders
Risings in Wexford and Ulster
French army landed in Killala Bay, Co. Mayo
French fleet captured off Donegal; Tone arrested
Tone tried and sentenced to hang; attempted suicide; later died

1800
Act of Union

1800 AD

You will learn to ...
- ⊘ Explore the impact of the physical force tradition on Irish politics
- ⊘ Explore the impact of the 1798 Rebellion
- ⊘ Explore the Nature of History

KEY WORDS
- Cause
- Empathy
- Bias
- Parliamentary tradition
- Course
- Source
- Chronology
- Impact
- Consequence
- Evidence
- Physical force

Political Traditions in Modern Ireland

There were two main political traditions in Ireland – **nationalism** and **unionism**.

- **Nationalism** sought to gain **independence** from Britain while **unionism** wanted to **maintain British rule** in Ireland.

Nationalists **disagreed** about how they would achieve independence.

- Some believed in **parliamentary means** – that is, using the British Parliament to pass laws to give independence to Ireland. This tradition used **peaceful means** to achieve its aim of an independent Ireland. **Leaders** associated with this tradition in the 18th and 19th centuries included Henry Grattan, Daniel O'Connell, Isaac Butt, Charles Stewart Parnell and John Redmond.

- Others supported **physical force** as a means of achieving independence. This would mean organising **armed rebellion** or **uprising** to defeat the British army in Ireland. **Leaders** associated with this tradition in the 18th and 19th centuries included Wolfe Tone, Robert Emmet, William O'Brien, James Stephens and Jeremiah O'Donovan Rossa.

These political traditions were **dominant at different times** during those centuries. The traditions also continued into the 20th century, and we will look at this later.

Political traditions in modern Ireland

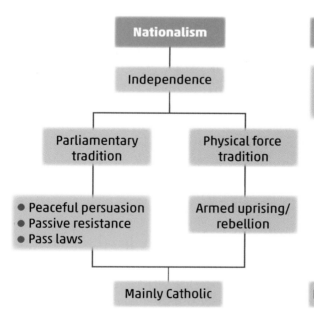

HISTORICAL CONCEPTS

⊘ Outline political traditions in modern Ireland

Timeline of Nationalist political traditions in Modern Ireland

CHRONOLOGICAL AWARENESS

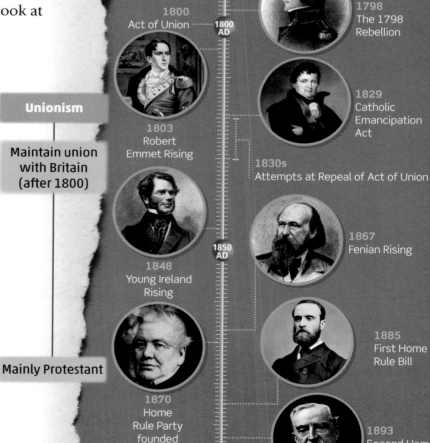

1750 AD

1782
Irish Parliament, known as Grattan's Parliament, makes laws

1791
United Irishmen founded

1800
Act of Union

1800 AD

1798
The 1798 Rebellion

1829
Catholic Emancipation Act

1803
Robert Emmet Rising

1830s
Attempts at Repeal of Act of Union

1850 AD

1867
Fenian Rising

1848
Young Ireland Rising

1885
First Home Rule Bill

1870
Home Rule Party founded

1893
Second Home Rule Bill

1900 AD

1912
Third Rome Rule Bill

Q What events are listed as part of the physical force tradition? What events are listed as part of the parliamentary tradition?

⊘ List the causes of the 1798 Rebellion
⊘ Examine the causes of the 1798 Rebellion

HISTORICAL CONCEPTS

Ireland in 1790

The Protestant Ascendancy

At the end of the 18th century, Ireland was ruled by a parliament in Dublin that was under the control of Great Britain. The Irish Parliament was controlled by the **Protestant Ascendancy**, that is, by members of the Church of Ireland (or Anglican Church). Even though they made up only 15 per cent of the population, they owned most of the land of Ireland, which they got during the plantations.

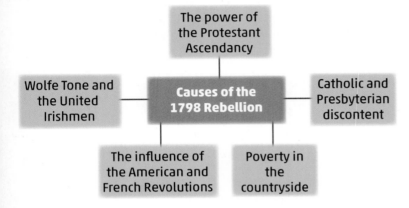

The power of the Protestant Ascendancy

Wolfe Tone and the United Irishmen

Causes of the 1798 Rebellion

Catholic and Presbyterian discontent

The influence of the American and French Revolutions

Poverty in the countryside

Catholic and Presbyterian discontent

The Protestant Ascendancy used the **penal laws** to maintain its power in Ireland. These were laws that **discriminated** against Catholics and Presbyterians. Catholics, who formed 75 per cent of the population, lived all over Ireland, but Presbyterians, who formed 10 per cent, lived mainly in Ulster.

Although some of the penal laws had been abolished (repealed), Catholics and Presbyterians still protested about the remaining laws. They also had to pay **tithes** (one-tenth of their crops) to support the Anglican clergy.

Poverty in the countryside

The majority of people in Ireland lived in the **countryside**. Most of the people were tenant farmers and landless labourers. The population of Ireland doubled in the 18th century, so many farms were **subdivided**. As a result, many people were **very badly off**.

The influence of the American Revolution

The Americans had won their **independence** from Britain in 1783. This was an example for some in Ireland, led by Henry Grattan, who wanted the Irish Parliament to have more power. In the circumstances, the Irish Volunteers won the right for the Irish Parliament to make its **own laws** (legislative independence) in 1782.

The influence of the French Revolution

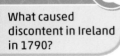

What caused discontent in Ireland in 1790?

The principles of the French Revolution – **liberty**, **equality and fraternity** (brotherhood, nationality) – were popular in Ireland, especially among **Presbyterians** in Belfast. Some political leaders wanted the French revolutionary principles put into practice in Ireland.

The United Irishmen

The **Society of the United Irishmen** was founded in **Belfast** on 18 October 1791. They wanted to reduce English power in Ireland.

- To do that they sought the *'complete and radical reform of the representation of the people in Parliament.'*
- They wanted to include *'Irishmen of every religious persuasion'*, including Catholics, in that reform.

Part of a swearing in ceremony for United Irishmen

'What is that in your hand?'
'It is a branch'.
'Of what?
Of the tree of Liberty.'
'Where did it first grow?'
'In America.'
'Where does it bloom?'
'In France.'
'Where did the seed fall?'
'In Ireland.'

Oath taken by United Irishmen

'I ---- do voluntarily declare that I will persevere (carry on) and endeavour (try) to form a Brotherhood of affection amongst Irishmen of every religious persuasion. I do further declare that I will persevere and endeavour for a Parliamentary Reform, and for an equal representation of all the people in Ireland. So help me God.'

1. How did the words in the ceremony connect Ireland with a **wider revolutionary movement**?
2. What, do you think, is the wider revolutionary movement?
3. What are the **aims** of the United Irishmen according to the Oath?
4. How does the oath show that the United Irishmen began as a **peaceful organisation**?

Wolfe Tone

Theobald **Wolfe Tone**, a Dublin lawyer, was present at the founding meeting of the United Irishmen. He came to prominence when he wrote a pamphlet, *An Argument on behalf of the Catholics of Ireland* (1791).

Tone supported the British government getting rid of some more of the penal laws but he was **disappointed** that the government did not get rid of them all.

⊘ Explain the role of Wolfe Tone

The influence of war

War broke out between Britain and France in 1793 and this **changed everything**. Now the British **feared** a French invasion so they stopped any further reforms and brought in a policy of **repression**.

The United Irishmen were banned so they became a **secret, oath-bound society**. Instead of seeking parliamentary reform, they started planning **an anti-English rebellion** and a **republic**.

Q What were the aims of the United Irishmen? Why did their aims change? What part did Tone play?

Wolfe Tone sought help

Tone went to **America** first, and then to **France**. He asked the French revolutionary government for help. They provided a fleet of 43 ships and 15,000 soldiers, with one of their most able commanders, **General Hoche**. They failed to land in **Bantry Bay** in 1796 due to bad weather. Tone, on board one of the ships, was very disappointed.

'We have now been six days in Bantry Bay within 500 yards of the shore without being able to land. .... all our hopes are now reduced to getting back safely to Brest (France), and I believe we will set sail for that port the instant the weather will permit.'

A drawing by James Gillray, an English artist, on *End of the Irish Invasion;– or– the Destruction of the French Armada* (1797)

Q Can you **identify** the ships? Does this drawing support or oppose the French attempted invasion in Bantry Bay in 1796? Is this **mocking** the invasion? Is this **propaganda**? Explain your answers by referring to to evidence in the drawing.

Analysing Sources

How did Tone's ideas change?

Source 1

I do not mean to take away from the application of his Majesty's rights: I owe him allegiance (loyalty), and if occasion should require it, I would be ready, cheerfully, to spill my blood in his service.

(*An Argument on Behalf of the Catholics of Ireland* [1791])

Source 2

My argument is simply this: That Ireland requires a strength in the people to counteract (cancel out) the influence of [the British] Government: that this strength may be safely and peaceably achieved through the reform of Parliament: and finally that no reform is honourable, or just, which does not include, the extension of elective franchise (vote) to the Roman Catholics.

(*An Argument on Behalf of the Catholics of Ireland* [1791])

Source 3

July 14th [1791]. I sent down to Belfast, resolutions suited to this day, and reduced to three heads. 1st. That English influence in Ireland was the great grievance (complaint) of the country. 2nd. That the most efficient way to oppose it was by a reform in Parliament. 3rd. That no reform could be just which did not include the Catholics.

(*Tone's Diary*)

Source 4

To subvert (undermine) the tyranny (oppression) of our very bad Government, to break the connection with England, the never-failing source of all our political evils, and to assert the independence of my country – these were my **objects** (aims). To unite the whole people of Ireland, to abolish the memory of all past dissentions (disagreements), and to substitute the common name of Irishman in place of the denominations (religions) of Protestant, Catholic, and Dissenter (Presbyterian) – these were my **means** (methods).

(*The Autobiography of Theobald Wolfe Tone* [1937])

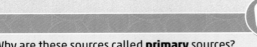

Q

1. Why are these sources called **primary** sources?
2. For whom is Tone prepared to **spill his blood** in Source 1?
3. According to Tone in Source 2, how will **parliamentary reform** help Ireland? What must be included as part of that reform?
4. Do Tone's views in Source 3 match those in Source 2?
5. According to Tone in Source 4, what is the source of Ireland's 'political evils'? What connection does Tone want to break? How does he intend to achieve his objects (aims)?
6. What changes do you notice in Tone's views?
7. **Summarise** the changes in Tone's views. Explain your answers in each case by using evidence from the sources.

Tone arrived in Ireland

Tone got further help from the French government. However, he was captured on board the French fleet off the coast of Donegal. He was taken to Dublin, tried for treason and found guilty. He was sentenced to death. His request to be shot like a soldier was refused, so he committed **suicide**.

Massacre at Scullabogue

On 5 June 1798, 126 people – men, women and children – were killed at Scullabogue, Co. Wexford. They were mostly Protestants. They had been rounded up from the locality and held prisoners some days previously. First, 37 of them were taken and shot, and some piked, in groups of four. Then the remainder, who were held in a barn, were attacked and the barn set on fire. Anyone trying to escape was piked and blocked. The **Massacre at Scullabogue** has caused controversy ever since.

DID YOU KNOW?

The 1798 Rebellion is commemorated by many ballads, including 'Boulavogue', 'The Boys of Wexford' and 'The Rising of the Moon'.

Go onto YouTube and look up 'Reasons for the failure of the 1798 Rebellion'

CHRONOLOGICAL AWARENESS

Timeline for 1798 Rebellion

May	Rebels victory at Battle of Oulart Hill Rebels control Enniscorthy and Wexford
June	Rebels defeated at the Battle of New Ross Massacre at Scullabogue Henry Joy McCracken rebelled in Co. Antrim Rebels defeated at Battle of Vinegar Hill
August	General Humbert landed in Killala, Co. Mayo
September	General Humbert defeated at Ballinamuck, Co. Longford
October	Tone captured in French ship off Donegal
November	Tone committed suicide

Analysing Sources
Massacre at Scullabogue

CONTROVERSIAL ISSUES

pp. 93–94

Source 1

Massacre at Scullabogue, a drawing by George Cruikshank (1792-1878), from William Maxwell, *History of the Irish Rebellion in 1798; with memoirs of the Union, and Emmett's insurrection in 1803* (1845)

Q

1. Is this drawing a **primary** or a **secondary** source?
2. What is happening at the barn?
3. What is happening to the people that are trying to get out of the barn?
4. What **weapons** are being used by the attackers?
5. How would you describe the **mood** of the crowd?
6. Is this source **reliable**?
7. Is it **propaganda**?
8. What **impression**, do you think, the drawing would make on people who saw it in the 19th century? Explain your answers in each case by referring to evidence in the drawing.

Q

1. What does the writer in Source 2 say happened to 'suspected government loyalists' in Wexford?
2. What sometimes happened to prisoners, according to this source?
3. What part did **sectarianism** play in the massacre, according to Source 2?
4. Why is this a **secondary** source? Explain your answers in each case, using evidence from the sources.

Q Source 2

What conclusions can we draw from this summary of the evidence? We must first acknowledge that the rounding up of suspected government loyalists (supporters) was common practice everywhere in Wexford during the rebellion, and the killing of prisoners was not unknown either; in this sense what happened at Scullabogue was part of a larger pattern, although on a larger scale and carried out in an especially brutal manner. Beyond this though, the evidence strongly suggests that the killings took place as an immediate reaction to atrocities in the battle of New Ross, raging six miles away. ... Finally, while it cannot be denied that sectarian hatred (hatred between religions, groups) had some part to play in the affair, I suspect that as we learn more about the crime and the people who carried it out, ... the sectarian dimension (aspect) will then come to appear far more incidental (less important) to the affair than it has seemed up to this.

(Daniel Gahan, *The Scullabogue Massacre 1798*, in History Ireland, 1996)

Q Source 3

The killings were not a matter of mob-frenzy ... but a military-style operation carried out by a small number of men, perhaps as few as seventeen [watched by a much larger group] ... So far as we know all of [the Catholics] were imprisoned and killed because of their connections with local Protestants. ... Apart from [the wife and son of a yeoman], none [of the total killed] had any known connection with the military; they were only 'loyalists' in the general sense that this was used as a synonym (same or nearly same meaning) for 'Protestant' ... Most died mainly because they belonged to recently established and deeply resented local Protestant settlements.

(Tom Dunne, *The Killings at Scullabogue*, in Rebellions: Memoir, Memory and 1798 [2010])

Q

1. How were the killings carried out, according to Source 3?
2. Why were Catholics killed?
3. What did the word 'loyalists' mean, according to Source 3?
4. Why did most of the people die?
5. Do Sources 2 and 3 come to the same conclusions about the Scullabogue Massacre? Explain your answers in each case by referring to evidence in the sources.

Q Source 5

The reporting of these (Wexford) events in Belfast from 7 July (1798) to 11 June the following year (1799) laid great stress on the brutal, annihilating (destroying) anti-Protestantism of the Catholic masses: 'if the gates of hell were opened there would not come a worse enemy than our neighbours were.'

(Paul Bew, *The Politics of Enmity 1789–2006* [2007])

Memorial for victims of Scullabogue Massacre, unveiled in May 1998

Q Source 4

Catholics 11%

Protestants 89%

Known occupations	
Farmers	5
Weavers	4
Shoemakers	2
Servants	2
Masons	2
Others – Butcher, Labourer, Butler, Piper, Excise official, Steward, Tailor, Cattle buyer, Slater, and Schoolmaster	

Q

1. What conclusions about the people who were killed can you draw from the information in Source 4?
2. Does this information help you understand what happened in Scullabogue?
3. According to Source 5, what was the impact of the events in Wexford on Belfast?

The Impact of the Rebellion

Death and destruction

There is uncertainty about the number **killed** in the 1798 Rebellion. Numbers range from about 10,000 to 30,000. There was widespread **destruction** in towns, such as New Ross, where fighting took place.

⊘ Explore the impact of the 1798 Rebellion at the time and on later Irish history

HISTORICAL SIGNIFICANCE

The Act of Union

The **Act of Union** (1800) was passed which ended the parliament in Dublin. Instead, all Irish members of parliament (M.P's) and Irish Lords sat in the parliament in **Westminster**. Ireland was now **ruled directly** from London.

◀ p. 96

Memory

For decades, families who had supported the Rebellion sought safety in suppressing their memories; Anna Kinsella (a historian) points out that the earliest known 1798 memorial in Co. Wexford was erected as late as 1875 in Bunclody. (*The Irish Times*, 10 January 1998)

Catholics and Protestants in conflict

'The bloodshed and murder confirmed two awful lessons. For Catholics, that the state (government) and its allies, (especially perhaps its Orange allies) would, if provoked, impose a bloody terror on the countryside. For Protestants, on the other hand, it became easy to claim that Catholics could not be trusted: given a chance they would use their power, as at Scullabogue, to destroy the other community. Both sides now believed the worst of each other.' (Paul Bew, *The Politics of Enmity 1789–2006*, [2007])

Republic and physical force

The United Irishmen movement influenced **later generations**. The United Irishmen put forward the concept (idea) of a **republic** as the right form of Irish independence. They also had fought and died for the republic. For some people in later years, **armed rising** (physical force) was the only way a republic would be gained.

Boolavogue

At Boolavogue as the sun was setting
O'ér the bright May meadows of Shelmalier
A rebel hand set the heather blazing
And brought the neighbours from far and near
Then Father Murphy from old Kilcormack
Spurred up the rock with a warning cry
'Arm, arm' he cried, 'for I've come to lead you
For Ireland's freedom we fight or die'

Boolavogue was composed in 1898, on the centenary of the 1798 Rebellion

Listen to the song being sung on YouTube.

1. What is the message of this verse of 'Boolavogue'?
2. Is the song propaganda?
3. What do you think about the song, after listening to it?

The physical force tradition in the 19th century

🔍 The Rising of 1803

This rising was organised by Robert Emmet who was hanged for his part in it. Even though the rising was a failure, Emmet's speech from the dock at his trial became famous. 'Not only did Emmet fail to take Dublin; he came nowhere near any success at all ... A ... mob was soon rampaging through the streets of Dublin with pikes and blunderbusses. It eventually found itself surrounding the coach of Lord Kilwarden, the Lord Chief Justice, and a remarkably humane man, who with his son-in-law was now savagely piked to death.'

(R. Kee, *The Green Flag* [1972])

🔍 The Young Irelanders Rising of 1848

'What is often described as the rising of 1848 in Ireland was not in any practical sense a rising at all.' The leaders, including William Smith O'Brien, were sent into exile in Van Diemen's Land (Tasmania).

(R. Kee, *The Green Flag* [1972])

🔍 'I have but one request to ask at my departure from this world – it is the charity of its silence. Let no man write my epitaph; for as no man who knows my motives and character dares now to vindicate (justify) them, let not prejudice or ignorance asperse (criticise) them. Let them rest in obscurity and peace until other times and other men can do justice to them. When my country takes her place among the nations of the earth, then and not till then, let my epitaph be written.'

(Robert Emmet at his trial)

William Smith O'Brien, one of the main organisers of the 1848 Rising

The main event of the Rising of 1848 was an attack on a group of Royal Irish Constabulary (RIC) besieged in the Widow McCormack's house in Ballingarry, Co. Tipperary

One result of the 1848 Rising was the tricolour flag of green, white and orange, which later became the national flag of Ireland. 'The white in the centre signifies a lasting truce between the "orange" and the "green".' (Thomas Francis Meagher)

The Fenian Rising of 1867

The **Irish Republican Brotherhood** (IRB) organised the Fenian Rising of 1867. The efforts at a rising in Ireland failed, but the IRB continued to exist. Members of the IRB organised the **1916 Rising**.

p. 98

Physical force tradition in 19th century

INVESTIGATE A REPOSITORY OF HISTORICAL EVIDENCE

Investigate the National 1798 Rebellion Centre, Enniscorthy
www.1798centre.ie

❯ Preparing for CBA1

A project related to an aspect of the history of your locality or place (or personal/family history)

LOCAL PROJECTS FROM THE 1798 REBELLION AND LATER RISINGS

Your locality can include your county

- Any United Irishmen leaders from your locality
- Any battles or incidents in your locality
- Any leaders from 19th century rebellions from your locality
- Any battles or incidents from 19th century rebellions in your locality
- Any family ancestor involved in 19th century rebellions

❯ Preparing for CBA2

❰ p. 98
Web Resources and Reading

A project on the life and experiences of a person of historical interest

PERSONS OF INTEREST FROM THE 1798 REBELLION AND THE PHYSICAL FORCE TRADITION IN THE 18TH AND 19TH CENTURIES

- Theobald Wolfe Tone
- Father John Murphy
- Henry Joy McCracken
- Robert Emmet
- James Stephens

- Lord Edward Fitzgerald
- Bagenal Harvey
- Henry Munro
- William Smith O'Brien
- Jeremiah O'Donovan Rossa

- General Hoche
- General Humbert
- Michael Dwyer
- John Mitchel
- Thomas Francis Meagher

Focus Task

Historical Debate
> 'The 1798 Rebellion showed physical force was a failure.' Use your textbook, the internet and your school library to present the case, for and against, the motion.

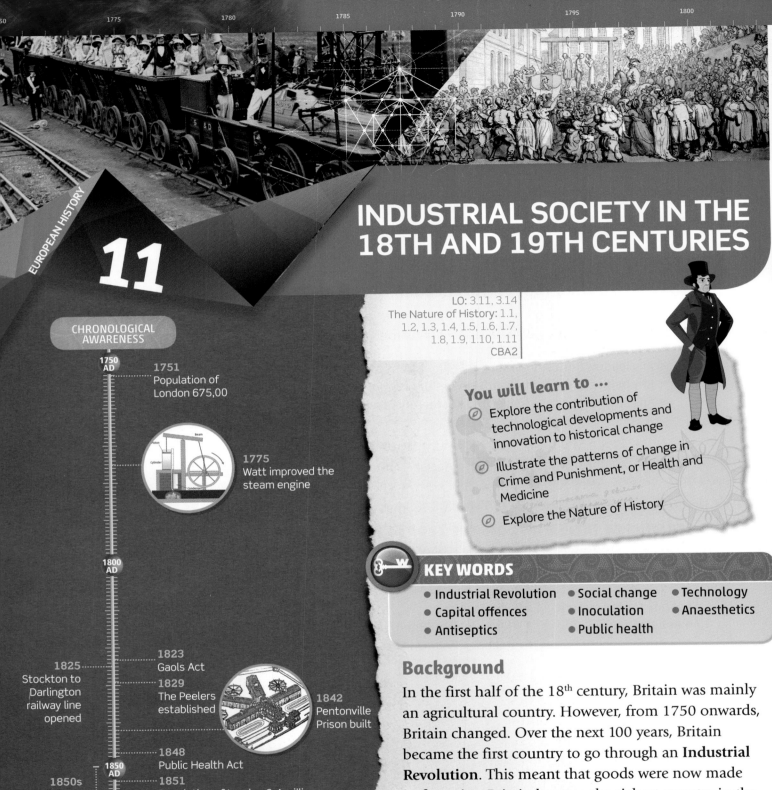

11

INDUSTRIAL SOCIETY IN THE 18TH AND 19TH CENTURIES

LO: 3.11, 3.14
The Nature of History: 1.1, 1.2, 1.3, 1.4, 1.5, 1.6, 1.7, 1.8, 1.9, 1.10, 1.11
CBA2

You will learn to ...

⊘ Explore the contribution of technological developments and innovation to historical change

⊘ Illustrate the patterns of change in Crime and Punishment, or Health and Medicine

⊘ Explore the Nature of History

KEY WORDS

- Industrial Revolution
- Social change
- Technology
- Capital offences
- Inoculation
- Anaesthetics
- Antiseptics
- Public health

CHRONOLOGICAL AWARENESS

1750 AD

1751 Population of London 675,00

1775 Watt improved the steam engine

1800 AD

1825 Stockton to Darlington railway line opened

1823 Gaols Act

1829 The Peelers established

1842 Pentonville Prison built

1848 Public Health Act

1850 AD

1851 Population of London 2.4 million

1850s Nightingale in Crimean War

1860s Pasteur discovered germs spread disease

1868 End of transportation to Australia

1878 Koch grew bacteria

1895 Roentgen discovered the use of X-rays

1900 AD

Background

In the first half of the 18th century, Britain was mainly an agricultural country. However, from 1750 onwards, Britain changed. Over the next 100 years, Britain became the first country to go through an **Industrial Revolution**. This meant that goods were now made in **factories**. Britain became the richest country in the world, and it also experienced great **social changes** (in the way people lived). New towns and cities grew up, and by 1850 more than half the people of Britain were living in cities.

These changes were partly caused by **technological change**, and they contributed to **patterns of change** in crime and punishment, and health and medicine.

Technology and Historical Change

New Technology – The Invention of the Steam Engine

Explore the contribution of the steam engine to historical change in the 19th century

There were many **causes** of the Industrial Revolution which began in Britain in the middle of the 18th century.

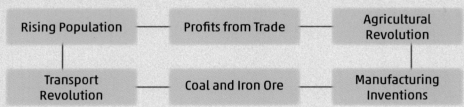

| Rising Population | — | Profits from Trade | — | Agricultural Revolution |
| Transport Revolution | — | Coal and Iron Ore | — | Manufacturing Inventions |

p. 101

One of the most important causes was **the invention of the steam engine**. The steam engine contributed to huge **historical change** in the 18th and 19th centuries.

Steam power

The steam engine was the **most important invention** of the Industrial Revolution. Steam engines built by **Thomas Newcomen** were first used to pump water out of mines. But **James Watt** made improvements to the early steam engines. His most important improvement was to add a **flywheel**. The old steam engines had only an up-and-down motion (movement). Watt's engine had a **rotary (turning) motion**. Now steam engines could be used with belts to **power other machines**. The steam engines were now used to power factories.

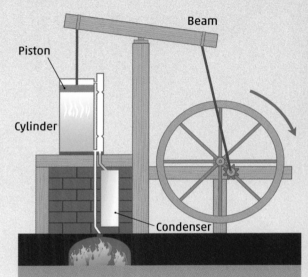

Watt's steam engine: Watt improved the steam engine, which meant it could now be used to drive machinery in factories

From domestic industry to the factory system

The steam engine was used to **power new inventions** for making thread and cloth, such as Crompton's spinning mule or Cartwright's power loom. These inventions speeded up the **manufacture of cloth**. The new machines were also bigger than the old spinning wheel and hand loom. These bigger machines were powered by **waterwheels**, and later by **steam engines**.

This meant that they could be used only in **mills** and **factories**, not in houses. This led to the **growth of factories** in cities in Britain.

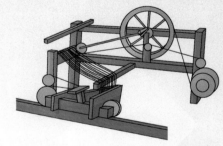

Samuel Crompton's spinning mule

Edmund Cartwright's power loom

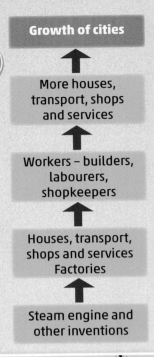

Q

How did the invention of the steam engine lead to the growth of factories and cities?

Growth of cities

↑

More houses, transport, shops and services

↑

Workers – builders, labourers, shopkeepers

↑

Houses, transport, shops and services Factories

↑

Steam engine and other inventions

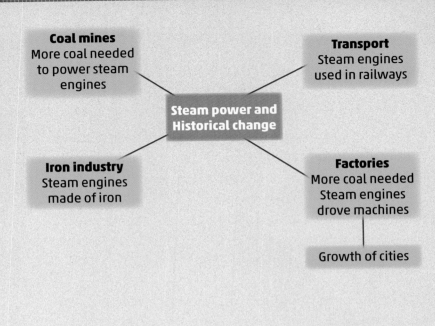

Steam power and Historical change

Coal mines
More coal needed to power steam engines

Transport
Steam engines used in railways

Iron industry
Steam engines made of iron

Factories
More coal needed
Steam engines drove machines

Growth of cities

A re-enactment of the opening of the Stockton to Darlington railway line in 1825

Railways

The invention of the steam engine speeded up the **transport revolution**. Britain depended on carts and canals for transporting goods. The development of the railways changed all that. The first **railroads** were built to haul coal from coal mines. But these railroads used **huge stationary steam engines**. When **Richard Trevithick** designed a small engine on wheels, the **Railway Age** had begun.

In 1825, the **first goods train** ran between **Stockton** and **Darlington**. This train was built by **George Stephenson**. Five years later, the **first passenger line** was built between **Manchester** and **Liverpool**. George and Robert Stephenson's **Rocket** ran on that line.

The impact of the railways

The growth of railways in Britain had a huge impact:

- Faster, cheaper and more comfortable transport.
- Decline of coaches and canals.
- Growth of industry – more coal, iron and engines.
- Growth of towns and cities – more people came to shop; people lived in suburbs.
- Growth of tourism – daytrips to seaside resorts.

The steam engine was the single most important invention, which spurred on the great historical changes of the industrial revolution.

Crime and Punishment

Crime and Punishment in Nineteenth-Century Industrial Society

Britain experienced **great social changes** from the late 18th century through the 19th century. The population increased dramatically from about 7 million in 1750 to 42 million in 1900. More and more of this population **lived in towns and cities**. As the cities grew, the rich and poor separated – the rich went to live in the suburbs, while the poor lived in overcrowded conditions in the city centres. These changes were accompanied by increased crime, drunkenness and violence.

Population of cities		
	1750	**1851**
London	675,000	2.4 million
Liverpool	35,000	376,000
Manchester	45,000	303,000

⊘ Illustrate patterns of change in Crime and Punishment in the 19th century

Who made the law?

During the 18th century, governments looked on punishment as **a deterrent** to stop people committing crimes. In Britain, this was the time of the **Bloody Code** when more and more crimes were punished by execution. By the early 19th century, over 200 offences such as sheep stealing, poaching and theft were **capital offences**, that is, punishable by hanging.

It was clear that this was not working as the crime rate continued to rise so the government changed its approach and its laws. They were influenced by **John Howard**, who wrote *The State of the Prisons in England and Wales*, and by **Elizabeth Fry**, who visited women in Newgate Prison in 1813. They advocated improved prison conditions and introducing worthwhile activities for the prisoners.

Sir **Robert Peel**, who was Home Secretary in the 1820s and later Prime Minister, began the process of change. He had to overcome resistance by Members of Parliament to the changes. Some believed that governments should not interfere or intervene in the economy or society. They also did not want to see increased taxation.

Sir Robert Peel, who introduced many reforms in dealing with crime and punishment in Britain in the 19th century

Who enforced the law?

Prior to the 19th century, **policing** was the responsibility of the local community with volunteer constables and watchmen. The increasing crime rate in **London** led to changes in policing. In 1829, Sir Robert Peel founded the first professional police force there. The new police – called **Peelers** – had a distinctive uniform but they were only armed with a baton or truncheon. Their main job was to patrol the streets to **prevent crime**. Very soon, the example of London spread to all parts of Britain. Later, specialist detective sections were set up to **solve crimes**.

Q

1. What role did Robert Peel play in Irish history?
2. What changes did he introduce in dealing with crime?

What were the crimes?

Some of the old crimes, such as poaching, became less important but **newer crimes** developed in this rapidly changing society. These included bank robbery, as more banks were set up, or thefts from the workplace as more goods were being traded. There was also white-collar crimes of corruption and cheating. But the close living conditions of the time resulted in **petty theft** being the most common crime.

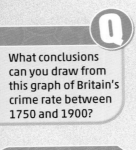

What conclusions can you draw from this graph of Britain's crime rate between 1750 and 1900?

NUMERACY

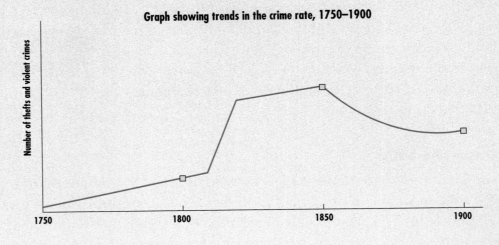

Graph showing trends in the crime rate, 1750–1900

Number of thefts and violent crimes

1750   1800   1850   1900

What were the punishments?

Attitudes to punishment changed during the 19th century. People still looked on punishment as a deterrent, but they began to think that punishment should **match** the crime. They also thought that capital punishment (hanging, execution) was too severe except for the most serious crimes. Now also people began to think that punishment should **improve** the offender. These attitudes led to ending the Bloody Code, and new forms of punishment being tried.

Transportation was one of the new forms of punishment. The first criminals were transported to Australia in 1787. There, criminals worked for the settlers for seven years, providing free labour, and in return they got free food and board. After that, most former criminals stayed in Australia because they could not afford the passage home. By 1868, when transportation ended, over 160,000 people had been transported to Australia.

Transportation ended because people in Australia did not want to see any more criminals. But more importantly, in Britain **prisons** became the new alternative to transportation.

Prisons

Prior to the 19th century, prisons were only used to hold people awaiting trial. Conditions there were usually bad, and disease spread quickly in them. All types of prisoners were grouped together in the one space. Robert Peel began the process of prison reform with his **Gaols Act 1823**. This act separated prisoners by **gender** and **category of crime**. The act also said gaolers should be paid, and that prisoners should not be held in chains.

Later improvements included the building of 90 new prisons between 1842 and 1877. The first of these was **Pentonville Prison**, London. While conditions in the gaols improved, the manner in which prison life was organised made life difficult for the prisoners. Prisons were run on the **Separate system**, that is, all prisoners were kept separate in their own cells. Prisons were also run by the **Silent system**, which was hard labour in silence – 'hard labour, hard fare and hard board'.

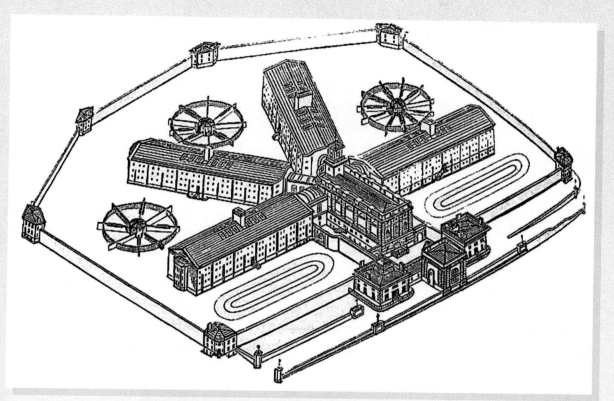

Pentonville Prison built in 1842. Here there were individual cells for prisoners with washing facilities, hammock bed, a window for light and a loom for work. Prisoners were exercised with masks to prevent talking with other prisoners.

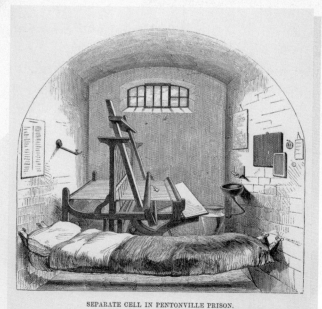

SEPARATE CELL IN PENTONVILLE PRISON.
WITH HAMMOCK SLUNG FOR SLEEPING, AND LOOM FOR DAY-WORK.

CONVICTS EXERCISING AT PENTONVILLE PRISON.

HISTORICAL EMPATHY

What is your understanding of the life of prisoners in Pentonville Prison in the mid-19th century?

These are two verses of Oscar Wilde's long poem, the 'Ballad of Reading Gaol', about the execution of a soldier while Wilde himself was a prisoner there. What prison conditions is he referring to in these verses?

Q

What changes were made in punishments for crime during the 19th century?

How did 19th century punishments compare with punishments in medieval times?

The Ballad of Reading Gaol

We tore the tarry rope to shreds
With blunt and bleeding nails;
We rubbed the doors, and scrubbed the floors,
And cleaned the shining rails;
And, rank by rank, we soaped the plank,
And clattered with the pails.

We sewed the sacks, we broke the stones,
We turned the dusty drill
We banged the tins, and bawled the hymns,
And sweated on the mill;
But in the heart of every man
Terror was lying still.

During the first half of the 19th century, **hangings** were held in public. This practice had gone back as far as the Middle Ages because people believed that public hangings acted as a deterrent to crime. However, instead of deterring crime, public hangings had become scenes of laughter and drunkenness. As a result, the last public hanging in Britain was conducted in 1868.

Hangings also became more effective in killing the victims. In the 1870s, the **long drop technique** for hanging was introduced. This resulted in the neck of the victim being snapped causing instant death.

A public hanging in London at the end of the 18th century. How would you summarise the attitude and behaviour of the crowd?

Health and Medicine

Health and Medicine in Nineteenth-Century Industrial Society

⊘ Illustrate patterns of change in Health and Medicine in the 19th century

Health and medicine in the 19th century

There were very significant developments in health and medicine in the 19th century. By the end of the century doctors knew much more about disease and its origins, how to prevent its spread and how to cure patients.

The most significant discovery was made in the 1860s by **Louis Pasteur** who discovered that **germs caused disease**.

In Germany, **Robert Koch** (1878) learned to grow bacteria and he was able to distinguish which bacteria caused certain diseases, for example, TB and cholera. Another important discovery was the existence of viruses which also caused disease.

DID YOU KNOW?
One side effect of Louis Pasteur's work was **pasteurisation** – in which milk is heated to a certain temperature to kill off any bacteria and keep it fresh for longer.

Louis Pasteur

Cures and remedies

Medical discoveries were improved by better **diagnosis**. This was helped by better **microscopes** to see tiny organisms (1826), and the use of the **stethoscope** (1816) to listen to a patient's chest. At the end of the century in 1895, **William Roentgen** discovered the use of **X-rays**, which were used to investigate broken bones and other complaints.

One of the major discoveries of the 19th century was the use of **inoculation** to prevent disease. This meant that doctors could inject a weakened strain of the disease into patients and this provided immunity (protection) against the full disease. Edward Jenner developed a vaccine for smallpox in 1796 when he injected people with cowpox which protected them against smallpox. Later in the 19th century, Pasteur developed the use of inoculation to combat rabies, a deadly virus transmitted through dog bites.

However, some cures were not successful so people still relied on medicines sold in bottles that had no effect.

Surgery

At the beginning of the 19th century, surgery was often done in a very brutal, painful way. It resulted in a high death rate, either through the surgery itself or through disease picked up afterwards.

The use of anesthetics was encouraged when Queen Victoria gave birth to her eighth child with the help of chloroform

Surgical procedures improved during the century to such an extent that the death rate due to surgical operations was reduced substantially. The development of **anaesthetics** (which protected patients from pain) and **antiseptics** (which protected patients from infection) helped to reduce the death rate and the suffering.

Some of these developments came from America where laughing gas and ether were used as anaesthetics. In Britain, **James Simpson** used **chloroform** as an anaesthetic (1847) and this allowed surgeons to take greater care with their operations.

Some doctors were aware of the importance of cleanliness, even before Pasteur's discovery about bacteria. After his discovery, **Joseph Lister** (1865) reduced the death rate amongst his patients by using a **carbolic spray** to protect against infection. Other improvements included the development of a sterile operating theatre and the use of specialist clothing and face masks for the doctors and nurses.

Hospitals

Hospitals were not safe in the early 19th century. In fact patients often entered with one disease and died from another inside. However, as the century progressed, there were many changes to hospitals, including the building of many new hospitals. These hospitals were better managed, in particular, in relation to cleanliness.

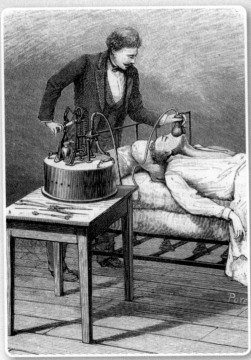

Chloroform being administered to a patient

There was also the influence of **Florence Nightingale**. After her experience in the Crimean War, she returned to London and wrote *Notes on Nursing*, about how nurses could be better trained. She also set up the first nurse training school in Britain. Later she wrote *Notes on Hospitals*, which encouraged the better management of hospitals.

The **place of women** in medicine was limited to nursing. However, a few women qualified as doctors in spite of great obstacles. For example, **Sophia Jex-Blake** studied medicine in Edinburgh but had to gain her qualification in Switzerland, and began to practice as a doctor in Ireland. She later founded the London School of Medicine for Women in 1874.

Public health

Improvements in **public health** played an important part in reducing the death rate as bad living conditions were to blame for some deaths. For example, Britain was hit by a succession of **cholera outbreaks**, which ensured that action had to be taken to prevent future outbreaks.

Average ages of death during the Industrial Revolution		
	Manchester	**Rutland (country area)**
Labourers	17	33
Middle class	38	50

How, according to this table, did being rich or poor, or living in a city or country area, affect life expectancy in 19th century Britain?

Cholera* deaths in Britain	
1831–32	50,000
1848	60,000
1854	20,000

*Cholera is caused by drinking contaminated water

THE "SILENT HIGHWAY"-MAN.
"Your MONEY or your LIFE!"

The Silent Highwayman (1858) – cartoon depicting Death rowing up the Thames. This was during the time when London experienced the Great Stink from the River Thames, into which sewerage drained

One of the most important promoters of public health was **Edwin Chadwick**. His report on the *Sanitary Conditions of the Labouring Population* in 1842 highlighted the link between bad living conditions, ill-health and life expectancy. He wanted government action to improve living conditions. The outbreak of cholera in 1848 forced the government to act. It passed the **Public Health Act 1848**, which allowed local councils to improve conditions in their own towns.

Later acts of parliament improved sanitation, housing regulations and forced local councils to improve conditions in their towns and cities. These acts reduced deaths from **typhus** (spread by fleas or lice) in London from 716 in 1868 to none in 1900.

What, do you consider, were the most important developments in medicine in the 19th century?

New sewers

Flush toilets

Public Health Acts

Better housing conditions

Factors that improved public health

Street cleaning

Slum clearance

Compulsory vaccination against smallpox

Improved living conditions in 19th-century cities and towns

- Main streets were paved
- Street cleaning was improved
- Iron and steel pipes and mains water supplies were introduced
- Sewage disposal was introduced
- Regulations were brought in to build better houses
- Compulsory vaccines were introduced
- Slum clearance was started

INVESTIGATING A REPOSITORY OF HISTORICAL EVIDENCE FOR THE STEAM ENGINE

How did the railways change the lives of people in Victorian Britain?
http://webarchive.nationalarchives.gov.uk/20090124061522/www.learningcurve.gov.uk/
victorianbritain/happy/default.htm

INVESTIGATING A REPOSITORY OF HISTORICAL EVIDENCE FOR CRIME AND PUNISHMENT

Crime and Punishment,
www.nationalarchives.gov.uk/education/candp/default.htm
A Victorian Prison,
Go onto www.nationalarchives.gov.uk 'Victorians 1850–1901', then 'A Victorian Prison'.

INVESTIGATING A REPOSITORY OF HISTORICAL EVIDENCE FOR HEALTH AND MEDICINE

Cholera: From 'great stink to safe to drink?
www.nationalarchives.gov.uk/education/sessions/cholera-great-stink-safe-drink/
Florence Nightingale,
www.nationalarchives.gov.uk/education/resources/florence-nightingale/

》 Preparing for CBA2

A project on the life and experience of a person of historical interest

PERSONS OF INTEREST IN 19TH CENTURY INDUSTRIAL SOCIETY

- James Watt
- John Howard
- Mary Seacole
- Louis Pasteur
- George and Robert Stephenson
- Elizabeth Fry
- Edwin Chadwick
- Joseph Lister
- Robert Peel
- Florence Nightingale
- Sophia Jex-Blake
- Robert Koch

Focus Task

HISTORICAL RESEARCH

> Select one of the following inventions from the Industrial Revolution: flying shuttle: spinning jenny: the power loom: Bessemer converter. Research the invention and its impact on historical change. Include in your research a comparison with the impact of the steam engine.

> Louis Pasteur
Investigate the contribution of Louis Pasteur to science and medicine.

《 p. 105
Web Resources
and Reading

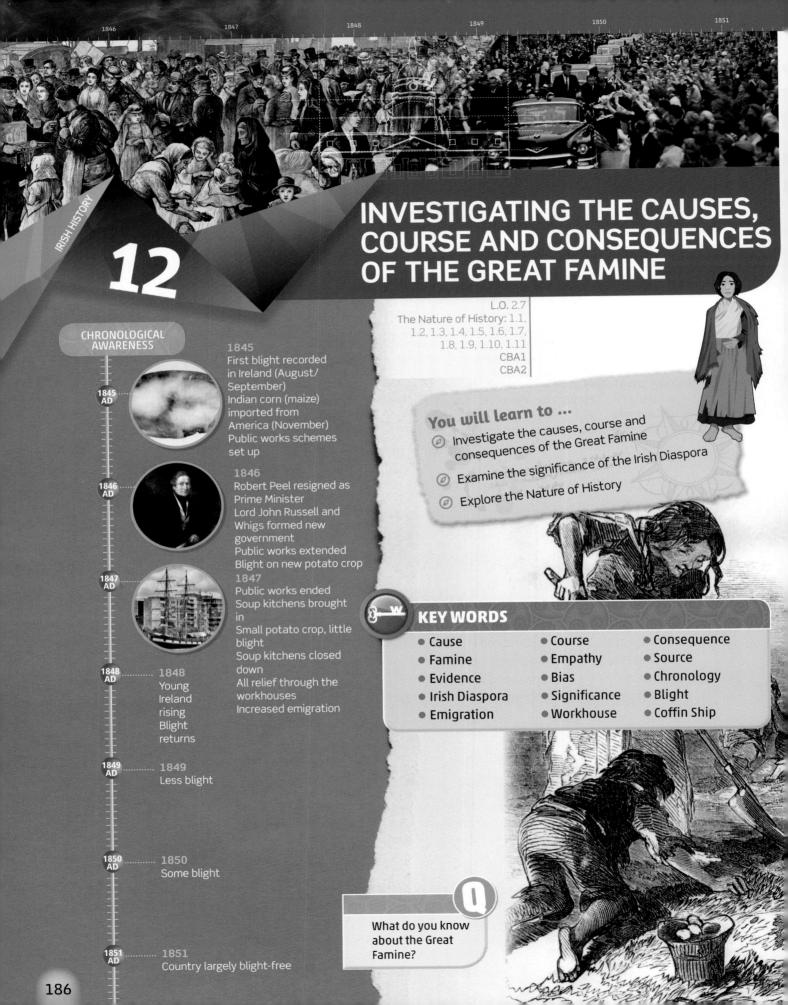

12

INVESTIGATING THE CAUSES, COURSE AND CONSEQUENCES OF THE GREAT FAMINE

L.O. 2.7
The Nature of History: 1.1, 1.2, 1.3, 1.4, 1.5, 1.6, 1.7, 1.8, 1.9, 1.10, 1.11
CBA1
CBA2

CHRONOLOGICAL AWARENESS

1845
First blight recorded in Ireland (August/September)
Indian corn (maize) imported from America (November)
Public works schemes set up

1846
Robert Peel resigned as Prime Minister
Lord John Russell and Whigs formed new government
Public works extended
Blight on new potato crop

1847
Public works ended
Soup kitchens brought in
Small potato crop, little blight
Soup kitchens closed down
All relief through the workhouses
Increased emigration

1848
Young Ireland rising
Blight returns

1849
Less blight

1850
Some blight

1851
Country largely blight-free

1845 AD
1846 AD
1847 AD
1848 AD
1849 AD
1850 AD
1851 AD

You will learn to ...
◎ Investigate the causes, course and consequences of the Great Famine
◎ Examine the significance of the Irish Diaspora
◎ Explore the Nature of History

KEY WORDS
- Cause
- Famine
- Evidence
- Irish Diaspora
- Emigration
- Course
- Empathy
- Bias
- Significance
- Workhouse
- Consequence
- Source
- Chronology
- Blight
- Coffin Ship

Q What do you know about the Great Famine?

Preparing to emigrate

Ireland in 1840

In 1840, Ireland was **ruled directly** from London. The British government ruled through a **Lord Lieutenant** in the Vice-regal Lodge in the Phoenix Park, and a **Chief Secretary** in Dublin Castle.

Examine the causes of the Great Famine

Ireland's population grew rapidly in the 18th and early 19th centuries. In 1841, there were 8.2 million people living in the country. Most of the people lived in the countryside. Only three cities had populations of more than 50,000 – Dublin, Cork and Belfast. Of these, only Belfast was industrialised, like cities in England.

The land

Landlords owned most of the land. They were descended from the **planters** who received land in the plantations of the 16th and 17th centuries. They rented the land to **tenant farmers**. In turn, these farmers worked their land, and some employed **labourers** to help them.

The **landlord's agent** collected rent twice a year. Tenants could be **evicted** for any reason, but they were usually only evicted for non-payment of rent.

Some labourers were **cottiers**. Cottiers rented a small plot of ground – called **conacre** – from a farmer. In return they worked on the farm to pay off the rent. Other labourers were **landless**. These were the poorest people, living in mud cabins on the edge of towns, or renting rooms in lodging houses.

Example of a mud cabin, as painted by the artist William Evans of Eton, Killary, near the Mouth of the Bundoracha River, Co. Galway

Social Classes in Ireland in 1840s

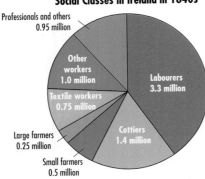

Professionals and others
0.95 million

Other workers
1.0 million

Labourers
3.3 million

Textile workers
0.75 million

Large farmers
0.25 million

Small farmers
0.5 million

Cottiers
1.4 million

Poverty in the country

There was much **poverty** in the country in the 1840s. The growing population, failed harvests and dependence on farming were all causes of poverty. Many people **emigrated** as a result of the poverty. In all, 1.5 million people emigrated from Ireland to the United States, Canada and more so to England, in the thirty years **before** the Great Famine.

For poor people who lived in Ireland, there was the **workhouse**. The British government passed a **Poor Law Act** in 1838. This set up **Poor Law Unions** (or districts), each with a **workhouse**. People who needed help had to move to the workhouse.

Poor Law Unions and Workhouses in Ireland. In which Poor Law Union is your school located? Do you know where the workhouse for your area was located? What use is being made of the building now?

The causes of the Great Famine

Ireland experienced the Great Famine between 1845 and 1850. The principal **causes** of the famine were:

p. 110

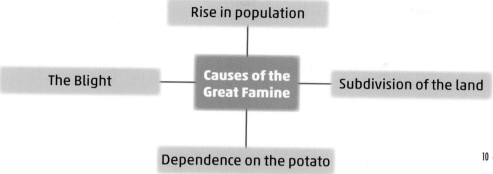

```
                    Rise in population

                         |
The Blight ───── Causes of the ───── Subdivision of the land
                  Great Famine
                         |

              Dependence on the potato
```

Rise in population

The population of Ireland **grew** from 6.8 million in 1821 to 8.2 million in 1841, in spite of emigration. Some areas of the country, such as counties in **Connacht**, were **more densely populated** than others. As the population increased, people became **poorer**. The poorest were the labourers, cottiers and small farmers with less than five acres. (See pie chart p. 188)

Subdivision of the land

Most of the people depended on farming because the manufacturing industry was not developed like in Britain. As the population grew, fathers **subdivided** their land between their sons, and gave a dowry to their daughters. Other farmers sublet their land as **conacre** to pay for labourers. As the farms got smaller, families became **poorer**.

Rising population in Ireland before the famine

Dependence on the potato

Poorer families **depended** on the potato to live. Their three meals a day consisted of potatoes only. By the 1840s, the potato was almost the only food for about 4 million families.

Daily diet of the poorer classes in Ireland in the 1840s – adult males		
Breakfast	**Dinner**	**Supper**
2 kgs of potatoes and skimmed milk	2 kgs of potatoes and skimmed milk	2 kgs of potatoes and skimmed milk – none in a bad season

Blight

Blight is a **disease** that attacks and rots potatoes. When the blight destroyed the potato crop, those who depended on the potato had no other food and so they starved.

A potato with blight

The progress of the famine

The **blight** was reported in America in 1843. By the autumn of **1845**, it was in Ireland. Only some areas were affected, and the early crop had escaped. For this reason, very few people died.

The blight hit again in **1846**. This time the entire crop was destroyed so starvation and hardship affected many people. The blight was less severe in **1847**. However, the seed potatoes used for planting had been eaten so the crop was smaller. Starvation was widespread.

In **1848**, the blight struck again with greater force. People had planted extra potatoes, but the potatoes rotted. Many people who had survived the earlier years died or emigrated. The blight struck again in **1849** and **1850**, but the worst effects of the famine were over.

Analysing Sources

Famine in Skibbereen

HISTORICAL EMPATHY

Q Source 1

Letter describing a visit to Skibbereen

Being aware that I should have to witness scenes of frightful hunger, I provided myself with as much bread as five men could carry, and on reaching the spot I was surprised to find the wretched hamlet (village near Skibbereen) apparently deserted. I entered some of the hovels to find out the cause, and the scenes that presented themselves were such no tongue or pen can convey the slightest idea of. In the first, six famished and ghastly skeletons, to all appearance dead, were huddled in a corner on some filthy straw, their sole covering what seemed a ragged horse-cloth, naked above the knees. I approached in horror, and found by a low moaning they were alive, they were in fever – four children, a woman, and what had once been a man. It is impossible to go through the details, suffice to say, that in a few minutes I was surrounded by at least 200 of such phantoms (ghosts). By far the greater number were delirious (feverish), either from famine or fever. Their demonic (crazed) yells are still yelling in my ears, and their horrible images are fixed upon my brain.

(N. M. Cummins, J.P, Cork, 17 December 1846)

Source 2

THE FAMINE IN IRELAND.—FUNERAL AT SKIBBEREEN.—FROM A SKETCH BY MR. H. SMITH, CORK.—(SEE NEXT PAGE.)

Funeral at Skibbereen

Q

1. Why did the writer in Source 1 find the village 'apparently deserted'?
2. What did he find in one of the hovels?
3. Is the writer of Source 1 **shocked** at what he saw?
4. How is his **evidence** supported by the drawing of the funeral in Source 2?
5. How many people are buried in the famine grave, according to the plaque in Source 3?
6. What was the **percentage decline** in the population of Skibbereen Union between 1841 and 1851, based on Source 4?
7. Are these sources **primary** or **secondary** sources?
8. What, do you think, would be the impact of Sources 1 and 2 on the people who read and saw them at the time?
9. Identify **one fact** and **one opinion** in Source 3.
10. What is the **purpose** of the plaque in Source 3?
Explain your answers in each case by referring to evidence in the sources.

Source 3

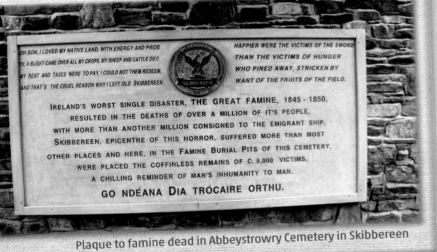

OH SON, I LOVED MY NATIVE LAND, WITH ENERGY AND PRIDE
TIL A BLIGHT CAME OVER ALL MY CROPS, MY SHEEP AND CATTLE DIED
MY RENT AND TAXES WERE TO PAY, I COULD NOT THEM REDEEM,
AND THAT'S THE CRUEL REASON WHY I LEFT OLD SKIBBEREEN.

HAPPIER WERE THE VICTIMS OF THE SWORD
THAN THE VICTIMS OF HUNGER
WHO PINED AWAY, STRICKEN BY
WANT OF THE FRUITS OF THE FIELD.

IRELAND'S WORST SINGLE DISASTER, THE GREAT FAMINE, 1845 - 1850,
RESULTED IN THE DEATHS OF OVER A MILLION OF IT'S PEOPLE,
WITH MORE THAN ANOTHER MILLION CONSIGNED TO THE EMIGRANT SHIP.
SKIBBEREEN, EPICENTRE OF THIS HORROR, SUFFERED MORE THAN MOST
OTHER PLACES AND HERE, IN THE FAMINE BURIAL PITS OF THIS CEMETERY,
WERE PLACED THE COFFINLESS REMAINS OF C. 9,000 VICTIMS,
A CHILLING REMINDER OF MAN'S INHUMANITY TO MAN.

GO NDÉANA DIA TRÓCAIRE ORTHU.

Plaque to famine dead in Abbeystrowry Cemetery in Skibbereen

COMMEMMORATION

Source 4

The population of Skibbereen Union, 1841–51

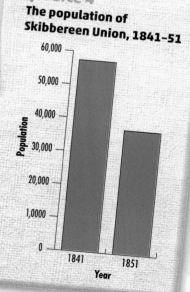

Population / Year

1. Why did the father in the verse of *Dear Old Skibbereen* say he left the town?
2. What is the reaction of the son?
3. Google the words of the rest of the song, and listen to a recording of it on YouTube. What is the **purpose** of the song, do you think? What impact/influence would the words and music of the song have on its listeners?
4. Is the song in Source 5 **propaganda**? Explain your answers in each case, by referring to evidence in the source.

Q Source 5

Dear Old Skibbereen (a song probably composed in America about 1880)

My son, I loved our native land with energy and pride
Until a blight fell on my crops, my sheep and cattle died,
The rents and taxes were too high, I could not them redeem,
And that's the cruel reason why I left Old Skibbereen.

....

Oh father dear, the day will come when in answer to the call
Each Irishman with feelings stern will answer one and all,
I'll be the man to lead the van, beneath our flag of green,
And loud and high we'll raise the cry, 'Remember Skibbereen!'

Consider how the British government coped with the Great Famine

What did the British Government do?

The government of **Sir Robert Peel** acted quickly in 1845 when reports of the blight came in. Peel ordered the importation of £100,000 (the equivalent of €10.2 million in 2018) worth of **Indian corn** (or maize), enough to feed 1 million people. This was sold through government depots. It helped to reduce the impact of the famine in 1845. Peel also set up **public works schemes** so that poor people could earn money by working on roads and piers.

British government policy towards the Great Famine **changed** when **Lord John Russell** replaced Peel as Prime Minister in 1846. The new government believed in a **policy of laissez-faire**.

They believed that the government should **not interfere** in the workings of the economy. Government interference, they said, would only make matters worse because it would encourage landlords and tenants to do little to improve the situation. They also believed that '**Irish property (the landlords) should pay for Irish poverty**'.

Government relief

- 1845   Government bought Indian corn and set up public works
- 1846   Laissez-faire policy; public works schemes; workhouses
- 1847   Soup Kitchen Act; workhouses
- 1848   Workhouses; public works; outdoor relief
- 1849   Workhouses; public works; outdoor relief
- 1850   Workhouses; public works; outdoor relief

Russell's government expanded the **public works schemes** for roads and piers. By 1847, 750,000 people were employed in these schemes. The government also passed the **Soup Kitchen Act** (1847), after seeing the success of the **Quakers' soup kitchens**. Soup was cooked in large boilers and given to the people. Three million people were fed each day. But the government closed down the soup kitchens after six months, in September 1847. They said all relief (help) would be provided through the **workhouses**.

Famine relief

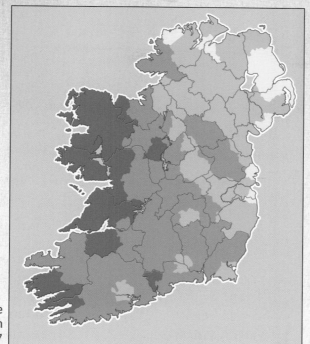

Over 60%

30–60%

5–30%

Less than 5%

p. 111

Map showing the percentage of people taking up rations in the summer of 1847

Q

1. Which area of the country had the highest percentage of people taking up rations in 1847?
2. Name three counties in that area.
3. How many counties had over 30% of the people taking up rations in 1847?
4. Which areas had less than 5% of the people taking up rations in 1847?
5. What was the percentage in your locality or county?
6. According to the poster, how should children be fed?
7. How should 'grown people' be fed?
8. According to the poster, is Indian meal better than wheaten bread?
9. Is this a **primary** or **secondary** source?
10. Was the poster a good way for telling people about Indian meal?
11. From the graph, in what years were grain imports greater than grain exports?
    Explain your answers.

THE USE OF
Indian Meal as an article of Food

Various Manners of using Indian Meal, as Human Food.

Suppawn, or Porridge, that is to say, boiling milk, or water, thickened with Indian Corn meal. Put into water, this is a breakfast, supper, or dinner for little children; put into milk, it is the same for grown people. In milk it is a good strong meal, sufficient for a man to work upon.

It takes about three pounds and a half of Indian corn flour to make porridge for ten persons, less than half a pound of corn flour for a meal for one man, and a warm comfortable meal that fills and strengthens the stomach. Three pounds and a half of wheaten flour would make four pounds and a half of bread, but it would be dry bread, and bread alone; and not affording half the sustenance or comfort of the porridge.

NUMERACY

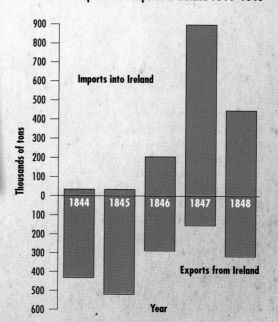

Grain Imports and Exports in Ireland 1844–1848

Imports into Ireland

Exports from Ireland

Thousands of tons

900
800
700
600
500
400
300
200
100
0
100
200
300
400
500
600

1844 1845 1846 1847 1848

Year

1. Which of these recipes would you prefer and why?

2. Would you consider soup kitchens the 'best solution' to the Great Famine? Explain your answers.

Soup kitchens recipes

Quaker Soup

100 gallons of water

75 lbs of meat (salt beef or pork)

35 lbs of dried peas

21 lbs each of oatmeal and barley

$1\frac{1}{2}$ lbs pepper

14 lbs of salt

Recipe for Government Soup

$21\frac{1}{2}$ lbs beef

$6\frac{1}{4}$ lbs dripping

25 lbs each of flour and barley

9 lbs salt

100 onions

$1\frac{1}{2}$ lbs brown sugar

Workhouses

Workhouses had been set up before the famine to help poor people. By 1848, there were almost 200,000 people in the workhouses, built for about 100,000 people. Although new workhouses were opened, overcrowding continued, conditions were bad and disease spread quickly. The government also provided '**outdoor relief**' for another 800,000 people.

Overall, the British government's response was **influenced** by the view that local authorities should only look for government help when they really needed it. Many government ministers also blamed Irish landlords and they felt the landlords should pay for sorting out the problems. But the government could have continued to import Indian corn and keep the soup kitchens open.

DID YOU KNOW?

Between 1848 and 1850, over 4,000 orphaned girls from workhouses around Ireland emigrated to Australia under the Earl Grey Scheme.

1. What did Trevelyan mean when he said, 'Local distress (suffering) cannot be helped out of national (government) funds without great abuses and evils'?

2. What did Trevelyan mean when he said, 'All (people) are interested in getting as much as they can'?

3. What does 'make a poor mouth' mean?

4. What do you think Trevelyan is most concerned about?

5. Do you think Trevelyan favoured helping people with government spending during the Great Famine? Explain your answers using evidence from the document.

Charles Trevelyan was the most senior civil servant who made decisions about famine relief in Ireland

Local distress (suffering) cannot be helped out of national (government) funds without great abuses and evils ... All (people) are interested in getting as much as they can. It is nobody's concern to put a check on the spending. ... Ireland is not the only country which would have been thrown off its balance by the attraction of 'public money'. All classes 'make a poor mouth,' as it is called in Ireland. They conceal (hide) their advantages, exaggerate their difficulties, and relax their effort. The cottier does not sow his holding (land), the proprietor (owner) does not employ his poor in improving his estate, because by doing so they would disentitle themselves to (forfeit) their 'share of the relief.'

(Charles Trevelyan, 'The Irish Crisis', *Edinburgh Review*, January 1848)

Disease

The weakened people suffered from many diseases. Indeed, more died from disease than from starvation. **Typhus** and **relapsing fever**, or 'yellow fever', were the most serious sicknesses. Where starvation affected the poor, these diseases affected everybody, rich and poor alike.

Emigration

Thousands emigrated each year during the famine to **Britain**, the **United States** and **Canada**. About 215,000 people left for America in 1847, and over 200,000 emigrated each year for the next five years. Landlords who wanted to clear their estates helped some. Others, sent one family member over to work in order to pay for the passage of the rest of the family later.

The **ships** were often unsuitable for the difficult voyage to North America. Conditions were so bad on some ships that they were called '**coffin ships**'.

The Jeanie Johnston made her maiden voyage on 24 April 1848 from Blennerville, Co. Kerry to Quebec with 193 passengers. Over the next seven years, the ship made 16 voyages to North America carrying over 2,500 emigrants without loss of life to the New World. A replica of the original *Jeanie Johnston* is docked in Custom House Quay, Dublin.

Analysing Sources
Emigration

HISTORICAL JUDGEMENT

Source 1
Emigration from Ireland, 1843–1851

Source 2
Emigration from Cork

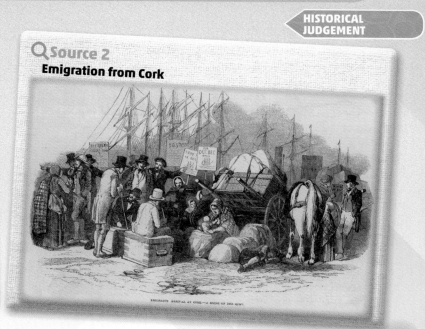

195

Source 3
Advertisement for Packet Ships

NATION.

Weekly Communication with the United States.

Year 1849.

REGULAR LINE OF PACKET SHIPS:
FOR NEW YORK.

Names of Ships.	Commanders.	Tons Register.	To Sail
Columbus,	M'Cenan	1800	7th Sept.
Yorkshire,	Byer,	2300	16th do.

FOR BOSTON.

| Nathl. Kembal, | Stone, | 1600 | 15th Sept. |
| Living Age, | Snow, | 1800 | |

FOR NEW ORLEANS.

| W. D. Sewall, | Jack | 1500 | 15th Sept. |

PHILADELPHIA LINE OF PACKETS.
Sailing on the 1st of every Month.

Robert Burton,	Deacon	1700	1st Oct.
Europe	Miercken	1150	1st Nov.
Mary Pleasants,	Browne,	1800	1st Dec.
Shenandoah,	West	1600	1st Jan.

"COPES."
PHILADELPHIA LINE OF PACKETS,
Sailing on the 12th of every month.

Susquehanna	.. Dunavy	1600	.. 12th Sept.
Tuscorora	.. Turley	1800	.. 12th Oct.
Wyoming	.. Miercken	1800	.. 12th Nov.
Saranak	.. Julius	1600	.. 12th Dec.

These Ships are of the first class, coppered and copper-fastened, fast sailers, and commanded by men of experience in the Trade, afford excellent accommodation for Passengers, and sail punctually.

The Passengers proceeding by the above Ships will be found in 7lb. of Bread per week; 10lbs. of Meat; Vinegar and Medicine, agreeably to the American Law.

Apply to HARNDEN and Co. LIVERPOOL, or ROCHE, BROTHERS and Co., 30, EDEN-QUAY, DUBLIN.

In LIMERICK, 3, WELLESLEY-BUILDINGS, and to JAMES ROCHE, NENAGH.

N.B.—The Public will please take notice, that we have no Office in Dublin, except at 30, EDEN-QUAY.

AMERICAN LINE OF PACKET SHIPS.

Source 4
Stephen de Vere who travelled on a ship to Canada

Before the emigrant has been a week at sea he is an altered man. How could it be otherwise? Hundreds of poor people men, women, and children of all ages from the driveling idiot of ninety to the babe just born, huddled together without light, without air, wallowing in filth and breathing a fetid atmosphere, the fever patients lying between the sound. The meat was of the worst quality. The supply of water shipped on board was abundant, but the quantity served out to the passengers was so scanty that they were frequently obliged to throw overboard their salt provisions and rice, because they had not water enough both for the necessary cooking and the satisfying of their raging thirst afterwards. No cleanliness was enforced; the beds never aired; the food contracted for was supplied, though at irregular times; but false measures were used to measure out the food.

Source 5
A cartoon from Punch magazine, 1848

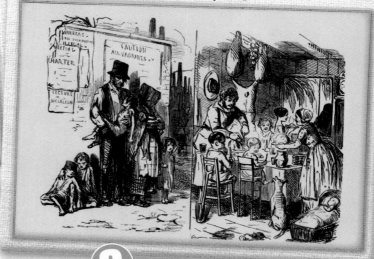

1. Are each of the sources here **primary** or **secondary** sources?
2. Which source would you consider the most **reliable**?
3. In Source 1, which year had the **highest** emigration figures?
4. How do the emigration figures in Source 1 compare with the progress of the blight?
5. How would you describe the people leaving Cork in Source 2?
6. What **cities** are they emigrating to?
7. How do the names of the cities in Source 2 compare with the names in Source 3?
8. What does the **advertisement** in Source 3 say about its ships?
9. How are the people fed on board?
10. How does the account in Source 4 **compare** with the advertisement in Source 3?
11. What **message** is Source 5 giving to those who might be thinking of emigrating? Explain your answers using evidence from the sources.

An emigrant's experience

Isabella McDougall:

Born in 1832, Isabella McDougall was just one of a huge number who left Ireland during the famine years. As a 16-year-old orphan in a workhouse in Banbridge, County Down, Isabella sailed for Australia aboard one of the first of Earl Grey's orphan ships, a scheme to transport orphaned girls from Irish workhouses to Australia. Many of the Earl Grey orphans became known as 'workhouse sweep-ins' by those already there. She landed in Sydney in 1848, and was then transferred to Maitland. She began work as a nursery maid until her marriage to Edward Spicer, an ex-convict, in 1849. Together, they travelled to Armidale, and later Inverell, where Edward worked as a shepherd. They had 13 children before Edward died in 1872, at which point Isabella had to find a way to support herself and her large family. Luckily, she found work as a boarding house mistress in Inverell, until she married for a second time – this time to Angus Mackay, a farmer from Swan Vale. Isabella died in 1904, while on a visit to Glen Innes.

Thomas Quinn:

As a child, he was one of many to have been affected by the Famine. His family were tenant farmers on the Strokestown Estate in Roscommon, owned by Major Denis Mahon. When Quinn was seven years old, Mahon forced over 3,000 of his starving tenants to emigrate, paying their passage to the cheapest destination – Canada. Travelling in 1847 on the so-called 'coffin ships' with no money and barely any clothes, they were easy victims for disease. Quinn's own parents died of typhus on the journey, just two amongst the 196 other passengers on board who did not survive the journey. The ship was quarantined at Grosse Ile in Quebec, which had become overwhelmed by sick and destitute arrivals from Ireland. Quinn and his brother were fortunate enough to be adopted by a French-Canadian family and both went on to become priests with Thomas Quinn rising to high office. He was adamant to defend his roots through religion, remembering some of his father's last words: 'Remember your soul, and your liberty.'

(Source: EPIC, Irish Emigration Museum, Dublin)

Q
1. How do the experiences of Isabella McDougall and Thomas Quinn differ?
2. What aspects of famine emigration are illustrated by their life stories?

Go onto 'YouTube and look up Miss Stout's History Class The Famine'.

The Consequences of the Famine

Fall in population

The population of Ireland fell by at least two million between 1845 and 1851. In all, one million died from hunger and disease, while one million emigrated.

The **cottiers** and **agricultural labourers** were worst hit. The counties along the **western seaboard** suffered the greatest fall in population. The population continued to decline after the famine due to **emigration** and a **low birth rate**.

Emigration continued to America, Canada and Britain, and this along with earlier emigration created the **Irish Diaspora** – the scattering of the Irish population around the world.

Explore the consequences of the Great Famine

Q

What **conclusions** can you draw from the graph on Ireland's population from 1801 to 1911? How does the information on Irish emigration **explain** some of the decline in population up to 1911? What other factors caused the population to decline after 1851?

p. 115

Ireland's Population, 1801–1911

Before the Famine Population Increase 1801–45

After the Famine Population Decline 1845–1911

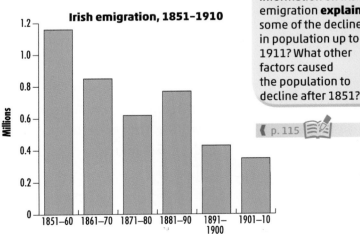

Irish emigration, 1851–1910

Subdivision ended

The practice of subdividing the land ended. Instead, the eldest son got the land, and other sons and daughters were forced to **emigrate**. The eldest son only got the farm when his father died, so he married late. This reduced **the birth rate** in Ireland. There was also **clearance of estates** during the famine and this, combined with the ending of subdivision, resulted in larger farms.

Decline in the Irish language

The Irish-speaking areas in the West and South-West of Ireland were the worst hit by death and emigration. This contributed to the decline of the Irish language.

1. Which areas had the **highest percentage** of Irish speakers in 1851?
2. Identify **three differences** between the percentage of Irish speakers in 1851 and 1961.
3. Why, do you think, the numbers of Irish speakers continued to decline after the famine?

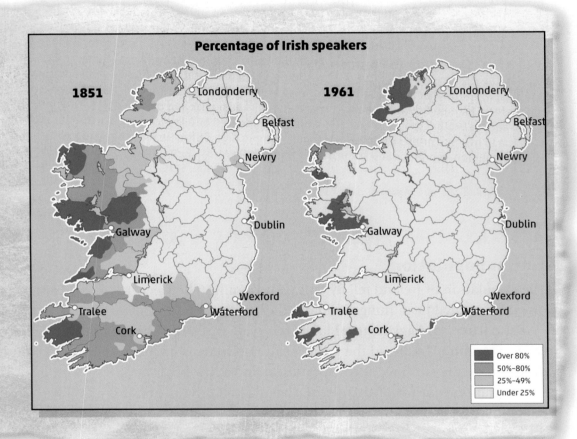

Percentage of Irish speakers

1851   1961

Londonderry
Belfast
Newry
Galway
Dublin
Limerick
Tralee   Wexford
Waterford
Cork

Over 80%
50%–80%
25%–49%
Under 25%

Politics

The English government was **blamed** for the famine. Emigrants took their hatred of England with them to America. They later supported the Fenians, the Land League, Home Rule, the rebels in the 1916 Rising and the IRA when these groups opposed the British government.

Significance of the Irish Diaspora

◎ Evaluate the significance of the Irish Diaspora

The **Irish Diaspora** 'comprises emigrants from Ireland and their descendants around the world'.

During and after the Great Famine, the bulk of Irish emigration went to **America**. Irish emigrants there poured into east coast cities such as **New York** and **Boston**. They lived in crowded tenements, cellars and attics. They experienced **diseases** such as typhus and cholera from bad living conditions. They worked in poorly paid jobs; women worked as domestic servants and men worked in hard-labouring jobs such as canal and railroad construction. They also suffered from **discrimination** and **anti-Irish hatred**.

However, within a generation the Irish had **climbed the social ladder**. The next generation availed of jobs such as policemen, firefighters and teachers. They were better educated and more successful. They laid the **foundation** for the future success of the Irish in America. The **links** between the Irish-Americans and Ireland remain strong in modern times, through politics, tourism and culture.

THE USUAL IRISH WAY OF DOING THINGS.

'The Usual Irish Way of Doing Things' (1871), an American cartoon showing the Irish as drunken and violent, with ape-like features. This shows the racist feelings against the Irish in America in the 19th century.

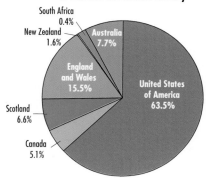

Percentage of Irish-born living abroad in the late nineteenth century

- South Africa 0.4%
- New Zealand 1.6%
- Australia 7.7%
- England and Wales 15.5%
- United States of America 63.5%
- Scotland 6.6%
- Canada 5.1%

(Source: Atlas of the Great Irish Famine)

NUMERACY

Irish-born population in the US, 1850–2014

Millions

2000000 – 1500000 – 1000000 – 500000 – 0

1850 1860 1870 1880 1890 1900 1910 1920 1930 1960 1970 1980 1890 2000 2014

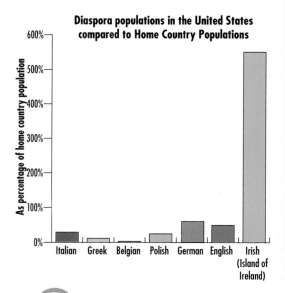

Diaspora populations in the United States compared to Home Country Populations

As percentage of home country population

600% – 500% – 400% – 300% – 200% – 100% – 0%

Italian Greek Belgian Polish German English Irish (Island of Ireland)

Q What **conclusions** can you draw from the information in these graphs about Irish emigration?

Include information from the graphs in support of your answer.

'When my great grandfather left here to become a cooper in East Boston, he carried nothing with him except two things: a strong religious faith and a strong desire for liberty. I am glad to say that all of his great-grandchildren have valued that inheritance.'

(President Kennedy, visiting his ancestral home in Wexford in 1963)

Irish-Americans increased their influence in American politics through the Democratic Party, one of America's two main political parties. President Kennedy was the first Catholic Irish-American president. Name some of the other Irish-American presidents before and after Kennedy. What province in Ireland can claim the most of these? Why?

Tom Brady

John McEnroe

Jack Dempsey

Ben Hogan

Maureen O'Hara

Irish-born and people of Irish descent have contributed to many aspects of life in other countries, particularly America, Australia and Britain. The early emigrants often suffered discrimination in these countries – 'No Irish Need Apply' – but later generations contributed to politics, music and entertainment, art and literature, the sciences and engineering, and sport. Investigate the Irish ancestry of ne of the people pictured here.

Henry Ford

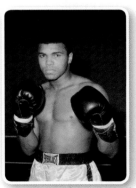

Muhammad Ali

Georgia O'Keeffe

Anne Rice

INVESTIGATING A REPOSITORY OF HISTORICAL EVIDENCE FOR THE GREAT FAMINE

The Irish Emigration Museum,
www.epicchq.com
The Jeanie Johnston,
www.jeaniejohnston.ie
Dunbrody Famine Ship Experience,
www.dunbrody.com

〉 Preparing for CBA1

A project related to an aspect of the history of your locality or place (or personal/family history)

LOCAL PROJECTS FROM THE GREAT FAMINE

Your locality can include your county

- Emigration in your locality during the Great Famine
- Famine Population in your locality
- Government famine schemes in your locality
- A local workhouse
- Experiences of a notable local person who helped in the Great Famine
- The Earl Grey Scheme in your locality
- Landlords and the famine in your locality
- Emigration from your locality in later years
- How newspapers reported the Great Famine in your locality (for a short period)

Visit ...
The Strokestown Park Irish National Famine Museum, Roscommon and the Skibbereen Heritage Centre to learn more about the Great Famine.
Epic, The Irish Emigration Museum, Custom House Quay, Dublin;
The *Jeanie Johnston*, Custom House Quay, Dublin; and the Dunbrody Emigrant Ship, New Ross to see how Irish emigrants made the journey to America.

〉 Preparing for CBA2

A project on the life and experience of a person of historical interest

PERSONS OF INTEREST FROM THE GREAT FAMINE

- Sir Robert Peel
- Dr Dan Donovan (Skibbereen)
- Jonathan Pim
- Archbishop MacHale, Tuam

- Rev. Robert Traill
- Patrick Kennedy (Wexford)
- Lord John Russell
- Archbishop Murray, Dublin

- Charles Trevelyan
- Joseph Bewley
- Queen Victoria
- Asenath Nicholson

 p. 113 Web Resources and Reading

Focus Task

Historical Investigation
- 〉 Investigate songs of Irish emigration, in Irish or in English. Select five of those songs.
- 〉 When were they composed and who composed them?
- 〉 What are their themes?
- 〉 Are there themes not mentioned which you would expect from emigrant songs?
- 〉 Are those songs still popular today?

IRISH HISTORY

THE PARLIAMENTARY TRADITION IN IRISH POLITICS
– Daniel O'Connell and C. S. Parnell

13

L.O. 2.2
The Nature of History:
1.1, 1.2, 1.3, 1.4, 1.5, 1.6,
1.7, 1.8, 1.9, 1.10, 1.11
CBA1
CBA2

CHRONOLOGICAL AWARENESS

1820 AD

1823
O'Connell founded the Catholic Association

1829
O'Connell won Catholic Emancipation

1830 AD

1833
The Slavery Abolition Act

1832
O'Connell supported the Great Reform Act in Westminster

1840 AD

1843
Year of Repeal; monster meetings

1840
O'Connell founded the Repeal Association

1847
Death of O'Connell

1845
Beginning of the Great Famine

1850 AD

1860 AD

1867
The Fenian Rising

1870 AD

1875
Parnell elected to parliament

1879
New Departure, Land League and land campaign

1880 AD

1880
Parnell leader of Home Rule Party

1886
First Home Rule Bill

1890 AD

1891
Death of Parnell

You will learn to ...

- Investigate the role and significance of Daniel O'Connell in the parliamentary tradition

- Investigate the role and significance of Charles Stewart Parnell in the parliamentary tradition

- Explore the nature of history

Q Why were images of Daniel O'Connell and Charles Stewart Parnell used on the old currency notes?

Banc Ceannais na hÉireann   £20
Fiche Punt
WTV 893636 09 12 99
Daniel O'Connell 1775 1847

na hÉireann   £100
Céap Punt
AAK 792483 22 08 96
Charles Stewart Parnell 1846 1891

KEY WORDS

- Parliament
- Politics
- Repeal
- Significance
- Catholic Emancipation
- Home Rule
- Unionism

What is the Parliamentary Tradition?

⊘ Describe the parliamentary tradition in Ireland

Parliament House in Dublin in the 18th century

Dáil Éireann

'Ireland has a tradition of parliamentary government whose roots predate the written history of the country.'

In **Celtic society**, legends and annals provide examples of chieftains and kings who were elected. But it was the coming of the **Normans** to Ireland in 1169 that led to the introduction of the same type of parliament as they had already established in England. This parliament was abolished in the **Act of Union**, 1800. During the 19th century, campaigns for **Repeal** (of the Act of Union) and **Home Rule** fought to bring back the parliament to Dublin.

When **Sinn Féin** grew in popularity after the 1916 Rising, they won the 1918 general election with a policy of abstaining from the parliament in Westminster, and seeking greater independence for Ireland.

Sinn Féin representatives set up their own parliament in Dublin in 1919, called the first **Dáil Éireann**. Following the **Anglo-Irish Treaty** of December 1921, the third Dáil was elected in June 1922.

Since 1922 **Leinster House** has been the seat of Dáil Éireann and Seanad Éireann.

Features of the parliamentary tradition
Peaceful, lawful methods
Mass demonstrations
Pressure on the British government
Laws passed in parliament

Daniel O'Connell, The Liberator

Daniel O'Connell was the most important political leader in Ireland in the first half of the 19th century. He was opposed to the use of violence for political purposes. Instead he believed in working through the laws and parliament to achieve changes.

⊘ Investigate the role and significance of Daniel O'Connell

Daniel O'Connell by John Gubbins, Oil on canvas, c. 1817–18. This portrait shows Daniel O'Connell (1775–1847) with his hand on a petition seeking 'freedom of conscience' for Catholics.

Derrynane House, ancestral home of the O'Connell's. Daniel O'Connell inherited Derrynane House on his uncle's death in 1825.

O'Connell and non-violence

O'Connell was born in Co. Kerry in 1775. He was educated at home, in Belgium, France and in London. He witnessed scenes from the **French Revolution** as he travelled through France in 1793, at the time the King of France was beheaded. These events made a big impression on him. He said France was *'deluged (flooded) in blood; liberty (freedom) was sacrificed.'*

Events in Ireland during the **1798 Rebellion** also horrified him. He said, *'May every virtuous revolutionist remember the horrors of Wexford!'*

He said later in life; *'The principle of my political life … is, that all improvements in political institutions can be obtained by persevering (persisting) in a perfectly peaceable and legal course, and cannot be obtained by forcible means (violence, armed rising), or if they could be got by forcible means, such means create more evils than they cure, and leave the country worse than they found it.'*

After his education in London, O'Connell became a famous barrister who won many court cases. He earned the nickname, **'The Councellor'**. One of his biographers said, *'No man of the people had ever spoken as he did in the king's courts.'* (Seán Ó Faoileáin)

Q Why was O'Connell opposed to the use of violence?

O'Connell often made insulting comments about his opponents. *'The poor old Duke [of Wellington]! What shall I say of him? To be sure he was born in Ireland, but being born in a stable does not make a man a horse.'*

How did O'Connell achieve Catholic Emancipation?

In one of the last of the penal laws, Catholics could not take their seats in parliament, even if they were elected. O'Connell fought a long campaign to overturn this law. In 1823, he founded the **Catholic Association** to lead his campaign for Catholic Emancipation. He organised a **Catholic Rent** (a penny a month) to finance the campaign. He also held peaceful meetings in both Ireland and Britain, to put pressure on the British government.

He got elected to **Clare** in 1828, and this forced the government to pass the **Catholic Relief Act** (1829), which allowed Catholics take their seats in parliament. O'Connell's fame spread far and wide, including in Europe, where many admired his peaceful methods of achieving his goals. He became known as **'The Liberator'**.

Q What was Catholic Rent? Where did O'Connell win an election? What did Catholic Emancipation mean?

DID YOU KNOW?
John D'Esterre challenged Daniel O'Connell to a duel in 1815 because of a speech made by O'Connell. O'Connell, who did not support violence, accepted the duel, and killed D'Esterre.

Analysing Sources
Catholic Emancipation

HISTORICAL JUDGEMENTS

Source 1

O'Connell agitated (campaigned) for Catholic Emancipation for 30 years. Two contrasting things appalled (shocked) him about the oppression (coercion) of the Catholics. The first was how generations of being downtrodden (kept down) turned them into what he called 'hereditary bondsmen (slaves)', almost accepting of their plight (condition).

On the other hand, O'Connell was appalled at how easily the oppressed could themselves become tyrannical shedders of blood (of others) on a large scale: he saw this in France as a schoolboy and in Ireland in 1798.

(Adrian Hardiman, *The counsellor and the Liberator, a man of his time*, The Irish Times, 21 April 2014)

Source 2

Daniel O'Connell and his supporters in an English cartoon (1828)

COMMEMMORATION

Source 3

O'Connell was honoured by the new Irish Free State in 1929, on the centenary of Catholic Emancipation

1. Are Sources 1 to 3 **primary** or **secondary**?
2. Does the author of Source 1 **admire** O'Connell?
3. What two things **appalled** O'Connell, according to Source 1?
4. How are O'Connell's supporters represented in the cartoon?
5. What is the significance of the signpost?
6. What does the cartoon fear will happen after Catholic Emancipation?
7. Is the cartoon in Source 2 in **favour or opposed** to Catholic Emancipation?
8. Do you think a similar stamp to Source 3 was issued in Northern Ireland to honour the same centenary? Explain your answers in each case.

What did O'Connell contribute to the abolition of slavery?

O'Connell also achieved great fame, at home and abroad, as an **abolitionist**, who wanted to abolish slavery. He helped pass the **Slavery Abolition Act 1833**, which abolished slavery in the British empire. When **Frederick Douglass**, a former American slave, came to Ireland in 1845, he looked on O'Connell as a hero. He said, *'The fire of freedom was burning in his mighty heart.'* O'Connell also favoured Jewish emancipation.

Frederick Douglass, who visited Ireland in 1845 and admired O'Connell's work in helping to abolish slavery

p. 119 ▶

Q

1. What does O'Connell say about the 'Irish heart'?
2. What did he say was not learned in Ireland?
3. Why would he 'recognise [them] as Irishmen no longer'?
4. What points is he making to try to persuade them not to support slavery?

O'Connell wrote to the Irish Repeal Association in Cinncinati, Ohio, in 1843 criticising their views on slavery.

How can the generous, the charitable, the humane, and the noble emotions of the Irish heart have become extinct amongst you? How can your nature be so totally changed as that you should become the apologists (supporters) and advocates (promoters) of the execrable (terrible) system which makes man the property of his fellow man, condemns to ignorance, immorality and irreligion, millions of our fellow creatures …? It was not in Ireland that you learned this cruelty … if you remain and dare continue to support the system of slavery that is supported there, we will recognise you as Irishmen no longer!

The Repeal of the Act of Union

After his success in winning Catholic Emancipation, O'Connell led a campaign to **Repeal the Act of Union**, so that a parliament would be established in Dublin. He set up the **Repeal Association** in 1840, with Repeal Rent. *'… I want to make all Europe and America know it – I want to make England feel her weakness if she refuses to give the justice we [the Irish] require – the restoration of our domestic parliament …'*

He said 1843 would be the **Year of Repeal**. In spite of huge peaceful rallies, 'monster meetings', held all over the country, his campaign **failed**. The British government feared that giving Repeal to Ireland would lead to the break-up of the union of England, Scotland and Wales. O'Connell cancelled a monster meeting at **Clontarf** when the British government banned it, because he feared it would result in violence.

Leader of Home Rule Party

When Isaac Butt died in 1879, one of his supporters, William Shaw, was elected leader of the Home Rule Party. However, the 1880 general election changed everything, as many supporters of Parnell got elected as Home Rule MPs. Parnell got elected for Cork city and replaced Shaw as **leader of the Home Rule Party**.

Kilmainham Gaol and treaty

There were increased **agrarian outrages** (incidents, crimes) in the countryside as a **Land War** between tenants and landlords broke out. The **Land League** demanded that **Gladstone**, the British Prime Minister, bring in land reform. He introduced the **Land Act** of 1881, which provided fair rents for the tenants, and a land court to decide the rents. **Parnell** favoured the Act, but publicly asked tenants to test it in the courts. Parnell and other leaders were interned in **Kilmainham Gaol** (1881).

While Parnell was in jail, there was an increase in disturbances in the countryside. Gladstone realised that it would be better if Parnell were released. At the end of six months, Parnell agreed the **Kilmainham Treaty** (1882) with Gladstone. Gladstone improved the Land Act, while Parnell promised that he would use his influence to stop the violence. This led to a break between Parnell and the Fenians. It also meant that Parnell had used **outside agitation** and **pressure in parliament** to improve conditions for tenants.

Home Rule Bill

Parnell now concentrated on Home Rule. He **re-organised the party**. He founded the **Irish National League**, which was organised in each constituency. He controlled the organisation with a tight discipline. Members now sat together in parliament and worked together as a united group. The party paid Home Rule MPs and they had to take a **pledge** or oath to vote with the party.

Parnell's arrest and entry into Kilmainham Gaol

More people got the vote in general elections, which meant Parnell increased his support. After the 1885 general election, Parnell and the Home Rule Party held the **balance of power** in Westminster between **Liberals** and **Conservatives**. He could have put either into government, but Parnell supported Gladstone and the Liberal Party after Gladstone's promise to bring in a Home Rule Bill.

Gladstone's **Home Rule Bill** (1886) provided for parliament in Dublin to deal with internal Irish affairs, while parliament in Westminster would deal with external affairs. However, it was **defeated** in the House of Commons. The Conservative Party, and some of Gladstone's Liberal Party, backed by unionists in the North of Ireland, combined to defeat the Bill.

Q How did Parnell re-organise the Home Rule Party? How did he hold the balance of power after the 1885 general election?

Analysing Sources

INVESTIGATING SOURCES

Source 1
The Balance of Power

Source 2

Parnell on Home Rule

We cannot ask for less than the restitution (restoration) of Grattan's parliament (loud cheers) with its important privileges and wide and far-reaching constitution ... But no man has the right to fix the boundary to the march of a nation (great cheers). No man has the right to say to his country, 'thus far shalt thou go and no further,' and we have never attempted to fix the *ne plus ultra* (the highest point) to the progress of Ireland's nationhood, and we never shall (cheers).

(Parnell speaking in Cork, *Freeman's Journal*, 22 January 1885)

Q

1. What is the **message** of the cartoon in Source 1?
2. What must Parnell **decide**, according to the cartoon?
3. What is Parnell **asking** for in Source 2?
4. What does he mean when he says 'no man has the right to fix the boundary to the march of a nation'?
5. Are both of these sources **primary** sources?
6. How **useful** are cartoons such as Source 1 as sources for historians?
7. How **useful** are newspapers such as Source 2 as sources for historians?
8. How **reliable** are both cartoons and newspapers as sources for historians? Explain your answers in each case.

Nationalist (or Home Rule) MPs elected in 1886

1. This map was published in *Parnell: A Documentary History*, by Noel Kissane. Is it a **primary** or a **secondary** source?
2. What does the source tell you about the **success** of the Home Rule Party (or Irish Party) in that election?
3. What area of the country had **no Home Rule Party MPs** elected? Can you explain why?
4. Where was Parnell elected as MP?
5. Who was elected for your area? Do you know anything about him?
6. Why are there no women featured in the map?
7. How **useful** is this method for showing who got elected in elections? Explain your answers in each case.

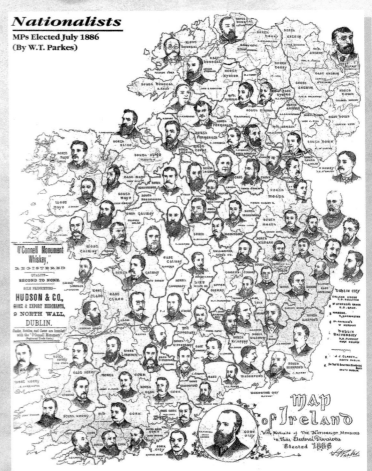

Nationalists

MPs Elected July 1886
(By W.T. Parkes)

map of Ireland

Piggott forgeries

Soon after, the London *Times* published letters in articles called *Parnellism and Crime*. These letters seemed to show that Parnell supported the **Phoenix Park murders**, when two high-ranking officials in the British government were brutally murdered by a Fenian group in 1882. Parnell said the letters were **forgeries**. And so it was proved by a Special Commission, which showed the letters had been forged by Richard Piggott, a journalist. Parnell's name was cleared and his **popularity** was at its highest.

Q Source 1
Parnell and Gladstone

HISTORICAL JUDGEMENTS

Q Source 2
Parnell cleared

We entirely acquit Mr Parnell and the other respondents of the charge of insincerity in their denunciation of the Phoenix Park murders, and find that facsimile letter on which this charge was chiefly based as against Mr Parnell is a forgery.

(Report of the Special Commission, February 1890)

Q Source 3
Parnell and Gladstone

Q

1. What is the **message** of this cartoon in Source 1? Does it favour Parnell and Gladstone?
2. What is at stake, according to the cartoon?
3. What was Parnell cleared of by the Special Commission in Source 2?
4. What is the message of Source 3? Does it favour Parnell and Gladstone?
5. What did you learn about the **use of cartoons** as sources from studying Source 1 and Source 3? Explain your answers fully.

Parnell's downfall

However, Parnell's downfall came soon after because of the **O'Shea Divorce Case**. Parnell had been having an affair with **Katherine O'Shea** since 1880, and they had a number of children. In 1890, her husband, Captain O'Shea, filed for divorce, and named Parnell in the proceedings.

The divorce case provided **scandal** but, after it, Parnell still retained the support of his party. The situation changed when **Gladstone** said his Liberal Party could no longer bring forward a Home Rule Bill if Parnell continued as leader of the Home Rule party. This led to a **split** in the party, the majority voting against Parnell.

After this, Parnell fought a number of by-elections in Ireland. In the process his health deteriorated. He returned to Brighton where he lived with Katherine O'Shea, and died there in October 1891, aged 45. He was buried in **Glasnevin Cemetery** after a huge funeral procession through the streets of Dublin.

Katherine O'Shea, mistress of C. S. Parnell

The significance of Parnell

- Parnell was a very able politician who led the majority of the people in Ireland through many difficult political situations in the late 1870s and the 1880s.
- Parnell was a **Protestant leader and landlord**, who led a Catholic tenant population.
- Parnell and Davitt led the Land League in the **Land War**, which forced Gladstone to bring in **land reform** for the tenants in the 1881 Land Act.
- Parnell created a **disciplined political party**, which others imitated later.
- Parnell forced Gladstone and the Liberal Party to bring in the **First Home Rule Bill**.
- Parnell seemed to side with the Fenians who wanted a completely separate Ireland. As a result, after his death, he was often included in the republican or physical force tradition, in contrast to O'Connell who was clearly against the use of violence or armed rising.

Parnell Monument, O'Connell St., Dublin, erected in 1911 to honour Parnell

1. Who wrote this letter?
2. Why did he write the letter?
3. What is 'the ugly and irritating fact' he refers to?
4. What sports and activities does he say were 'dead and buried' and 'entirely forgotten'?
5. What are the 'foreign and fantastic field sports'?
6. Why does he object to them?
7. Is this letter a **primary** or a **secondary** source?

8. Does this letter **explain** why some people would support the GAA?
9. Why, do you think, was it **important** for the GAA to get support from patrons?
10. How does the letter help you understand the **impact of the GAA** on Irish life in the 19th century?
11. Why would historians consider this letter to be **'historically significant'**?
Use evidence from the letter to support your answers.

The Impact of the GAA
The GAA as part of the cultural revival

◎ Examine the impact of the GAA on Irish life

The GAA was part of the **cultural revival** at the end of the 19th century in Ireland. The cultural revival promoted all things **Irish** or **Gaelic**. It wanted to reduce English influence in all aspects of Irish life. This was also emphasised by the **Gaelic League** (founded in 1893) as both wanted to **de-anglicise** Irish society.

Not surprisingly, by the early years of the 20th century, many people were members of both organisations.

As one historian of the GAA said:

'By 1910 or so dual membership had become normal for the majority of athletically-minded urban-based nationalists; for many of them their first contact with the GAA came through their involvement in the League.' (Marcus de Búrca)

Chapter 1 – Aims and Ethos

1.1 Name
The name of the Association is: 'The Gaelic Athletic Association'.

1.2 Basic Aim
The Association is a National Organisation which has as its basic aim the strengthening of the National Identity in a 32 County Ireland through the preservation and promotion of Gaelic Games and pastimes.

1.3 National Games
The Association shall promote and control the National games of Hurling, Gaelic Football, Handball and Rounders, and such other games, as may be sanctioned and approved by Annual Congress.

1.4 Additional Aims
(a) The Association shall actively support the Irish language, traditional Irish dancing, music, song and other aspects of Irish culture. It shall foster an awareness of love of the national ideals in the people of Ireland, and assist in promoting a community spirit through its clubs.
(b) The Association shall promote its aims amongst communities abroad through its International Units.
(c) The Association shall support the promotion of Camogie and Ladies Gaelic Football.
(d) The Association shall use all practical endeavours to support Irish Industry especially in relation to the provision of trophies and playing gear and equipment.

(Source: GAA Official Guide 2017, Part 1)

1. What is the basic **aim** of the GAA, according to the GAA Official Guide 2017?
2. What **national games** are listed?
3. What **other activities** will the GAA support, according to Additional Aims?
4. How will the GAA connect with the **Irish Diaspora**?
5. What **ladies games** will the GAA support?
6. How will it support **Irish industry**?
7. How do these aims **compare** with the views of Archbishop Croke in p. 218?
8. How do these aims **compare** with the aims of the Cultural Revival?

How did the GAA spread?

The GAA had an **immediate impact** on Irish life. According to Cusack, it *'swept the country like a prairie fire'*, as clubs were established in many counties. Clubs were founded in Munster, Leinster and Connacht, and more slowly in Ulster. Some of the more successful early events were **athletics meetings**, but gradually hurling and football took over as the main interest of the GAA. The GAA athletics meetings, and hurling and football matches drew large crowds. There was a rise in **local pride** as clubs, based on **parishes**, played other clubs.

GAA CLUBS 1887–1890					
	1887	1888	1889	1890	1891
Leinster	175	214	297	323	271
Munster	380	255	289	258	152
Connacht	80	31	74	206	87
Ulster	-	6	37	88	47
Total	635	506	697	875	557

(from de Búrca)

Trouble for the GAA

However, the GAA's early years were also troublesome. First, **Cusack** was fired as secretary due to personality clashes. There was also a disastrous tour to America in 1888 – the **American Invasion** – aimed at promoting Gaelic sports there, but which lost money for the new Association. Then there was conflict between IRB/Fenian members and Home Rulers, which resulted in a **split** in the Association.

The foundation of the GAA had already attracted the attention of the **Irish Republican Brotherhood** (IRB or Fenians) as four of the seven who attended the founding meeting in Thurles were Fenians. The IRB looked on the GAA as a cover for training young men for any future rising.

Decline and revival

However, the involvement of the IRB led to a **split** in the Association. Some of the GAA supported Parnell in his conflict with the majority of the Home Rule Party (see p. 214). In 1891, when he died, 2,000 GAA men carrying hurleys draped in black marched in his funeral to Glasnevin cemetery. These divisions between IRB and Home Rule supporters, backed by the Catholic Church, led to a **decline** in the GAA, which lasted for about a decade. The number of clubs fell from nearly 900 in 1890 to 118 in 1893.

By the early 20th century, a **revival** of the GAA was taking place. In spite of divisions, All-Irelands were held every year except one. The first All-Irelands were held in 1887, and apart from 1888, All-Irelands were held each year thereafter. The number of clubs grew again after the decline of the 1890s. By 1901 the number of clubs had risen from 118 in 1893 to 411 in 1901, though still well short of nearly 900 in the late 1880s.

p. 126
Hill 16 or Hill 60?

Croke Park

A major step in the expansion of the GAA was the purchase of playing fields in Jones Road, Dublin in 1913, which soon became **Croke Park**, after Archbishop Croke. This became the **headquarters** of the GAA.

During the 20th century, the stadium underwent a number of **developments**. In 1915, a sloped terrace was developed behind the goals. The **Hogan Stand** was added in the 1920s and the **Cusack Stand** in the 1930s. A new Hogan Stand was built in the 1950s. The modern development of Croke Park took place from the 1990s into the early 21st century.

The modern development of Croke Park

As the most important sporting venue in Ireland, Croke Park has contributed not only to all the major football and hurling matches each year, but also to many other **great occasions**. These included the Muhammad Ali – Al 'Blue' Lewis fight in 1972, the International Rules matches between Ireland and Australia, major rugby and soccer matches while the Aviva Stadium was being built, the Special Olympics in 2003, sell-out music concerts and American football matches. These events were an important contribution to **Dublin's economy**.

Croke Park names

Q Source 1

The spread of the GAA, 1901–08

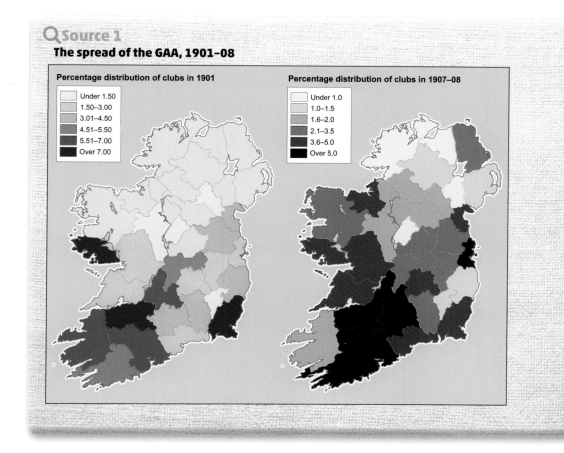

Percentage distribution of clubs in 1901

- Under 1.50
- 1.50–3.00
- 3.01–4.50
- 4.51–5.50
- 5.51–7.00
- Over 7.00

Percentage distribution of clubs in 1907–08

- Under 1.0
- 1.0–1.5
- 1.6–2.0
- 2.1–3.5
- 3.6–5.0
- Over 5.0

SPACE AND TIME

Q

1. In what part of the country was the GAA **strongest** in 1901?
2. Where was it weakest in 1901?
3. Where was the GAA **weakest** in 1907–08?
4. Can you suggest **reasons** for this?
5. Identify **three counties** that had the highest distribution (spread) of clubs in 1907–08.
6. Investigate **reasons** for the distribution of clubs in 1907–08.
7. What **conclusions** can you draw about the **growth and impact** of the GAA in the early 20th century from your study of the maps?

Q Source 2

Comparing the Rules

Some playing rules of Gaelic Football, adopted in December 1884	Some Modern Rules of Football and Hurling
There shall not be less than 15 or more than 21 players aside.	The field of play shall be rectangular, and its dimensions shall be as follows:
The ground shall be at least 120 yards (110m) long by 80 yards (73m) in breadth and properly marked by boundary lines.	Length – 130m minimum and 145m maximum.
Goal-posts shall stand at each end in the centre of the goal-line.	Width – 80m minimum and 90m maximum.
The time of actual play shall be one hour.	A team shall consist of 15 players.
The match shall be decided by the greater number of goals. A goal is scored when the ball is kicked through the goalposts under the cross-bar.	The playing time shall consist of two periods of 30 minutes each, but time shall be added on in each period for incidental or deliberate delays.
Some playing rules of Hurling, adopted in December 1884	[There are Exceptions when] the playing time shall consist of two periods of 35 minutes each.
The ground shall, when convenient, be at least 200 yards (183m) long by 150 yards (137m) broad, or as near to that size as can be got.	In all hurling games and hurling practice sessions, it shall be mandatory for, and the responsibility of, each individual player to wear a helmet with a facial guard.
There shall not be less than 14 or more than 21 players at the side in regular matches.	A **goal** is scored when the ball is played over the goal-line between the posts and under the crossbar by either team.
The time of play shall be one hour and 20 minutes.	A **point** is scored when the ball is played over the crossbar between the posts by either team.
No nails or iron tips allowed on the boots (strips of leather fastened to the soles will prevent slipping).	The team with the greater final total of points is the winner.
The dress for hurling and football to be knee-breeches and stockings and boots or shoes.	

Q

1. Why, do you think, the GAA had to bring in rules?
2. What **differences** do you notice between the GAA rules of the 1880s and the modern rules in Source 2?
3. Why, do you think, was there a need to change the rules?

Q Source 3
Leinster Hurling Final, 1921

Michael Collins throwing in the sliotar to start the 1921 Leinster hurling final between Dublin and Kilkenny, which was played in Croke Park on 11 September 1921

Q Source 4
All-Ireland Hurling Final, 2017

Action from the 2017 All-Ireland Hurling Final between Galway and Waterford

Q

What **differences** do you notice between hurling played in 1921 (Source 3) and modern hurling (Source 4)? What **similarities** do you notice?

The GAA and the Rising

The GAA was part of the **separatist tradition**, which was linked with the cultural revival. Some believed that the revival of Gaelic culture could not be achieved without a fully independent country. These men and women, who were involved in the GAA and the Gaelic League, became involved in **political activity**.

There were also those who looked on the GAA as a cover for training young men for a future rising. This **Fenian or IRB** involvement had resulted in the Special Branch of the **Royal Irish Constabulary** (RIC) reporting on the activities of the GAA members and clubs. GAA members took part in the **centenary of the 1798 Rebellion**. They also opposed Royal visits to Ireland. The GAA **banned** members of the RIC from playing GAA (1897), and it **banned** GAA members from playing or watching 'foreign games', such as cricket, hockey, rugby and soccer (1905). As well as Parnell's funeral, the GAA was also involved in famous funerals such as that of James Stephens (1901) and John O'Leary (1907), both Fenians.

It was not surprising that members of the GAA took part in the **1916 Rising**, which grew out of the separatist tradition and the cultural revival.

HISTORICAL JUDGEMENT

The GAA and the 1916 Rising: 'The organisation claimed it played a major role, but the truth is more complex', writes Paul Rouse (26 November 2015)

In the decades after 1916, the history of the Easter Rising was rewritten by men and women who wished to claim for themselves – or for the organisations they loved – a central part in the Rising. In sporting terms, the great example of this is provided by the GAA. The Association and its historians claimed that, unique among Irish sporting organisations, the GAA had provided the great bulk of the men who fought in 1916.

Like all the best myths, this is rooted in a certain truth: ... As William Murphy has written, GAA players were indeed more likely to have participated in the Easter Rising in Dublin than most other sectors of society. It appears that there were some 302 players from 53 clubs.

This total of 302 represents a little less than one-fifth of the estimated 1,500 to 1,800 rebels of Easter Week. There can be no denying that it represented a significant contribution.

Allowing for this, it is also the truth that in the immediate aftermath of the Rising the GAA behaved in a way that was entirely at odds with an organisation apparently in sympathy with rebellion.

For example, the response of the GAA was to flat-out deny any involvement in 1916. It issued a statement saying that all allegations 'that the Gaelic Athletic Association had been used in furtherance of the objectives of the Irish Volunteers are as untrue as they are unjust'.

... More than that, there were also many more GAA men fighting in British army uniforms in France than there were in the GPO.

Any rounded account of the GAA's involvement in 1916 must acknowledge this basic truth – and accommodate it in any meaningful history of the Easter Rising.

(Dr Paul Rouse, lecturer in Irish History and Sports History at the School of History at University College Dublin (UCD); www.independent.ie.)

1. How many GAA players took part in the 1916 Rising, according to this article?
2. How did the GAA react to the Rising?
3. Why were more GAA men in France at this time?
4. Summarise the GAA's part in the 1916 Rising.

See Croke Park and Bloody Sunday, p. 247

Spreading the GAA

Handball is one of the four national sports. The GAA helped to set up the Irish Amateur Handball Association in 1924. Handball has an international dimension as Irish players compete against players from the USA, Canada, Australia and the UK, where the sport was taken through emigration. It is open to both males and females. Handball progressed in the 1960s when indoor courts were constructed. It is not a popular spectator sport.

Rounders is similar to baseball, and it is another of the four national sports promoted by the GAA. It is played by both males and females, and as a non-contact sport, it is open to many people.

The GAA has maintained links between the Irish Diaspora and the Irish in Ireland. The links between Gaelic games and Irish emigrants in the USA and the UK go back to the beginning of the GAA in the 19th century. This continued through the 20th century. Gaelic Park in New York, for example, became a centre for Irish emigrants who went to watch football and hurling matches on Sundays. The links were maintained through visiting county teams and All-Star selections. Modern emigration has strengthened those links, and expanded them now into Australia, Europe and Asia where GAA clubs have sprung up. These links between the GAA and the Irish Diaspora have helped tourism in the country.

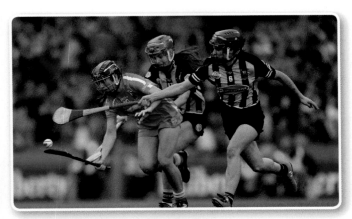

Camogie and Ladies Football

Camogie and Ladies Gaelic football are run **independently** of the GAA, but with its **active support**.

The **Camogie Association** (Cumann Camógaíochta na nGael) was founded in 1904 after a challenge camogie match had taken place in 1903. The inspiration for the development of camogie came from the **Keatings Branch** of the Gaelic League, in Dublin. The sport was developed from **hurling**.

Camogie spread gradually. By 1912, there were 22 clubs:
Dublin – 11; London – 2; Wexford – 3; Meath – 2; Louth – 3.
The first All-Ireland Championship was held in 1932.

It took much longer before ladies football was organised. The **Ladies Gaelic Football Association** was founded in 1974 after a number of tournaments were held in the years before that, and county boards were set up in some counties. The first All-Ireland championship was held that year. Both camogie and ladies football have benefitted from coverage by TG4. They have provided a **Gaelic outlet** for ladies to match the men's hurling and football. If they were absent, more younger ladies would be playing soccer and rugby as alternatives.

The impact of GAA Clubs

The GAA depended on a **club and county structure**. The local club was based on the **parish**. Players grew up with their clubs and the clubs became the focus of matches on Sundays. **Competition** between neighbouring clubs and counties provided a strong motivation. Participation in games encouraged teamwork and discipline. Involvement in the club at all levels helped **blur class distinctions** in the countryside.

Many **priests** were active in the administration of local clubs. This strengthened the relationship between the GAA and the Catholic Church.

As the 20th century progressed, the club became the focus of **social activity**, particularly in country areas. The club house often became the community centre for meetings, dances and concerts.

All the activity relating to the club was **voluntary** – whether administering or coaching, or maintaining the club grounds. It was also **amateur** as there were no payments involved. Voluntary and amateur became important **characteristics** of GAA life.

The structure of the GAA has encouraged and promoted **democracy** in Ireland. Its decisions come through its clubs, county boards and annual congress. This has consolidated the democratic (and parliamentary) tradition in the country.

USING EVIDENCE

Q Source 1

GAA: The surviving, thriving third pillar of nationalist Ireland

Is there an organisation anywhere comparable to the GAA? Run almost totally on a voluntary basis, it reaches into practically every community on the island of Ireland and with a success no other institution does.

It is the only one of those three great pillars of nationalist Ireland – itself, the Catholic Church and Fianna Fáil – to continue thriving uninhibited at home and abroad as the third decade of the 21st century beckons.

A huge source of the GAA's strength is attachment and loyalty to the local club, of which there are over 2,200 in all 32 counties of Ireland. There are a further 462 clubs abroad, 'wherever green is worn', – 83 in the UK; 71 throughout Europe; 132 in the US; 19 in Canada; 64 in Australia; and 22 in the Middle and Far East.

The centrality of so many clubs to life in small town/rural Ireland is not lost on the GAA either, for whom they are a critical strand in its success.

(Patsy McGarry, *The Irish Times*, 24 July 2017)

Q Source 2

Voluntary work
Volunteers cut grass, put out fertiliser, brush off water from the goal areas, clean up after players, put out flags, line fields, pick up rubbish after people, fix netting, and fencing, repair plumbing, put up lights, collect at gates, run lottos, raise funds, organise games and trips away, communicate with players and public, attend meetings, attend meetings after meetings, take gear to the laundry, bring it back, coach, train, exhort, encourage, drive, hire, dig, delegate, negotiate, volunteer.
(Jerome O'Brien, GAA Oral History Project Archive, 2008)

Q Source 3

Development of fields
The great story of my life is the story of the acquisition of fields and the development of those fields for GAA purposes and for Gaelic games alone.
Immediately roots were put down the club became the corner stone of life in a parish and so it has continued to this day. It is quite extraordinary to travel Ireland today and to see the church, the school and the GAA grounds occupying pride of place in the villages and the small towns of Ireland and in the rural places.
(Pat Fanning, President of the GAA (1970–73), GAA Oral History Project, 2008)

1. What are the **three great pillars** of nationalist Ireland, according to Source 1?
2. Which of the three continues 'thriving uninhibited'?
3. How many clubs are there in 'all 32 counties of Ireland', according to Source 1?
4. How many clubs are there abroad?
5. Which place has the **greatest number** of those clubs? Can you **explain** why that place has the greater number of clubs?
6. According to Source 1, what is a 'critical strand' in the **success** of the GAA?
7. What does Source 2 tell you about the role of volunteers in the GAA?
8. What does Pat Fanning in Source 3 say is the great story of his life?
9. Are these sources **primary** or **secondary**?
10. Select **two opinions** and **one fact** using the three sources?
11. What are the **strengths** and **weaknesses** of **oral history**? Explain your answers using evidence from the sources.

How has the GAA 'moved with the times'?

The impact of the GAA is partly explained by the way the organisation has 'moved with the times': it has kept pace with changes in Irish society.

One example of that is the lifting of the **Ban** in **Rule 27** on members playing in or attending soccer, rugby, cricket and hockey matches. This Rule was deleted in 1971 and it reflected a feeling that **barriers in society** should be brought down. It also reflected a **more inclusive society**, which developed during the 1960s. It showed how well the **democratic process** worked in the GAA.

The Troubles and Rule 21

The **Troubles** in the North made life difficult for the GAA there. The GAA played an important role for nationalists in Northern Ireland. It allowed nationalists to express their **identity**. Nationalists could meet through the GAA's social activities.

Loyalists (extreme unionists) looked on the GAA as 'a nursery school' for republicans and nationalists. Some GAA members were murdered by loyalist organisations, security forces harassed its members and some of its grounds, in particular **Crossmaglen, Co. Armagh** were taken over by them.

What was the influence of Cultural Nationalism?

Ireland went through a **cultural revolution** at the end of the 19ᵗʰ century and the beginning of the 20ᵗʰ century. A number of organisations and movements promoted the idea of an **Irish Ireland** or **Gaelic Ireland**. Even though they were not political groups, they influenced the political thinking of many people. Some leaders, especially those who later led the 1916 Rising, believed that the only way a Gaelic Ireland could be achieved was by **full independence** from Britain.
The groups included:

Michael Cusack, founder of GAA

Douglas Hyde, founder of Gaelic League

- The **Gaelic Athletic Association** (GAA), founded in 1884 to promote Gaelic games, including hurling and football (see Ch. 14).
- The **Gaelic League**, founded in 1893 to promote the use of the Irish language and to de-Anglicise Ireland.
- The **Anglo-Irish literary movement**, which promoted Irish literature in the English language using Irish folktales and history.

W.B. Yeats, Anglo-Irish Literary Revival

The Home Rule Crisis, 1912–14

Background

The **Conservative Party** ruled Britain from 1895 to 1906. During that time, unionists in Ireland were happy because they knew that a Home Rule Bill would not be passed. But, in 1906, the **Liberal Party** took over government. They supported Home Rule.

⊘ Consider the Home Rule Crisis, 1912–14

The Parliament Act, 1911

In 1910, after two elections, the Liberals needed the support of the **Home Rule Party** to stay in government (power). The Liberals also passed a new law in 1911 – the **Parliament Act**. Up to this, the House of Lords could vote against (and defeat) Bills coming from the House of Commons. Now under the Parliament Act, the House of Lords could delay laws for **only two years**.

With the Liberals depending on the Home Rule Party and with the power of the House of Lords weakened, Home Rule for Ireland seemed likely.

The Third Home Rule Bill, 1912

The Liberal Party had tried to pass two Home Rule bills in the 19ᵗʰ century. Both of these had been defeated. In 1912, the Liberals, led by Prime Minister **Asquith**, introduced the **Third Home Rule Bill**. According to this bill:
- A parliament in Dublin would deal with **internal Irish affairs**.
- The parliament in Westminster would deal with **external affairs**.

The Unionist Party and the Conservatives were opposed to the bill, but the House of Lords could not delay the bill for more than two years. **So Home Rule would become law in 1914.**

Unionist opposition

The unionist leaders, Carson and Craig, believed that if they opposed the bill strongly enough, the British government would be forced to drop it. They began to organise strong opposition to the bill.

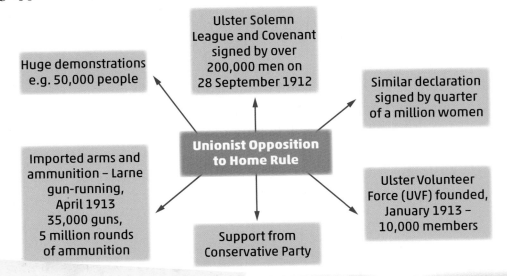

Huge demonstrations e.g. 50,000 people

Ulster Solemn League and Covenant signed by over 200,000 men on 28 September 1912

Similar declaration signed by quarter of a million women

Imported arms and ammunition – Larne gun-running, April 1913 35,000 guns, 5 million rounds of ammunition

Unionist Opposition to Home Rule

Ulster Volunteer Force (UVF) founded, January 1913 – 10,000 members

Support from Conservative Party

Ulster's Solemn League and Covenant.

Being convinced in our consciences that Home Rule would be disastrous to the material well-being of Ulster as well as of the whole of Ireland, subversive of our civil and religious freedom, destructive of our citizenship and perilous to the unity of the Empire, we, whose names are under-written, men of Ulster, loyal subjects of His Gracious Majesty King George V., humbly relying on the God whom our fathers in days of stress and trial confidently trusted, do hereby pledge ourselves in solemn Covenant throughout this our time of threatened calamity to stand by one another in defending for ourselves and our children our cherished position of equal citizen-ship in the United Kingdom and in using all means which may be found necessary to defeat the present conspiracy to set up a Home Rule Parliament in Ireland. ¶And in the event of such a Parliament being forced upon us we further solemnly and mutually pledge ourselves to refuse to recognise its authority. ¶In sure confidence that God will defend the right we hereto subscribe our names. ¶And further, we individually declare that we have not already signed this Covenant.

The above was signed by me at _____
"Ulster Day." Saturday, 28th September, 1912.

_____

God Save the King.

1. What did the **signatories** of the Ulster Solemn League and Covenant 'pledge to defend'?
2. What was 'the present conspiracy' mentioned in the document?
3. From the document, identify **two reasons** why unionists **opposed** Home Rule.
4. Why, do you think, the document said, 'God Save the King'?
5. Investigate the **significance** of the symbol of the red hand on the top left-hand corner of the document (See Ch. 8).
6. Why is this document regarded as a **primary source** for historians?
7. Is this document **useful**?
8. Is this document **reliable**?
   Explain your answers using the evidence in the document.

Nationalist reaction

Nationalists also organised themselves. In November 1913, **Eoin MacNeill**, Professor of History at University College, Dublin, wrote an article called **'The North Began'**. He suggested that nationalists should follow the example of the Northern unionists and form their own Volunteer force. This would put pressure on the British government to bring in Home Rule.

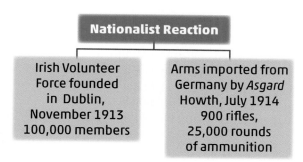

The threat of civil war

At this time, the **Third Home Rule Bill** was making its progress through the British parliament at Westminster. Attempts at compromise or agreement between nationalists and unionists failed. It looked as if Ireland was heading for **civil war**.

But the crisis came to a sudden end. On 4 August 1914, Britain declared war on Germany. **World War I** had begun. The Home Rule Bill became law on 18 September, but it was immediately **suspended** and not revived until 1919.

Reaction to World War I

Nationalist Split

The Irish Volunteers **split** over Ireland's part in World War I. The vast majority of the Irish Volunteers followed the views of **John Redmond**, leader of the Home Rule Party. These became known as the **National Volunteers**. Redmond said Irishmen should take part in the war to **defend Home Rule**.

Unionists in Northern Ireland

Unionists, north and south, joined the British army to take part in the war. In the north, **Carson** asked the Ulster Volunteer Force to *'answer immediately his Majesty's call'* to arms. In some places, Irish Volunteers and Ulster Volunteers marched together and cheered each other.

However, the Ulster Volunteers were able to enlist in their own **Ulster Division**, while National Volunteers were sent to **different regiments**. There was equally heavy recruitment from both nationalists and unionists in the early months of the war. But the different treatment of Ulster Volunteers compared to National Volunteers, along with the delay in implementing Home Rule, caused nationalist recruitment to slow down.

Analysing Sources
Different attitudes to Ireland and World War I

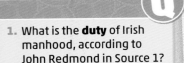

1. What is the **duty** of Irish manhood, according to John Redmond in Source 1?
2. How are the 'interests of Ireland' at stake in the war?
3. Does John Redmond believe that Irishmen should 'stay at home to defend the shores of Ireland'?
4. What does he believe Irishmen should do?
5. According to Arthur Griffith, what is the **duty** of Irish nationalists?
6. Does Arthur Griffith agree with John Redmond?
7. Identify one **fact** and one **opinion** in either of the sources above?
8. Are these sources **biased**?
9. Are these sources **propaganda**?
10. Do these sources help you **understand** why the Irish Volunteers split? Explain your answers using evidence from the sources.

Source 1

'The duty of the manhood of Ireland is twofold. Its duty is, at all costs, to defend the shores of Ireland against foreign invasion. It is a duty more than that, of taking care that Irish valour (bravery) proves itself on the field of war as it has always proved itself in the past. The interests of Ireland – the whole of Ireland – are at stake in this war. The war is undertaken in defence of the highest principles of religion and morality and right, and it would be a disgrace forever for our country ... if young Ireland confined their efforts to remaining at home to defend the shores of Ireland from an unlikely invasion.

I say to you, therefore, ... 'Go on drilling and make yourselves efficient for the work, and then account yourselves as men, not only in Ireland itself, but wherever the firing line extends, in defence of right, of freedom and of religion in this war.'

(John Redmond, speaking to Irish Volunteers in Co. Wicklow, on 20 September 1914)

Source 2

'Ireland is not at war with Germany ... England is at war with Germany, and Mr Redmond has offered England the services of the National Volunteers to defend Ireland. ... Our duty is in no doubt. We are Irish nationalists and the only duty we have is to stand for Ireland's interests, irrespective of the interests of England, or Germany, or any other foreign country.'

(Arthur Griffith writing in his newspaper, *Sinn Féin*, 1914)

Nationalist Split over WWI

National Volunteers	Irish Volunteers
• Followed John Redmond	• Followed Eoin MacNeill
• Supported Irishmen fighting abroad	• Opposed to Irishmen fighting abroad
• Defended Home Rule	• Defended Ireland in Ireland
• About 110,000 men	• About 10,000 men

The 1916 Rising

> Examine the causes, course and impact of the 1916 Rising

Plans for a Rising

The **IRB** (Irish Republican Brotherhood) leaders began to make plans for a rising soon after the start of World War I. The IRB believed that *'England's difficulty was Ireland's opportunity.'* They felt that this was a good time for a rising because the English government's attention would be distracted from Irish affairs by the World War. The IRB formed a **Military Council** to organise the Rising.

Military Council plans

The Military Council needed **arms and ammunition** and they needed **men** for the Rising.

But they also wanted to keep their plans **secret**, because of the danger that spies would provide information to the British government.

In January 1916, the Military Council decided that the Rising would take place at **Easter**.

Arms from Germany

Roger Casement got arms from Germany, England's enemy in the war. The Germans gave him 20,000 rifles, ten machine guns and ammunition. These were loaded on board the *Aud*, which set sail for Ireland.

Involving the Irish Volunteers

Eoin MacNeill and the Irish Volunteers were needed to provide men for the Rising. But MacNeill was opposed to a rising.

Just before Easter 1916, the Military Council showed MacNeill a document – the 'Castle Document' – that said the British government was planning to disarm the Irish Volunteers. As a result, MacNeill allowed the Irish Volunteers to go ahead with drills and manoeuvres planned for Easter Sunday.

It now seemed as if all the plans were working out. Arms would be landed in Co. Kerry, and distributed to Volunteer groups out on training exercises on Easter Sunday. The Rising would be a **national (countrywide) rising**.

Then the plans began to **go wrong**.

The plans go wrong

- On the Friday before Easter, the *Aud* was captured off the Kerry coast. It was sunk by its captain off Cork harbour and all the arms and ammunition were lost.
- **Roger Casement** was captured in Kerry after coming ashore from a German submarine.
- **Eoin MacNeill** found out that the Castle Document was a **forgery**. He then **cancelled** the Volunteer manoeuvres for Easter Sunday.

PROFILE – PATRICK PEARSE, LEADER OF 1916 RISING

- Pearse was born in Dublin in 1879.
- He joined the Gaelic League and edited their newspaper, *An Claidheamh Soluis*.
- He founded a school, St Enda's, in Dublin.
- He joined the Irish Volunteers and the Irish Republican Brotherhood (IRB) in 1913.
- He was a member of the Military Council of the IRB in planning the 1916 Rising.
- He read the *Proclamation of the Irish Republic* outside the General Post Office (GPO) on Easter Monday, 1916.
- He was executed after the Rising, and buried in Arbour Hill Cemetery, Dublin.

Analysing Sources

Pearse and the Use of Violence

HISTORICAL EMPATHY

Q

1. In Source 1, what will be achieved by **violence or armed rebellion**, according to Pearse?
2. What 'mistakes' could happen at the beginning, according to Pearse?
3. What is Pearse's view about **bloodshed**?
4. Would all nationalist leaders at that time agree with Pearse's views on violence and bloodshed?
5. Who are the 'Defenders of the Realm' in Source 2?
6. What is Pearse's main **message** here?
7. What does Pearse mean by the last sentence?
8. Why are both of these sources **primary** sources? Are they **biased**? Are they **propaganda**?
9. How do these sources help you **explain the causes** of the 1916 Rising?
   Explain your answers using evidence from the sources.

Q Source 1

Ireland unarmed will attain just as much freedom as it is convenient for England to give her: Ireland armed will attain ultimately just as much freedom as she wants ... We must accustom ourselves to the thought of arms, to the sight of arms, to the use of arms. We may make mistakes in the beginning and shoot the wrong people; but bloodshed is a cleansing and a sanctifying thing, and a nation which regards it as the final horror has lost its manhood.

(Source: Patrick Pearse, *The Coming Revolution* [1913])

Q Source 2

Life springs from death; and from the graves of patriot men and women spring living nations. The Defenders of the Realm ... think they have pacified Ireland. They think they have purchased half of us and intimidated (frightened) the other half ... but the fools, the fools, the fools! – they have left us our Fenian dead, and while Ireland holds these graves, Ireland unfree shall never be at peace.

(Patrick Pearse's speech at the funeral of O'Donovan Rossa, an old Fenian, who died in August 1915)

The Rising goes ahead

The Military Council decided that the Rising would go ahead on **Easter Monday**, influenced by Pearse's ideas of a *Blood Sacrifice*, that their deaths would inspire the rest of the Irish people and reawaken the national spirit. However, the Rising would now be confined **mainly to Dublin**. It also had **no hope of military success**.

On Easter Monday morning, 1,500 Volunteers took over **key buildings** in the city centre. The **General Post Office** (GPO) became the headquarters of the Rising. Here, Pearse read out the **Proclamation of the Irish Republic** on the street outside.

Marlborough Barracks

Royal Barracks

GPO HQ

Four Courts

River Liffey

Islandbridge Barracks

Mendicity Institute

Dublin Castle

Boland's Mills

Curragh

South Dublin Union

Jacob's Factory

St Stephen's Green

Beggar's Bush Barracks

Wellington Barracks

Grand Canal

Kingstown (Dun Laoghaire)

Portobello Barracks

■ British barracks — — — British military cordon

▲ Rebel positions ┅┅┅ Railway lines

POBLACHT NA H EIREANN.
THE PROVISIONAL GOVERNMENT
OF THE
IRISH REPUBLIC
TO THE PEOPLE OF IRELAND.

IRISHMEN AND IRISHWOMEN: In the name of God and of the dead generations from which she receives her old tradition of nationhood, Ireland, through us, summons her children to her flag and strikes for her freedom.

Having organised and trained her manhood through her secret revolutionary organisation, the Irish Republican Brotherhood, and through her open military organisations, the Irish Volunteers and the Irish Citizen Army, having patiently perfected her discipline, having resolutely waited for the right moment to reveal itself, she now seizes that moment, and, supported by her exiled children in America and by gallant allies in Europe, but relying in the first on her own strength, she strikes in full confidence of victory.

We declare the right of the people of Ireland to the ownership of Ireland, and to the unfettered control of Irish destinies, to be sovereign and indefeasible. The long usurpation of that right by a foreign people and government has not extinguished the right, nor can it ever be extinguished except by the destruction of the Irish people. In every generation the Irish people have asserted their right to national freedom and sovereignty: six times during the past three hundred years they have asserted it in arms. Standing on that fundamental right and again asserting it in arms in the face of the world, we hereby proclaim the Irish Republic as a Sovereign Independent State, and we pledge our lives and the lives of our comrades-in-arms to the cause of its freedom, of its welfare, and of its exaltation among the nations.

The Irish Republic is entitled to, and hereby claims, the allegiance of every Irishman and Irishwoman. The Republic guarantees religious and civil liberty, equal rights and equal opportunities to all its citizens, and declares its resolve to pursue the happiness and prosperity of the whole nation and of all its parts, cherishing all the children of the nation equally, and oblivious of the differences carefully fostered by an alien government, which have divided a minority from the majority in the past.

Until our arms have brought the opportune moment for the establishment of a permanent National Government, representative of the whole people of Ireland and elected by the suffrages of all her men and women, the Provisional Government, hereby constituted, will administer the civil and military affairs of the Republic in trust for the people.

We place the cause of the Irish Republic under the protection of the Most High God, Whose blessing we invoke upon our arms, and we pray that no one who serves that cause will dishonour it by cowardice, inhumanity, or rapine. In this supreme hour the Irish nation must, by its valour and discipline and by the readiness of its children to sacrifice themselves for the common good, prove itself worthy of the august destiny to which it is called.

Signed on Behalf of the Provisional Government,

THOMAS J. CLARKE,
SEAN Mac DIARMADA,   THOMAS MacDONAGH,
P. H. PEARSE,   EAMONN CEANNT,
JAMES CONNOLLY.   JOSEPH PLUNKETT.

1. According to the Proclamation, from whom does Ireland receive her 'old tradition of nationhood'?
2. Name **one** of the groups that 'organised and trained her manhood'.
3. Give **one** piece of **evidence** to show that the Rising received support from outside of ireland.
4. What does the document accuse the 'alien government' of doing?
5. Give **two** pieces of **evidence** from this document to show how the leaders hoped that this document would encourage people to support the Rising.
6. Give **one fact** and **one opinion** from the document.
7. Is this document **propaganda**?
8. Is this document a **primary** source?
9. How does this document **explain the causes** of the 1916 Rising?
10. How does this document **differ** from the Ulster Solemn League and Covenant, p. 234?
    Explain your answers by referring to evidence in the source.

The British government reaction

The British government was taken by surprise by the Rising. Reinforcements (extra soldiers) were brought in from the Curragh and from England. A **military cordon** (barrier) was thrown around the centre of Dublin. By Wednesday, the rebels were outnumbered 20 to one. Artillery was brought in, and a gunboat, the *Helga*, was brought up the Liffey to shell the GPO.

End of the Rising

By the end of the week, the city centre was in ruins, the rebel positions surrounded, widespread looting was occurring and many civilians had been killed. On Saturday, Pearse **surrendered** unconditionally.

The rebels were rounded up and held as prisoners. Then, between 3 May and 3 August 16 leaders were executed, mostly in Kilmainham Gaol in Dublin.

Why did the Rising fail?

Which of these reasons, do you think, was the most important in explaining the **military failure** of the Rising?

Irish Volunteers outnumbered	British army had greater fire power	Rising largely confined to Dublin
The capture of the *Aud*	Bad tactics of the Volunteers	Irish Volunteers failed to get the support of the people

What serious mistake did the British government make?

The British government made a **serious political mistake** in executing the leaders of the Rising and in rounding up so many people who had nothing to do with the Rising. Irish public opinion began to favour the Rising. This, along with later events, (see The Rise of Sinn Féin, p. 242) resulted in those who were involved in the Rising becoming **more popular** and eventually leading the main political organisation in Ireland in 1918.

The results of the Rising

p. 133 ›

DEATHS
- 500 people killed including...
  - 130 British army and Royal Irish Constabulary (RIC)
  - 64 Volunteers
  - 300 civilians
  - About 2,500 injured

RISE OF SINN FÉIN
- Sinn Féin were not involved in the Rising, but newspapers called it the 'Sinn Féin Rising'

DESTRUCTION IN DUBLIN
- The equivalent of €3.8 million worth of damage was done

MILITARY IN CONTROL
- Martial law (military law) imposed
- 170 people tried
- 2,000 people interned (imprisoned without trial)

PEOPLE'S REACTION
- Anger over food shortages and destruction
- People supported Home Rule party and sent soldiers to the war
- Home Rule in danger

EXECUTIONS
- 15 executed in Kilmainham Gaol, including seven signatories of the Proclamation

CHANGING REACTIONS
- Executions and internments began to change people's minds in favour of the Rising.

Analysing Sources

Reporting the 1916 Rising

JOB OF THE HISTORIAN

The *Irish World* newspaper was published in New York between 1878 and 1951. The Irish Times and Evening Herald were published in Dublin.

The *Evening Herald*, 5 May 1916

THE IRISH WORLD, 13 MAY, 1916

THE MEN BUTCHERED BY ENGLAND

The Most Cultured of Ireland's Sons Murdered Because They Loved Their Native Land—Put to Death as Common Felons After Surrendering as Prisoners of War—Their Heroic Bravery and Unselfish Patriotism Appealed not to a Callous and Brutal Enemy—Irish Poets and Prose Writers Executed a Few Hours After They Laid Down Their Arms—Dead. They Still Serve Their Loved Ireland—The Memory of What They Did Will Be an Inspiration for Their Countrymen—England Will Yet Be Taught That They Did Not Die in Vain.

The Irish World, 13 May 1916

SINN FEIN REBELLION IN IRELAND.

The *Weekly Irish Times*, 5 and 13 May 1916

How England Goaded Ireland Into Rebellion

Orders On File at Dublin Castle Show That England Contemplated the Arrest of the Officers of Every Irish Ireland Organization and of Every Irishman Suspected of Loving His Country—England Demanded Absolute Submission of Irishmen Under Threats of Massacre—The Irish Volunteers Preferred to Face the Enemy and Die.

The Irish World, 13 May 1916

THE WEEKLY IRISH TIMES, APRIL

EXECUTION OF THIRTEEN OF THE REBEL LEADERS.

◆

SIXTY OTHERS SENTENCED TO PENAL SERVITUDE.

◆

COUNTESS MARKIEVICZ GETS A LIFE SENTENCE.

The *Weekly Irish Times*, April 1916

IRISH REPUBLIC DECLARED

◆

THE PROCLAMATION OF THE REBELS

The *Weekly Irish Times*, 5 and 13 May 1916

THE HEART OF DUBLIN DEVOURED IN FURIOUS CONFLAGRATIONS.

◆

TWO AND A HALF MILLIONS WORTH DESTROYED IN 200 BUILDINGS

◆

FIRE BRIGADE DRIVEN OFF THE STREETS BY RIFLE FIRE

The *Weekly Irish Times*, 5 and 13 May 1916

MILITARY AND POLICE CASUALTIES OVER FIVE HUNDRED

◆

124 OFFICERS AND MEN KILLED.

◆

217 VICTIMS BURIED IN GLASNEVIN CEMETERY.

The *Weekly Irish Times*, 5 and 13 May 1916

Q

1. What are the **main headings** in the *Evening Herald* in relation to the 1916 Rising?
2. What are the **main headings** in the *Irish World* in relation to the 1916 Rising?
3. What are the **main headings** in the *Weekly Irish Times* in relation to the 1916 Rising?
4. Which of the newspapers is **most factual**?
5. Which of the newspapers is **most biased**?
6. Why were newspapers such an **important source** of news in the early 20th century?
7. How would the reporting of any of the newspapers have **influenced your view** of the Rising, if you were living in 1916?
8. Are these newspapers **primary** sources?
9. How **useful** are they for historians researching the 1916 Rising?
10. Why would historians have to research many **different** newspapers? Explain your answers using evidence from the sources.

Go onto YouTube and look up 'Miss Stout's History Class The 1916 Rising'

Visit ...
GPO Witness History, www.gpowitnesshistory.ie
Kilmainham Gaol Museum, www.kilmainhamgaolmuseum.ie
Arbour Hill Cemetery, Dublin

Timeline of Nationalism and Unionism, 1916–23

1916	Easter Rising and execution of leaders
	Battle of the Somme
1917	Sinn Féin grew in popularity
	Sinn Féin changed its aims
1918	Conscription for Ireland
	German Plot
	End of World War I
	General election victory for Sinn Féin
1919	War of Independence began
1920	Government of Ireland Act
	Northern Ireland Parliament established
1921	Truce in War of Independence
	Anglo-Irish Treaty
1922	Irish Civil War
	Irish Free State established
1923	End of Civil War

The Rise of Sinn Féin

Sinn Féin rose in **popularity** over the next two years.

- **Éamon de Valera** took over from Arthur Griffith as **President of Sinn Féin**. He was also **President of the Irish Volunteers**.
- Sinn Féin won by-elections in 1917 and 1918.
- The British government tried to introduce **conscription** (compulsory military service) to Ireland in 1918. Sinn Féin gained popularity by leading a victorious **anti-conscription campaign**.
- Sinn Féin campaigned in the 1918 general election for a **republic** with complete independence from Britain. They won 73 out of 105 seats in Ireland. They followed a policy of **abstentionism** (they would form their own parliament in Dublin rather than going to Westminster).

1910 AND 1918 GENERAL ELECTION RESULTS		
	1910	1918
Home Rule Party	73	6
Sinn Féin	0	73
Unionists	19	23

⊘ Explore how the Independence Struggle, 1919–21, was conducted

The Independence Struggle, 1919–21

Between 1919 and 1921, nationalists in Ireland organised a strong campaign to gain independence from Britain. The campaign took two forms:

1. Sinn Féin organised **passive resistance**, a policy of opposing the British government without using violence.
2. The Irish Volunteers (who now became known as the **Irish Republican Army**, or **IRA**) organised a **guerrilla warfare campaign**.

How did passive resistance work?

On 21 January 1919, Sinn Féin held a meeting of the **First Dáil Éireann** (parliament) in the Mansion House, Dublin. Only 27 TDs attended, because the remainder were either in jail or on the run.

On that day, the **First Dáil** issued:

- The Declaration of Independence
- A Message to the Free Nations of the World
- A programme to improve living and working conditions

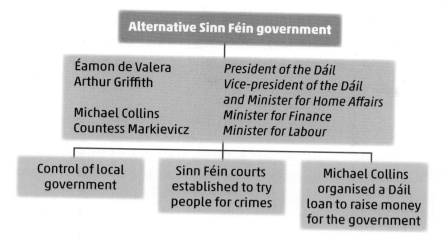

The actions of the **Sinn Féin government** showed that they could run an independent government. The actions also helped to win the battle over public opinion.

The War of Independence, 1919–21

On the same day that the First Dáil met, 21 January 1919, an **RIC** (Royal Irish Constabulary) patrol was ambushed in **Soloheadbeg**, Co. Tipperary. A local IRA unit led by Dan Breen and Seán Treacy carried out the ambush. The IRA men attacked police who were guarding a supply of gelignite going to a nearby quarry. Two policemen were shot dead. These were the **first shots** of the War of Independence.

Guerrilla warfare

The IRA used **guerrilla war tactics** against the British government forces. These were ambush, or 'hit and run' tactics. The IRA's main target was the **RIC**. They attacked isolated barracks in the countryside to get arms and ammunition. The IRA also intimidated the RIC members and their families.

Seán Keating's (1889–1977) painting of a flying column from the North Cork Brigade IRA, **Men of the South,** painted in 1921

SOURCES

1. What **evidence** is there to suggest that the men are not professional soldiers?
2. What **type of warfare** did these men carry out?
3. How would you describe the **look** on the men's faces?
4. Is there any **evidence** in the painting which would support the view that the British government had difficulties defeating men like these?
5. Is this a **primary** or a **secondary** source?
6. What **type** of primary or secondary source is it?
7. Is this painting **biased** or **objective**? In your opinion, is the painter opposed to or a supporter of the IRA?
   Explain your answer using evidence from the painting.

For more information, consult the website **www.historyireland.com** and search for 'Men of the South Revisited'.

Flying columns

As the IRA increased in numbers, local units called **flying columns** were formed. The men in these units lived off the countryside getting food and shelter from the local people. Flying columns took part in large-scale ambushes.

The role of Michael Collins

Collins operated an **intelligence network**, using spies to gather information. He got information from secretaries, porters and policemen. He used this information to direct operations by the IRA.

He also organised a special group in Dublin called '**The Squad**'. Their job was to kill spies and detectives.

The British response

The British government, led by **David Lloyd George**, Prime Minister, recruited **ex-soldiers** in Britain to overcome a shortage of recruits in the RIC. Members of the new force became known as the '**Black and Tans**', because they wore a mixed army and RIC uniform.

The government also recruited **ex-officers**. These were known as the **Auxiliaries**. Very often these forces carried out **reprisals** against local people because of attacks on themselves. These actions helped the IRA, which got greater support from the people. The British government also introduced the **Government of Ireland Act 1920**. Under the Act, two parliaments were to be set up, one in Dublin and one in Belfast. Sinn Féin rejected this Act.

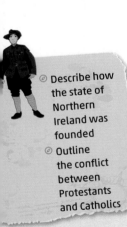

- Describe how the state of Northern Ireland was founded
- Outline the conflict between Protestants and Catholics

The Foundation of Northern Ireland

After World War I

There was a different attitude to World War I amongst **Northern unionists** compared to **nationalists**. Northern unionists took **pride** in their part in the war. Many commemorated the **Battle of the Somme** on 1 July each year when thousands of men from the Ulster Division had fought and died.

There was also commemoration amongst many nationalists for some years after the war. But over the decades, nationalists' part in the war was played down and largely forgotten.

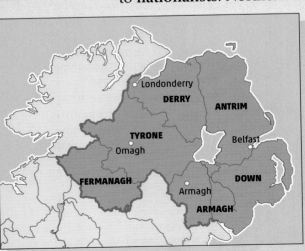

The six counties of Northern Ireland

The Government of Ireland Act, 1920

The state of Northern Ireland was formed under the **Government of Ireland Act 1920**. This Act **partitioned** (divided) the country. It established a parliament for Northern Ireland and a parliament for the Irish Free State in the South. Southern unionists refused to accept this. But unionists in Northern Ireland formed their own government and parliament after a general election in 1921.

The **Northern parliament** had power over internal Northern Ireland affairs, such as education, health, policing and roads. The parliament at Westminster controlled trade, international relations, peace and war.

This was the way Northern Ireland was **ruled** for the next 50 years.

Unionist control

The **Unionist Party**, led by **James B. Craig** as Prime Minister, dominated the political system. It won all elections with clear majorities. The party had close links with the **Orange Order**, which organised parades and marches to maintain unionist domination (control).

James Craig

BELFAST DURING THE RECENT RIOTS: DISTURBANCES DURING WHICH 18 WERE KILLED AND 200 WOUNDED.

Select three of the pictures here and describe what is happening in each of them.

Protestant and Catholic conflict

In the early 1920s, serious **conflict** arose between **Protestants** (unionists) and **Catholics** (nationalists). Unionists believed that Catholics wanted to destroy Northern Ireland.

- Unionists were opposed to a united Ireland because they feared being **discriminated** against in a nationalist/Catholic-dominated country
- They also felt that the Northern Ireland economy would suffer more by being cut off from the British market

The **Royal Ulster Constabulary** (RUC) was formed in 1922 as an armed police force. It had a mostly Protestant membership. It was helped by the **B-Specials**, a part-time police force. They could use the **Special Powers Act** (1922) to arrest and imprison anyone. Nationalist felt that the B-Specials and the Special Powers Act were used to keep them down.

Riots

In the **sectarian riots** in the early 1920s between Protestants and Catholics, Catholics suffered more than Protestants:

- More Catholics were **killed**
- Thousands of Catholics **lost their jobs** – in the most famous incident, Catholics were driven out of the **Harland and Wolff** shipyards (July 1920)
- Catholic houses and businesses were **burned**

The **IRA** continued a campaign in the north during 1922. RUC were attacked and killed, big houses were burned, and railway stations were attacked. There were continued killings of Catholics and Protestants in Belfast.

The outbreak of the Civil War in the south ended the violence. Over a period of two years from 1920 to 1922, 557 people had been **killed** in Northern Ireland – almost 60 per cent of these were Catholics.

Major incidents of the War of Independence

Put these events of the War of Independence in **chronological order**:

 CHRONOLOGICAL AWARENESS

Terence MacSwiney, Lord Mayor of Cork, died on hunger strike in Brixton Prison, London, after 74 days	Ambush at Kilmichael	Members of the RIC murdered Tomás MacCurtain, Lord Mayor of Cork, in front of his family	Bloody Sunday – Collins' Squad killed 11 British agents sent specially to catch him. Black and Tans shot into Croke Park during a football match, killing 12 people
	Ambush at Crossbarry		

p. 136 ▶

IRA attack on the Custom House, Dublin; over 80 IRA captured

Write a report on major incidents of the War of Independence based on the events here.

Casualties due to IRA violence, 1920–22

Most

Least

✳ Raids by Black and Tans or Auxiliaries

— Border between North and South after Government of Ireland Act 1920

Incidents in the War of Independence
1. The burning of Cork City
2. Ambush at Crossbarry, Co. Cork
3. Ambush at Kilmichael, Co. Cork
4. The attack on the Custom House, Dublin

Tuam

Balbriggan

Dublin ④

Ennistymon

Mallow

① Cork
③ ②

Analysing Sources

What happened at Croke Park on Bloody Sunday?

Source 1

Historian's view

Today two theories exist as to what happened in Croke Park. At a time when there was considerable infiltration of the GAA by the IRA, the authorities claimed that the first shots were fired by IRA men hiding in the crowd of spectators in order to create a panic and evade arrest. The alternative theory is that Auxiliary/RIC forces went to Croke Park in reprisal for the attacks that morning on British secret service men at the hands of Collins' squad. According to the RIC/Auxiliary witness accounts, on their arrival at Croke Park a number of civilians appearing to be a picquet (on duty, on guard), were seen outside at the entrance close to the turnstiles and began firing at the forces as they dismounted from their convoy. It is this piece of information that is central to the authorities according blame to the civilians.

(Source: The GAA through History and Documents, 1870–1920 [2008])

Source 2

Witness Statement 15

At Croke Park on 21st November I was in the second lorry of the police convoy. As soon as we got to the top of the Canal Bridge I saw a group of about ten civilians. Some in the middle of the street and some on the sides between the bridge and the turning down to the turnstiles. By their demeanour (behaviour) and formation, they gave us an impression that they were a picquet (on guard). Those men immediately on our arrival turned round and started to run towards the nearest entrance gates; as they ran they turned round and fired at the first car. Those were the first shots I heard. I noticed three or four of them firing.

Source 3

Witness Statement 22

On Sunday 21st inst., I was on duty outside the main entrance [to] Croke Park in Jones's Road … three small Crossley lorries pulled up in Jones's Road. There were about ten or 12 men dressed in RIC uniforms in each. When they got out of the cars they started firing in the air which I thought was blank ammunition, and almost immediately firing started all round the ground. Some of the men who got out of the lorries went into the field and others remained on the road.

Source 4

Opinion of Military Court of Inquiry into what happened

I consider that the first shots were fired by members in the crowd, and that these shots led to the panic.

I consider that the firing on the crowd was carried out without orders, was indiscriminate (random), and unjustifiable, with the exception of any shooting that took place inside the enclosure.

(Major-General Boyd, Commanding Dublin District, 11 December 1920)

1. According to Source 1, what did the authorities **claim** happened at Croke Park?
2. In Source 1, why did the Auxiliaries go to Croke Park, according to the second theory?
3. What is the **main point** made by Witness Statement 15 in Source 2?
4. What is the **main point** made by Witness Statement 22 in Source 3?
5. What **conclusions** were made by the Military Court of Enquiry in Source 4?
6. Which of the **two theories** in Source 1 are supported by either of the Sources 2 and 3?
7. Can you **explain** why the witnesses in Source 2 and 3 disagree?
8. Are these sources **biased**?
9. What, do you think, happened in Croke Park on that day?
   Explain your answers using evidence from the sources.

Peace

By 1921, both sides wanted **peace**

- The **IRA** was running short of men and ammunition
- The **people** wanted peace
- The **British government** was being criticised at home and in America for the actions of the Black and Tans and the Auxiliaries
- The war was **costing** the government a great deal of money

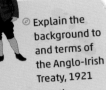

Go onto YouTube and look up 'Miss Stout's History Class First Year History'

De Valera returned from America where he had been during most of the War of Independence. He agreed the terms of a ceasefire with Lloyd George. The **ceasefire** came into operation on 11 July 1921.

The Anglo-Irish Treaty, 1921

Delegations

⊘ Explain the background to and terms of the Anglo-Irish Treaty, 1921

⊘ Consider the arguments for and against the Anglo-Irish Treaty, 1921

⊘ Analyse the impact of the Anglo-Irish Treaty

After the truce, the British government and Sinn Féin began negotiations. The Sinn Féin government selected a **delegation** to represent them at the talks in London. The delegates were **Arthur Griffith, Michael Collins, Robert Barton, Eamonn Duggan** and **George Gavan Duffy**.

De Valera refused to go because:

- He was head of state
- He **wanted to control extremists at home**

Lloyd George headed the British delegation. He was assisted by **Winston Churchill, Austin Chamberlain** and **Lord Birkenhead**.

Different aims

Sinn Féin had two main goals in the negotiations:

- To achieve a **republic** (complete independence from Britain)
- To have **no border, or partition**, between the north and south of Ireland

The main British aim was:

- To keep Ireland **within the British Empire** (or Commonwealth, as it was known).

Negotiations

From October to December 1921, the two delegations negotiated in London. Finally, on 6 December 1921, they signed the 'Treaty between Great Britain and Ireland', or the **Anglo-Irish Treaty**.

The terms of the Anglo-Irish Treaty

1. Ireland would be known as the **Irish Free State**.
2. Ireland would still be a **dominion** (part of) the British Commonwealth.
3. The King of England would be represented in Ireland by a **Governor-general**.
4. Members of the Dáil and Seanad (Senate) would take an **oath of allegiance** to the Irish government and the King of England.

5. Britain would have the use of **three ports** (the 'Treaty ports') – Berehaven, Cobh and Lough Swilly.

6. A **Boundary Commission** would be established to decide on the border between the north and south of Ireland.

The Treaty debates

There was **widespread debate** in Ireland over the terms of the Treaty. The Dáil debated the Treaty from December 1921 to January 1922.

 p. 137

ARGUMENTS FOR AND AGAINST THE TREATY

PRO-TREATY
- The IRA was not able to carry on a war any longer.
- The Treaty was a stepping stone to full independence. Collins said: *'It gives us freedom, not the ultimate freedom that all nations desire and develop to, but the freedom to achieve it.'*
- The Treaty gave Ireland much more independence than Home Rule.
- In favour: Collins and Griffith

ANTI-TREATY
- The Treaty did not give Ireland the republic they had fought for.
- Better terms could have been negotiated.
- The oath of allegiance recognised the king as head of state.
- Against: De Valera and Cathal Brugha

The debate sometimes became very **emotional**. It concluded on 7 January 1922, when the Treaty was accepted by **64 votes to 57**. De Valera resigned as President of the Executive Council. He and his supporters left the Dáil. The Pro-Treaty side now took over the government, with **Arthur Griffith** replacing de Valera as president.

For and Against the Treaty

CONTROVERSIAL ISSUES

Source 1
A print attributed to Countess Markievicz

Source 2
A Pro-Treaty poster

1. Who are Churchill's puppets, according to Source 1?
2. What is the **main point** being made by the print?
3. What **evidence** suggests that this is an anti-Treaty print?
4. What **terms** of the Anglo-Irish Treaty could be used **in support** of the main point of this print?
5. What **terms** of the Anglo-Irish Treaty could be used **against** the main point of this print?
6. In Source 2, select what you consider are the **four main points** made in support of the Treaty.
7. Which source is more **effective** in getting its point across?
8. Why would historians consider both sources as **propaganda**? Explain your answers by referring to evidence in the sources.

⊘ Explore how the Civil War was conducted

The Irish Civil War

After the Dáil debates, the divisions between the **Pro-Treaty** and **Anti-Treaty** sides grew wider. Very often, families and friends disagreed.

The slide towards **Civil War** began when a group of Republicans (Anti-Treaty) took over the **Four Courts** in the centre of Dublin in April 1922. This was a **direct challenge** to the government. The government was also under pressure from the **British government** who feared that war would break out again.

A **general election** in June 1922 gave a huge majority **in favour** of the Treaty. This put the Free State government in a stronger position. When the Republicans in the Four Courts captured a Free State general, Griffith and Collins decided to attack them.

Pro-Treaty	Anti-Treaty
Regulars	Irregulars
Free State government	Republicans
Government forces	

General election results June 1922	
Sinn Féin (Pro-Treaty)	58
Sinn Féin (Anti-Treaty)	36
The rest (including the Labour Party) – Pro-Treaty	34
Total – Pro-Treaty	92
Total – Anti-Treaty	36

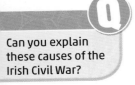

Can you explain these causes of the Irish Civil War?

The fighting begins

Fighting in Dublin

The **Free State army**, led by Collins, borrowed artillery from the British army to shell the Four Courts. Within two days, the 200 Republicans inside surrendered. Fighting continued in the centre of Dublin for a few more days, but the government forces defeated the Republicans easily.

How did Hitler and the Nazis Gain Power in Germany?

⊘ Outline briefly the causes of Hitler's rise to power

Hitler joined the **German Workers' Party** after World War I. He soon took over the leadership of the party and changed its name to the **National Socialist German Workers' Party** (NSDAP), popularly know as the **Nazi Party**.

During the 1920s, the Nazi Party was small. But after the **Great Depression** hit Germany in 1929, the popularity of the Nazi Party soared. Soon the Nazi Party became the **largest party** in the Reichstag (German parliament), and in January 1933, Hitler became **Chancellor** (prime minister) of Germany.

Adolf Hitler, leader of Nazi Party

Joseph Goebbels, responsible for propaganda

Heinrich Himmler, head of the SS

Hermann Goering, Chief of the Luftwaffe (German Air Force)

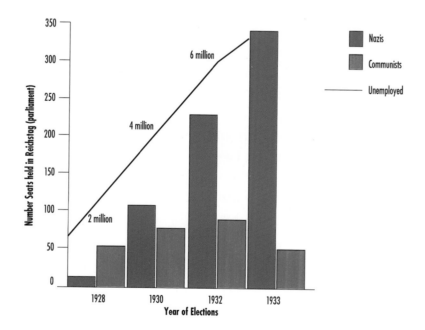

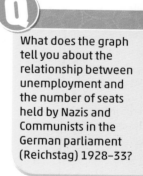
Q What does the graph tell you about the relationship between unemployment and the number of seats held by Nazis and Communists in the German parliament (Reichstag) 1928–33?

The Weakness of the Weimar Republic
A democratic government ran Germany during the 1920s. It was blamed for defeat in World War I and the harsh peace treaty afterwards, the Treaty of Versailles.

The Great Depression
Unemployment rose in Germany from 1 million in 1929 to 6 million in 1932. The government was not able to cope with this, and many blamed them for making matters worse.

The Largest Party
Hitler gained popularity and his party increased the number of seats in the Reichstag from 12 in 1928 to 230 in 1932, making it the largest party in Germany.

Causes of Hitler's rise to power

Hitler's leadership of the Nazis
Hitler intended to achieve power by democratic means (elections) and then establish dictatorship.

The SA and SS
Hitler's Nazi party was supported by two para-military groups – the SA (Brownshirts) and the SS (Blackshirts). The SA and SS attacks on communists and socialists led to riots in the streets. They intimidated all opposition.

Propaganda
Hitler used many different forms of propaganda to get across his message.

Hitler's policies
His policies appealed to many: his **nationalism** appealed to all Germans; his **anti-communism** appealed to business people and industrialists; his promise to **revive the economy** appealed to the unemployed.

How did each of the following help Hitler's rise to power:
1. Weimar government
2. Great Depression
3. Hitler's policies
4. Propaganda
5. SA and SS?

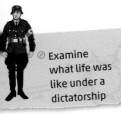

⊘ Examine what life was like under a dictatorship

Germany – Life in a Fascist Dictatorship

As soon as he became Chancellor, Hitler called a general election for March 1933. When a Dutch communist set fire to the **Reichstag** (parliament) building, Hitler used this incident to ban the Communist Party and to give extra powers to the police. After the election, Hitler passed the **Enabling Law** in 1933, which allowed him to **rule by decree** (dictate orders).

Hitler then **banned** all political parties except the Nazi Party. Trade unions were also banned.

Hitler created a **police state**:

- The **SS** and the **Gestapo** (secret police) could arrest anybody, read mail and listen to phone calls.
- The **judges** in the law courts took oaths of loyalty to Hitler. Informers were encouraged to spy on their families.
- Press, radio and cinema were **controlled**.

- Those **opposed** to Hitler were rounded up and put into concentration camps such as Dachau, set up in 1933.

Within a short time, Hitler and the Nazi Party had created a **dictatorship**.

The Nazis organised concentration camps to hold prisoners without trial. The prisoners included Jews and anybody the Nazis thought were opposed to their rule. The number of prisoners increased from 1933 to 1939. During World War II, the number and size of the concentration camps increased rapidly. There were also six extermination camps developed for killing Jews and other minority groups whom the Nazis hated (see Ch. 20).

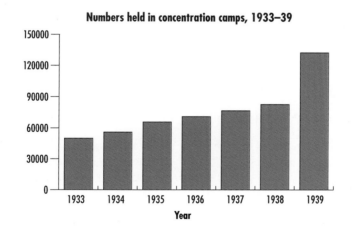

Numbers held in concentration camps, 1933–39

Q

How were opponents of Hitler treated in Nazi Germany?

What happened on the Night of the Long Knives?

Hitler decided to eliminate the **SA**, led by Ernst Röhm, because they threatened his power. On the **Night of the Long Knives** (30 June 1934), the SS were used to kill the leadership of the SA. At least, 85 people were shot and thousands of SA arrested. Hitler was now in total control of his organisation and of the state. In August 1934, when President Hindenburg died, Hitler combined the positions of President and Chancellor as one office and became **Der Führer** ('the Leader').

Analysing Sources

The Night of the Long Knives

Q Source 1

Hitler can't walk over me as he might have done a year ago; I've seen to that. Don't forget that I have three million men, with every key position in the hands of my own people, Hitler knows that I have friends in the Reichswehr (German army), you know! If Hitler is reasonable I shall settle the matter quietly; if he isn't I must be prepared to use force – not for my sake but for the sake of our revolution.

(Ernst Röhm, leader of the SA, speaking in January 1934)

Q Source 2

In the circumstances I had to make but one decision. If disaster was to be prevented at all, action had to be taken with lightning speed ... If anyone reproaches (criticises) me and asks why I did not resort to the regular courts of justice for conviction of the offenders, then all I can say is, 'I alone during those 24 hours was the supreme court of justice of the German people. I ordered the leaders of the guilty shot.'

(Hitler speaking in the Reichstag after the Night of the Long Knives)

Q Source 3

A British cartoon commenting on the Night of the Long Knives

Q Source 4

HITLER AND GOERING SMASH NAZI REVOLT.

SWIFT AND RUTHLESS COUP.

FLIGHT BY NIGHT TO MEET THE REBELS.

STORM TROOP LEADERS SHOT DEAD.

THE GERMAN COUP.

Whatever one may think of Herr Hitler as a statesman, nobody can deny his courage as a man. As the full details of Saturday's events in Germany come to light this quality of the Fuehrer stands our in strong relief against a welter of bloodshed and intrigue. Altogether, some two hundred leaders of the Brown Shirts were arrested, and seventeen of them were shot out of hand.

The Irish Times, Monday, 2 July 1934

Q

1. In Source 1, what was **Röhm's attitude** to Hitler?
2. Should Hitler have felt **threatened** by his attitude?
3. Who did Hitler say was 'the supreme court of justice of the German people' in Source 2?
4. In the cartoon in Source 3, can you identify the two people beside Hitler?
5. What does the caption, 'They salute with both hands now' mean?
6. What is the **message** of the cartoon?
7. What does the *Irish Times* think about Hitler in Source 4?
8. Are all the sources **biased**?
9. Which sources, do you think, are **most reliable**?
10. Which sources are **most useful** for studying Nazi Germany? Explain your answers using evidence in the sources.

Living under Nazi Propaganda

Propaganda was very important to Hitler and the Nazis, because it helped them to control what people knew and thought. Joseph **Goebbels** was appointed Minister for National Enlightenment and Propaganda. He was in charge of press, radio, cinema, theatre and art.

⊘ Consider how Nazi propaganda influenced life in Germany

Newspaper editors had to keep out of the papers *'anything which is in any manner misleading to the public, tends to weaken the strength of the German Reich (Empire) … or offends the honour and dignity of Germany.'*

Goebbels provided **cheap radios** – the People's Radio – so that people could listen to broadcasts of Hitler's speeches. He also installed **loudspeakers** along streets to ensure that more people could hear the speeches.

A **cult of personality** was developed around Hitler. Hitler was glorified as the Führer, with posters all over Germany. Special festivals, such as Hitler's birthday were introduced, and *'Heil Hitler'* was used as a salute or greeting.

Great **rallies** in Nuremberg – the Nuremberg Rallies – and **torchlight parades** were used as propaganda occasions. Even the **Olympic Games** in Berlin in 1936 were used as a Nazi showcase.

A mother and child listening to the People's Radio

Leni Riefenstahl directing a cameraman filming the Nuremberg Rally

A scene from *Triumph of the Will*, Riefenstahl's film on the 1934 Nuremberg Rally

Analysing Sources

The Cult of the Leader

Q Source 1

Hitler's appeal

A far more powerful factor in the New Germany than the appeal of Hitler's doctrine, however, was the appeal of Hitler himself. Many Germans believed that Hitler was actually endowed with superhuman qualities. I remember Frau Fleischer telling me that in Germany there was no need for people to have opinions; they had the Führer's opinions and the Führer was inspired.

(Virginia Cowles (a Sunday Times journalist), Looking for Trouble [1941])

Q Source 2

Nature of Propaganda

All propaganda must be popular and its intellectual level must be adjusted to the most limited intelligence among those it is addressed to. Consequently, the greater the mass it is intended to reach, the lower its purely intellectual level will have to be. But if the aim is to influence a whole people, we must avoid excessive intellectual demands on our public.

(Hitler's views on propaganda)

Q Source 3

Nuremberg Rallies

The stadium (at Nuremberg) was packed with nearly 200,000 spectators. As the time of the Führer's arrival drew near, the crowd grew restless. Suddenly the beat of the drums increased and a fleet of black cars rolled into the arena. In one of them, standing in the front seat, his hand outstretched in the Nazi salute, was Hitler. The stadium looked like a shimmering sea of swastikas. Hitler began to speak. The crowd hushed in silence. Hitler's voice rasped into the night and every now and then the multitude broke into a roar of cheers. Some began swaying back and forth, chanting 'Sieg Heil' ('Hail Victory!') over and over again in a frenzy (emotion). I looked at the faces around me and saw tears streaming down people's cheeks. The drums had grown louder and I suddenly felt frightened.

(Virginia Cowles (a Sunday Times journalist), Looking for Trouble [1941])

Q

Q Source 4

Hitler poster

Ein Volk, ein Reich, ein Führer!

One People, one Empire, one Leader (1938), after the takeover of Austria by Germany

1. According to Source 1, what did many Germans think about Hitler?
2. Why was there no need for people to have their own opinion, according to Frau Fleischer in Source 1?
3. What does Hitler mean in Source 2, by 'all propaganda must be popular'?
4. According to Hitler, if you want to influence the whole people what must you do?
5. In Source 3, what was the reaction of the crowd to Hitler's speech?
6. What other aspects of Nazi **propaganda techniques** can you identify in Source 3?
7. Why do you think the journalist felt frightened?
8. What **symbols, words and images** are used in the poster in Source 4?
9. What is the **message** of the poster?
10. Is it **effective** propaganda?
11. How **useful** are these sources in explaining how the Nazis controlled the minds of many German people?
    Explain your answers using evidence from the sources.

Analysing Sources

How to Analyse Posters

Propaganda – The Cult of the Leader

Flagbearer

Upraised arm – strength

Determined

Inspired

Oak – strength

Heavenly light from sky – religious – godly

Leader

Military style uniform

Crowd support – followers

Symbols

Slogan to emphasise working for Germany

Long Live Germany (1932). Posters played an important part in Nazi propaganda.

ANALYSING POSTERS

- Images
- Words
- Symbols

Q

1. Who **made** the poster?
2. Who is it **aimed** at (its audience)?
3. What is its **purpose**?
4. What is its **message**?
5. What **propaganda techniques** are used? – use of **images**, **words** and **symbols**?

⊙ Explore how youth were treated in Nazi Germany

How did the Nazis Control the Young?

In education, **loyalty** to the Führer was taught from kindergarten to university. History books were rewritten to glorify Germany's past, and physical education was emphasised. Nazi ideas were also taught in **other subjects**, such as maths.

Boys and girls joined **youth organisations**. There was the **Hitler Youth** for boys and the **League of German Maidens** for girls, in which they were **indoctrinated** (brainwashed) with Nazi ideas.

However, some young people rebelled against the Nazi ideas. These were the **Edelweiss Pirates**. They listened to American and British music, and tried to disrupt Hitler Youth patrols.

School in Nazi Germany

Young German Folk	Young Girls	Hitler Youth	League of German Maidens
Boys 10–14	Girls 10–14	Boys 14–18	Girls 14–18

SOURCES

Nazi education and youth

Source 1
A Nazi school timetable

	Lesson 1	Lesson 2	Lesson 3	Dinner	Lesson 4	Lesson 5	Lesson 6
Boys	German	History/ Geography	Race science/ Nazi ideas	Sport and music	Physics and Chemistry	PE: boxing, football and marching	Maths
Girls	German	History/ Geography	Race science/ Nazi ideas	Sport and music	Biology/ Health and sex education	Cookery	Maths

Source 2
Using maths to teach anti-Semitism
The Jews are aliens in Germany. In 1933 there were 66,060,000 inhabitants of the German Reich of whom 499,862 were Jews. What is the percentage of aliens in Germany?
(A question from a maths textbook)

Source 3
A children's Recitation or prayer

My Leader!
(The child speaks:)
I know you well and love you
    like father and mother
I intend to obey you always
    like father and mother
And when I am grown up, I shall help you
    like father and mother
And you should be proud of me
    like father and mother
(From a Nazi children's colouring book)

Source 4

'Youth serves the Führer. All ten-year-olds in the Hitler Youth.'

How does this poster promote the idea of loyalty and obedience to Hitler?

What symbols, words and images are used to get across its message?

Q

1. Referring to the **timetable** in Source 1, how did **Nazi ideas** influence it?
2. How does **your timetable** differ from those in Nazi Germany?
3. How were boys and girls treated **differently** to each other in schools in Nazi Germany?
4. Using Sources 2 and 3, explain how the **content of school subjects** can be used for **propaganda**?
5. Are schools used for propaganda today?
6. How effective is the **poster** in Source 4 for getting across Nazi ideas?
7. Are all these sources **propaganda**?
8. How **useful** are these sources for researching education and youth in Nazi Germany?
   Explain your answers using evidence from the sources.

What was Life Like for Women in Nazi Germany?

⊘ Explore the life of women in Nazi Germany

The Nazis promoted **the ideal role for women** as mothers, with large families. The Nazi ideal for women was *Kinder, Kuche, Kirche* (children, kitchen, church). They encouraged women to give up their jobs when they married. Women in state jobs such as teachers and civil servants were sacked. They discouraged women from smoking and wearing make-up. They organised **Mothers' Schools** so that women would be trained in household work. The Nazis also made **Mother's Day** into a national holiday.

The Nazis wanted to increase the German **birth rate**, which was falling, as they needed soldiers for their plans. One of their first actions when they came into power was to introduce **'marriage loans'**.

A Nazi portrayal of the ideal family. How does this portray the ideal Nazi family?

People of German nationality who marry may be granted a marriage loan of up to 1,000 Reichmarks … provided:
- *That the future wife has spent at least six months in employment*
- *That the future wife gives up her job*

(Law for the Reduction of Unemployment [1933])

❰ p. 144 CBA2

1. What was the **Nazi ideal** for women?

2. What was *Kinder, Kuche, Kirche*?

3. **Why** did the Nazis want to increase the birth rate?

4. **What methods** did they use to try to increase the birth rate?

◉ Examine the life of Jews in Nazi Germany

p. 145 ❭

Marriage loans were not the only means the Nazis used to increase the birth rate. They also provided maternity benefits, family allowances and medals for mothers with large families. As a result, the birth rate increased between 1933 and 1939.

But the Nazis also **sterilised** (made infertile) some women, *'for the prevention of hereditary diseased offspring'* (to prevent children born with disabilities).

Life for the Jews in Nazi Germany

Racist ideas influenced the Nazis very much. The Nazis believed the Germans were the pure-blooded **Aryan** race – the **Master Race** (*Herrenvolk*). They said they were a superior race to the **inferior Jews** (and others). They regarded the Jews as the *Untermenschen* – subhuman. Jewish children were badly treated in schools, newspapers spread stories about the Jews, and Nazi organisations were used to harass Jews.

Hitler had a great hatred of the Jews (**anti-Semitism**). He now used the power of the government to persecute them, while **Goebbels** used propaganda films to increase racist feeling in Germany. Jewish shops were **boycotted** in 1933. Jews were banned from the civil service, from the universities and from journalism. The **Nuremberg Laws** were passed in 1935 *'for the promotion of German blood and honour'*.

Cross of Honour of the German Mother (Mother's Cross) presented to mothers with large families

Nazi Stormtroopers (SA) arrested a woman and her partner prior to the Nuremberg Laws. The sign on the woman reads: 'I am the biggest pig of all. I only sleep with Jews!' The sign around the man says: 'I am a Jewish boy who only brings German girls to my room.'

Analysing Sources

Nazis and the Jews

Source 1

Influence of Jews

The Jew is the real cause of our loss of the Great War (World War I). The Jew is responsible for our misery and he lives on it. He has corrupted our race, fouled our morals, undermined our customs and broken our power.

(Joseph Goebbels [1930])

Source 3

Children's schoolbook

A children's schoolbook compares the ideal German with the Jew

'The German and the Jew.
Take a good look at the two
In the picture drawn for you.
A joke – you think it is only that?
Easy to guess which is which, I say:
The German stands up, the Jew gives way.'

Source 2

Some of the laws against the Jews

> A citizen of the Reich (German empire) is a subject of German or kindred blood.
> Marriages between Jews and citizens of German or kindred blood are forbidden.
> Jews are allowed only certain first names ... Jews with first names different from those listed must register and use as signature the first name 'Israel' (for men) and 'Sara' (for women) in addition to their own first names.
> As of January 1939, Jews are forbidden to own shops or engage in trade.
> Jews are not permitted to attend German schools. They may only attend Jewish schools.
> Jews are banned from all theatres, shows, concert and lecture halls, museums, sports fields, bathing areas ...
> Jews over six years of age must wear the '**Star of David**' in public.

Q

1. In Source 1, for what does Goebbels **blame** the Jews?
2. What have Jews done to Germany, according to Goebbels?
3. In Source 2, which of the **laws against** the Jews would you consider most **severe**?
4. What **impact** would those laws have on the Jews in Nazi Germany?
5. How is the Jewish man **portrayed** in Source 3?
6. How is the 'German' **portrayed** in Source 3?
7. What **influence** would these (and other) pictures in the school textbook have on children?
8. Why did the Nazis think it was important to **teach** these ideas in schools?
9. Are these sources **biased**?
10. Are these sources **propaganda**?
    Explain your answers using evidence from the sources.

Night of the Broken Glass

In 1938, when a Polish Jew killed a German diplomat in Paris, this incident was used as an excuse for a night of violence against Jewish people (a **pogrom**). On 10 November 1938, in the **Night of the Broken Glass** (Kristallnacht – 'Night of the Crystal Glass'), Jewish shops and synagogues were attacked, about ninety Jews were killed and others were arrested and sent to concentration camps. Hitler insisted that a fine be imposed on the Jewish community to pay for the damage. By 1939, half of Germany's 600,000 Jews, including **Albert Einstein**, had emigrated to other countries.

But worse was to follow when **World War II** broke out (see Ch. 20).

KEY WORD

● Pogrom = organised violence against an ethnic group

267

Analysing Sources

Reports on the Night of the Broken Glass

Source 1

Mob law rules

Mob law ruled in Berlin throughout the afternoon and evening as hordes of hooligans took part in an orgy of destruction. I have never seen an anti-Jewish outbreak as sickening as this. I saw fashionably dressed women clapping their hands and screaming with glee while respectable mothers held up their babies to see the 'fun'. No attempt was made by the police to stop the rioters.

(*Daily Telegraph* [London], 12 November 1938)

Source 2

Revenge for murder of a German

The death of a loyal party member by the Jewish murderer (in Paris) has aroused spontaneous (unplanned) anti-Jewish demonstrations throughout the Reich. In many places, Jewish shops have been smashed. The synagogues, from which teachings hostile to the State and people are spread, have been set on fire. Well done to those Germans who have ensured revenge for the murder of an innocent German.

(*Der Stürmer* [Berlin], 10 November 1938)

Source 3

Kristallanacht in Leipzig

At 3 a.m. on 10 November, the Nazis let loose a savage attack which had no equal before this in Germany or anywhere else in the world since savagery began. Shop windows were shattered, stores were looted and the dwellings of Jews attacked. Three synagogues in Leipzig were set on fire and all sacred objects destroyed. In one of the Jewish sections an eighteen-year old boy was hurled from a three-story window to land on both legs broken on a street littered with broken beds.

(US consul in Leipzig 1938)

Source 4

Jewry's Lot

Dr Goebbels is at great pains to insist that the anti-Jewish pogroms are a result of a spontaneous (unplanned) outburst among the rank and file of the German nation. Actually, of course, they are nothing of the sort. Last Thursday's excesses obviously were well organised, and they were carried out in the main by youthful members of the Hitler *Jugend* (Youth). Dr. Goebbels' propaganda has been so efficient that anti-Jewish prejudice has been worked up ... Sooner or later, we are convinced, the inherent decency of the German people will reassert itself; otherwise the outlook not alone for the Jews, but for civilisation, will be dreadful.

(*The Irish Times* [Dublin], 14 November 1938)

Q

1. In Source 1, what did the **journalist think** about what he saw in Berlin?
2. In Source 2, why does the newspaper say 'Well done to those Germans'?
3. In Source 3, what **damage** was done to Leipzig?
4. Does the *Irish Times* agree with Goebbels about the **cause** of the pogrom in Source 4?
5. What is the *Irish Times* concerned could happen?
6. Is the attitude of the *Irish Times* to Nazi Germany changing compared to Source 4 in p. 260?
7. Do any of these sources show **bias**?
8. Is any of these sources **more objective** than the others?
9. How **helpful** were these sources in understanding what happened on the Night of the Broken Glass?
   Explain your answers using evidence from the sources.

What was Life Like for Christians?

Hitler attacked the Christian churches. He saw the **Catholic Church** as owing loyalty to another leader, the Pope. Catholic schools were closed; Catholic priests were harassed and arrested, and Catholic youth movements were closed.

Pope Pius XI responded by criticising the Nazis in a famous statement, *With Burning Anxiety* (1937).

Hitler also attacked **Protestants** who did not agree with him. He set up a Protestant national church. But most Protestants did not agree with it. One of their leaders, Pastor **Martin Niemöller** was sent to a concentration camp in 1937.

Hitler and the Nazis made it very difficult for Christians to practice their religion.

⊘ Describe how Christians were treated in Nazi Germany

What was Life Like for Workers?

Hitler promised 'work for all', so when he came to power in 1933, he began the 'Battle for Work' to eliminate **unemployment**. The number of unemployed then stood at 6 million. By 1939, there was no unemployment.

Hitler provided work in **public works schemes** to build **motorways** (called autobahns) and **housing** schemes.

Rearmament began, with ships, submarines, planes and arms being manufactured for the expanding German armed forces.

The Nazis set up:

- *Strength through Joy*, an organisation to organise leisure activities for the workers
- *Beauty of Labour* to improve working conditions such as better lighting and canteen food

Hitler also expanded the **motor industry**. He encouraged the design and manufacture of the Volkswagen (the 'people's car') so that everyone in the future could afford a car. However, cars were not delivered before World War II began in 1939.

Hitler's efforts to supply all the food and raw materials Germany needed were not successful. He planned to conquer lands in Eastern Europe to obtain **lebensraum** (living space), and the extra food and raw materials that he needed.

⊘ Explore what life was like for workers in Nazi Germany

The opening of a German autobahn (motorway)

Analysing Sources

Were workers better or worse off under Hitler?

Source 1

Unemployment in Germany, 1928–39

1928	1929	1930	1931	1932	1933
8.4%	13.1%	15.3%	23.3%	30.1	26.3

1934	1935	1936	1937	1938	1939
14.9%	11.6%	8.3%	4.6%	2.1%	0.6%

Source 2

Food consumption, 1929–37

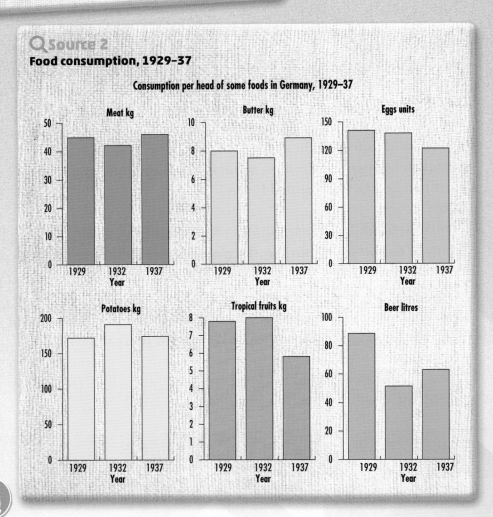

Consumption per head of some foods in Germany, 1929–37

Go onto YouTube and look up 'History File Nazi Germany: Life in Hitler's Germany'

Q

1. What did Hitler and the Nazis do to **reduce unemployment** in Source 1?
2. According to Source 2, did German **food consumption** increase or decrease between 1929 and 1937?
3. Using Sources 3 and 4, did German workers earn more per hour at the end of the 1930s compared to when the Nazis came to power in 1933?
4. Were workers **better or worse off** under Hitler?

Source 3

Average weekly wages	
1932	86 marks
1938	109 marks

Source 4

Average hours of work in industry (per week)	
1933	42.9
1939	47

There was more encouragement for larger families **after World War II** because of the huge loss of population. There were more allowances for large families, and mothers of such families were honoured as **Mother-Heroines**.

Health and Education

Health care was provided **free** for the people. Large numbers of hospitals were built. Thousands of doctors were trained. There were more doctors per head of the population in the Soviet Union than in Britain or the USA. By 1970, 70% of doctors were female.

Communists wanted **free and compulsory education** for all young people. Stalin wanted all children to be educated so that they would be 'of the greatest possible service to the country.' It was not always possible to achieve this, because of a shortage of teachers and buildings.

There was also a **huge literacy campaign**. By 1950, almost all those aged over eight and under 50 could read and write.

Education was also used for **propaganda** purposes. Children were taught that Stalin was the *Great Leader*. A new textbook, *A Short History of the USSR*, was written for schools, which exaggerated Stalin's role in the Communist Revolution of 1917.

Children also joined **youth organisations**, which taught them ideas about communism through their activities in sports and summer camps.

Communist Youth Organisations		
Little Octobrists 7 to 9 years	**Young Pioneers** 10 to 14 years	**Komsomol** 15 to 28 years

⊘ Explain how different aspects of life changed in Soviet Russia

Housing presented problems. As millions of people moved from the countryside into the cities, the building of houses and apartments could not keep up with the demand. As a result only 6% of families in Moscow lived in apartments of more than one room in the 1930s.

What was Life Like in Soviet Russia during World War II?

⊘ Explain how World War II affected the lives of the people in Soviet Russia

In 1941, the **German army** attacked the Soviet Union (see Ch. 19). They advanced rapidly into Russia. But they were halted before they reached **Moscow** by the Russian winter. In 1942, the Germans advanced towards **Stalingrad**. A brutal battle in Stalingrad resulted in victory for the Russian army. After that, the German army was forced to retreat towards Germany.

The **Russian people** suffered a great deal during the war, especially people living in German conquered lands or in the cities of Moscow, Leningrad and Stalingrad.

In **Leningrad** alone, 700,000 people starved or froze to death as they resisted the siege of the city by the Germans.

The government imposed a **rationing system** because of shortages of food and clothing. Workers involved in war industries got higher rations than others. Everybody, including older people and teenagers, could be ordered to work for the war effort. It is estimated that about **17 million Soviet civilians** died in the war, less than half from enemy action, and the rest from cold, hunger or the strain of the war.

Analysing Sources
Life in Soviet Russia during World War II

EVIDENCE

Q

What do these sources tell you about the life of ordinary people in the Soviet Union during World War II? Explain your answer.

Q Source 1

Russian peasants leaving their village ahead of German army

Who are the experts on life in a Communist country?

Go onto YouTube and look up 'Stalin and the Modernisation of Russia'.

Q Source 2

I watched my mother and father die. I knew perfectly well that they were starving. But I wanted their bread more than I wanted them to stay alive. And they knew that. That's what I remember about the blockade: that feeling that you wanted your parents to die because you wanted their bread.
(A survivor of the siege of Leningrad)

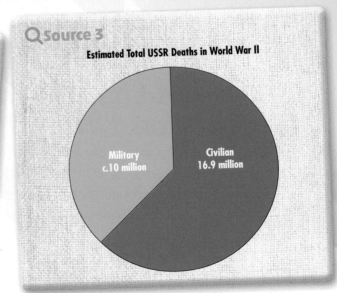

Q Source 3

Estimated Total USSR Deaths in World War II

Military c.10 million

Civilian 16.9 million

INVESTIGATING A REPOSITORY OF HISTORICAL EVIDENCE FOR SOVIET RUSSIA

GULAG: Soviet Forced Labour Camps and the Struggle for Freedom
www.gulaghistory.org

》 Preparing for CBA2

A project on the life and experience of a person of historical interest

PERSONS OF INTEREST IN SOVIET RUSSIA

- Lenin
- Nikita Khrushchev
- Lyudmila Pavlichenko
- Joseph Stalin
- Leon Trotsky
- Trofim Lysenko
- Lavrentiy Beria
- Dora Kaplan

❮ p. 152
Web Resources
and Reading

Focus Task

Historical Investigation

> Investigate the building of the White Sea Canal in the Soviet Union between 1931 and 1933. What does it tell you about life in Stalin's Russia?

EUROPEAN HISTORY

18

THE DRIFT TO WAR
– The Causes of World War II

L.O. 3.4
The Nature of History: 1.1,
1.2, 1.3, 1.4, 1.5, 1.6, 1.7,
1.8, 1.9, 1.10, 1.11.
CBA2

You will learn to …
- ⊘ Discuss the causes of World War II
- ⊘ Explore the Nature of History

KEY WORDS
- Cause
- Rearmament
- Remilitarisation
- Sources

CHRONOLOGICAL AWARENESS

1930 AD

1931
Japan invaded Manchuria

1933
Hitler in power

1935
Germany introduced conscription
Broke the Treaty of Versailles
Mussolini and Italy invaded
Abyssinia

1936
German troops
remilitarised the
Rhineland

1938
Anschluss with
Austria
Munich Conference
Sudetenland
(Czechoslovakia)
taken by Germany

1939
Rest of
Czechoslovakia
taken over by
Germany
Nazi-Soviet Pact
Hitler demanded
the Polish
Corridor
Germany
invaded Poland
World War II
began

1940 AD

1941
German invasion
of the Soviet
Union
Japanese bombing
of Pearl Harbor
World War II
expanded

1950 AD

Stepping Stones to Glory – Rearmament, Rhineland
Fortification, Danzig … Boss of the Universe

What is the message of this cartoon?

The Causes of World War II

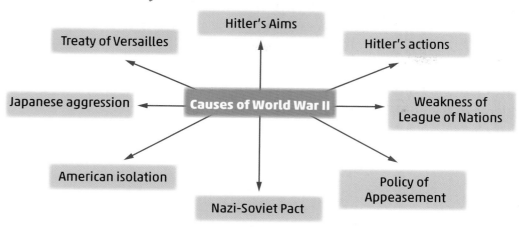

- Treaty of Versailles
- Hitler's Aims
- Hitler's actions
- Japanese aggression
- **Causes of World War II**
- Weakness of League of Nations
- American isolation
- Nazi-Soviet Pact
- Policy of Appeasement

@ Discuss the causes of World War II

Analysing Sources

What were the Causes of World War II?

The Treaty of Versailles 1919

After World War I, Germany was forced to sign the **Treaty of Versailles** with the victorious Allies, Britain, France and America. Germans **resented** (disliked) the terms of the Treaty.

HISTORICAL JUDGEMENTS

 p. 155

Source 1

Terms of the Treaty of Versailles

- Germany had to sign a 'war guilt clause', acknowledging that it caused World War I.
- Germany had to pay compensation (**reparations**) to the Allies.
- The German army could not enter the Rhineland (**demilitarised**).
- Part of Germany was cut-off from the main country by the **Polish Corridor**.
- The German armed forces were **reduced**.
- Germany was **prevented** from uniting with Austria.

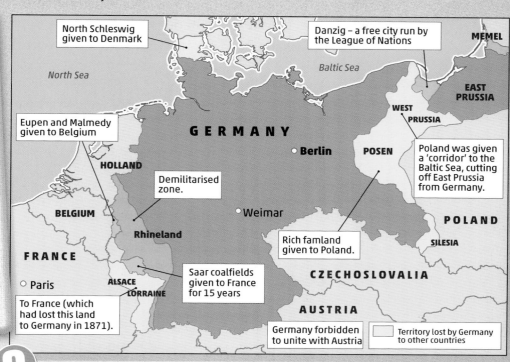

- North Schleswig given to Denmark
- Danzig – a free city run by the League of Nations
- MEMEL
- North Sea
- Baltic Sea
- EAST PRUSSIA
- WEST PRUSSIA
- Eupen and Malmedy given to Belgium
- **GERMANY**
- Berlin
- POSEN
- Poland was given a 'corridor' to the Baltic Sea, cutting off East Prussia from Germany.
- HOLLAND
- Demilitarised zone.
- Weimar
- POLAND
- BELGIUM
- Rhineland
- Rich famland given to Poland.
- SILESIA
- FRANCE
- CZECHOSLOVAKIA
- Paris
- ALSACE LORRAINE
- Saar coalfields given to France for 15 years
- To France (which had lost this land to Germany in 1871).
- AUSTRIA
- Germany forbidden to unite with Austria
- Territory lost by Germany to other countries

Q

Why did the Germans resent (dislike) the terms of the Treaty of Versailles?

Hitler's aims in foreign policy

Hitler wanted to make Germany **great** again. He wanted to use his foreign policy to expand German power. But his aims in foreign policy were bound to disturb the peace of Europe.

The **Nazi Party Programme** (1920) said:

- We demand the union of all Germans to form a **Greater Germany** (Grossdeutchland)
- We demand the **abolition** of the **Treaty of Versailles**
- We **demand land** for settling our surplus population (**lebensraum**) [in Eastern Europe and the Soviet Union]

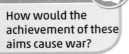

How would the achievement of these aims cause war?

Hitler's actions – destroying the Treaty of Versailles

Hitler set about destroying the Treaty of Versailles once he had achieved full power in Germany. He began **rearmament**, which broke the Treaty of Versailles (1935). Then. he sent the German army into the **Rhineland** (remilitatisation) (1936). He **supported** Mussolini (Italy) in his invasion of Abyssinia (1936). Then, Hitler united Germany and Austria (**Anschluss**) in 1938.

The Munich Conference, 1938

Next, he laid claim to the German-speaking section of Czechoslovakia, the **Sudetenland**. When the Czech government refused to hand it over, the **Munich Conference** (1938) was held to sort out the difficulty. Other European leaders, **Chamberlain** of Britain, **Daladier** of France and **Mussolini** met with Hitler. They **excluded** the Czech government and **Stalin's Soviet Union** from their meeting. They agreed to force Czechoslovakia to **hand over** the Sudetenland to Germany. Chamberlain returned home to Britain claiming that he had achieved 'peace in our time'.

However, six months later in 1939, Hitler took over the **rest of Czechoslovakia**.

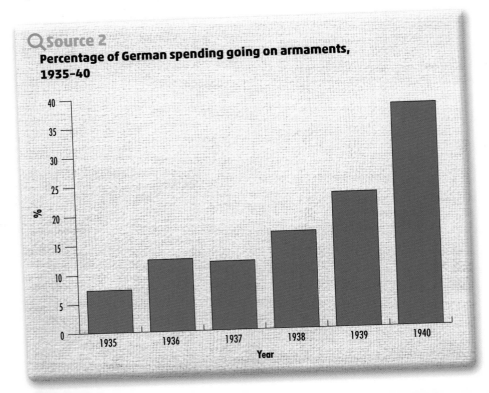

Source 2

Percentage of German spending going on armaments, 1935–40

Source 3
German Rearmament

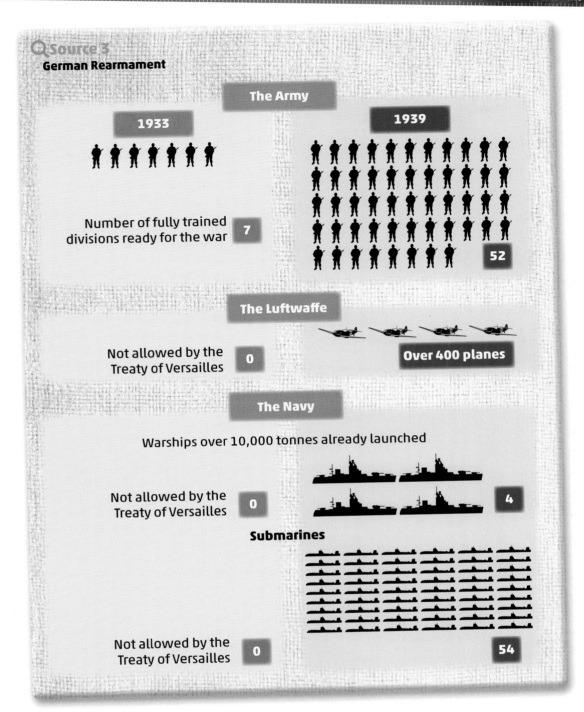

The Army

1933 | 1939

Number of fully trained divisions ready for the war `7` `52`

The Luftwaffe

Not allowed by the Treaty of Versailles `0` **Over 400 planes**

The Navy

Warships over 10,000 tonnes already launched

Not allowed by the Treaty of Versailles `0` `4`

Submarines

Not allowed by the Treaty of Versailles `0` `54`

Source 4
Hitler speaking in a private conversation in 1936
German and Italian rearmament is proceeding more rapidly than rearmament can in England. In three years Germany will be ready.

1. How did German rearmament break the Treaty of Versailles?
2. How did German rearmament contribute to causing World War II?
   Refer to Sources 2, 3 and 4 in your answers.

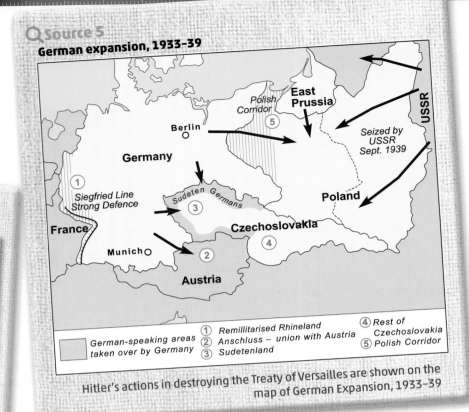

East Prussia

Polish Corridor

USSR

Berlin

Germany

Seized by USSR Sept. 1939

Siegfried Line Strong Defence

Sudeten Germans

France

Poland

Czechoslovakia

Munich

Austria

German-speaking areas taken over by Germany

① Remilllitarised Rhineland
② Anschluss – union with Austria
③ Sudetenland
④ Rest of Czechoslovakia
⑤ Polish Corridor

Hitler's actions in destroying the Treaty of Versailles are shown on the map of German Expansion, 1933–39

Q

1. Where did Germany **expand** in the 1930s according to Source 5?
2. Select the actions in the Timeline (p. 284) which **match** the actions of Hitler in 1 to 5 in the map.
3. How did those actions **contribute to the causes** of World War II?

Source 6
Remilitarising the Rhineland, 1936

THE GOOSE-STEP

"GOOSEY GOOSEY GANDER,
WHITHER DOST THOU WANDER?"
"ONLY THROUGH THE RHINELAND—
PRAY EXCUSE MY BLUNDER!"

British cartoon, 1936

Q

1. What is the **message** of this cartoon?
2. Does it agree with Hitler's actions in the Rhineland?
3. How was **remilitarising** the Rhineland **another step** towards causing the war?

Q

1. Is this newspaper happy with the Munich agreement?
2. In 'Never to Go To War Again', what did Chamberlain and Hitler agree about sorting out any future disagreements between the two countries?
3. What, do you think, about Chamberlain's views?

Source 7
Peace in Our Time

The Munich Conference, 1938

The **Munich Conference** was held to sort out disagreement over the **Sudetenland**, which was part of Czechoslovakia. The Czech government refused Hitler's demand for this **German-speaking province**. So Hitler threatened war. Four leaders – **Hitler, Chamberlain, Daladier** and **Mussolini** – met in **Munich**. They agreed to force Czechoslovakia to hand over the Sudetenland to Germany.

Weakness of the League of Nations

The League of Nations was set up after World War I

- to promote international **co-operation** and
- to achieve international **peace**.

But the League of Nations **failed** to stop Hitler, Japan or Mussolini. The League had a number of **weaknesses**.

- America did **not join** the League
- Decisions of the League had to be **unanimous** (all agree) so it was often difficult for the League to agree on what to do
- The League had **no army** to enforce its decisions. It relied on **economic sanctions** (block trade).

Q Source 9

The Invasion of Abyssinia, 1935

Mussolini, leader of fascist Italy, wanted to create a great Italian empire. He invaded **Abyssinia** (Ethiopia) in 1935 and easily defeated the badly armed native tribesmen. He was criticised by the **League of Nations** but the League failed to take effective action against him. On the other hand, **Hitler** supported him.

THE AWFUL WARNING.

FRANCE AND ENGLAND *(together ?)*. { "WE DON'T WANT YOU TO FIGHT, BUT, BY JINGO, IF YOU DO, WE SHALL PROBABLY ISSUE A JOINT MEMORANDUM SUGGESTING A MILD DISAPPROVAL OF YOU."

British cartoon after the Italian invasion of Abyssinia, featuring Mussolini, the Italian fascist leader

Q Source 8

The Manchurian Crisis, 1931–33

Japan invaded Manchuria, in Northern China, in 1931. The **League of Nations** failed to agree on economic sanctions for Japan. Japan withdrew from the League and continued to occupy Manchuria. Later, the Japanese took over much of China.

Der Krieg im fernen Often

Japan besetzt die Mandschurei.

Japan siegt am Nonnifluß

Der Völkerbund greift ein

Japan räumt die Mandschurei! — —

German cartoon on Japanese invasion of Manchuria (1936): Japan plants a flag in Manchuria; Japanese soldier bayonets Manchurian man; League of Nations send note to Japan; Japan conquers Manchuria

Q

1. What is the **message** of the cartoon in Source 8?
2. How did the Manchurian Crisis show up the **weaknesses** of the League of Nations?

Q

1. Can you **identify** Britain and France in the cartoon in Source 9?
2. Does the cartoonist believe that Britain and France (the two main powers in the League of Nations) will take action against Mussolini and Italy over his invasion of Abyssinia?
3. What lessons could be learnt by Germany and Japan from the way the Manchurian and Abyssinian Crises were handled? How did the League's **handling** of those crises **contribute to the causes** of World War II?
   Explain your answers by using evidence from the cartoon.

Policy of Appeasement

Why did Chamberlain favour a policy of appeasement?

Britain and France gave into Hitler's demands because they followed a **policy of appeasement**. They believed that if they gave into Hitler's demands, they would prevent war. Instead, Hitler saw this as a sign of **weakness** so he continued to make **more demands**. However, the policy also allowed Britain **to begin rearmament** so that by 1939 Britain was better prepared for war than it had been a few years earlier.

Q Source 10

When I think of those four terrible years (1914–18) and I think of the seven million men who were cut down in their prime ... then I am bound to say in war there are no winners, but all are losers. It is those thoughts that have made me strain every nerve to avoid a repetition of the Great War (World War I) in Europe.

(Neville Chamberlain, Prime Minister of Britain, speaking before the Munich Conference, 1938)

Q Source 11

British cartoon, 1938, after the Munich Conference: 'Europe can look forward to a Christmas of Peace.' (Hitler)

*Deutschland Uber Alles – Germany Above All

1. Who is Santa Claus in Source 11?
2. Who do the children represent?
3. What is the **message** of this cartoon?
4. Does the cartoonist agree with the policy of appeasement?
5. Is the cartoonist **biased**?
   Explain your answers by referring to evidence in the cartoon.

p.160

Analysing a cartoon
www.johndclare.net/RoadtoWWII3_ppt2.pps

1. Does this cartoon agree with Chamberlain (Source 10) or the cartoon in Source 11?
2. How did the policy of appeasement contribute to causing World War II?

Q Source 12

A Swiss cartoon (1938) shows Hitler as the giant, Gulliver, surrounded by other political leaders, British (front right), French (front left), League of Nations (centre left)

Nazi-Soviet Pact, 1939

Nazis and Communists were **bitter enemies**. But Hitler and Stalin, the leader of the Soviet Union, did not want to fight each other yet. So they signed the **Nazi-Soviet Pact** in 1939.

- They agreed to a **ten-year non-aggression pact** (they agreed not to attack each other)
- They also secretly agreed to **divide Poland** between them

The pact meant that Hitler could attack Poland without having to fight the Soviet Union. It also meant that Stalin could prepare for a future war with Hitler.

Source 13

Soviet cartoon (1939): Chamberlain (Britain) and Daladier (France) direct Hitler away from their own countries towards the USSR (CCCP)

Source 14

Does the cartoon in Source 13 **explain why** Stalin and the Soviet Union made a pact with Hitler?

The Polish Corridor

The **Polish Corridor** separated Germany from one of its provinces, East Prussia. Hitler demanded the return of the **Polish Corridor** but the Polish government refused. Britain and France supported Poland. However, Hitler believed they were too far away and would not be able to help Poland. He **declared war** on Poland on **1 September 1939**.

1. What **symbols** are used in the cartoon in Source 14?
2. Does this cartoon expect that Germany and the Soviet Union will still go to war in spite of the Nazi-Soviet Pact?
3. How did the Nazi-Soviet Pact **contribute** to the causes of World War II?

Supreme Commander of the Armed Forces Most Secret Directive No. 1 for the Conduct of War

Now that all the political possibilities of disposing by peaceful means of a situation on the Eastern frontier (border), which is intolerable for Germany, are exhausted, I have decided on a solution by force.

Date of attack: 1 September 1939

Time of attack: 4.45 a.m.

Japanese aggression in the East

Japan **expanded** into China in the 1930s. The League of Nations **failed** to stop Japanese expansion. The Japanese also expanded into Indo-China (Vietnam). This brought it into conflict with America, which imposed **economic sanctions** on Japan. The Japanese decided they needed to destroy the strong **US Pacific Fleet** based in Hawaii. The Japanese attacked **Pearl Harbor** in December 1941. **This brought America into World War II.**

Q Source 15
Japanese aggression

Japan needed coal, oil, iron and other raw materials for her expanding industries

Japan's population of 70 million was growing but there was not enough land

Japan's government was controlled by the armed forces; they wanted to expand into mainland Asia

Japan took over other areas of China in later 1930s

Japanese aggression

Japan took over Manchuria in 1931–32

Japan needed more markets to sell her products

Q

1. Why did Japan want to expand its territory in the 1930s?
2. How did Japanese expansion contribute to the causes of World War II?

American isolation

America did **not join** the League of Nations after World War I. The country stayed **isolated** from conflicts around the world, even though America was the most powerful country in the world at that time. In this way, America hoped to avoid another world war.

However, America was **forced to take action** because of **Japanese expansion in Asia.**

Q

Does Source 16 explain **why** Germany declared war on the US?

Q Source 16
America is a decayed country. I like an Englishman a thousand times better than an American. Everything about the behaviour of American society reveals that it is half Jew, and the other half negro. How can one expect a state like that to hold together – a country where everything is built on the dollar.
(Hitler's views on America before the war)

INVESTIGATING A REPOSITORY OF HISTORICAL EVIDENCE FOR THE CAUSES OF WORLD WAR II

The Road to World War II,
Go onto www.johndclare.net and click on 'Road to WWII'.
Was Hitler a passionate lunatic?
Go onto www.nationalarchives.gov.uk and click on 'Education', then 'Second World War 1393-1945',
then 'Adolf Hitler'.

》 Preparing for CBA2

A project on the life and experience of a person of historical interest

PERSONS OF INTEREST IN THE CAUSES OF WORLD WAR II

- Adolf Hitler
- Franklin D. Roosevelt
- Neville Chamberlain
- Emperor Hirohito
- Benito Mussolini

《 p. 156
Web Resources
and Reading

Focus Task

Summarise

> Draw up a table in a page of your copybook with the heading **The Causes of World War II**. Fill in the information in short note form opposite each of the categories to **explain how each of the factors contributed to causing World War II**. Refer to the sources in support of your conclusions.

HISTORICAL
JUDGEMENT

The Causes of World War II	
Treaty of Versailles	
Hitler's aims	
Hitler's actions	
League of Nations	
Policy of Appeasement	
Nazi-Soviet Pact	
Japanese aggression	
American isolation	

Go onto YouTube
and look up '20th
Century History File
Why Appeasement'.

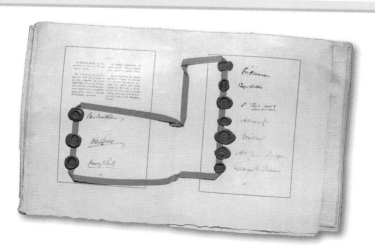

The Treaty of Versailles

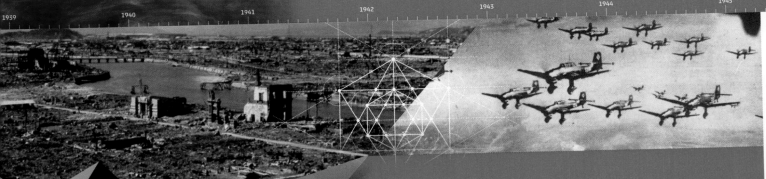

WORLD WAR II, 1939–45
– Course and Impact

19

L.O. 3.4; 3.14
The Nature of History: 1.1, 1.2, 1.3, 1.4, 1.5, 1.6, 1.7, 1.8, 1.9, 1.10, 1.11.
CBA2

You will learn to ...

- Discuss the course of World War II
- Discuss the immediate and long-term impact of the war on people and nations
- Explore the Nature of History
- Explore the contribution of technology to historical change

CHRONOLOGICAL AWARENESS

1939 AD
1939
Nazi-Soviet Pact
Germany invaded Poland
World War II began

1940 AD
1940
The Invasion of France
The Battle of Britain

1941 AD
1941
German invasion of Soviet Union
America entered the war

1942 AD
1942
The Battle of Midway
The Battle of Stalingrad

1943 AD

1944 AD
1944
D-Day

1945
VE-Day
VJ-Day
1945 AD World War II ended

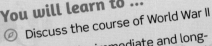

KEY WORDS

- Blitzkrieg
- Radar
- Scorched earth
- Phoney War
- Blitz
- D-Day
- Evacuation
- Turning point
- Atomic bomb

Q

What role did bombers play in World War II?

German Victories, 1939–42

The invasion of Poland, 1939

On 31 August 1939, members of the **German SS** dressed in Polish army uniforms attacked a German radio station. Hitler used this as an **excuse** and invaded Poland on 1 September 1939. Two days later, Britain and France declared war on Germany. **World War II had begun.**

⊘ Discuss the progress and reasons for German victories, 1939–42

Blitzkrieg in Poland

The German army used new war tactics against Poland, which led to a quick victory. These tactics, called **blitzkrieg**, or 'lightning war', were later used against France and Russia. Their success depended on speed and surprise, and Poland was defeated in five weeks.

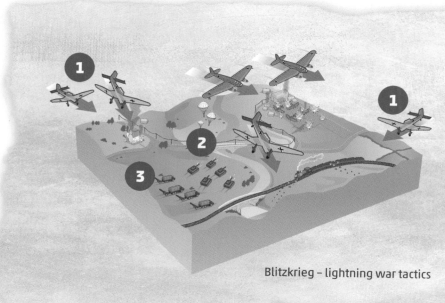

Blitzkrieg – lightning war tactics

1. **German air force (Luftwaffe) bombers** destroyed most of the Polish air force while it was still on the ground. German bombers also destroyed roads, railways and bridges.

2. **German panzer (tank) divisions** moved quickly into Poland, bypassing towns and cities and cutting off the Polish army from its supplies.

3. **Motorised German infantry** defeated the weakened Polish army. When Poland was largely defeated, the Soviet Union invaded from the east. Germany and the Soviet Union **divided the country** between them as they had secretly agreed to do in the **Nazi-Soviet Pact of 1939.**

The Phoney War

Many people expected the fighting to continue, but instead came the **Phoney War** – a period over the winter of 1939–40 when enemy troops faced each other across the Franco-German border but did not fight. Instead, Germany, Britain and France were getting ready for the next round of war.

Norway and Denmark conquered

Hitler moved next to conquer Denmark and Norway. He wanted to ensure that the German **iron ore supply**, which came through Norway from Sweden, was secure for the rest of the war.

In April 1940, Hitler and his army overran **Denmark** in one day. At the same time, a German invasion fleet landed at **ports** along the Norwegian coast. German **paratroopers** were also dropped to control bridges, airports and radio stations. Within a short time, Norway was captured, and Vidkun **Quisling**, a Norwegian sympathetic to Hitler, was made Minister President of Norway.

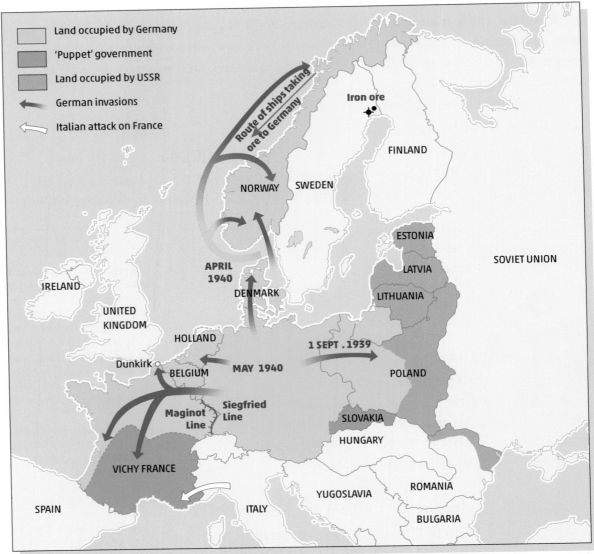

Hitler's conquests, 1939–40

The invasion of France, 1940

On 10 May 1940, Hitler began his attack on France. He again used **blitzkrieg tactics** of control of the air, rapid tank movement and infantry mopping up. He caught the French and British by **surprise**, as German tank divisions advanced quickly through the **Ardennes Mountains** in Luxembourg. They cut off French and British troops who had invaded Belgium. The defeated armies were pushed back to **Dunkirk** on the English Channel.

Dunkirk

At this point, Hitler ordered his troops to halt and this gave the British and French time to organise the mass evacuation of troops from Dunkirk. In **Operation Dynamo**, Britain sent all available boats – naval vessels, tug boats, even paddle steamers – to

As the Russians retreated, they used a **scorched earth policy**. They destroyed crops and communication lines so that the Germans could not use them.

Then Hitler's early progress was halted by the **Russian winter** of 1941–42. Lorries, tanks and aeroplanes seized up, and soldiers froze to death on duty. The Germans captured **Kiev**, but failed to capture Moscow and Leningrad.

The Battle of Stalingrad: A turning point

In 1942, Hitler's armies advanced towards **Stalingrad** and the **oil fields** of the Caucasus. Their advance was stopped at the **Battle of Stalingrad**. The German army, under **von Paulus**, fought vicious street battles with the Russian army defending the city. Stalin insisted the city must not be lost.

The Russians then attacked from the sides in a **pincer movement** and cut off the German army in the city from their supplies. Hitler continued to supply them with **airdrops**, but the army suffered greatly in

Joseph Stalin, Soviet leader

A female Soviet sniper

Go onto YouTube and look up 'A German soldier who took part in Operation Barbarossa'.

the freezing winter of 1942–43. Eventually, over 100,000 German soldiers were forced to surrender in February 1943. The German defeat at the Battle of Stalingrad was **another major turning point in the war.**

America joined the war

Events in the **Far East** caused the United States to join the war. Japan wanted to create its own empire and relations between America and Japan worsened in the 1930s. In December 1941, Japan attacked **Pearl Harbor** in Hawaii, where the American **Pacific fleet** was based. Fortunately, for America, the main part of the fleet was at sea when the attack occurred.

Soon after **Hitler declared war** on America as part of an agreement with Japan. The US entry into the war was **another major turning point.**

US President Roosevelt

Damage at Pearl Harbor

The war at sea: The Battle of the Atlantic

Even before America entered the war, the country provided supplies of food, military goods and industrial products to Britain. In the words of the American President, **Roosevelt**, America became the **'arsenal of democracy'**.

All the supplies came to Britain across the Atlantic Ocean, so Germany used its submarines (**U-boats**) to sink Allied shipping. Fleets of U-boats, called **wolfpacks**, left the French and Norwegian coasts and raided Allied **convoys** crossing the sea. In 1942, U-boats sank 6 million tons of shipping, and thousands of sailors lost their lives.

The **Allies defeated the U-boat threat** by:

- Increased shipbuilding
- Use of air reconnaissance, radar, sonar and depth charges
- Use of **Ultra**, the code-breaking operation, which provided information to direct **convoys** away from the paths of wolfpacks.

U-boat

War in the air

The Americans and British organised **bombing raids on Germany**. Their targets were large German cities such as **Hamburg** and **Berlin**, and the industrial cities of the **Ruhr**. American **Flying Fortresses** and British **Lancaster bombers** raided Germany by day and night. Even though the bombing failed to destroy German morale (spirit), war production was disrupted.

Germany tried to counter-attack by using **V1 flying bombs** and **V2 rockets** to bomb British cites. However, they came into use too late in the war to have a great effect.

Nazi-controlled Europe

Most of the continent of Europe had been conquered by Germany and its allies by 1942. The **SS** and the **Gestapo** (secret police) enforced Nazi rule. More than 7.5 million foreign workers were used as **slave labour** to keep the German economy going during the war. As the German army swept across Europe, millions of **Jews**, especially in Eastern Europe, came under Nazi rule. Hitler's plan – the **Final Solution** – was to kill all Jews. By 1945, 6 million Jews were killed by the Nazis in the **Holocaust** (see Ch. 20). In spite of harsh Nazi control, there was **active resistance** to Hitler, through spying, sabotage and ambushes.

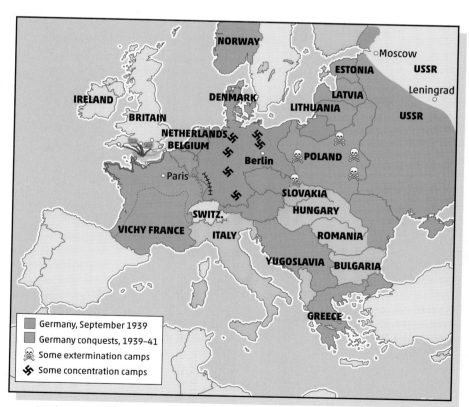

Nazi-controlled Europe: Most of the continent of Europe had been conquered by Germany and its allies by 1942

The Allies Advance, 1942–45

The Allies advanced on Germany from **different directions**.

- In the **South**, British and American troops invaded Sicily and then moved on to mainland Italy. They gradually fought their way up along the mountainous peninsula. Fighters in the Italian resistance (**partisans**) captured **Mussolini** and killed him.

- In the **east**, after victory of the Battle of Stalingrad, the Soviet army continued to push the Germans back. The Russians won the **Battle of Kursk**, the largest tank battle in the war, and advanced as FAR as Warsaw by the end of 1944. They refused help to the Polish Resistance in the **Warsaw Uprising**, and the Poles were brutally crushed by the German army.

D-Day, June 1944

Stalin demanded that the Allies open a **second front** in the west. America and Britain went ahead with **Operation Overlord** – the invasion of the continent of Europe on **D-Day, 6 June 1944.**

The Soviet army advanced on Germany from the east and the American and British armies from the west, and up through Italy

Go onto YouTube and look up 'Miss Stout's History Class, D-Day Landings'.

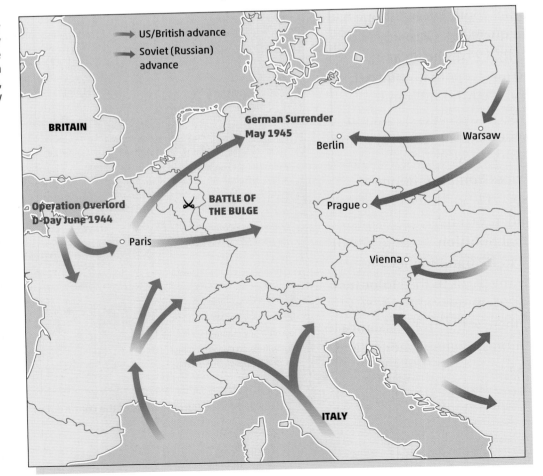

The Allies selected France's **Normandy coast** for their invasion because of its beaches, shallow water and closeness to Britain. They surprised the Germans who expected an attack over the shorter sea route from Britain to Calais.

On 6 June General **Eisenhower**, the commander of the D-Day operations, gave the order to attack

- Thousands of Allied planes bombed the German defences – part of Hitler's **Atlantic Wall**
- **Paratroopers** were dropped behind enemy lines
- 130,000 soldiers were landed on five beaches by warships and landing craft – **Utah**, **Omaha**, **Gold**, **Juno and Sword**.

Allied troops advanced up the beaches at a cost of about 4,000 dead on the first day against about 1,000 Germans killed. They established **beachheads** so that thousands more troops could be brought in to continue into France.

Later, Allied troops set up **artificial harbours** (called **mulberry piers**) to bring in tanks and trucks, and they built a **pipeline under the ocean** (Pluto) to supply oil.

The Allies then advanced across northern France to Paris. The British and Americans suffered a setback at the **Battle of the Bulge** in Luxembourg. But the German advance there was quickly halted.

General Eisenhower, commander of D-Day operatives

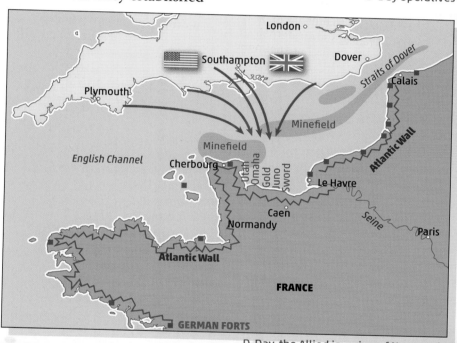

D-Day, the Allied invasion of Normandy

Analysing Sources

The bombing of Dresden

On 13–14 February 1945, the Allies bombed the city of Dresden, in Germany. In three waves of attacks, 3,300 bombs were dropped on the city. The bombing created a firestorm, and about 25,000 people were killed, though there were some claims that up to 250,000 people were killed.

Source 1

Dresden, the seventh largest city in Germany and not much smaller than Manchester, is also by far the largest unbombed built-up city the enemy has got. In the midst of winter, with refugees pouring westwards and troops to be rested, roofs are at a premium. The intentions of the attack are to hit the enemy where he will feel it most, behind an already partially collapsed front, to prevent the use of the city in the way of further advance, and incidentally to show the Russians when they arrive what Bomber Command can do.

(RAF report, January 1945)

Source 2

We bombed Dresden because it was a prime target that night. We were called during the day by the Russians, who particularly called for a raid on Dresden. There were something like 80,000 (German troops) at the time on their way to the Russian front, less than a hundred miles away. So at short notice, we were put on to Dresden, which was bombed perfectly normally. The fact that it caught fire rather easily was the Germans' fault. They had no air-raid precautions and they didn't believe in building anything other than wooden residences in Dresden. They also happened to have the German civil service in Dresden. They'd moved them out of Berlin for safety – so we did some heavy bombing.

(British Air Vice-Marshal Donald Bennett (RAF), speaking after the war)

Source 3

Before the 13 February, there had not been any air activity over Dresden. It was considered a safe city and we believed that culture-loving people would never destroy a jewel like Dresden. At about half past nine [all] hell broke loose. It was like looking into a huge burning oven ... flames flicked all round us. There were bodies everywhere and the gasmasks that people were wearing were melting into their faces. In every cellar we looked into, we saw people sitting dead because the fires had sucked the oxygen out and suffocated them. I looked around and saw the whole city in ruins.

(Karin Busch, a German schoolgirl, from Max Arthur, *Forgotten Voices of the Second World War* [2004])

1. Why did the RAF plan to bomb Dresden, according to Source 1?
2. Why did the RAF bomb Dresden, according to Source 2?
3. When did the RAF decide to bomb Dresden, according to Source 2?
4. What is the **conflict** between the **evidence** in Source 1 and Source 2?
5. Which is more **reliable**, Source 1 or 2?
6. What were the **effects** of the bombing, based on Sources 3 and 4?
7. Does the **evidence** in Source 4 explain the effects in Source 3?
8. Are these sources **primary** or **secondary**?
9. How **useful** are these sources for researching the bombing of Dresden?
   Explain your answers by using evidence from the sources.

Source 4

Hitler's suicide

As the Russians advanced from the east and the Americans and British from the west, Hitler was trapped in his **bunker** in Berlin. He and his wife, **Eva Braun**, and close followers, including **Goebbels**, committed suicide in April 1945. Early the next month Germany surrendered unconditionally. The war in Europe was over and **VE (Victory in Europe) Day** was celebrated on 8 May 1945.

The war in the Far East

Japan had been at war off-and-on since it invaded **Manchuria** in 1931. Japan invaded the **rest of China** in 1937. Then in 1941, Japan invaded **Indo-China** and prepared to attack the East Indies and the Philippine Islands.

Celebrating VE Day in London

As Britain and America imposed sanctions on Japan, the country suddenly attacked the American naval base at **Pearl Harbor** in Hawaii in December 1941, and advanced on the British naval base in **Singapore**. Germany and Italy also declared war on America. The war which began in Europe was now widened into a **global war**.

Within a short time, the Japanese advanced rapidly and conquered a huge area of the Pacific Ocean (see map of Japanese expansion).

Japanese Expansion 1941–42

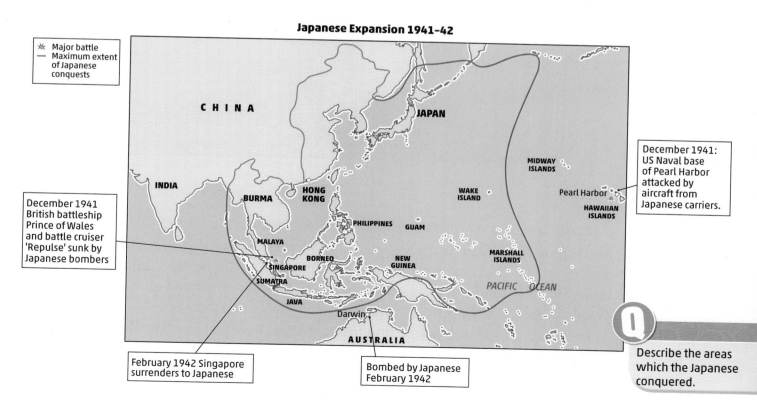

✳ Major battle
— Maximum extent of Japanese conquests

December 1941 British battleship Prince of Wales and battle cruiser 'Repulse' sunk by Japanese bombers

December 1941: US Naval base of Pearl Harbor attacked by aircraft from Japanese carriers.

February 1942 Singapore surrenders to Japanese

Bombed by Japanese February 1942

Q Describe the areas which the Japanese conquered.

Turning point in the Pacific War

In June 1942, the US navy defeated the Japanese navy in the **Battle of Midway**. This halted the Japanese expansion in the Pacific. Now the Americans began the process of driving out the Japanese from the Pacific islands which they had conquered.

Japanese resistance

The Japanese **resisted fiercely** American advances in the Pacific, and British, Chinese and Soviet advances in mainland Asia. The British drove the Japanese back in **Burma**, while the Chinese pushed the Japanese out of areas in **China**. The Soviets advanced in **Manchuria**.

The Americans came up against great resistance as they advanced through the islands of the Pacific. In the **Battle of Iwo Jima**, in 1945, the Americans had to root out Japanese defenders who used a network of caves, tunnels and dugouts to resist the attack. Only 1,000 Japanese soldiers survived out of 23,000 defenders.

Flag raising at Iwo Jima

Atomic bombs on Hiroshima and Nagasaki

Go onto YouTube and look up 20th Century History File 'Pearl Harbor to Hiroshima'.

As the Americans came nearer to Japan, they feared they would have to invade the country to force its surrender. This led to the decision to drop **atomic bombs** on **Hiroshima** first, and then **Nagasaki**. Both cities were destroyed and about 120,000 people were killed.

The terrible death and destruction forced the Japanese Emperor, **Hirohito**, to surrender on 15 August 1945. **VJ-Day** was celebrated in the streets of Britain and America, especially.

World War II was over.

Technology and Historical Change

The Discovery and Use of Nuclear Energy – Its Impact on Historical Change

◎ Explore the contribution of technological developments and innovation to historical change

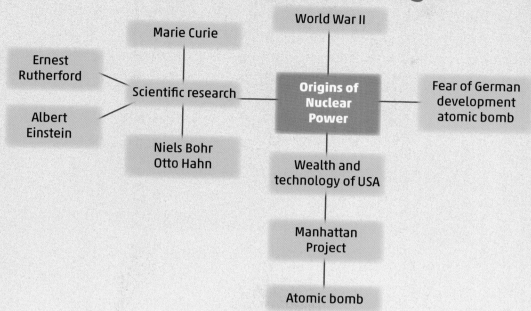

◀ p. 251 📝

The development of nuclear energy in the first half of the 20th century had a huge impact on **historical change** in the second half of the century.

The science of **nuclear technology** was developed between the end of the 19th century and the middle of the 20th century. Scientists such as William Roentgen, Henri Becquerel, Marie and Pierre Curie and Ernest Rutherford made discoveries which added to knowledge about nuclear energy. Some scientists showed how nuclear power could be developed by splitting atoms. Other scientists during the 1930s added to their ideas so that by 1938 Hahn and Strassmann in Germany had used nuclear fission to split atoms and release their energy.

These developments in nuclear energy or power had a huge effect on **historical change** during and after World War II.

CHRONOLOGICAL AWARENESS

Timeline of Nuclear Technology

1895	William Roentgen discovers X-rays
1898	The Curies use the term 'radioactive'
1911	Rutherford developed his ideas on the structure of the atom
1905	Albert Einstein published his theory of relativity, which states that mass can be changed into energy
1911	Radioactive tracers developed, later used for medicine
1938	Hann and Strassmann demonstrated nuclear fission in Germany
1942	Manhattan Project set up to develop nuclear or atomic bomb
1945	First atomic explosion in New Mexico
	Atomic bombs dropped on Hiroshima and Nagasaki
1952	First Hydrogen bomb developed
1954	First nuclear powered submarine, Nautillus, launched
	First nuclear power station operational in Soviet Union
1962	Cuban Missile Crisis
1979	Three Mile Island accident
1986	Chernobyl accident
2011	Fukushima incident

World War II

Most of the ideas about nuclear energy were developed in European countries. When World War II broke out in 1939, there were efforts in Britain and Germany to develop an atomic bomb. However, it took the wealth and technology of the USA after they entered the war in December 1941 to develop the first of those bombs. As part of the **Manhattan Project**, the USA used its best scientists and some from other countries to set off the first explosion of a nuclear bomb in the desert of New Mexico. The success of this experiment led to dropping the atomic bombs on **Hiroshima** and **Nagasaki** in Japan, in August 1945 (See p. 313).

(See p. 313)

1. Powder charge is fired
2. Powder charge sent uranium 'bullet' through gun barrel
3. The uranium 'bullet' crashed into larger amount of uranium, creating a nuclear chain reaction which exploded the bomb

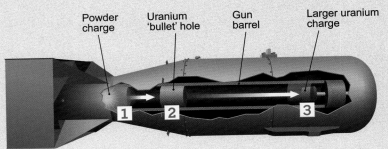

A cross-section of *Little Boy*, which was dropped on Hiroshima

The dropping of the bombs on Hiroshima and Nagasaki helped bring about the **end of World War II** in the East. They resulted in huge numbers of deaths in Japan, and vast destruction. But they also saved an unknown number of US and Allied lives, which would have been lost if they had been forced to invade Japan.

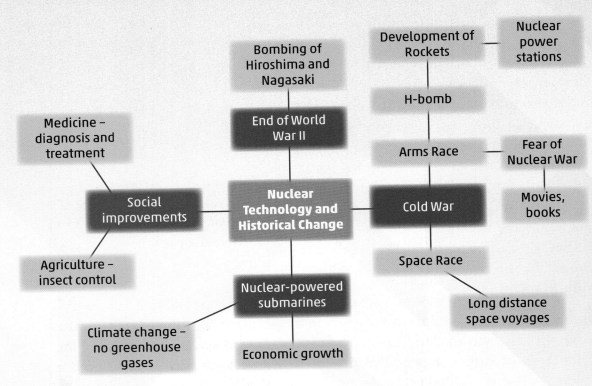

Cold War

The Cold War between the USA and the USSR developed after World War II (See Ch. 22). The danger of World War III breaking out and the use of nuclear weapons in such a war created great fear amongst the people in all countries that might be affected by such a war. This fear was added to by the development of the much more powerful **Hydrogen bomb** (H-bomb), and by huge InterContinental Ballistic Missiles (ICBMs), which would carry these bombs.

These fears came to a head in the **Cuban Missile Crisis**, which brought the world to the brink of war (See p. 351). As a result of this crisis, efforts were made to control the spread of nuclear power and to limit testing of nuclear weapons.

However, the existence of so-called 'rogue states', such as North Korea, in the 21st century has increased the danger of a nuclear war.

The fear of a nuclear war resulted in the establishment of the Campaign for Nuclear Disarmament (CND) in Britain in 1957. The CND organised the annual London to Aldermaston (location of Britain's atomic research establishment) march.

Peaceful use of nuclear energy

The peaceful use of nuclear energy also influenced historical change.

The first nuclear power station was built in Obninsk, in the Soviet Union in 1954. This was followed by others in the most powerful countries in the world – USA, Britain, France and China. The power stations contributed to the **economic growth** of the 1950s through to the 1970s.

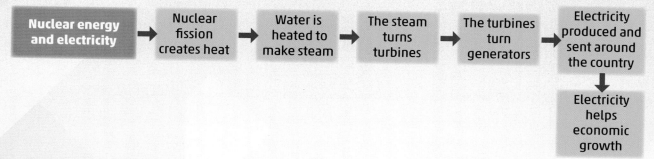

Two accidents slowed down the development of nuclear power stations. One was in **Three Mile Island**, Pennsylvania, USA, in 1979 – where the cooling system in one reactor broke down, leading to an escape of radioactive fallout. There were no deaths or injuries linked to the accident.

The second accident was an explosion in **Chernobyl** in the USSR in 1986 which resulted in a cloud of radioactive material falling in the area, with some of it drifting as far as Ireland and Scotland. Two Chernobyl plant workers died as a result of the accident, and a further 28 people died within a few weeks as a result of radioactive poisoning. About 100,000 people living within a 30-kilometre radius of Chernobyl were evacuated and relocated elsewhere.

The advent of climate change towards the end of the 20th century and during the 21st century led to a re-examination of the role of nuclear power stations. Since they do not produce greenhouse gases, they do not contribute to global warming.

However, a third accident in **Fukushima**, Japan, in 2011, caused by a tsunami and inadequate safety precautions led to further questions about the safety of nuclear power plants. Those favouring nuclear power argued instead that it had saved 1.8 million lives by offsetting air-pollution related deaths, which would have been caused by fossil fuels.

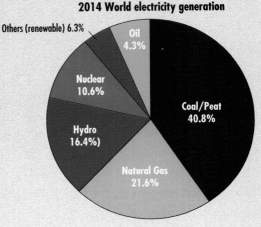

2014 World electricity generation

Others (renewable) 6.3%
Oil 4.3%
Nuclear 10.6%
Coal/Peat 40.8%
Hydro 16.4%)
Natural Gas 21.6%

Nuclear power makes a small but significant contribution to world electricity generation

Some countries, such as France, rely heavily on nuclear power to generate their electricity, largely because they have limited fossil-fuel sources, such as coal or oil

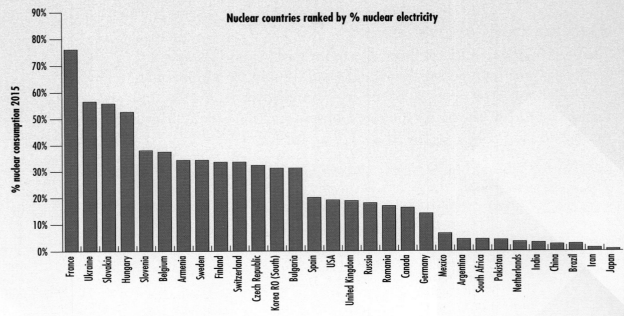

Nuclear countries ranked by % nuclear electricity

% nuclear consumption 2015

France, Ukraine, Slovakia, Hungary, Slovenia, Belgium, Armenia, Sweden, Finland, Switzerland, Czech Republic, Korea RO (South), Bulgaria, Spain, USA, United Kingdom, Russia, Romania, Canada, Germany, Mexico, Argentina, South Africa, Pakistan, Netherlands, India, China, Brazil, Iran, Japan

Social Improvements

Nuclear technology also influenced **medical improvements**. CT scans are used to **diagnose** injuries and illnesses, while radioactive substances are used to **treat** cancers. **Insect control** – using radiation to sterilise insects – has been used to contain the spread of viruses by mosquitoes, and to limit damage to crops.

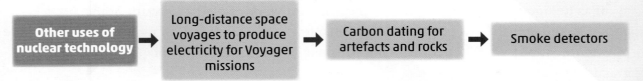

Other uses of nuclear technology → Long-distance space voyages to produce electricity for Voyager missions → Carbon dating for artefacts and rocks → Smoke detectors

Analysing Sources

Should the atomic bombs have been dropped on Hiroshima and Nagasaki?

HISTORICAL EMPATHY

The atomic bombs were triggered to explode about 600 metres above the ground. There was intense heat from the explosions. People directly below the bomb were immediately evaporated, leaving just their shadows burnt into the ground. Others further away became burnt corpses. Many of those that survived were badly burnt.

Source 1

Hiroshima after the atomic explosion, August 1945

Source 2
A victim of the Hiroshima explosion

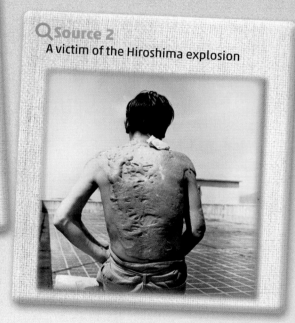

Source 3

The total strength of the Japanese army was estimated at about 5 million men. The air force or Kamikaze, or suicide attacks had already caused serious damage to our seagoing forces. There was a very strong possibility that the Japanese government might decide on resistance to the end. The Allies would have been faced with the enormous task of destroying an armed force of five million men and five thousand suicide aircraft. We estimated that if we were forced to carry this plan to its conclusion, the major fighting would not end until the latter part of 1946 at the earliest.

(Henry Stimson, the US Secretary of State for War in 1945, writing in 1947)

Source 4

The Americans dropped atom bombs on the Japanese cities of Hiroshima and Nagasaki killing hundreds of thousands of civilians. Officially the USA 'claimed' that the bombings were aimed at bringing the end of the war nearer and avoiding unnecessary casualties. But they had entirely different reasons. The purpose of the bombings was to intimidate other countries, above all the Soviet Union.

(Vadim Nekrasov, *The Roots of European Security* (1984), a Russian history book)

Source 5

On the first day of July (1945), Sato (the Japanese Ambassador in Moscow) sent a long message to Tokyo. He strongly advised accepting any terms. The response of the Japanese Cabinet (government) was that the war must be fought with all the energy that the nation was capable of so long as the only alternative was unconditional surrender.

(A Japanese telegram intercepted by US Intelligence in 1945)

Source 6

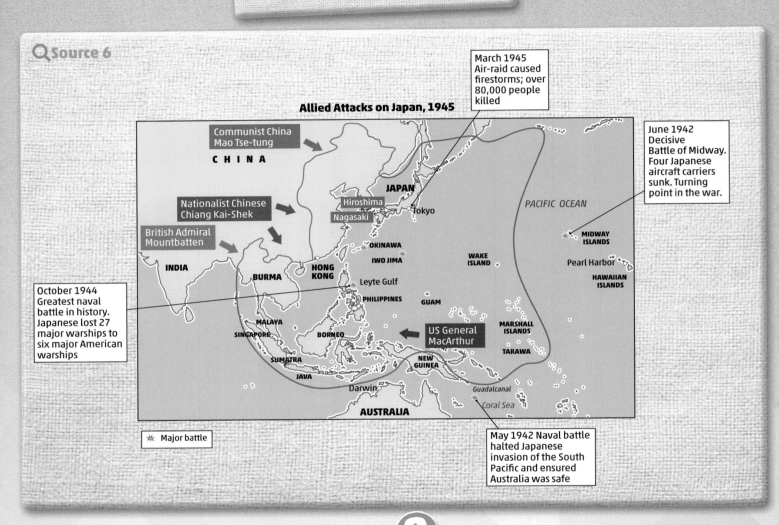

Allied Attacks on Japan, 1945

March 1945 Air-raid caused firestorms; over 80,000 people killed

June 1942 Decisive Battle of Midway. Four Japanese aircraft carriers sunk. Turning point in the war.

October 1944 Greatest naval battle in history. Japanese lost 27 major warships to six major American warships

May 1942 Naval battle halted Japanese invasion of the South Pacific and ensured Australia was safe

Communist China Mao Tse-tung
Nationalist Chinese Chiang Kai-Shek
British Admiral Mountbatten
US General MacArthur

CHINA — JAPAN — Hiroshima — Nagasaki — Tokyo — PACIFIC OCEAN — MIDWAY ISLANDS — Pearl Harbor — HAWAIIAN ISLANDS — OKINAWA — IWO JIMA — WAKE ISLAND — INDIA — BURMA — HONG KONG — Leyte Gulf — PHILIPPINES — GUAM — MARSHALL ISLANDS — MALAYA — SINGAPORE — BORNEO — TARAWA — SUMATRA — NEW GUINEA — JAVA — Darwin — Guadalcanal — Coral Sea — AUSTRALIA

✳ Major battle

Q

1. What do Sources 1 and 2 show about the **effects** of the bombing of Hiroshima?
2. **Why** did the US drop the atomic bomb, according to Source 3?
3. Does Source 4 agree with the reasons given in Source 3?
4. Which does the **evidence** in Sources 5 and 6 support – the reasons given in Sources 3 or 4?
5. Are the sources **primary** or **secondary**?
6. Are some of the sources more **reliable** than others?
7. Which side of the **argument** do you agree with – should the atomic bombs have been dropped on Hiroshima and Nagasaki or not? Explain your answers using evidence from the sources.

Why did the Allies win the war?

p. 172

1. Population and armies

The Allies had a **larger population** and **larger armies** than the Axis powers.
The Allied countries, including USA and the USSR, had a population of over one billion, whereas the Axis countries, including Japan, had a population of over 600 million. By 1945, the Allied armies numbered over 28 million soldiers, while the Axis powers had 15.5 million soldiers.

2. American wealth

America, 'the arsenal of democracy', produced 300,000 aircraft and 86,000 tanks. It gave $48 billion (€61 billion) in war supplies to Britain and $11 billion (€14 billion) to Russia.

3. Oil production

Hitler's territories produced just 60 million barrels of oil per year; the Allies produced 2,200 million barrels per year.
Japan had very little oil of its own. So it depended on oil in the countries it conquered. By 1945, it had little oil because it lost control of those countries.

4. Hitler's decisions

Hitler decided on the invasion of the Soviet Union to gain lebensraum but this was a mistake. Hitler also declared war on America when he need not have done so.

5. Winning the key battles

The Allies won the key battles that were **turning points in the war** – the Battle of Britain, El Alamein, Stalingrad in Europe, and Midway and Iwo Jima in the Pacific. The invasion of Europe – D-Day – was a success. The dropping of the atomic bombs ended the war with Japan.

6. Winning the War at Sea

The Allies won the **War at Sea** in the Atlantic, which kept the shipping lanes open and brought men and supplies from the Commonwealth and from America to Britain. The American Pacific fleet dominated the Pacific Ocean.

7. Winning the War in the Air

The Allies won the **War in the Air**, in which German and Japanese factories, railways, roads and cities were bombed.

What was the Impact of World War II?

Economic revival

Destruction

Refugees

Short-term impact of WWII

Death

War Crime Trials

Long-term impact of WWII

Fate of Germany

United Nations

Fate of Japan

End of European Supremacy

Growth of Superpowers

Cold War

Towards European Unity

Short-term impact

Deaths and injuries

NUMERACY

p.174

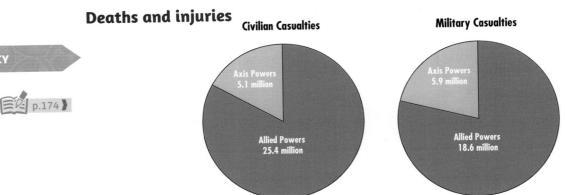

Civilian Casualties

Axis Powers 5.1 million

Allied Powers 25.4 million

Military Casualties

Axis Powers 5.9 million

Allied Powers 18.6 million

Civilian casualties

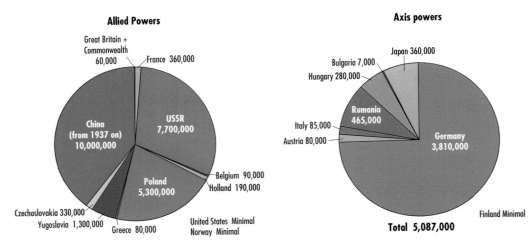

Allied Powers

Great Britain + Commonwealth 60,000

France 360,000

China (from 1937 on) 10,000,000

USSR 7,700,000

Poland 5,300,000

Belgium 90,000
Holland 190,000

Czechoslovakia 330,000
Yugoslavia 1,300,000

Greece 80,000

United States Minimal
Norway Minimal

Total 25,410,000

Axis powers

Japan 360,000

Bulgaria 7,000
Hungary 280,000

Rumania 465,000

Italy 85,000

Austria 80,000

Germany 3,810,000

Finland Minimal

Total 5,087,000

Military casualties

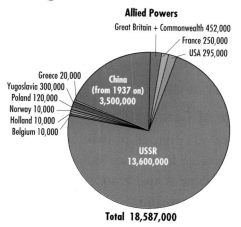

Allied Powers

Great Britain + Commonwealth 452,000
France 250,000
USA 295,000
Greece 20,000
Yugoslavia 300,000
Poland 120,000
Norway 10,000
Holland 10,000
Belgium 10,000
China (from 1937 on) 3,500,000
USSR 13,600,000

Total 18,587,000

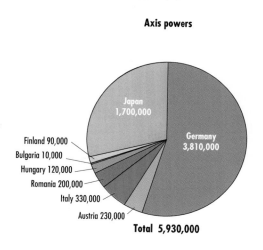

Axis powers

Japan 1,700,000
Germany 3,810,000
Finland 90,000
Bulgaria 10,000
Hungary 120,000
Romania 200,000
Italy 330,000
Austria 230,000

Total 5,930,000

> **Q**
> 1. Which countries suffered the highest number of civilian casualties?
> 2. Which countries suffered the highest number of military casualties?
> 3. What explanations can you give for your answers to (1) and (2)?

Destruction and economic revival

Cities, industries, roads, railways and harbours were destroyed throughout Europe and the Far East. After the war, the American Government provided **Marshall Aid** to help **European governments** rebuild their countries.

The Americans controlled **Japan** after the war. They introduced economic policies, which benefitted the Japanese economy. The economy also benefitted from the outbreak of the **Korean War** in 1950, when Japan became the main supplier to America.

Refugees

There was huge **movement of people** after the war was over.

- By 1950, about 11.5 million Germans were either expelled or left voluntarily from countries in Eastern Europe.
- **Jews** leaving the concentration camps found that their properties were taken over by others. Many had to live in camps until they were able to move to Israel in the late 1940s.
- Two million **Poles** had to leave Polish territory given to the Soviet Union. Other nationalities were also on the move, many trying to leave Eastern Europe as the Soviet Union began to take control of their countries.

German refugees migrating after World War II

War Crimes Trials

War Crimes Trials were held in many countries after the war. The most significant trials occurred in **Nuremberg**, where high-ranking Nazi leaders were tried and some of them

Goering (to the far left) and other Nazi leaders at the Nuremberg Trials

executed. Japanese leaders were tried for war crimes in **Tokyo**. Some of those also were executed, and others were imprisoned.

Long-term impact

The fate of Germany

Germany was divided in **two**: East Germany was controlled by the Soviet Union, whereas America, Britain, and France controlled West Germany (see p. 346).

The fate of Japan

Japan was occupied by US forces until 1952. By then, the Japanese economy had revived. A treaty was signed between the US and Japan, which ended the occupation but allowed the US to retain bases in Japan.

The growth of the superpowers

The **US** and the **USSR** (Soviet Union) emerged from the war as **superpowers**, far more powerful than other large countries such as Britain and France.

The Cold War

Relations between the Allies worsened after the war. America, Britain and France feared the spread of Soviet communism, while the Soviet Union installed Communist governments in the countries of Eastern Europe. This caused the **Cold War** to develop (see Ch. 22).

Who are the experts on German victories in WWII?

Who are the experts on why Germany and Japan lost World War II?

Who are the experts on the impact of World War II?

The End of European Supremacy

European supremacy was **ended**; after the war Britain and France were not strong enough to hold onto their empires. From the late 1940s to the 1960s, their empires were **decolonised** (see Ch. 24).

Moves towards European Unity

European leaders wanted **peace**. Since both world wars had begun in Europe, European leaders promoted the movement towards European unity that eventually led to the **European Union** (see Ch. 27).

The United Nations

Go onto YouTube and look up 'The Impact of World War II'.

The League of Nations had failed to prevent World War II so a new organisation, the **United Nations**, was set up. On this occasion, the most powerful countries – the USA and the USSR – became members of that organisation to promote international co-operation and to maintain peace.

Darfur genocide

In the early years of this century, the Sudanese government organised militia, which killed about 400,000 people in the Darfur area.

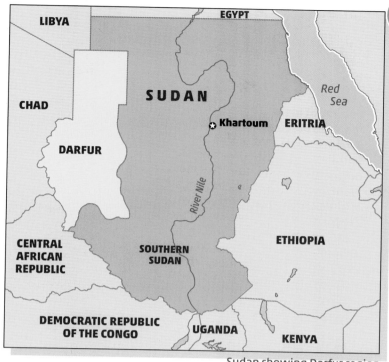

Sudan showing Darfur region

Q

1. What do these stories about genocide in the modern world tell you about its **significance**?
2. How do these stories **differ** from the treatment of native people and slaves during and after the Age of Exploration? (See Ch. 6)

What were the Causes of the Holocaust?

What was the Holocaust?

The **Holocaust** was the deliberate killing of millions of Jews and others by the Nazis before and during World War II.

⊘ Consider the causes of the Holocaust

What caused the Holocaust?

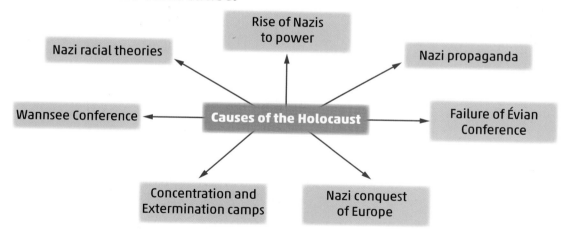

Rise of Nazis to power

Nazi racial theories

Nazi propaganda

Wannsee Conference ← **Causes of the Holocaust** → Failure of Évian Conference

Concentration and Extermination camps

Nazi conquest of Europe

The Nazis and the Jews

Hitler and the Nazis were strongly influenced by **racial ideas** or **racism**. They directed their **hatred** towards the Jews (**anti-Semitism**) and other groups. When they took power in Germany in 1933, they used **propaganda** against the Jews. They passed **harsh laws** against them, and also organised **pogroms** (See pp. 266–68). Other countries in Europe and outside **failed** to help the Jews. When the Nazis conquered large parts of Europe in World War II, they **captured** millions more Jews. During the war, the Nazis organised the **mass extermination** of the Jews in the **Holocaust**.

Analysing Sources

Nazi racial ideas

HISTORICAL JUDGEMENT

SECONDARY SOURCES

See Chapter. 16

Go onto YouTube and look up 'History File Nazi Germany P3 The Master Race'.

Source 1
Nazi racial ideas
The Nazis based their hatred of the Jews on **racial ideas** or **racism**. They said all characteristics were handed down through **race**. They said they were the **superior Aryan race** against the **'parasitic' 'inferior' Jews**. As the **Master Race**, the Nazis said the Germans were the creators of a 'high culture'. They claimed that, *'The decline of a people's culture is always the result of race mixing and a decline in racial quality.'*

Source 2
What is anti-Semitism?
Anti-Semitism is the term used when people are prejudiced against Jews just because they are Jewish. Anti-Semitism is a modern racial term that was invented in 1879 by a German journalist called Wilhelm Marr. However, anti-Jewish feelings are much older than that.
About 2,000 years ago, Jesus, according to the story in the Gospels, was executed for treason. He was crucified, which was the Roman method of execution. Christian teaching did not blame the Romans; it blamed the Jews. As his followers later regarded Jesus as God, killing him became known as the crime of 'deicide' (killing of God). This was the basis of Jew hatred.

(www.theholocaustexplained.org)

Source 3
Nazi propaganda
The Jewish race is much inferior to the Negro race.
All Jews have crooked legs, fat bellies, curly hair and a suspicious look.
The Jews were responsible for the [First] World War.
All Jews are communists.

(German school textbook)

Source 5
Hitler's views
Hitler remarked: 'Out with the Jews from all the professions and into the ghetto with them; fence them in somewhere they can perish as they deserve while the German people look on, the way people stare at wild animals.'
(General Wiedemann, Hitler's adjutant, 1935)

Source 4
The Aryan race

A Nazi poster showing the kinds of men that Nazis considered Aryan: Nordic, Falian, Easter Baltic; Western, Dinaric, Eastern.

 Q

1. What were Nazi ideas about **race**, according to Source 1?
2. According to Source 2, what was the **original cause** of anti-Semitism?
3. Who would be **influenced** by the ideas in Sources 3 and 4?
4. In Nazi racial ideas, who were the **Aryans**, as mentioned in Source 1 and Source 4?
5. What was **Hitler's attitude** to the Jews in Source 5?
6. **Summarise** Nazi attitudes to the Jews based on Sources 1 to 5.
7. How could these **attitudes** lead to genocide?

❯ Preparing for CBA2

A project on the life and experience of a person of historical interest

PERSONS OF INTEREST IN THE HOLOCAUST

- Adolf Hitler
- Adolf Eichmann
- Tomi Reichental
- Nicholas Winton
- Ettie Steinberg

- Heinrich Himmler
- Reinhard Heydrich
- Oskar Schindler
- Monsignor Hugh O'Flaherty

- Rudolf Höss
- Anne Frank
- Mary Elmes
- Irma Grese

❮ p. 180
Web Resources
and Reading

Focus Task

Historical Research

Investigate the Nazi treatment of other minorities, besides the Jews.

- ❯ www.auschwitz.org
- ❯ www.ushmm.org

1939 1940 1941 1942 1943 1944 1945

21

THE IMPACT OF WORLD WAR II ON IRELAND, NORTH AND SOUTH

CHRONOLOGICAL AWARENESS

1939 AD

1939
World War II began

Southern Ireland declared neutrality

Northern Ireland involved in World War II

Irish Republican Army (IRA) raid on Irish army magazine in Phoenix Park, Dublin

1940 AD

1940
James Craig, Prime Minister of Northern Ireland, died

J.M. Andrews became Prime Minister

German bombing of Campile, Co. Wexford, three people killed

1941 AD

1941
Bombing of Belfast, 7–8 April, 15–16 April, 4–5 May and 5–6 May 1941

1942 AD

Bombing of North Strand, Dublin, 31 May, 1941

Irish Shipping set up

1943 AD

1943
Basil Brooke became Prime Minister of Northern Ireland

1944 AD

1945 AD

1945
World War II ended

L.O. 2.8
The Nature of History: 1.1, 1.3, 1.4, 1.5, 1.6, 1.7, 1.8, 1.9, 1.10, 1.11
CBA1
CBA2

You will learn to ...

- ◎ Describe the impact of World War II on the lives of people in the South of Ireland
- ◎ Describe the impact of World War II on the lives of people in the North of Ireland
- ◎ Explore the Nature of History

KEY WORDS

- Neutrality
- Shortages
- Evidence
- Primary
- Objective
- Emergency
- Blitz
- Fact
- Secondary
- Rationing
- Source
- Opinion
- Biased

EAMON DEFYING THE LIGHTNING

Q British cartoon on Irish neutrality: what is the message of the cartoon? Is it in favour of Irish neutrality?

Life in Southern Ireland during World War II

Ireland in 1939

When World War II broke out in September, 1939, the South of Ireland (also called Éire) was part of the British Commonwealth. However, in the years since independence was achieved, the South of Ireland had won greater freedom from Britain.

Éamon de Valera was Taoiseach, and a new Constitution for the country had been established in 1937. This made the country a republic in all but name.

⊘ Consider why the South of Ireland was neutral during World War II

⊘ Describe how World War II impacted on the lives of people in the South

Neutral or not

When war broke out in September, 1939, the South of Ireland declared itself **neutral**. This meant that the South of Ireland would not fight in the war and would not support either side. This showed how **independent** the country was now. The South of Ireland also **favoured neutrality** because:

- Northern Ireland was still part of the United Kingdom
- Ireland was too weak to fight stronger countries

PROFILE – ÉAMON DE VALERA, TAOISEACH

- De Valera was born in New York but grew up in Bruree, Co. Limerick.
- He took part in the 1916 Rising as commander of Boland's Mills.
- He opposed the Anglo-Irish Treaty in 1921–22.
- He founded Fianna Fáil and became head of government in 1932.
- He led the country for the next 16 years, including as Taoiseach during World War II.
- He was elected President of Ireland in 1959.

Speaking in the Dáil in September, 1939, de Valera said, *'The government stands before you as the guardians of the interest of our people, and it is to guard those interests as best we can that we are proposing to follow the policy of neutrality.'*

IRELAND NEUTRAL

Oireachtas Is Unanimous For Emergency Measures

THE Government intended to pursue its policy of keeping the country out of war, the Taoiseach informed the Oireachtas on Saturday, when a special session of the Dáil and Seanad passed, without division, all stages of the First Amendment of the Constitution Bill and the Emergency Powers Bill. Resolutions were passed declaring a state of national emergency. The Bills were later signed by the President.

Both Houses sat until early yesterday morning to get the measures through. The Seanad adjourned sine die at 4.45 a.m. and the Dáil at 5, until October 18.

Mr. de Valera said that so long as the country, or any part of

GERMANY'S NEUTRALITY ATTITUDE TO IRELAND

MR. DE VALERA intimated to Press representatives while the Dáil was in session yesterday morning that the German Minister had called on him on Thursday last and informed him of Germany's peaceful attitude towards Ireland and said that if on a European war the German Government would respect Ireland's neutrality, provided it was adhered to.

Mr. de Valera replied that the Irish Government wished to remain at peace with Germany, as with all other Powers, and referred to a statement published in the Press on February 20 last, that the aim of Government policy was to maintain and preserve Ire-

MINISTERS TAKE OVER NEW DUTIES

THE Taoiseach announced last night a reorganisation of the Government, as follows:—

Minister for Supplies—Sean Lemass.
Minister for Co-Ordination of Military and Civil Defence—Mr. Frank Aiken.
Minister for Industry and Commerce—Tomas O Deirg.
Minister for Defence—Mr. Oscar Traynor.
Minister for Lands and Posts and Telegraphs—Mr. Gerald Boland.
Ministry of Local Government and Ministry of Education — The Tánaiste.

THE Taoiseach, Mr. de Valera, in a broadcast address to the nation from Radio-Éireann last night, said: "I am speaking to you to-night because I thought you would expect me to. I have been too busy to prepare any connected manuscript, so I must speak to you from notes. I know you will understand. You know from the News bulletins to which you have been listening that the great Europe-

A report from *The Irish Press* newspaper

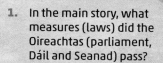

1. In the main story, what measures (laws) did the Oireachtas (parliament, Dáil and Seanad) pass?

2. How long did the Dáil and Seanad sit to get the measures through?

3. Did any person vote against declaring 'a state of national emergency'?

4. Is this a **primary** or a **secondary** source?

5. Would you consider the reporting to be **biased** or **objective**?
   Explain your answers using evidence from the newspaper.

Neutrality in action

The government passed the **Emergency Powers Act**, which gave it great power to control the country. The **'Emergency'** was the word used to describe the situation in the South of Ireland during World War II.

The government also built up the **defence forces**, in case the South of Ireland was invaded during the war. These were increased from about 20,000 to almost 250,000 part-time and full-time soldiers. The Irish government also **censored** radio and newspaper reports, to maintain a neutral position.

A ration book

Even though Ireland was neutral, the Irish government **favoured the Allies** (Britain, France and the United States). This policy meant that Allied planes were allowed to fly out over Donegal from Northern Ireland, to patrol the Atlantic.

Shortages and rationing

The South of Ireland was short of raw materials during the war. **Seán Lemass**, as **Minister for Supplies**, had to buy and charter ships to bring supplies to the country. **Rationing** of food, clothes, footwear and petrol had to be introduced because of the shortages. **Coupons** from ration books were exchanged for goods in the shops.

Ireland had surplus food, but some foods had to be imported. A series of compulsory tillage orders were enacted to increase the growing of crops such as wheat. However, there were still shortages, which could not be made up by imports.

People overcame the **shortages** by other means. Tea leaves were used over and over again. Bread was baked using Irish wheat, and some people called it 'black bread'. Goods could always be bought on the 'black market', but they were very expensive.

"Glory be! The Glimmer Man!"

Gas inspectors (or glimmer men) checked out the use of gas in houses. What does this cartoon say about the attitude of people to the glimmer men?

Seán Lemass, Minister for Supplies

Life in Northern Ireland during World War II

Crucial role of the North

In Northern Ireland, the story was **different** to the South. Northern Ireland, as part of the United Kingdom, took an **active part** in the war. Even though **conscription** (compulsory enlistment in the army) was **not enforced** in Northern Ireland because of nationalist objections there, **rationing** was. Moreover, the German occupation of France and the neutrality of Southern Ireland meant that Northern Ireland played a **crucial role** in World War II.

Planes based in Northern Ireland were used to **patrol** the North Atlantic and look for German U-boats and to protect **convoys** bringing supplies to Britain and Northern Ireland.

When the **United States** joined the war in December 1941, Northern Ireland became an important base for American troops. At one time, 120,000 American sailors and airmen were based in the country. Some were manning ships to protect the Atlantic trade, while others were preparing for D-Day.

⊘ Describe the impact of World War II on life in Northern Ireland

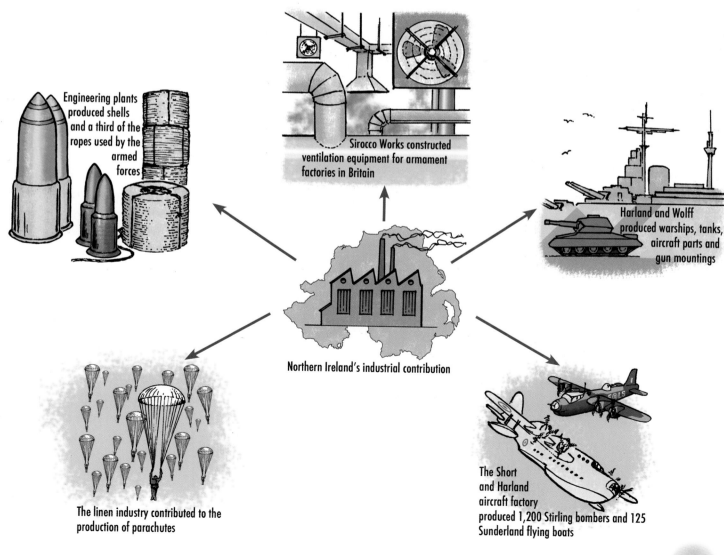

Engineering plants produced shells and a third of the ropes used by the armed forces

Sirocco Works constructed ventilation equipment for armament factories in Britain

Harland and Wolff produced warships, tanks, aircraft parts and gun mountings

Northern Ireland's industrial contribution

The linen industry contributed to the production of parachutes

The Short and Harland aircraft factory produced 1,200 Stirling bombers and 125 Sunderland flying boats

337

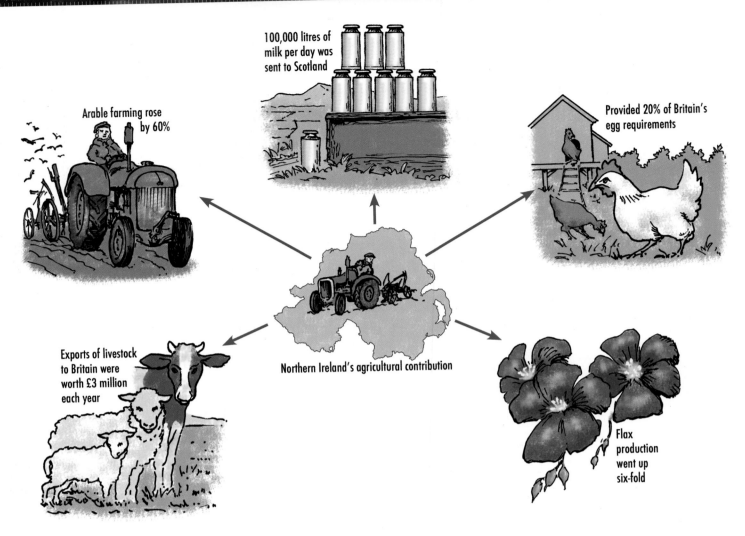

100,000 litres of milk per day was sent to Scotland

Arable farming rose by 60%

Provided 20% of Britain's egg requirements

Exports of livestock to Britain were worth £3 million each year

Northern Ireland's agricultural contribution

Flax production went up six-fold

The North's industries

Northern Ireland's **industries** grew, so unemployment fell from pre-war levels of 25% to 5% during the war. Warships and merchant ships were built at **Harland and Wolff**, over 1,600 aircraft were built by **Shorts**. Tanks, parachutes, rope and shells were all produced for the war effort.

The North's **farmers** also prospered. They received guaranteed prices for their food on the British market. Food was shipped from Belfast port to Britain every day, as compulsory tillage orders increased the acreage under flax, oats and potatoes.

Northern Ireland's contribution to World War II

Historian Thomas Hennessy said, 'Northern Ireland's main contribution came in the areas of food production and munitions. Farmers provided Britain with £3 million worth of cattle and sheep per year, 20% of home-produced eggs and 25,000 gallons of liquid milk in four out of six wartime winters. Belfast's shipyards produced 140 warships, 123 merchant ships and repaired 3,000 ships. Munitions producers manufactured 75 million shells, 180 million incendiary bullets, 50,000 bayonets, and a variety of other military material. ... Northern Ireland's only Victoria Cross was won by James Magennis, a Belfast Catholic in the Royal Navy, in July 1945.'

Belfast attacked – the Belfast Blitz

Belfast was **poorly defended** during the war, with only 22 anti-aircraft batteries, no searchlights and no night fighters to guard it. It was an easy target for German bombers. The Northern government thought Belfast was too far away from Germany.

The city and its industries were heavily attacked **four times** in April and May, 1941, during the **Belfast Blitz**. In all, over 1,100 people were killed in these attacks.

Half the houses of the city were destroyed, leaving thousands homeless and also showing the great poverty in the working-class areas of Belfast. On two occasions the Southern government sent **fire brigades** to Belfast to help the people there.

As a result of the raids, thousands of people left the city, some to the South of Ireland, most to towns outside of Belfast. Also thousands left each night to shelter in the surrounding countryside until morning.

James Magennis, VC

What do you think of the advice given in this poster 'IF THE INVADER COMES'?

IF THE INVADER COMES

ADVICE TO CIVILIANS:

KEEP CALM and STAY PUT

Don't leave your own area.

Stay in your own home unless you are officially ordered to move. Take orders only from the Military, the Police or other authorised persons you know.

Disregard any Instructions you may receive by telephone until you have checked them.

IGNORE RUMOURS. They are probably spread by the enemy.

Issued by the Ministry of Public Security, Northern Ireland, 27th July, 1940.

MPS1/2/4

VE-Day

Victory in Europe Day was celebrated in the streets of **Belfast** and elsewhere in Northern Ireland.

In **Dublin**, Trinity College students celebrated the victory of the Allies in Europe. However, they provoked a **counter-demonstration** by UCD students who took exception to the way the Trinity College students flew flags from the roof of the university building – they had placed the Irish flag lowest of the flags hoisted on the mast.

Analysing Sources

The Belfast Blitz

Source 1

On the Easter Tuesday we had all spent the day at the zoo, nice afternoon. I can remember going to bed about nine o'clock and being wakened by the sound of sirens and grandfather shouting. Tremendous noise and explosion and a couple of ceilings came down and we went out downstairs through the shop (shoemakers), where the whole front of the shop disappeared virtually. We ran to the air raid shelter in Hillman Street. The smell and the noises. I was only out in the open for five minutes running from the house to the shelter but felt a whole multitude of emotions especially seeing St James Church in flames. Luckily we all got across and had shoes on because there was glass everywhere. St James Church was just a mass of flames and the school was also on fire.

When we got into the shelter there were about fifty people there already on seats all round the walls and people started to sing 'Run Rabbit Run'. There were maybe ten to fifteen children in the shelter and the adults were trying to put on a good face for the children and keep the spirits up.

(Ken Stanley, Antrim Road, Belfast quoted in Stephen Douds, *The Belfast Blitz, The People's Story* [2011])

Q

1. Is there **evidence** in Source 1 to suggest that some aspects of life in Belfast were normal before the raid?
2. How serious a danger were the Stanley family in during the bombing?
3. What 'smell' and what 'noise' do you think he was referring to?
4. Why did the crowd in the shelter sing 'Run Rabbit Run'?
5. How badly damaged was Belfast, according to the report in the Northern Whig in Source 2?
6. How **objective** is the reporting in this newspaper?
7. Based on the **evidence** in this **chapter**, would the Germans consider they were justified in bombing Belfast?
8. Select **one fact** and **one opinion** from any of the sources.

Go onto YouTube and look up 'Southern Ireland during World War 2'.

Visit ...

Soldiers and Chiefs, National Museum, Collins Barracks, Dublin

The Ulster Museum and the Northern Ireland War Memorial Museum, to learn more about the impact of the war on Belfast

Who are the experts on the impact of World War II on Irish life?

Source 2

The Space Race

The Cold War influenced the Space Race. The Soviets (Russians) led the Space Race by putting the first satellite and the first man into space. **Khrushchev**, the Soviet leader, claimed that, *'The Sputniks (Soviet space satellite) prove that communism has won the competition between Communist and capitalist countries. The economy, science, culture and the creative genius of people in all areas of life develop better and faster under communism.'*

The success of the Soviets forced the Americans to invest heavily in getting the first man on the Moon (see Ch. 24).

Timeline of the nuclear arms race, 1945–60

1945	USA dropped first atomic bomb (A-bomb)
1949	USSR tested its first atomic bomb
1952	USA tested its first Hydrogen bomb (H-bomb)
1957	USSR tested intercontinental ballistic missile (ICBM) to carry H-bombs to the USA
1958	USA set up intermediate missiles in NATO countries within range of USSR
1959	USA developed ICBMs
1960	USA launched first nuclear-powered submarine
1962	Cuban Missile Crisis

Q Source 1

Timeline of Space Race

1957	USSR launched Sputnik 1 – first satellite in space
	USA Vanguard exploded on launch
1958	USA launched Explorer 1
1961	Yuri Gagarin (USSR) – first person in space
	Alan Shepard – first American in space
1962	John Glenn – first American to orbit the Earth
1963	Cosmonaut Valentina Tereshkova (USSR) – first woman in space
1966	Luna 9 (USSR) – first satellite to soft-land on the moon
1969	Apollo 11 – Neil Armstrong and 'Buzz' Aldrin – first men to walk on the Moon

Q Source 2

Conflict in the Cold War

The Cold War was important because it led to conflicts which brought the world to the **edge of a world war**. Between the end of the 1940s and 1991, many major incidents occurred involving the USA and USSR, and some of these **took the world to the brink of war**.

Three of the most serious incidents were:

The Berlin Blockade   **The Korean War**   **The Cuban Missile Crisis**

1. How do these sources above show the rivalry between the USA and the USSR in the Space Race?
2. Who won the Space Race? Explain your answers.

Recognise the importance of the Berlin Blockade in international relations

What was the Importance of the Berlin Blockade, 1948–49?

Background

Decisions about Germany

The Allied leaders held conferences at **Yalta** and **Potsdam** near the **end of World War II**. The leaders decided that:

- **Germany** would be divided into **four occupied zones** – American, Soviet, British and French.
- **Berlin** would also be divided into **four sectors**.
- The division of Germany and Berlin would be **temporary**.

After World War II, Germany was divided into four zones. Berlin, which was in the Soviet zone, was divided into four sectors.

Truman, US President

Stalin, Soviet leader

How should Germany be treated after the War?

Differences arose among the Allied countries about how Germany should be treated.

Soviet view	American and British view
The Soviet Union demanded huge **reparations** (compensation) from their zone in Eastern Germany because they had suffered a great deal in the war.	The Americans and the British wanted to **revive** the German economy and establish a **democratic government**.

Clash over a new currency

The Americans and British went ahead with their plan to revive the German economy. They launched a new currency – the **Deutschmark**.

The Soviet Union responded by cutting off road, rail and canal links to West Berlin on 24 June 1948. Power supplies that came from the Soviet zone were also cut off. The **Berlin Blockade** had begun.

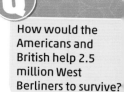

How would the Americans and British help 2.5 million West Berliners to survive?

A British cartoon showing the Western attitude to the Soviet blockade of Berlin. What images are used in this cartoon? What is its message? Is it effective in getting across its message? (Note symbols, words and images.)

US plane carrying supplies into West Berlin during the Berlin Blockade

The Berlin Airlift

The Western countries decided to supply Berlin by using three 20-mile-wide **air corridors** that the Soviet Union had not cut off. In a huge operation – codenamed **Operation Vittles** – they flew large cargo planes into three airports in West Berlin. They flew in food, medical supplies, drums of petrol, even coal. In spite of bad weather and harassment by Soviet planes, the Western Allies continued to supply Berlin for the next 11 months.

THE BERLIN AIRLIFT, JUNE 1948 TO MAY 1949				
	USAF	RAF	CIVIL	TOTAL
Flights to Berlin and back	131,918	49,733	13,897	195,548
Tons flown	1,101,405	255,526	79,470	1,436,401

Conditions in Berlin

In West Berlin, food was **rationed**, but West Berliners refused to give in. Most of the city's industry was closed down and over 125,000 people lost their jobs. The people lit their homes with candles and went to bed at sunset. Huge meetings were held regularly in the city to keep up the spirits of the people.

The blockade lifted

Stalin and the Soviet leadership realised that they could not win when they saw that supplies were being maintained and that the spirit of West Berliners remained strong. On 12 May 1949, Stalin and the Soviet Union lifted the blockade.

The **danger of a world war** developing over Berlin was **ended**.

Q

1. What **symbols** are used in this cartoon in Source 1, and what do they mean?
2. What is the **message** of the cartoon in Source 1?
3. What **danger** does it show could happen?
4. Did that danger happen?
5. How does Source 2 help you **understand** why the Western Allies were successful in the Berlin Airlift?

Source 1

THE BIRD WATCHER

A British cartoon on the Berlin Blockade and Airlift (1948)

Source 2

Planes were taking off every thirty seconds, soldiers were unloading trucks, the maintenance shops were a beehive of activity, the mess halls and clubs were open. It was a twenty-four hour operation. The commanding officer stood in the control tower with his stop-watch, checking the timing of the planes. To most people it seemed an impossible task to meet the needs of 2,000,000 people by airlift. But, except for water, Berlin was supplied with everything by air.

(Account by US airman, 1948)

Why was the Berlin Blockade important?

- The Berlin Blockade showed that while the Soviet Union was prepared to raise **tensions**, it was **not prepared** to go to war with the West. In spite of the Russian land blockade, Russian air traffic controllers continued to direct Allied planes into Berlin.
- **Two countries** were established in Germany for the foreseeable future.
  - The Western Allies set up a democratic West Germany, the **Federal Republic of Germany**, with its capital in Bonn. They also revived the West German economy with the help from the **Marshall Plan**.

- The Soviet Union established the **German Democratic Republic** in East Germany, which was Communist-controlled.

- The USA, Canada and ten Western European countries formed the **North Atlantic Treaty Organisation** (NATO) to defend each other. The Soviet Union responded by forming a military alliance, called the **Warsaw Pact**, with countries in Eastern Europe.

- **The building of the Berlin Wall, 1961:** During the 1950s, West Germany prospered while East Germany was poorer. Thousands of East Germans migrated through East Berlin into West Berlin and West Germany. They wanted a better life with more job prospects and greater freedom. East Germany, supported by the Soviet Union, suddenly built a **wall** between **East and West Berlin** in 1961 to stop the migration and the movement of people to the West.

- The building of the wall was a great **propaganda coup** for the West because it highlighted the freedoms of the West against the lack of freedom in the East. The wall continued to divide Berlin until it was knocked down in 1989 as the Cold War came to an end, and Germany was reunited soon after (see p. 355).

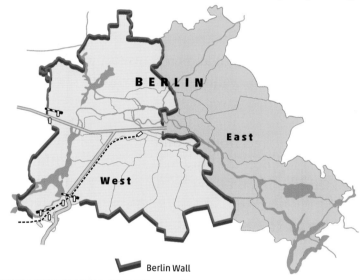

Berlin Wall

Go onto YouTube and look up Miss Stout's History Class The Berlin Blockade.

What was the Importance of the Korean War, 1950–53?

Recognise the importance of the Korean War in international relations

Background

At the end of World War II, Korea was divided along the **38th parallel** between North Korea and South Korea. North Korea was supported by the Soviet Union, and it established a **Communist** government. South Korea was supported by the United States.

In June 1948, the United Nations called for free elections in both North and South Korea. However, elections only went ahead in the South, and a new **Republic of Korea** was established, with its capital in Seoul. Soon after this, the **Democratic Republic of Korea** was set up in the North, with its capital in Pyongyang.

The war begins

In June 1950, the North Korean army **invaded** the South. This Soviet-equipped army advanced rapidly, taking Seoul and pushing the South Koreans into the south-eastern corner of the country.

US and UN help

The US President, **Truman**, ordered sea and air transport for the South Koreans. The United Nations passed a resolution calling on its members *'to furnish such assistance to the Republic of Korea as may be necessary to repel the armed attack'*.

General **Douglas MacArthur** led the UN forces, consisting mostly of American soldiers but also including soldiers from 15 other countries. They landed at Inchon and drove the North Koreans back over the border. However, MacArthur then advanced into North Korea and headed for the Yalu River border with China.

Chinese leader, Mao Zedong

China in the war

In response to MacArthur's advance, **Mao Zedong**, the leader of Communist China, ordered huge numbers of Chinese troops into the war in November 1950. The American and UN forces were pushed back, and the Communist armies again occupied part of South Korea.

MacArthur dismissed

President Truman dismissed MacArthur because he feared MacArthur would involve America in a much larger war, which would bring the Soviet Union into the war.

Peace at last

The war dragged on until 1953. The election of a new president in America, **Eisenhower**, and the death of **Stalin** in the Soviet Union resulted in a speedy end to the conflict June, 1953. Both sides agreed to maintain the border along the 38th parallel.

Why was the Korean War important?

- The war resulted in a **huge loss of life** on both sides. 54,000 US soldiers were killed, and 100,000 injured. South Korea lost 400,000 soldiers. About 500,000 North Koreans and between 250,000 and 500,000 Chinese soldiers were killed.

- The war almost resulted in a much wider conflict that could have become a world war.

- America acquired a **new ally in Asia** – Japan, which just five years prior to the war had been enemies in World War II.

- **North Korea** became a rigid, conservative dictatorship, which contrasted with the prosperous **South Korea**.

- The authority of the **United Nations** was upheld on this occasion.

 p. 198

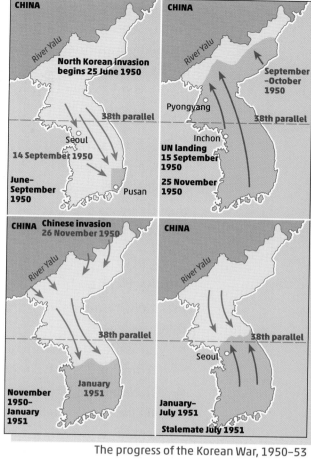

CHINA — North Korean invasion begins 25 June 1950 — 38th parallel — Seoul — 14 September 1950 — June–September 1950 — Pusan — River Yalu

CHINA — September–October 1950 — Pyongyang — 38th parallel — Inchon — UN landing 15 September 1950 — 25 November 1950 — River Yalu

CHINA — Chinese invasion 26 November 1950 — River Yalu — 38th parallel — November 1950–January 1951 — January 1951

CHINA — River Yalu — 38th parallel — Seoul — January–July 1951 — Stalemate July 1951

The progress of the Korean War, 1950–53

Why was the Cuban Missile Crisis Important?

In the 1950s, Cuba had a close relationship with America. America bought Cuba's main crop, **sugar**, and American companies controlled much of Cuban industry. The US government supported the dictator of Cuba, **Batista**.

But in 1959, a small Communist group, led by **Fidel Castro**, overthrew Batista. Castro **nationalised** (put under government ownership) the sugar plantations and took over other American businesses. In response, the American government refused to buy Cuban sugar. Castro turned to the Soviet Union (Russia) for help. The Russian leader, **Khrushchev**, agreed to help. The Soviet Union bought Cuban sugar and sold weapons to Cuba.

Recognise the importance of the Cuban Missile Crisis, 1962 in international relations

Kennedy

Khrushchev

Castro

The Bay of Pigs

The American Central Intelligence Agency (CIA), with the sanction of President Kennedy, supported an invasion of Cuba by Cuban exiles living in America. However, the invasion of the **Bay of Pigs** in Cuba in 1961 was a **disastrous failure**. It drove Castro closer to the Soviet Union.

Soviet missile bases

In 1962, the Russian leader, Khrushchev, decided that his country would build **missile bases** in Cuba. Soon afterwards, an American **U-2 spyplane** photographed Soviet **missile bases** being constructed in Cuba. If they were built, they would bring all major US cities within range of Soviet missiles.

Danger of war

President **Kennedy** addressed the American people on television. He informed them that:

- A missile attack launched from Cuba on any country in the Western hemisphere (North and South America) would be seen as an attack by the USSR on the USA.
- He ordered a blockade of Cuba by the US navy until the missiles were removed. He also put US troops on **alert**.

Khrushchev (Soviet leader) and Kennedy (US President) arm-wrestle over the Cuban Missile Crisis. What is the message of this cartoon? How does it compare with the message of the cartoon on p. 347?

Neither side was prepared to give in and the world seemed headed for a **nuclear war** as Soviet ships steamed towards Cuba. Some ships were stopped but were allowed to go on because they did not have parts for nuclear weapons.

Robert Kennedy described his brother, President Kennedy, during the crisis: *'I think those few minutes (as they waited to see what the Russian ships would do) were the time of greatest concern for the President. Was the world on the brink of a holocaust? Was it our error? A mistake? His face seemed drawn, his eyes pained, almost grey. We stared at each other across the table.'*

A conservative society

In the new **Irish Free State**, women over the age of 21 got the vote in 1922. However, Ireland was a **conservative** (old-fashioned, traditional) **society** from the 1920s to the 1960s.

- Most men and women thought that a **'woman's place was in the home'**, taking care of the family. This reflected thinking in most Western countries at that time.
- **Divorce** and **contraception** were banned, and women were not allowed sit on juries.
- A **'marriage bar'** was brought in in 1932, which meant women had to give up certain jobs when they got married, for example, teaching and the civil service.
- The **Irish Constitution of 1937** supported the traditional attitude to women by recognising women's special role 'within the home'.

The Irish Constitution, 1937 on the role of women

41.2.1 In particular, the State recognises that by her life within the home, woman gives to the State a support without which the common good cannot be achieved.

41.2.2 The State shall, therefore, endeavour (try) to ensure that mothers shall not be obliged by economic necessity to engage in labour to the neglect of their duties in the home.

In your own words, what do these articles say?

p. 207

The 1960s Onwards – How did Women's Lives Change?

The position of women **changed gradually** in the 1960s.

- Girls had greater access to education
- Outside ideas influenced life in Ireland, particularly from **America** (see Ch. 24)
- The growing economy provided job opportunities
- Ireland joined the UN in 1955 and the EEC in 1973. The **EEC** often forced Ireland to bring in laws **to eliminate inequality**.

The **women's movement** demanded changes and greater equality for women. The government set up the **Commission for the Status of Women** in 1970, which issued a report in 1972 encouraging the government and other organisations to **eliminate** all aspects of inequality. The report led to the **marriage bar** being lifted and to the passage of laws that required equal pay for equal work. Later, the **Employment Equality Act 1977** outlawed discrimination on the basis of sex or marital status.

Explain the changing experiences of women in the later decades of 20th century Ireland

At the same time, the **Irish Women's Liberation Movement** (IWLM) was founded in Dublin in 1970. It drew its inspiration from the women's movement in America in the 1960s, and from authors such as Betty Friedan, who wrote *The Feminine Mystique*, demanding more from life than 'marriage, motherhood and homemaking'.

The IWLM published *Chains or Change* in 1971, a critical analysis of the position of women in Irish society at that time. The Movement got wide publicity through appearances on the *Late Late Show*, and actions such as the Contraceptive Train to Belfast to buy contraceptives, which were illegal in the South.

Analysing Sources
The Irish Women's Liberation Movement

HISTORICAL JUDGEMENT

Source 1

A publication of the Irish Women's Liberation Movement (1971)

Source 2

Members of the Irish Women's Liberation Movement on the platform of Connolly Station, Dublin 1971 prior to boarding the Belfast Train to buy contraceptives. Photograph: *The Irish Times*

Source 3

Article 40 of the Irish Constitution promises equal rights to all citizens of the Republic of Ireland. 1,434,970 Irish citizens (at the last count) are not given such rights. These are the women of Ireland. A married woman in Ireland is regarded as the chattel (property) of her husband. ... She must have permission from him for all kinds of things ...

He can change their **name** without consulting her. **She** may not.

.... The Constitution of this country promises a special place to **women in the home**. But the law has not fulfilled that promise. Irishwomen in the home have noticeably inferior status. And then, of course, if the woman wishes, or needs, to go out to **work**, she goes into unequal pay, the marriage bar, no amenities and penalising taxation.

(Irish Women's Liberation Movement, *Chains or Change* [1971])

Q

Source 4

Equal Rights for Irish Women!

Do you think it's just that ... for every 26p (5s 3d) that a woman earns, her male counterpart gets 47p (9s 6d)?

Do you think it's just that ... The Civil Service and all State Bodies, including Radio Telefís Éireann, sack women upon marriage?

Do you know that ... a mother is not permitted to sign a children's allowance receipt without her husband's permission?

(Irish Women's Liberation Movement, Chains or Change [1971])

1. What is the **message** of the cover of the Irish Women's Liberation Movement publication in Source 1?
2. To whom is the cover **appealing**?
3. How **effective** is the cover?
4. What is the **message** of the picture in Source 2?
5. Why, do you think, the women brought the press to the station before they left for Belfast?
6. According to Source 3, what **promise** made by Article 40 of the Irish Constitution has not been kept?
7. 'Irishwomen in the home have inferior status.' Give **one piece of evidence** from the source to support this view.
8. Give **two problems**, mentioned in this document, for women who wish or need to go out to work.
9. Select **one** of the statements in Source 4 and give your opinion on it.
10. How **effective** is the information in this source in persuading you that there should be equal rights for women?
11. From you study of women's experiences in 20th century Ireland, mention **two ways** in which women's lives have **changed** compared to the information in Sources 3 and 4?
    Explain your answers using the evidence from the sources.

Women in politics – the South

More women became involved in politics. Women became government ministers, for example **Máire Geoghegan-Quinn**, who became Minister for Justice, and **Gemma Hussey**, who was Minister for Education. **Mary Harney** became the **first woman leader** of a modern Irish political party in the South of Ireland when she became leader of the Progressive Democrats in 1993. She also became first woman Tánaiste.

The election of **Mary Robinson** as President of Ireland in 1990 had the greatest impact. Her success contributed to the election of another woman to succeed her as president, **Mary McAleese**. The contribution of these women, and that of **successful sportswomen** such as Sonia O'Sullivan, Catríona McKiernan (athletics) and Angela Downey (camogie) boosted the role of women in Irish society. Katie Taylor (boxing), Derval O'Rourke (athletics), Briege Corkery and Rena Buckley (camogie and football) continued that role in the 21st century.

Women in politics – the North

Women took an active role in Northern politics in the 1960s as civil rights issues came to the fore. **Angela McCrystal** was involved in the **Homeless Citizens League** in Dungannon to highlight discrimination in housing against Catholics. **Patricia McCluskey** and **Brid Rodgers** were involved in the **Campaign for Social Justice**, which provided the information to support the accusations in relation to discrimination in housing and gerrymandering (vote rigging) in local councils.

Both were also involved in the **Northern Ireland Civil Rights Association** (NICRA) in 1967, as was **Bernadette Devlin**. Devlin was later one of the leaders of the **People's Democracy** march from Belfast to Derry in 1969, which was attacked by loyalist groups on the way.

'Thus the founding of the Northern Ireland Civil Rights Association (NICRA) is as much the result of their [women's] groundwork as of the various trade union, republican and civil liberties groups that joined in establishing the organisation in April 1967.'

(Catherine Shannon)

Women featured in later events as the Troubles developed. Some, such as the **Price sisters**, were imprisoned for bombing activities; others such as **Mairéad Corrigan** and **Betty Williams** founded the *Peace People*.

However, the North, similar to the South, faced the same difficulty of increasing the numbers of women going forward for and winning elections for local and regional government. Nevertheless, **Anne Dickson** became the first leader of a major political party in Ireland when she became the leader of the **Unionist Party of Northern Ireland** (UPNI) in 1976, which had split from the main Unionist Party.

Sonia O'Sulllivan, athlete

Angela Downey, camogie player

Patricia McCluskey, civil rights activist

Katie Taylor, boxer

Bernadette Devlin, civil rights activist

Gemma Hussey, Minister for Education

Mary Harney, former Tánaiste

Mary Robinson, former President

Mary McAleese, former President

Analysing Sources

Women in Politics

Source 1
Women in Irish general elections by decade

Year	Candidates			Elected		
	Total number	Women candidates	Women as %	Total number	Women candidates	Women as %
1923	377	7	1.9	153	5	3.3
1933	246	6	2.4	153	3	1.9
1943	354	9	2.5	138	3	2.2
1954	303	6	1.9	147	5	3.4
1969	373	11	2.9	144	3	2.1
1977	375	25	6.6	148	6	4.1
1982*	365	31	8.5	166	14	8.4
1989	371	53	13.8	166	13	7.8
Total	2764	148	5.3	1215	52	4.2

Note: 1982* refers to the second general election in that year.
(Frances Gardiner, 'Political interest and participation of Irish women 1922–92' in Ailbhe Smyth (ed.), *Irish women's studies reader*, Dublin, 1993)

Source 2
Proportion of women in the national parliaments of the European Union member states

State	Year	% Female
Belgium	1995	15.3
Denmark	1994	33.0
Germany	1994	25.7
Greece	1993	5.3
Spain	1993	14.6
France	1993/92	5.6
Ireland	1997/92	12.4
Italy	1994	12.0
Luxembourg	1994	16.6
Netherlands	1994/95	30.2
Austria	1994	22.7
Portugal	1991	8.7
Finland	1995	33.5
Sweden	1994	40.4
UK	1992	7.4
Average		14.8

('Women and decision making' quoted in Department of Education, 'Facts and figures' in *Balance: A module in social education and equality issues*, Dublin, 1997)

1. When did a **significant increase** occur in the number and percentage of women seeking election in Irish general elections, according to Source 1?
2. How significant an increase was it?
3. What explanations can you give for the figures in this source?
4. How does Ireland **compare** with other EU states in relation to the proportion of women in national parliaments in Source 2?

Problems

In spite of all these changes in the experience of women, some problems still existed at the end of the 20th century:

- Women were still **exploited** in advertising
- Some **traditionally male clubs** and institutions were slow to accept women members on equal terms
- The pressures of modern society led to the **break-up of marriages** affecting both men and women
- There was still a **gap in pay** between males and females
- There was still a gap in the numbers of males and females in **management positions**.

INVESTIGATING A REPOSITORY OF HISTORICAL EVIDENCE FOR THE EXPERIENCES OF IRISH WOMEN IN THE 20TH CENTURY

RTÉ Archives, Milestones for Women,
www.rte.ie/archives/exhibitions/1666-women-and-society/
National Museum of Ireland – Country Life, Castlebar, Co. Mayo
www.museum.ie/Country-Life

》 Preparing for CBA1

A project related to an aspect of the history of your locality or place (or personal/family history)

LOCAL PROJECTS FROM THE EXPERIENCES OF IRISH WOMEN IN THE 20TH CENTURY

Your locality can include your county

- Any women in your locality active in the suffrage campaign or the independence struggle in the early 20th century
- The Irish Countrywomen's Association in your locality
- The Irish Housewives Association in your locality
- The Irish Women's Liberation Movement in your locality

》 Preparing for CBA2

A project on the life and experience of a person of historical interest

PERSONS OF INTEREST IN THE EXPERIENCES OF IRISH WOMEN IN THE 20TH CENTURY

- Louie Bennett
- Margaret Burke Sheridan
- Grace Gifford Plunkett
- Mainie Jellett
- Mary MacSwiney
- Mary Robinson
- Elizabeth O'Farrell

- Elizabeth Bowen
- Bernadette Devlin
- Maud Gonne McBride
- Mary Lavin
- Constance Markievicz
- Peig Sayers
- Jennie Wyse Power

- Kathleen Clarke
- Muriel Gahan
- Nora Herlihy
- Mary McAleese
- Patricia McCluskey
- Hanna Sheehy Skeffington
- Sonya O'Sullivan

HISTORICAL INVESTIGATION

Focus Task

p. 207 》
Web Resources and Reading

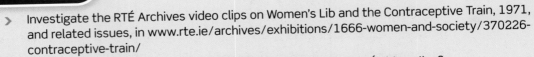

> Investigate the RTÉ Archives video clips on Women's Lib and the Contraceptive Train, 1971, and related issues, in www.rte.ie/archives/exhibitions/1666-women-and-society/370226-contraceptive-train/
> How are the issues on women's liberation presented in the RTÉ video clips?

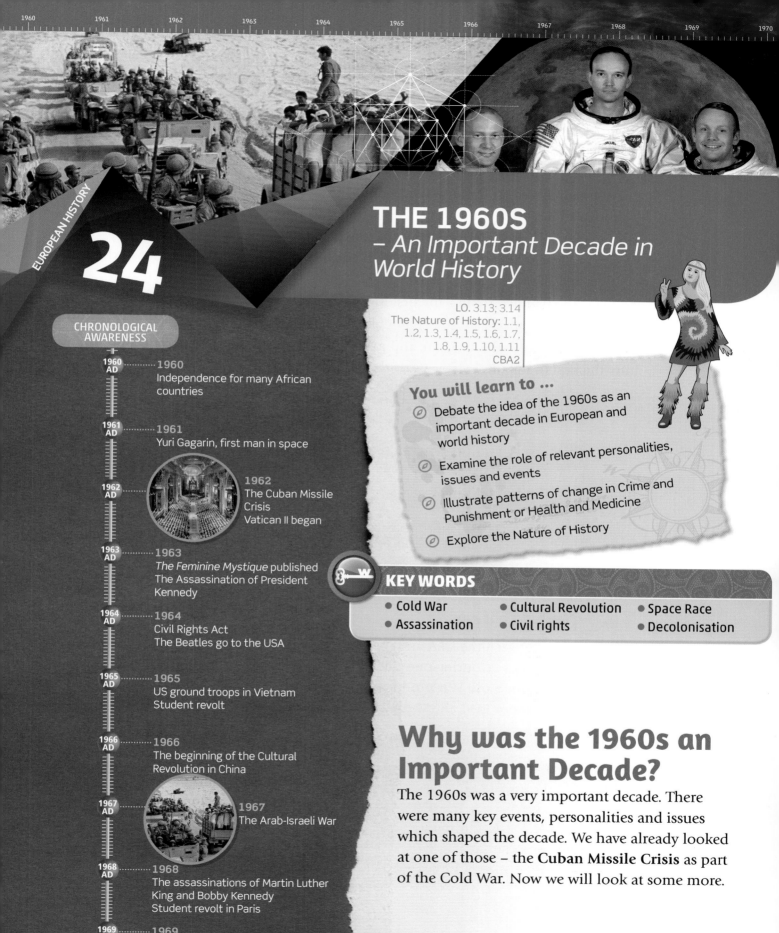

EUROPEAN HISTORY

24

CHRONOLOGICAL AWARENESS

1960 AD — 1960
Independence for many African countries

1961 AD — 1961
Yuri Gagarin, first man in space

1962 AD — 1962
The Cuban Missile Crisis
Vatican II began

1963 AD — 1963
The Feminine Mystique published
The Assassination of President Kennedy

1964 AD — 1964
Civil Rights Act
The Beatles go to the USA

1965 AD — 1965
US ground troops in Vietnam
Student revolt

1966 AD — 1966
The beginning of the Cultural Revolution in China

1967 AD — 1967
The Arab-Israeli War

1968 AD — 1968
The assassinations of Martin Luther King and Bobby Kennedy
Student revolt in Paris

1969 AD — 1969
First moon landing

1970 AD

THE 1960S
– An Important Decade in World History

LO. 3.13; 3.14
The Nature of History: 1.1, 1.2, 1.3, 1.4, 1.5, 1.6, 1.7, 1.8, 1.9, 1.10, 1.11
CBA2

You will learn to …

◎ Debate the idea of the 1960s as an important decade in European and world history

◎ Examine the role of relevant personalities, issues and events

◎ Illustrate patterns of change in Crime and Punishment or Health and Medicine

◎ Explore the Nature of History

KEY WORDS

- Cold War
- Assassination
- Cultural Revolution
- Civil rights
- Space Race
- Decolonisation

Why was the 1960s an Important Decade?

The 1960s was a very important decade. There were many key events, personalities and issues which shaped the decade. We have already looked at one of those – the **Cuban Missile Crisis** as part of the Cold War. Now we will look at some more.

⊘ Explain why the 1960s was an important decade

The 1960s was characterised by certain important **issues**:

- The **Cold War** in international relations between the USA and the USSR
- The growth of freedom in many aspects of life – **civil rights** in the USA, the **women's movement**, **decolonisation in Africa** and the **Youth Revolution**
- It was also characterised by the **assassination** of three important leaders in the USA – John F. Kennedy, Martin Luther King and Robert Kennedy
- **War** also played an important part in the 1960s, particularly the **Vietnam War** and the **Arab-Israeli War** of 1967

There were also **advances in science, technology and medicine**

- Science and technology contributed to advances in computers and videos, which had a greater impact on later decades
- Medicine had two **firsts** – the first human kidney transplant (1963) and the first human-to-human heart transplant (1968)

These issues produced the **events** and **personalities** that shaped the decade and made it into 'the best of decades'.

Choice of important issues and events in the 1960s

Cold War	Space Race	Vietnam War	Civil Rights in the USA
Decolonisation	Vatican II
China – the Cultural Revolution	Women's Liberation Movement	Youth Culture and Revolution

By the end of this chapter, you should decide:
- If any of these issues or events **does not deserve** to be called important.
- If there are **any other issues** in the 1960s which you think should be included.

The Cold War

⊘ Debate the importance of the Cold War

The Cold War between the USA and the USSR dominated international relations as countries took sides favouring one side or the other (see Ch. 20).

In the 1960s, the Cold War produced the **building of the Berlin Wall**, the **Cuban Missile Crisis** (see p. 351), the **Vietnam War** and the **Space Race**.

CHRONOLOGICAL AWARENESS

1961
The building of the Berlin Wall
USSR send Yuri Gagarin as first man in space
USA send their first astronaut, Alan Shepherd, into space
Kennedy's speech on Man on the Moon by the end of the 1960s

1963
USSR launches Valentina Tereshkova, first woman in space
The Assassination of President Kennedy

1969
Apollo 11 crew become first humans to land on the Moon

| 1961 AD | 1962 AD | 1963 AD | 1964 AD | 1965 AD | 1966 AD | 1967 AD | 1968 AD | 1969 AD |

1962
Cuban Missile Crisis

1964
USA launched first two-seat spacecraft

1965
US troops in Vietnam

1966
USSR achieved first soft landing on Moon

1968
Tet Offensive and My Lai Massacre in Vietnam
USA launched first manned mission to orbit the Moon

TEST OF NERVES

"LET'S GET A LOCK FOR THIS THING"

 See p. 349 for Building the Berlin Wall

 See p. 351 for Cuban Missile Crisis

President Kennedy (USA) and Premier Khrushchev (USSR) face each other over Berlin. What is the message of the cartoon? Does it favour either side?

Kennedy and Khrushchev trying to deal with the Cuban Missile Crisis. What is the message of this cartoon? How does it compare with the message of the previous cartoon?

Importance of the Cold War

- It was a **competition** between the **capitalist and democratic West** and the communist dictatorships of the East
- It brought the world to the **brink of nuclear war**, especially in the **Cuban Missile Crisis** (p. 351)
- It forced other countries to **take sides** for either the USA or the USSR
- It caused local crises such as the **building of the Berlin Wall** (p. 349)
- It resulted in spending **enormous sums of money** on military equipment

Q Do these factors make the Cold War important?

The Space Race

The **Space Race** between the USA and the USSR was part of the **Cold War**. It began in the 1950s when the USSR sent **Sputnik**, the first satellite, into space in 1957. This **shocked** America because it showed that Communist technology was superior to the American or capitalist technology. It also shocked America because it showed that the USSR had more powerful rockets capable of landing nuclear bombs on America.

The USSR jumped further ahead in 1961 when **Yuri Gagarin** became the first person to orbit the Earth.

Soon, the Americans were trying to catch up. **President Kennedy** made a commitment that year that America would

US astronaut, Buzz Aldrin, on the Moon

© Debate the importance of the Space Race

land a man on the Moon and return him safely to Earth before the 1960s were over. This resulted in the USA investing $25 billion dollars to get the **first man on the Moon**. This happened in 1969 when **Apollo 11** reached the Moon, and **Neil Armstrong** and **'Buzz' Aldrin** were the first men on the Moon.

The New York Times front page on the first Moon landing, 1969

PROFILE – PRESIDENT KENNEDY

- Elected first Catholic President of the USA in 1960
- Irish-American descent
- Committed USA to land men on the Moon in the 1960s
- Led the USA during the Cuban Missile Crisis
- Sent US special advisers to Vietnam to train local South Vietnamese Army
- Made historic visit to Ireland in 1963
- Assassinated a few months later in 1963 in Dallas, Texas

Importance of the Space Race

- It led to **huge investment** by both the USA and the USSR in space exploration
- It led to a **victory** for US technology in getting the first men on the Moon
- It increased our knowledge of space and led to the development of **space stations**
- **Technology** developed for space exploration led to CAT and MRI scanners for hospitals, freeze-dried food, better insulation, water purification technology, and other improvements.

The Vietnam War

During the 1960s, the USA became very seriously involved in a **war in Vietnam**. The USA had a **policy of containment** which stated that it wanted to contain communism wherever it was and prevent its expansion into other countries.

In South Vietnam, Viet Cong guerrillas backed up by communist North Vietnam attacked the government there. In turn, North Vietnam was supported by communist China and the USSR.

The US sent **advisers** to South Vietnam to train the South Vietnamese army. But by the middle of the 1960s, the USA had to decide to increase its involvement there or else pull out of South Vietnam.

In 1965, **President Johnson** of the USA took the advice of his generals. They said that if the US sent troops to help the South Vietnamese army and bombed the supply lines from North to South Vietnam, the superior technology of the USA would defeat the guerrilla warfare of the North Vietnamese and the Vietcong.

In spite of massive bombing and half a million US troops in Vietnam, the North Vietnamese, led by **Ho Chi Minh**, refused to give in. By 1968, there was a very strong anti-war campaign in the USA and the US lost 36,000 soldiers that year. Johnson realised that the US could not win the war so he began the process of cutting back US involvement and **negotiating peace**.

It took another five years before peace was finally agreed and the US pulled out of Vietnam in 1973. Within two years, North Vietnam had invaded South Vietnam and the country was united.

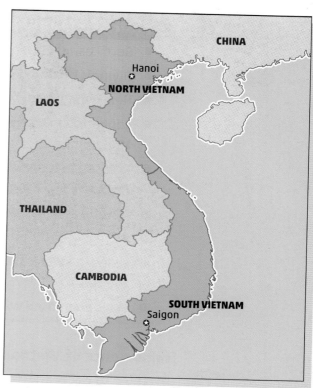

North and South Vietnam

US bombers in action during the Vietnam War

Viet Cong soldiers bringing in supplies

Soldiers fighting in Vietnam War

Q

How **useful** and **reliable** are photos as sources for historians?

PROFILE – MUHAMMAD ALI

- Born Cassius Clay in Louisville, Kentucky (1942)
- Olympic **boxing** gold medal winner (1960)
- Heavyweight boxing champion of the world
- Converted to **Islam** and changed his name to Muhammad Ali
- Refused to serve in **Vietnam War**, promoted **civil rights** for Black Americans
- His title as heavyweight champion was taken from him
- Ali regained his title later
- Listed in **100 Most Important People in 20th Century** and crowned **Sportsman of the Century**
- Later diagnosed with Parkinson's disease and died in 2016

Importance of Vietnam War

- It led to **deep divisions** in the USA between those who supported the Vietnam War and the anti-war movement.
- It led to thousands of US and Vietnamese **deaths** and widespread destruction in North and South Vietnam.
- It led to the **defeat** of the US army in the war.
- It showed that superior military technology was **not able** to defeat guerrilla warfare supported by the people

Q

What arguments can you present to say that the Vietnam War was not an important event of the 1960s?

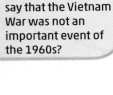

Debate the importance of civil rights in the USA

Civil Rights in the USA

Background

During the first half of the 20th century, black Americans suffered serious **discrimination** in the USA, particularly in the southern states. **Racist views** were widely held and put into practice there. Black Americans suffered in jobs, education, transport and voting. There was also **racial segregation** where blacks and whites were separated in public places such as restaurants. Even worse, some blacks were **lynched** in public hangings.

Civil Rights movement

After World War II, where black soldiers had fought for the freedoms of others, blacks demanded fairer treatment. In the 1950s, through a process of **passive resistance** and **legal challenges**, blacks had many victories.

One person emerged from the 1950s as the main leader of black America. He was **Martin Luther King**. He continued his campaign of passive resistance leading to a huge march of 250,000 people in Washington in 1963. Here he made his famous, **'I Have a Dream'** speech.

Q Source 3

The Feminine Mystique was an account of the frustrations and unhappiness of educated American women unable, as 'good wives and mothers', to use their education and stretch their intelligence – 'the problem that has no name' – and a criticism of the way in which American society forced women into the role of home-keepers and carers ...

(Arthur Marwick, *The Sixties* [1998])

Q

1. In Source 1, how does Debbie Reynolds in the *Tender Trap* see her role?
2. Why do the women in Source 2 feel stifled in their own homes?
3. Do the women written about in Source 2 see their role in the same way as Debbie Reynolds in Source 1?
4. What has provided 'the meat of dozens of speeches made by troubled presidents of women's colleges' in Source 2?
5. What frustrations does *The Feminine Mystique* refer to in Source 3?
6. What is it criticising?
7. Which of these sources are **primary** and which are **secondary**?
8. How **useful** are they in helping you to understand the problems women faced in the early 1960s?

 PROFILE – BETTY FRIEDAN

- University educated, housewife with three children
- Wrote *The Feminine Mystique* in 1963
- She said women were dependent on their husbands, and that they were frustrated
- She said women should be given a chance to develop their talents
- She founded the National Organisation of Women (NOW)
- She campaigned to achieve equal opportunities for women

Importance of Women's Liberation Movement

- **Laws** were changed to ban discrimination against women
- Women were more **aware** of discrimination and were more prepared to challenge it
- But issues in relation to **promotion** and **pay** were more difficult to overcome

Q Do you agree that the women's liberation movement was only important for middle class women but that poorer women did not benefit from it?

Youth Culture and Revolution

Prior to the 1960s, the role of youth was to carry on the **traditional culture of adults.** This all changed in the late 1950s and especially the 1960s.

By the 1960s, a **youth market** had developed as young people availed of opportunities for part-time and full-time jobs in the growing western economies. A break occurred between youth and

Teddy boys

 Debate the importance of youth culture and the youth revolution

Rockers

adults – the so-called **generation gap** – and music, clothes, soft drinks and food were produced which were geared to the younger generation.

Western countries followed advances in America. There, **Elvis Presley** and others led the **rock 'n roll revolution**. Very soon, Britain produced the **Beatles** and the **Rolling Stones**. Their long hair set a trend because it symbolised the differences with the clean-cut adult world.

Some aspects of youth culture were **more extreme** than others. **Teddy boys**, **mods** and **rockers**, and **hippies** rejected the traditional values of the adults, to differing degrees.

1968

A **more educated middle class youth** developed as more young people went to university. These took a **critical view** of issues in society, some following revolutionary ideas with heroes such as communist leaders Lenin, Trotsky and Che Guevara. They protested about the main issues that impacted on society – the Cold War, the nuclear arms race and the Vietnam War.

Hippies

In 1968, students staged **demonstrations** against the Vietnam War, the running of the government and their universities. There were over 200 demonstrations in the US alone. In **France** in that year, youth leaders protested against their traditional university education. This led to demonstrations and rioting in Paris, in which workers joined them. Even though the student protests ended, they contributed to the downfall of **President de Gaulle** in 1969.

The youth revolution was also reflected in **sexual activity**. The condom and the contraceptive pill, which was introduced in 1960, contributed to more widespread, premarital sex.

Q

1. What was the Beatles first US hit, according to the source?
2. How were the Beatles dressed when they arrived in America on 7 February 1964?
3. How big was their television audience for The Ed Sullivan Show?
4. What examples of fan hysteria are mentioned?
5. What was 'Beatlemania'?
6. What information does this source provide you about the **youth revolution**?

Q Source

Beatles arrive in New York

On February 7, 1964, Pan Am Yankee Clipper flight 101 from London Heathrow lands at New York's Kennedy Airport–and 'Beatlemania' arrives. It was the first visit to the United States by the Beatles, a British rock-and-roll quartet that had just scored its first No. 1 U.S. hit six days before with 'I Want to Hold Your Hand.' At Kennedy, the 'Fab Four' – dressed in mod suits and sporting their trademark pudding bowl haircuts – were greeted by 3,000 screaming fans, who caused a near riot when the boys stepped off their plane and onto American soil.

Two days later, Paul McCartney, age 21, Ringo Starr, 23, John Lennon, 23, and George Harrison, 20, made their first appearance on the *Ed Sullivan Show*, a popular television variety show. Although it was difficult to hear the performance over the screams of teenage girls in the studio audience, an estimated 73 million U.S. television viewers, or about 40 percent of the U.S. population, tuned in to watch. ... By the time the Beatles first feature-film, *A Hard Day's Night*, was released in August, 1964, Beatlemania was epidemic the world over.

(www.history.com/this-day-in-history/beatles-arrive-in-new-york)

The Beatles performing in New York

The Beatles performing on *The Ed Sullivan Show* in America

PROFILE – ELVIS PRESLEY

- US rock 'n roll star
- Became popular in late 1950s
- Drafted to serve in US army for two years
- He had huge hit songs in the 1960s: 'It's Now or Never', 'Are You Lonesome Tonight?'
- Starred in 27 poor quality movies in 1960s
- Developed an unhealthy lifestyle
- Died of a heart attack in 1977

Importance of the Youth Culture and Revolution
- It created **differences** between younger people and adults
- It created a **new market** for products
- It brought about changes in **behaviour** in society

Q Do you agree that the youth revolution only influenced fashion and music, and that they are not really important compared to other issues?

Vatican II

In 1958, a new Pope, **John XXIII**, was elected head of the Catholic Church. Shortly afterwards, he announced the holding of a **special council** for the Catholic Church to update the teachings and rules of the Church.

This Council became known as the **Second Vatican Council** or **Vatican II**. It was held between 1962 and 1965.

Pope John XXIII wanted the Catholic Church to adapt itself to changes in modern society. Even though he died during the Council, the new Pope, **Paul VI**, continued the work.

⊘ Debate the importance of Vatican II

As a result of Vatican II, there was greater **overall lay participation** in the running of the Catholic Church. The Mass, which had been said in Latin up to this, was now said in the **language of the people of the country**. In saying the Mass, the priest faced the people, rather than turning his back as before. The Catholic Church was now more open to modern methods of communication. The Church also improved relations between itself and other Christian churches, and with the Jews. It also reduced the dominance of Italian and European influence and opened the way for **Third World influences**, where most of its followers lived.

However, the goodwill generated by Vatican II was destroyed for many in 1968 when Pope Paul VI condemned artificial birth control. Other changes also occurred as thousands of priests left the priesthood in the decade after Vatican II.

Q

What is your view of the statement that 'Vatican II was only about religion, and religion is not that important'?

The importance of Vatican II

- It led to changes in the Catholic Church to meet the demands of **modern society**
- The changes impacted on people in the **largest religion** in the world
- It led to a greater role for **laity** in the Church
- It **reduced European influence** in the Catholic Church and opened it to Third World influences

PROFILE – POPE JOHN XXIII

- Italian-born Pope
- He called a Council of the Catholic Church, the Vatican Council
- He died during the Council
- But the Council led to **important changes** in the Catholic Church
- He was declared a saint of the Catholic Church in 2014

China – The Cultural Revolution

⊘ Debate the importance of the Cultural Revolution in China

China had become a communist dictatorship in 1949 when **Mao Zedong** won the Chinese civil war and set up the **People's Republic of China**.

In the 1960s, there were disagreements in China about how **Communism** should be organised there. Some leaders wanted more emphasis on factories and to allow peasants to have small plots of land to sell products for profit.

Mao Zedong was opposed to this. He wanted power to remain with the peasants in the **communes**. In 1966 he launched the **Cultural Revolution**. He called on university students and others to form **Red Guards** and he turned them against anybody who disagreed with his policies. Communist Party leaders, factory managers and others were sent out of the cities to learn from the peasants in the countryside.

The country was in chaos, schools and universities were disrupted, up to 1 million people were killed, millions more suffered and the economy declined. Despite this, Mao had complete control until his **death** in 1976.

After his death, the experiences of China during the Cultural Revolution taught many Communist leaders that this could not be repeated. Instead, the new leadership learnt lessons and they wanted to **modernise China** to catch up with other countries. The changes they brought in have led to China becoming the world's second largest economy, after the USA.

Poster of the Chinese Cultural Revolution

Importance of Chinese Cultural Revolution

- It caused **chaos** in China and led to **economic decline**
- It led to many **deaths**
- It taught Chinese leaders that there were **other better ways** to modernise China

Is it true to say the Chinese Cultural Revolution had no influence on the West so it's not important?

Go onto YouTube and look up 'Top 10 Defining Moments of 1960s America'. Next, look up 'Various Artists - Hits Of The 1960s - 100 Original Hit Recordings'.

Crime and Punishment

Crime and Punishment in Modern Times

Crime and punishment in modern times – Who made the laws?

During the 20th century, crime and punishment was influenced by **many factors**.

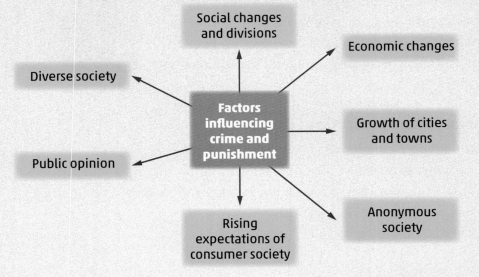

These factors have forced governments to change the laws – sometimes adding more crimes, other times decriminalising (removing criminal penalties from) some actions. Very often governments had to listen to **public opinion** on crime issues, though this was sometimes stirred up by newspapers, which printed sensational stories.

Who enforced the laws?

There were many changes in **policing** during the 20th century. These changes were necessary for police to keep up with changes in crime.

- Police became **motorised**. This allows police to cover wider areas but it took the policemen or women on the beat off the streets.
- Police remained **unarmed** except for batons, pepper sprays and tasers, but some units were armed with guns to deal with more aggressive criminal gangs.
- Some police became **specialised**, such as Drugs Units, Fraud Squads, and Traffic Control.
- Membership of the police forces has changed to ensure places for men and women, but also to reflect different **ethnic groups** in society.
- Police also use **Neighbourhood Watch**, to encourage communities to look out for their members.

Police have used the **benefits of science and technology** to catch and prosecute criminals. This includes fingerprinting (1901) and DNA testing late in 20th century, CCTV, radios and computers to communicate with each other.

 p. 265 ❯

What were the crimes?

In Britain, crime figures were lower in the first half of the 20th century. Then there was a rapid increase from the 1960s onwards.

The figures for some crimes have grown much more rapidly than others.

	Murders	Burglaries	Thefts
1900	312	3,812	63,604
2000	681	1,100,000	2,380,000

(Source: The National Archives, London)

NUMERACY

Q

What do these figures say about crime, if the population of Britain doubled during the same time?

p. 267

Many crimes are variations on older crimes. **Cybercrime**, for example online theft and fraud, are often new versions of older crimes. One difficulty with seeking justice in this area is that those who carry out these crimes are frequently located abroad.

Terrorism has got more notice in recent decades but it is not a new crime. For example, the IRA bombing campaign in Britain during the Troubles was carrying on from similar actions by the Fenians in the 19th century.

However, **new crimes** were also created as society changed. In a multi-cultural society, new laws were passed to protect different groups in society, based on race, religion or sexuality. This included the Race and Religious Hatred Act (2006). There were also new drug laws brought in as wider drug use affected society.

As **cars** became more widespread, new laws were brought in to control their misuse. Apart from speeding and breaking traffic lights, there were others:

- Driving under the influence of drugs
- Driving while using a mobile phone

As attitudes in society changed, some criminal acts were **abolished**. This included decriminalising homosexuality (1967) and abortion in certain situations (1967).

Suffragettes in the early decades of the 20th century were jailed for protesting in favour of votes for women. Some went on hunger strike and they were force-fed.

Prison population per 100,000 head of population, 1901–2016, selected years

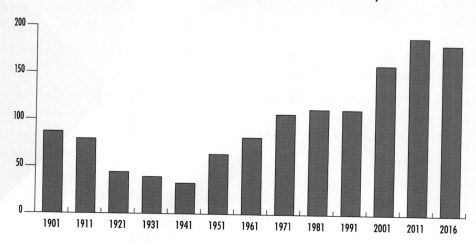

What were the punishments?

In Britain, there was a change in the way prisons were managed in the first half of the 20th century. The harsh system used in the latter half of the 19th century was changed. It was hoped that prisoners would come out of prison better people than they were when they went in.

The **separate system** of the 19th century was dropped and the hard work was reduced and then abolished. Prisoners were allowed ordinary haircuts and clothing rather than the shaven heads and prison clothes of the 19th century. Workshops were set up so that there were more opportunities for work, and prisoners could earn some money. They were also allowed more family visits.

The **death penalty** (capital punishment) was still carried out for murders. However, there was pressure on the governments to change this. There was concern that some innocent people were hanged by mistake. In 1964, the last two criminals were hanged and the next year the death penalty was abolished, except for in the case of treason. Nobody was hanged under this provision before all capital punishment was abolished in Britain in 2004.

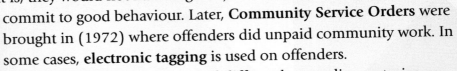

Capital punishment is still carried out in some states in the USA. There is a heated debate there over whether or not capital punishment should be abolished.	
Arguments for capital punishment	**Arguments against capital punishment**
Hanging deterred criminals from committing murder	Most murders are done on the spur of the moment, so deterrents won't work
Murderers deserved to die since they had killed a person/people	The governments are only acting revengefully
Murderers get a fair trial and justice is done	Many people who have been found guilty of murder have since proved their innocence

Conditions became more difficult from the 1960s onwards. As there was an increase in crime, the jails had more offenders who served longer sentences. This resulted in a greater prison population. The **difficult conditions** resulted in prison riots in the 1970s and later in 1990.

There were **new punishments** introduced rather than just prison. Some people could get **probation**, that is, they would not have to go to jail for minor offences if they could commit to good behaviour. Later, **Community Service Orders** were brought in (1972) where offenders did unpaid community work. In some cases, **electronic tagging** is used on offenders.

Young offenders were treated differently to earlier centuries. Rather than mixing them with adult criminals, new institutions were set up for them. The **Borstal system** began in 1902, with the purpose of reforming the young offender through training and counselling. Later, **juvenile courts** were set up.

Electronic tag on a young offender

However, later in the 20th century, there was criticism of the Borstal system because the re-offending rate was high. As a result, Borstals were closed in 1982, and **Youth Detention Centres** were set up. These were based on the 'short, sharp, shock'. In spite of this re-offending rates continued to be high.

Health and Medicine

Health and Medicine in the Modern World

⊘ Illustrate patterns of change in Health and Medicine in the Modern World

There were very significant discoveries in health and medicine in the modern world, which added to developments in the 19th century.

These discoveries have increased the life expectancy of men and women by many years.

The average life expectancy has increased during the 20th century, mainly because **child mortality** (death of children under five) has been reduced dramatically. Prior to this, the most dangerous time for anybody was in the first year of life, as children died from many curable diseases. Life expectancy was also extended by medical advances, which have cured and controlled many diseases to allow people to live longer.

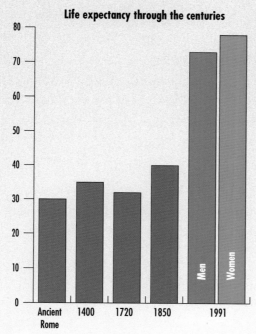

Life expectancy through the centuries

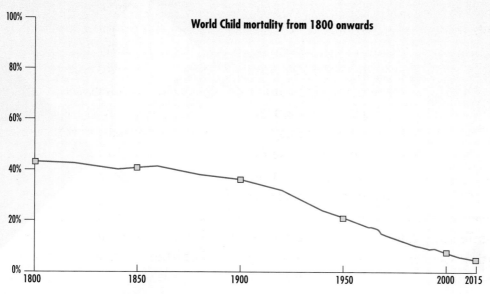

World Child mortality from 1800 onwards

◖ p. 259

During the 20th century, scientists and doctors added to our knowledge of the body and diseases. For example, they discovered:

- **Histamine**, which is produced by the body during an allergic reaction
- **Insulin**, which breaks down sugar in the bloodstream
- The **hormones**, which control femaleness (oestrogen) and maleness (testosterone)
- **Vitamins** and the role they play in certain diseases
- **DNA**, which carries the genetic information used to develop living organisms
- The **Human Genome** project, which mapped all the genes in the human body

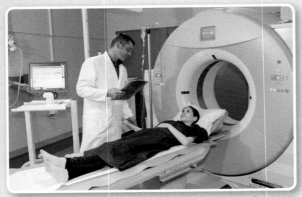

Modern MRI

Cures and remedies

There were a number of inventions that helped doctors understand better the workings of the body and to **diagnose** illnesses.

- **Electron microscope** to see bacteria and viruses
- **Endoscopes**, fibre optic cables to allow doctors see inside the body
- **Ultrasound**, a high frequency sound, to scan internal organs and for prenatal care
- **CAT scanners**, which developed 3D images of the inside of the body
- **MRI scanners**, which looked at the workings of the brain

Based on better knowledge of the working of the body and better diagnosis, doctors were able to develop **treatments** to deal with specific illnesses.

- **Insulin** was produced to alleviate the effects of diabetes

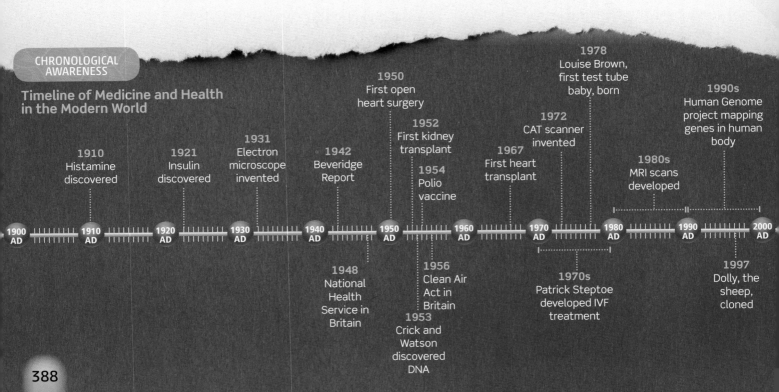

CHRONOLOGICAL AWARENESS

Timeline of Medicine and Health in the Modern World

1910
Histamine discovered

1921
Insulin discovered

1931
Electron microscope invented

1942
Beveridge Report

1948
National Health Service in Britain

1950
First open heart surgery

1952
First kidney transplant

1954
Polio vaccine

1956
Clean Air Act in Britain

1953
Crick and Watson discovered DNA

1967
First heart transplant

1972
CAT scanner invented

1978
Louise Brown, first test tube baby, born

1970s
Patrick Steptoe developed IVF treatment

1980s
MRI scans developed

1990s
Human Genome project mapping genes in human body

1997
Dolly, the sheep, cloned

1900 AD — 1910 AD — 1920 AD — 1930 AD — 1940 AD — 1950 AD — 1960 AD — 1970 AD — 1980 AD — 1990 AD — 2000 AD

- **Vitamin supplements** were used to cure some diseases such as rickets (which causes softening of the bones)
- **Hormone treatments** were developed for thyroid, growth and cancer

One of the most important discoveries was **penicillin**, discovered accidentally by Alexander Fleming in 1928, which was the **first antibiotic**. It was first mass produced during World War II and used to treat soldiers' infections in the war. However, its over use has resulted in the development of **superbugs**, such as MRSA, which are resistant to penicillin and other antibiotics.

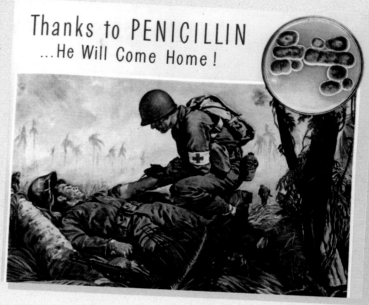

Thanks to PENICILLIN
...He Will Come Home!

Another important development was the **polio vaccine**, which eradicated polio from the Western World, and has almost eradicated it from the rest of the world.

There was more success with the battle against **smallpox**. This disease killed an estimated 300 to 500 million people in the 20th century before its complete eradication by 1980.

Medical discoveries also impacted on **human reproduction**. The invention of the contraceptive pill, first approved for use in 1960, was used to prevent pregnancy and to limit family size. On the other hand, in vitro fertilisation (IVF) was used to help childless women to have children. In 1978, Louise Brown became the first baby conceived by IVF.

Further developments in relation to the ability of doctors to decide on the characteristics of babies has raised **moral questions** about the extent to which humans should interfere in the process of choosing between 'inferior' and 'superior' characteristics, similar to Nazi experiments in Germany.

Louise Brown

Medicine had also to cope with a number of **pandemics** (widespread diseases) during the last hundred years or so. In 1918–19, the **Spanish flu** killed 20 to 40 million people worldwide. Towards the end of the 20th century, from the late 1970s, the **AIDS** epidemic, spread worldwide from Africa, resulted in increasing numbers of deaths up to 2005. Since then, due to medical advances, the annual number of deaths has declined from 2.3 million in 2005 to 1.2 million in 2014.

Conventional medicine is still not able to cure certain viral infections such as the common cold. Cancer is still a killer disease, even though much progress has been made in its diagnosis and treatment.

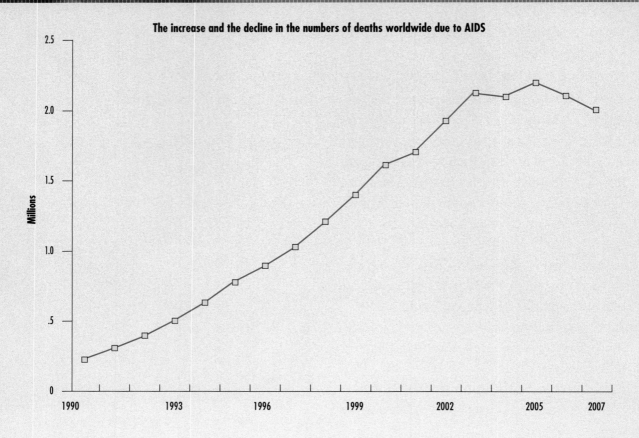

The increase and the decline in the numbers of deaths worldwide due to AIDS

Some people preferred to use **alternative medicines**, sometimes called Holistic medicine. These include treatments such as aromatherapy, hypnotherapy and acupuncture. There is also much support for herbal remedies and this has led to the growth of health shops.

Changing **lifestyles** have also presented **problems** for medicine. Heart disease and liver disease are two killer diseases in the modern world, which are largely caused by smoking, lack of exercise, obesity, bad diet and excessive alcohol. Medicine now has an educational role in trying to change people's lifestyles to prevent disease.

Surgery

Surgery made significant advances during the 20th century, partly due to the impact of **two world wars**, which produced injuries that doctors had to find new skills and methods to deal with. In World War I, surgeons used **skin grafts** to reconstruct damaged faces. They also benefitted from the discovery of blood groups before the war, and its use in blood transfusions during the war. After the war, in 1921, the British Red Cross created the first blood donor scheme.

There were further advances in World War II, when surgeons used **plastic surgery** to treat the faces of airmen burnt in the war.

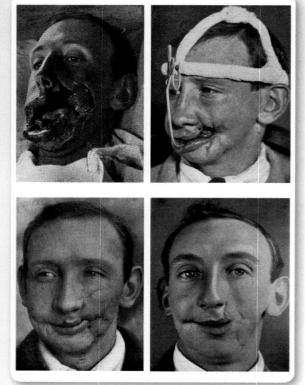

World War II facial reconstruction

25

THE 1960S
– An Important Decade in Irish History

ONE MAN ONE VOTE

LO: 2.12
The Nature of History: 1.1, 1.2, 1.3, 1.4, 1.5, 1.6, 1.7, 1.8, 1.9, 1.10, 1.11
CBA1
CBA2

You will learn to ...

- Debate the idea of the 1960s as an important decade in Irish history
- Examine the role of relevant personalities, issues and events
- Explore the Nature of History

KEY WORDS

- Economic change
- Social change
- Emigration
- Unemployment
- Modernising
- Civil rights
- Discrimination
- North-south relations

CHRONOLOGICAL AWARENESS

1958
First Programme for Economic Expansion published

1960 AD

1961 AD

1961
RTÉ's first TV broadcast on New Years' Eve

1962 AD

1963 AD

1963
Terence O'Neill became Prime Minister of Northern Ireland
President Kennedy visits Ireland

1964 AD

1965 AD

1966 AD

1966
50th Anniversary of 1916 Rising
Ulster Volunteer Force formed

1967
Northern Ireland Civil Rights Association (NICRA) formed
Free secondary education in Republic of Ireland introduced

1967 AD

1968
RUC stop Civil Rights march in Derry

1968 AD

1969
Terence O'Neill resigned as PM of Northern Ireland
Battle of the Bogside in Londonderry (Derry)
British troops sent to Northern Ireland

1969 AD

1970 AD

Why was the 1960s an Important Decade in Ireland?

The 1960s was a very important decade in Ireland. There were many **key events**, **personalities** and **issues**, which shaped the decade.

ONE MAN
ONE VOTE

⊘ Explain why
the 1960s was
an important
decade in
Ireland

The 1960s in Ireland were characterised by certain important **issues**:

- The Republic of Ireland had experienced serious **unemployment** and **emigration** during the 1950s, which contrasted with the prosperity of Europe and Britain. New **economic policies** were brought in to solve these problems.
- Ireland began to open a window to the wider world as prosperity increased during the 1960s. The economic changes led to important **changes in society**.
- Northern Ireland was ruled the same way it had been since 1920, with a unionist majority. Better education for Catholics and the example of the civil rights campaigns in America led to a **civil rights campaign** in Northern Ireland.

ONE MAN
ONE VOTE

⊘ Debate the
importance
of economic
changes in
Ireland in the
1960s

What Important Changes Occurred in Economic Policy in the 1960s?

Introduction – the 1950s

There was **high unemployment** and **high emigration** in Ireland in the **1950s** and the population fell. Government policy was based on protecting home industry by putting taxes on imports (protectionism). Emigration averaged 40,000 a year in that decade, workers' income fell and there were fewer people working. Changes were needed in the way the country was run.

Unemployment march in Dublin in the 1950s

Q

1. Why is this considered a **secondary source**?
2. What are the **strengths** and **weaknesses** of secondary sources?
3. What would the returning immigrant recognise after 30 years?
4. What was 'as common as ever'?
5. Give **one fact** and **one opinion** from this extract. Explain your answers by referring to evidence in the source.

🔍 **Source**

An immigrant returning to the Republic of Ireland in **the late fifties** after thirty years abroad would have had few recognition problems. The country had no television station, although the few homes on the east coast who could afford TV sets picked up programmes from the British stations. Shopping was still the homely experience it always had been, for there were no supermarkets or shopping centres. If he could afford to buy a car – which most people who remained in Ireland could not – the state would not oblige him to undergo any test of his driving proficiency. The ferocious literary and film censorship was as vigilant as it had been when he left. Those most conservative of Irish institutions, the churches, were very much as they had been in 1930 ... Late marriages, large families and high rates of emigration were as common as ever.

(Fergal Tobin, *The Best of Decades, Ireland in the Nineteen Sixties*, Gill and Co., Dublin, 198)

The Republic of Ireland

Seán Lemass became Taoiseach in 1959, and he promoted a new economic policy. This was called the **First Programme for Economic Expansion**.

He abolished the old policy of protection because it had failed and instead:

- Encouraged **exports**
- Gave **tax concessions** and **grants** to attract foreign industry to set up factories in Ireland.

This brought British and American companies to Ireland. Employment rose and emigration slowed down. Living standards also rose, as people were better off. The population began to increase from 1961 onwards.

There were other programmes for economic expansion during the 1960s, but these were not as successful. However, the economic changes that occurred in 1960s Ireland were the **basis for future progress** in the country.

The Population of the Republic of Ireland, 1926–1971

Important changes in education

The system of education also changed. School courses were changed and improved. New schools were built and older ones were refurbished. The Minister for Education, **Donagh O'Malley**, brought in a scheme for **free secondary education** and free transport, which was introduced in 1969. The first community and comprehensive schools were also built. These combined the academic subjects of the secondary school with the practical subjects of the vocational school. Numbers going to secondary school increased rapidly.

At the time, about a third – or 17,000 children – who finished primary school were dropping out of education; at 15 years of age fewer than 50 per cent were still in full-time education. By 16, only 36 per cent were still at school.

Within a decade of the policy change, participation rates in second-level had doubled.

Today, Ireland has one of the highest rates of second-level completion in the EU, with more than 90 per cent of the population completing the Leaving Cert.

(*The Irish Times*, 14 February 2017)

Analysing Sources

Q

1. Is Source 1 a **primary** or a **secondary** source?
2. What is meant by an 'era of change'?
3. From your reading of this chapter and the previous chapter, do you agree with the statement?
4. According to this source, what was 'the basic fault in our present educational structure'?
5. What does Donogh O'Malley propose to do to tackle the situation?

EVIDENCE AND SOURCES

NUMERACY

Q

1. What was the **increase** in the numbers of students sitting the Leaving Cert. exam between each of the following: **(a)** 1951 and 1956 **(b)** 1956 and 1961 **(c)** 1961 and 1966 **(d)** 1966 and 1972?
2. Which time period had the **largest** increase?
3. Based on Source 1, what **reason(s)** would you suggest for the largest change in numbers?
4. How do the changes in school numbers between **(a)** 1951 and 1961 **(b)** 1961 and 1972 **compare** with the changes in overall population above?
5. What do you think is the connection between education and economic growth in the country?
6. How do your answers to **(4)** and **(5)** help you **understand** the increase in student numbers?
7. Is the graph a **primary** or a **secondary** source?

Q Source 1

What of the future? We are, it must be remembered constantly, living through an era of change. Many of the former assumptions on which we based our lives are being questioned. The world of today and tomorrow would give scant attention to the uneducated and those lacking any qualification.

We will be judged by future generations on what we did for the children of our time. ... There was no difficulty in picking out the basic fault in our present educational structure – and that was the fact that many families could not afford to pay even part of the cost of education for their children. ... Every year some 17,000 of our children who finish their primary school course do not receive any further education. ... I believe that this is a situation which must be tackled with all speed and determination. ... I propose therefore, from the coming school year, beginning in September of next year, to introduce a scheme whereby, up to the completion of the Intermediate Certificate course, the opportunity for free post-primary education will be available to all families.

(Speech by Donogh O'Malley, Minister of Education, *The Irish Times*, 12 September 1966)

Q Source 2

Number of Students Taking the Leaving Certificate, 1951–72

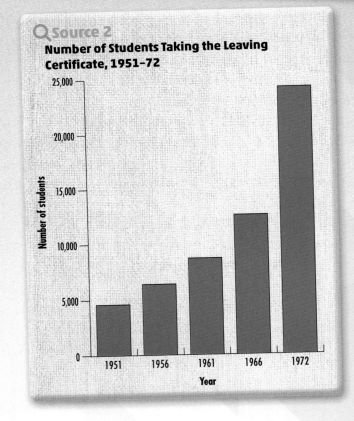

- Involved in 1916 Rising, War of Independence and Civil War
- Minister for Industry and Commerce in 1930s
- Minister for Supplies during World War II
- Introduced the **First Programme for Economic Expansion** – very successful
- Elected Taoiseach when Eamon de Valera got elected as President of Ireland
- Introduced the Second Programme for Economic Expansion but this was not as successful
- Met Terence O'Neill, Prime Minister of Northern Ireland, on two occasions
- He resigned as Taoiseach in 1966

What Important Social Changes Occurred?

The 1960s were the **'Swinging Sixties'** in contrast to the **depressed fifties**. People were **better off** in Ireland in the 1960s. There were many changes in the way people lived. The first shopping centres were built. These encouraged weekly rather than daily shopping, and they undermined the local grocery shop. More tourists came to the country, and more Irish people holidayed abroad, and these changes **opened up the country** to the wider world.

The **Catholic Church** brought in many reforms after Vatican II, the major church council (see p. 381). The Latin Mass was changed to the **vernacular** (English or Irish), the priest faced the people, there was greater **lay participation** in church services, folk masses were introduced and there were better relations with other religions (ecumenism).

Debate the importance of social changes in Ireland in the 1960s

The changes to the Mass in the Catholic Church – old rites (right) and new rites (left)

Teilifís Éireann (later RTÉ) was set up and television brought in new ideas to the country (1961). In programmes like *The Late Late Show* and *7 Days* many topics in Irish society were opened up for discussion and investigation. *'The critical achievement of Irish television in the 1960s [was that it] forced us to look at ourselves new.'* (Tobin)

When John F. Kennedy, President of the United States, came to Ireland in 1963, he said:

'You have modernised your economy, harnessed your rivers, diversified your industry, liberalised your trade, electrified your farms, accelerated your rate of growth and improved the living standards of your people.'

Irish racehorse Arkle, winner of three consecutive Cheltenham Gold Cups from 1964 to 1966

Gay Byrne presenting *The Late Late Show*

President Kennedy's visit to Ireland – meeting his relations in Wexford

DID YOU KNOW?
1966 was the 50th anniversary of the 1916 Rising. In advance of the celebration, a group of IRA men blew up the Nelson Monument in the centre of O'Connell Street, Dublin.

What Important Changes Occurred in Entertainment in the 1960s in Ireland?

Cinema and television

Cinema continued to be popular up to the 1960s, when **television** led to its decline. This was one of the consequences of the setting up of RTÉ. Sports programmes and soap operas attracted audiences, as did programmes such as *The Late Late Show*, on which controversial topics were discussed. It was easier and cheaper to stay at home watching television rather than going to the cinema.

Traditional music

There was a boom in Irish traditional music in the 1960s, which became popular with a new generation. **Seán Ó Riada** and his Ceoltóirí Cualainn modernised the sound of Irish traditional music. Ó Riada wrote the score for *Mise Éire* (1959), a documentary on the 1916 Rising and its aftermath, which was played by an orchestra. As part of the revival of Irish music, there was also a **ballad boom**. Here groups such as The Dubliners and the Clancy Brothers and Tommy Makem brought Irish folk songs to a wider audience. The continuing popularity of Irish traditional music **owes much to changes** made in the 1960s.

Seán O'Riada contributed to a revival of Irish traditional music

The Dubliners popularised many Irish folk songs

The 1960s was also the showband era, where Irish showbands played to huge audiences in dance halls across the country

What Changes made the 1960s Important in Northern Ireland?

ONE MAN ONE VOTE

⊙ Debate the importance of personalities, events and issues in Northern Ireland in the 1960s

A new Prime Minister, **Terence O'Neill**, took over in Northern Ireland in 1963. The North's traditional industries – shipbuilding, aircraft manufacture and linen – were in serious decline. He said his main goals were *'to make Northern Ireland economically stronger and prosperous … and to build bridges between the two traditions in our community.'*

In **industry**, the O'Neill government attracted new industries to the North – Ford, Goodyear and Imperial Chemicals. These industries were mostly located in the Protestant, eastern part of Ulster.

O'Neill also tried to improve **relations with Catholics**. He took over from a Prime Minister before him, Lord Brookeborough, who *'never crossed the border (with the South), never visited a Catholic school, and never received or sought a civic reception from a Catholic town.'*

- In contrast, O'Neill met the Catholic **Cardinal Conway**, Archbishop of Armagh
- He visited **Catholic schools**.

However, one of his decisions was to build a **new university** in Coleraine, a mainly Protestant town, rather than Derry/Londonderry, a mainly Catholic city.

PROFILE – TERENCE O'NEILL

- Became Prime Minister of Northern Ireland in 1963
- Attracted foreign industry to Northern Ireland
- Worked to improve relations with Catholics/ nationalists
- Met Taoiseach Seán Lemass (1965) and Jack Lynch (1967)
- Opposed by extreme unionists, led by Rev. Ian Paisley
- Brought in some reforms to Northern Ireland
- Resigned as Prime Minister in 1969

Why were the 1960s important for North-South relations?

There were also changes in the South, where Lemass changed government policy in relation to Northern Ireland. He believed that the best way to end the partition between the North and the South was to make Southern Ireland more prosperous. He met **Terence O'Neill**, Prime Minister of Northern Ireland, in Belfast and in Dublin in 1965. These were the first official meetings between the leaders of the two states since partition in 1920. However, by the end of the 1960s relations had worsened between North and South as the Troubles began (see Ch. 26).

Why were the 1960s important for relations between Catholics and Protestants in Northern Ireland?

Tensions began to grow in Northern Ireland. More extreme unionists were worried about O'Neill's efforts to improve relations with Catholics. The **Ulster Volunteer Force (UVF)** was formed in 1966, and a number of Catholics were killed. **Rev. Ian Paisley**, leader of the Free Presbyterian Church, was one of those very critical of O'Neill's efforts to improve relations with Catholics.

Catholics were also disappointed with O'Neill – they thought he should be bringing in more reforms. Catholics were still discriminated against in several areas.

Discrimination against Catholics in Northern Ireland

- The **property qualification** for voting in local elections meant that only property owners could vote – this favoured Protestants
- There was **gerrymandering** in constituencies so that unionists controlled councils in nationalist majority areas
- The allocation of **houses** by local councils favoured Protestants
- The allocation of **jobs** in the civil service and local councils favoured Protestants

The importance of Civil Rights

The disappointment of Catholics and nationalists led to the formation of the **Northern Ireland Civil Rights Association** (NICRA) in 1967. This was inspired by the civil rights movement in America. NICRA made the following demands:

- 'One man, one vote' in local elections
- An end to gerrymandering
- An end to discrimination in jobs and housing.

There were **marches** and **rioting** in Derry and Belfast. In October 1968, a civil rights march in Derry was stopped by the RUC. The television cameras captured the brutal treatment of its leaders by the police. This shocked people in the rest of Ireland and Britain.

The British government forced O'Neill and his government to bring in **reforms** in housing and local elections. However, this did not stop the demonstrations. O'Neill had to face opposition from extreme unionists, led by Ian Paisley, who demanded that he should not give in to Catholics. O'Neill was forced to **resign** in 1969 when he lost the support of his own party. The conflicts between nationalists and unionists got more serious, and developed into the **Troubles** from the end of 1969 onwards (see p. 403).

❯ Preparing for CBA1

A project related to an aspect of the history of your locality or place (or personal/family history)

LOCAL PROJECTS FROM 1960S IRELAND

Your locality can include your county

- Development of industry in the 1960s in your locality
- What your local newspaper said about developments in the 1960s in Ireland
- Changes in your local Catholic Church
- Interviews with local people concerning changes in the 1960s
- President Kennedy's visit to your locality
- Changes to local post-primary schools

❯ Preparing for CBA2

A project on the life and experience of a person of historical interest

PERSONS OF HISTORICAL INTEREST IN IRELAND OF THE 1960S

- Seán Lemass
- Declan Costello
- Michael O'Hehir
- Edna O'Brien
- Seán Ó Riada

- T. K. Whitaker
- Cardinal Conway
- Feargal Quinn
- Frances Condell
- Bridie Gallagher

- Archbishop McQuaid
- Gay Byrne
- Mick O'Connell
- Monica Sheridan
- Maureen Potter

HISTORICAL INVESTIGATION

Focus Task

p. 225 ❯
Web Resources and Reading

> Investigate the RTÉ Archives on the 1960s. What is your impression of the 1960s from a selection of the stories in the RTÉ Archives?

26

THE TROUBLES IN NORTHERN IRELAND

L.O. 2.5
The Nature of History: 1.1,
1.2, 1.3, 1.4, 1.5, 1.6, 1.7,
1.8, 1.9, 1.10, 1.11
CBA1
CBA2

NICRA

You will learn to ...

- ◎ Identify the causes of the Troubles in Northern Ireland
- ◎ Identify the course and consequences of the Troubles in Northern Ireland
- ◎ Examine their impact on North-South and Anglo-Irish relations

CHRONOLOGICAL AWARENESS

1609
The Ulster Plantation

1641
Massacre of Protestants

1690
Victory of William of Orange at the Battle of the Boyne

1800
Act of Union

1885–86
Sectarian riots in Belfast

1912
Foundation of Ulster Volunteer Force
Signing of Ulster Solemn League and Covenant

1916
Easter Rising

1920
Government of Ireland Act, setting up Northern Ireland

1969
The Battle of the Bogside
British army in streets of Northern Ireland
McGurk's Bar bombing by the UVF
IRA split into Official and Provisional IRA

1967
Foundation of NICRA (Northern Ireland Civil Rights Association)

1970
Provisional IRA began bombing campaign

1972
Bloody Sunday in Derry
Direct Rule from Westminster
Bloody Friday – IRA bombings in Belfast
Worst year for deaths in the Troubles

1973
The Sunningdale Agreement

1974
Ulster Workers' Council Strike

1978
Le Mon Bombing by the IRA

1979
Warrenpoint Ambush by the IRA

1981
Hunger Strike in Maze Prison
Death of Bobby Sands 1982
The Downing Street Declaration

1998
The Good Friday Agreement
The power-sharing government in Northern Ireland

2001
IRA began decommissioning weapons

KEY WORDS

- Parliamentary tradition
- Nationalist
- Loyalist
- Conquest
- The Troubles
- Gerrymandering
- Paramilitary
- Hunger strike
- Physical force tradition
- Unionist
- Sectarian
- Colonisation
- Discrimination
- Civil rights
- Internment

What were the Troubles?

The **Troubles** refers to the conflict which occurred in Northern Ireland from the late 1960s to 1998. The conflict involved the **unionist** and **nationalist** communities in the North.

⊘ Define the Troubles

It also involved their political representatives and various paramilitary groups on both sides, as well as British security forces. It resulted in over 3,000 deaths, migration of people and widespread destruction. It also involved the British and Irish governments in trying to find a solution that would end the Troubles.

What were they all about?

The Troubles initially began with Catholic/nationalist demands for improved **civil rights**. These were resisted by some unionists who felt that the demands would give more power to nationalists and would undermine Northern Ireland. Demonstrations and riots arose from clashes between nationalists and unionists (or Loyalists), and the police. These led the British government to bring in the British army to protect the nationalist community.

Paramilitary involvement in the conflict from both sides – the **IRA** on the nationalist side, and the **UVF (Ulster Volunteer Force)** and **UDA** (Ulster Defence Association) on the unionist side, dramatically increased the levels of violence. The IRA also went beyond civil rights demands by looking for a **united Ireland**.

⊘ Identify the causes of the Troubles in Northern Ireland

What Caused the Troubles?

The Troubles had both **long-term** and **short-term causes**. The long-term causes went back to the British use of conquest and colonisation in Ireland in the 16th and 17th centuries. The short-term causes were those which led to nationalist demands for reform in Northern Ireland in the 1960s.

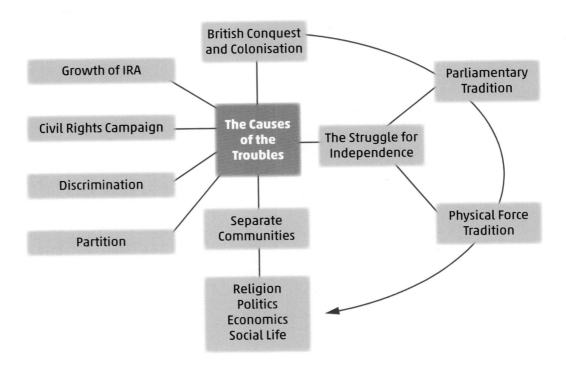

What were the long-term causes of the Troubles?

British conquest and colonisation

In the 16th and 17th centuries, the kings and queens of England used **war and plantation** to conquer Ireland.

They took land from the Gaelic and Anglo-Norman lords and gave it to Protestant planters from England and Scotland. By the end of the 17th century, the Protestant settlers controlled the land and government of Ireland (see Ch. 8).

The struggle for independence

By the end of the 18th century, many people in Ireland were calling for greater or full independence from Britain (see Ch. 10). These nationalists formed two different groups:

- One group favoured the **parliamentary tradition**. They wanted to achieve a separate parliament for Ireland by **peaceful means**.
- The second group favoured the **physical force tradition**. They wanted to achieve complete separation or independence from Britain by **armed rebellion**.

These were opposed by a third group, **unionists**. After the **Act of Union** in 1800, which brought in direct rule in Ireland from the parliament in Westminster, unionists wanted to maintain the unity of Britain and Ireland. The unionists were strongest in Ulster.

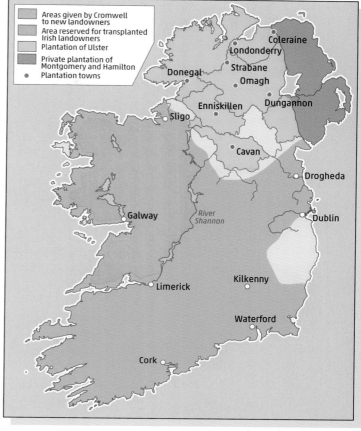

Map legend:
- Areas given by Cromwell to new landowners
- Area reserved for transplanted Irish landowners
- Plantation of Ulster
- Private plantation of Montgomery and Hamilton
- Plantation towns

Plantations in the 16th and 17th centuries resulted in the transfer of land and power from Gaelic and Anglo Irish lords to Protestant settlers

A Belfast mural featuring King William of Orange. In the Battle of the Boyne in 1690, the Protestant William of Orange defeated the Catholic King James. Protestants and unionists celebrate this victory on 12 July each year, as a victory that guaranteed the Protestant Ascendancy (power, control) in Ireland (see p. 142).

Analysing Sources

Separate communities

By the early 20th century, **two separate communities** had grown up in Northern Ireland. Protestants who had most of the power **feared** that Catholics in a united Ireland would **discriminate** against them.

CONTROVERSIAL ISSUES

Q Source 1
Separate Communities

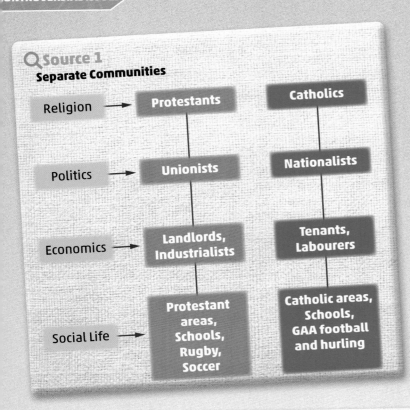

	Protestants	Catholics
Religion →		
Politics →	Unionists	Nationalists
Economics →	Landlords, Industrialists	Tenants, Labourers
Social Life →	Protestant areas, Schools, Rugby, Soccer	Catholic areas, Schools, GAA football and hurling

Q Source 2
Separate schools

The teachers liked to pretend it was a civilised outpost of England: rugby, cricket and English headmasters. There was little to suggest we were living in Ireland – no Irish history, no Irish literature, no Irish music. I could rhyme off the names of the English kings and queens but I hardly ever heard of Wolfe Tone and Daniel O'Connell.

(A Protestant grammar school in the 1950s: N. Longley, New Statesman, 1974)

Q Source 3
Separate schools

St Patrick's Academy Dungannon, where I went, was a patriotic school. It owed its proudly Irish slant to the Vice-Principal, Mother Benignus. She disliked the English. All her family had suffered at the hands of the British forces. She was very keen about Irish culture which drives lots of people away who couldn't take it for breakfast, dinner and tea.

She didn't hate Protestants. But her view was that you couldn't very well put up with them, they weren't Irish. We learned Irish history. The interpretations we were given were very different from Protestant history books.

(A Catholic grammar school in the 1960s: Bernadette Devlin, *The Price of My Soul*, 1969)

Q Source 4
Catholic and Protestant ghettos in Belfast

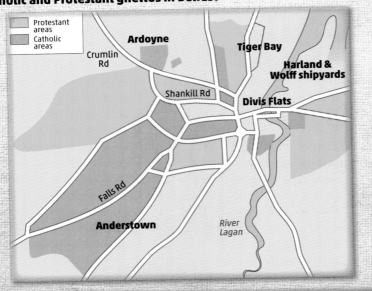

Protestant areas
Catholic areas

Ardoyne
Crumlin Rd
Tiger Bay
Harland & Wolff shipyards
Shankill Rd
Divis Flats
Falls Rd
Anderstown
River Lagan

Q Source 5
Different views of Cú Chulainn

Cú Chulainn was a legendary Irish hero who defended Ulster against the attack of the army of Queen Maedbh of Connacht. Nationalist and unionist wall murals feature Cú Chulainn for different reasons.

Q

1. Select three **differences** between Catholics and Protestants in Source 1, apart from religious differences.
2. How do Sources 2 and 3 differ about the school experience of Catholic and Protestant students?
3. Which of the **features** in Source 1 is/are supported by Sources 2 and 3?
4. What does Source 4 tell you about differences between Catholics and Protestants?
5. How do Protestant/unionists and Catholics/nationalists view the story of Cú Chulainn in Source 5?
6. Summarise the differences between Catholics and Protestants as shown in these sources.
7. Which of the sources here are **primary** and which are **secondary**?
   Explain your answers by referring to evidence in the sources.

> IDENTITY

> COMMEMMORATION

Partition

Between 1912 and 1920, unionists in the North of Ireland resisted all efforts to force them into a Home Rule Ireland. By 1920, they had won their battle when the **Government of Ireland Act** established a parliament in Belfast to deal with the internal affairs of Northern Ireland. At the same time there were **serious riots** in Belfast in which Catholics/nationalists suffered a greater number of deaths and injuries (See pp. 244–46).

From 1920 onwards, the unionists **dominated** the parliament of Northern Ireland and controlled the area in their own interest.

What were the short-term causes of the Troubles?

Discrimination

One of the ways the unionists maintained power in Northern Ireland was by **discriminating** against Catholics or nationalists. This happened in local government, housing and jobs (see p. 408).

Gerrymandering

One example of discrimination was **gerrymandering**. In this process, unionists rigged the votes so that areas with a Catholic majority still elected a majority of unionist councillors to local government. The most blatant **example** of that was in Derry/Londonderry. Unionists in gerrymandered councils controlled the allocation of houses and jobs.

Analysing Sources

Discrimination

Source 1
Gerrymandering

p. 232

North Ward
6476 voters
3946 Protestants
2530 Catholics
8 Unionist councillors

River Foyle

Waterside Ward
5549 voters
3697 Protestants
1852 Catholics
4 Unionist councillors

South Ward
11,185 voters
10,047 Catholics
1138 Protestants
8 Nationalist councillors

In Derry/Londonderry, unionists divided up the city in such a way that the minority unionist population was able to get a majority of unionist councillors elected to control the city council. You can examine the map and the figures here to show how the unionists controlled the local council.

Source 2

Many of you employ Catholics but I have not one about the house. In Northern Ireland the Catholic population is increasing. 97% of Catholics in Ireland are disloyal and disruptive. If we allow Catholics to work on our farms we are traitors to Ulster.

(Basil Brooke, future Prime Minister of Northern Ireland, speaking in 1933)

NUMERACY

Source 3
Protestant and Catholic Employment in Belfast Engineering Firms, 1982

Firm	Protestant employees (%)	Catholic employees (%)
Sirocco	98	2
Shorts	92–6	4–8
Mackies	90	10
Ford	91	9
Harland and Wolff	100	0

Q

1. In Source 1, use the figures to show how Unionists controlled the local council in Derry/Londonderry.
2. In Source 2, what was the **attitude** of Basil Brooke to Catholics?
3. What does he mean when he says 'If we allow Catholics to work on our farms we are traitors to Ulster'?
4. What are the **conclusions** to be drawn from the information in Source 3?
5. What do Sources 1 to 3 tell you about discrimination in Northern Ireland?

Civil Rights and the beginning of the Troubles

The disappointment of Catholics and nationalists led to the formation of the **Northern Ireland Civil Rights Association** (NICRA) in 1967. This was inspired by the civil rights movement in America (see p. 370). NICRA made the following demands:

- 'One man, one vote' in local elections.
- An end to gerrymandering.
- An end to discrimination in housing and jobs.

Its leaders included **Gerry Fitt**, **John Hume**, **Austin Currie** and **Bernadette Devlin**. There were marches and demonstrations, and rioting in Derry and Belfast.

The Prime Minister, **Terence O'Neill**, made efforts to improve relations with the Catholics. Despite this tensions began to grow in Northern Ireland. More extreme unionists were worried about O'Neill's efforts to improve relations with Catholics. The **UVF** was formed, and a number of Catholics were killed.

John Hume, Austin Currie, Paddy O'Hanlon and Bernadette Devlin – leaders of the Northern Ireland Civil Rights Association

On the other hand, Catholics were disappointed that O'Neill was not bringing in more reforms. Catholics were still discriminated against in several areas. Divisions between the two communities continued to grow.

The day the Troubles began

In October 1968, a **civil rights march in Derry** was stopped by the **Royal Ulster Constabulary (RUC)**. The television cameras captured the brutal treatment of its leaders by the police. This shocked people in the rest of Ireland and in Britain. The British Government forced O'Neill to bring in reforms in housing and in local elections, but this did not stop the demonstrations. O'Neill also had to face opposition from the extreme unionists, led by **Ian Paisley**, who demanded that he should not give in to Catholics. O'Neill was forced to resign in 1969 when he lost the support of his own party. He was succeeded by Major James Chichester-Clark.

Belfast people with belongings they have salvaged after being driven out of their home

Analysing Sources

The Day the Troubles began

Source 1
The Day the Troubles Began

RTÉ Archives | Archives Daily | Exhibitions ∨ | Collections ∨ | Profiles ∨ | About ∨ | Search ⊙

▷ **March Marks Beginnings of Troubles** 1968

WAR AND CONFLICT

(www.rte.ie)

Q

1. What **date** is given for the beginning of the Troubles?
2. What did NICRA **plan** on that day?
3. What group **opposed** them?
4. What decision did William Craig make?
5. What happened to the marchers?
6. To what extent were the **(a)** marchers and **(b)** police to **blame** for what happened?
7. Why is this called the 'Day the Troubles Began'?
8. Why, do you think, people said to Eamonn McCann, 'Things will never be the same again'?
9. How can you judge the **reliability** of this source?
10. Identify **one cause** and **one consequence** of any actions in this report. Explain your answers by using evidence from the source.

Source 2

Showdown on 5 October

After their first march on 24 August 1968 in County Tyrone, **NICRA** were invited by the Derry Housing Action Committee (DHAC) to hold a march in County Londonderry on 5 October. The **Apprentice Boys of Derry**, a Protestant society, announced plans to march the same route, on the same day. Northern Ireland's Minister for Home Affairs, **William Craig**, responded by issuing a banning order on all marches within the boundaries of the planned route.

On the day of the march, a few hundred civil rights protesters planned to walk from Duke Street, in the predominantly Protestant Waterside area of Derry, to the Diamond in the centre of the city. Duke Street had been declared out of bounds by Craig's order and marchers were confronted by rows of police officers from the RUC.

The police used batons and water cannons in an attempt to disperse the marchers and violent skirmishes broke out. Among those injured in the clash were **Gerry Fitt**, a Republican Labour MP, and three (Westminster) Labour MPs (Russell Kerr, Anne Kerr and John Ryan). Dramatic images were captured on camera by the media and broadcast around the world.

Television news coverage of these events brought the situation in Northern Ireland to international attention and serious rioting broke out locally. More civil rights demonstrations and counter-demonstrations followed in the weeks and months ahead, with many ending in clashes as the security situation slipped out of control. ... Eamonn McCann, one of the organisers of the (Derry) march, said that the thing he recalled most in the aftermath of the day was "the number of people who came up to me and said, using the exact phrase: 'Things will never be the same again'. And they were right."

(www.bbc.co.uk)

North-South relations

Relations between North and South improved during the 1960s (see p. 401). However, **tensions** rose in the late 1960s as the Troubles began. Attacks by RUC and loyalist paramilitaries on **Catholic ghettos** in Derry and Belfast resulted in nationalist (Catholic) families moving south. It also resulted in a television address by Taoiseach, Jack Lynch, where he said the Irish Government *'could no longer stand by and see innocent people injured'* (1969).

Relations worsened over the foundation of the IRA, unionist claims that the Irish Government wasn't doing enough to stop the IRA, and the events of Bloody Sunday (1972).

The Irish Government believed that partition was the cause of the Troubles. However, **this view changed** and the Irish Government wanted to see improved relations in the North, and that the unification of the country would only come though the **consent** (agreement) of the people.

Over the next 20 years, relations improved or disimproved depending on events in Northern Ireland. However, gradually, the Irish Government got a greater say in the affairs of Northern Ireland through the attempts at **peacemaking** – the Sunningdale Agreement, the Anglo-Irish Agreement and the Good Friday Agreement.

Battle of the Bogside

The Troubles escalate

Violence increased from 1969 onwards. In August of that year, major violence was sparked off by the Protestant **Apprentice Boys** march in Derry. This march led to a clash with the Catholics/nationalists of the **Bogside** in Derry. The nationalists barricaded their area and resisted efforts by unionists and the RUC to enter the area, in what became known as the **Battle of the Bogside**. Petrol bombs and stones were thrown at the RUC to keep them out of the Bogside. The rioting spread to other parts of Northern Ireland.

British troops

By now, nationalists had lost all respect for the RUC. The British Government sent in troops to **protect** the people of the Bogside. Troops were also sent into nationalist areas of Belfast after rioting broke out there. The people welcomed soldiers with cups of tea.

British troops receiving Christmas presents from local residents, 1969

John Hume

The SDLP

The **Social Democratic and Labour Party** (SDLP) was founded in 1970. It brought together different nationalist groups and became the largest nationalist party. Its first leader was **Gerry Fitt**, and he was succeeded by **John Hume**. Hume was an example of the parliamentary tradition in Irish politics.

The IRA

The **IRA** (Irish Republican Army) was badly organised at this time. It split into two groups: the **Official IRA**, which was moving away from violence, and the **Provisional IRA**, which believed in the traditional use of **physical force**, to force Britain to withdraw from Northern Ireland.

La Mon restaurant bombing in which an IRA bomb created a massive fireball which killed 12 people and severely injured about 30 more

The Provisional IRA was set up with the encouragement of members of the Southern Irish Government. Some government money was used illegally to purchase weapons for the 'Provos', as they became known later.

The IRA launched a **bombing campaign** in 1970, which resulted in the deaths of many civilians; they also targeted British soldiers and the RUC. The IRA also used stone-throwing youths to attack the British soldiers who responded with house searches. With these searches, the British army lost the support of the nationalist community.

Internment

As violence spread over the next couple of years, the unionist government of **Brian Faulkner**, who had taken over from Chichester-Clark, decided to bring in **internment**. This was the arrest and imprisonment without trial of people suspected of being involved in violence. In August 1971, 342 people were arrested in night-time raids.

The operation was a **disastrous failure**.

(i) The government had poor intelligence about IRA leaders, so many innocent people were arrested.

Helping the wounded through the streets of Derry on Bloody Sunday

(ii) Only some leaders of the IRA were arrested; the rest escaped internment.

(iii) There was widespread rioting and a huge increase in support for the IRA.

Bloody Sunday

Bloody Sunday in January 1972 also increased **nationalist anger**. On that Sunday, British soldiers fired on an anti-internment march in Derry.

13 people were killed. There were widespread protests and further rioting in Derry and Belfast. In Dublin, a crowd attacked and burned the British embassy.

Direct Rule from Britain

It was clear that the unionist governments had failed to tackle the problems of the North. More than 400 people had been killed in the four years since 1969. The British Government decided to **suspend** the government and parliament of Northern Ireland. **Direct rule** from Westminster was brought in in 1972. William **Whitelaw** was appointed the first Secretary of State to govern the North. This was the first time in 50 years that **unionists did not rule** Northern Ireland.

What is the message of this cartoon?

Attempts at peace

| Anglo-Irish relations and the Troubles | → | Sunningdale Agreement, 1973 | Anglo-Irish Agreement, 1985 | Downing Street Declaration, 1993 | Good Friday Agreement, 1998 |

◀ p. 236

The Sunningdale Agreement

By 1973, a new Conservative government in Britain drew up an agreement with the Southern Irish Government. This was the **Sunningdale Agreement**, signed by Edward **Heath**, Prime Minister of Britain, and Liam **Cosgrave**, Taoiseach. The agreement proposed a **power-sharing government** in Northern Ireland. Unionists and nationalists would rule together.

The agreement also proposed a **Council of Ireland**, which included representatives of the Southern Government to organise cross-border co-operation.

The new government was formed by the **Unionist Party** and the **SDLP**, which represented the majority of nationalists. It was led by **Brian Faulkner**, the leader of the Unionists, and **Gerry Fitt** of the SDLP.

The signing of the Sunningdale Agreement, 1973, Taoiseach Liam Cosgrave, shaking hands with Unionist leader, Brian Faulkner, with British Prime Minister, Ted Heath, next to Faulkner

Ian Paisley speaking during the Ulster Workers' Council Strike

The Ulster Workers' Council strike

Extreme unionists, led by **Ian Paisley**, were very much opposed to sharing power with nationalists. They also feared that the Council of Ireland would lead to a united Ireland.

The **Ulster Workers' Council** organised a general strike in May 1974 to bring down the power-sharing government. Electricity supplies were cut and roads were blocked. This led to the **collapse** of the power-sharing government. The North returned to direct rule from Westminster as the first effort to bring peace to the North failed.

The hunger strikes

In 1979, **Margaret Thatcher** replaced Edward Heath as Conservative Prime Minister. Very soon, she was faced with a major crisis. IRA prisoners in the **H-Blocks** of the Maze Prison demanded **political prisoner status** – that is, they wanted to be treated differently from criminal prisoners and allowed to wear their own clothes. When the government refused this demand, some of them, led by **Bobby Sands**, went on **hunger strike**.

The hunger strikes led to greater divisions between the two communities in the North. They also led to widespread **anti-British feeling** in the South. The British Government came under pressure to give in, but it did not. After sixty-six days, the first hunger striker, Bobby Sands, died. Over the next few months, nine more hunger strikers died. Then the Provisional IRA called off the hunger strike. The British Government restored political prisoner status after this.

By now, the IRA was developing a strategy of the '**Armalite and the ballot box**'. They continued bombing and shootings, but combined this with their political party, **Sinn Féin**, contesting elections.

Poster supporting the hunger strikers

Analysing Sources
Deaths during the Troubles

NUMERACY

Source 1
Conflict-related deaths by year

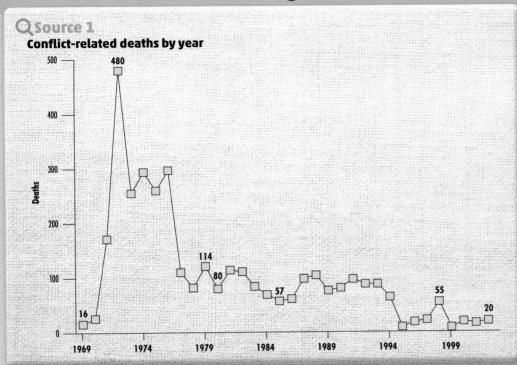

Source 2
Who was responsible for the killings in the Troubles?

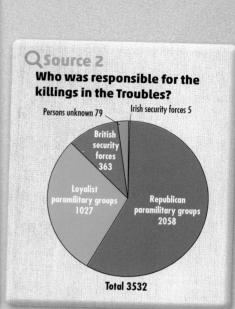

Persons unknown 79

Irish security forces 5

British security forces 363

Loyalist paramilitary groups 1027

Republican paramilitary groups 2058

Total 3532

Source 3
Casualties and losses
Civilians killed: 1,935
Total dead: 3,532
Total injured: 47,500
All casualties: around 50,000

Source 4

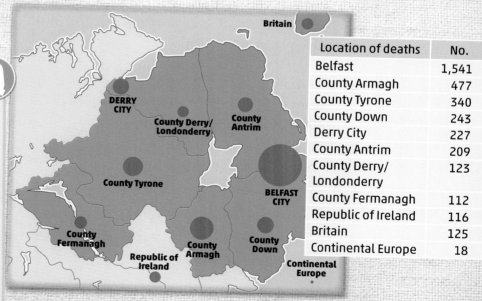

Location of deaths	No.
Belfast	1,541
County Armagh	477
County Tyrone	340
County Down	243
Derry City	227
County Antrim	209
County Derry/ Londonderry	123
County Fermanagh	112
Republic of Ireland	116
Britain	125
Continental Europe	18

Q

1. According to Source 1, which year had the **highest number** of deaths?
2. **Internment** was used in 1971 to stop the IRA. Did it work, according to Source 1?
3. Did the **Anglo-Irish Agreement** in 1985 have any effect on the pattern of violence?
4. Did the **Good Friday Agreement** in 1998 have any effect on the pattern of violence?
5. Which group caused the **most deaths** during the Troubles, according to Source 2? Why do you think they did?
6. Why do you think there were more civilians killed than paramilitaries or security forces in Source 3?
7. According to Source 4, which area had the highest number of deaths? Why, do you think, this was so?
8. Are these graphs primary or secondary sources?
9. What type of primary or secondary source are each of these sources? Explain your answer by referring to the sources.

| Economic consequences of the Troubles | → | Businesses wrecked by bombing | Foreign firms did not want to set up factories | Belfast city centre lost business | High unemployment amongst the youth |
| | → | Greater poverty in NI compared to the rest of Britain | Dependence on state welfare benefits | Increased employment in public services | |

Unionist opposition to the Anglo-Irish Agreement in 1985

The Anglo-Irish Agreement, 1985

The governments in London and Dublin now feared that Sinn Féin would gain support at the expense of the SDLP. This allowed **Garret Fitzgerald**, then Taoiseach, to persuade **Margaret Thatcher** that a new agreement was needed. This was the **Anglo-Irish Agreement of 1985**. It was signed by both leaders at Hillsborough Castle, near Belfast. The agreement gave the government of the Irish Republic a *say in running Northern Ireland*.

Unionists believed that they were **sold out** by the British Government and they were opposed to any say by the Irish government in the affairs of Northern Ireland. In spite of very strong unionist opposition to the agreement, the British and Irish governments refused to give in. The agreement was **a major step forward** and formed the basis for progress towards peace after that.

Taoiseach Garret Fitzgerald and British Prime Minister, Margaret Thatcher, signing the Anglo-Irish Agreement in 1985

Peace moves after 1985

After 1985, many efforts were made to find a solution to Northern Ireland's problems. The **British and Irish governments** worked to bring all the Northern parties together. Many people in Northern Ireland were **longing for peace**.

The **Downing Street Declaration** (1993) led to an IRA ceasefire, though it broke down later. The Declaration said there would be talks to discuss a new form of government for Northern Ireland. The British Government said that Irish unity was a matter for the Irish people, subject to the consent of the people of Northern Ireland.

John Hume, leader of SDLP

David Trimble, leader of Ulster Unionist Party

There were secret negotiations between **John Hume** and **Gerry Adams**, as Hume persuaded Adams of the necessity of ending the violence, and using the political process to achieve their aims.

The **US Government** was also involved through **President Clinton**. He sent US senator, **George Mitchell**, to work out a process for decommissioning arms and achieving a settlement everybody could support. This led to the **Good Friday Agreement**.

DID YOU KNOW?
The EU contributed over €1.3 billion between 1995 and 2013 through its PEACE programmes to improve community relations in Northern Ireland.

The **Good Friday Agreement** (1998) created a **power-sharing government** that included all political parties elected to the Northern Ireland Assembly. The agreement also stated that Northern Ireland would remain part of the United Kingdom until a majority both of the people of Northern Ireland and of the Republic of Ireland wished otherwise.

Initially, the dominant unionist and nationalist parties in the Northern Government were the **Unionist Party** and the **SDLP**. However, these were replaced after **general election results** in the early 21st century by the **Democratic Unionist Party** on the unionist side and by **Sinn Féin** on the nationalist side. These parties dominated the **power-sharing executive** (government) in Northern Ireland until the executive collapsed in January 2017. There are continuing negotiations to restore the executive.

INVESTIGATING A REPOSITORY OF HISTORICAL EVIDENCE FOR THE TROUBLES IN NORTHERN IRELAND

Discover Ulster-Scots Centre,
www.discoverulsterscots.com
Museum of Orange Heritage,
orangeheritage.co.uk
Ulster Museum,
www.nmni.com
Museum of Free Derry,
www.museumoffreederry.org
The Siege Museum,
www.thesiegemuseum.org
Apprentice Boys of Derry,
www.apprenticeboysofderry.org

〉 Preparing for CBA1

A project related to an aspect of the history of your locality or place (or personal/family history)

LOCAL PROJECTS FROM THE TROUBLES

Your locality can include your county

- Incidents/events relating to the Troubles in your locality
- Reaction in your locality to Bloody Sunday

〉 Preparing for CBA2

A project on the life and experience of a person of historical interest

PERSONS OF INTEREST IN THE TROUBLES

- Terence O'Neill
- Gerry Fitt
- Austin Currie
- Bobby Sands
- David Trimble
- Betty Williams

- Brian Faulkner
- John Hume
- Gerry Adams
- Margaret Thatcher
- Tony Blair
- Mairead Corrigan

- Ian Paisley
- Bernadette Devlin
- Martin McGuinness
- Garret Fitzgerald
- Bertie Ahern

HISTORICAL INVESTIGATION

Focus Task

p. 233 〉
Web Resources and Reading

Investigating Murals in Northern Ireland

〉 Examine the Mural Directory, A Directory of Murals in Northern Ireland at www.cain.ulst.ac.uk/mccormick/intro.htm.

〉 Select any two unionist/loyalist murals and any two nationalist murals and explain what each mural is about. What are the main differences between the unionist and nationalist murals?

27

THE EUROPEAN UNION AND IRELAND'S LINKS WITH EUROPE

LO 3.12, 2.13
The Nature of History: 1.1,
1.2, 1.3, 1.4, 1.5, 1.6, 1.7,
1.8, 1.9, 1.10, 1.11
CBA1
CBA2

CHRONOLOGICAL AWARENESS

1950 AD

1958 Treaty of Rome (1957) – EEC founded

1963 President de Gaulle of France vetoed British membership

1960 AD

1961 Ireland, Britain and Denmark applied for membership of EEC

1970 AD

1973 Ireland, Britain and Denmark joined the EEC

1979 European Monetary System (EMS) created

1981 Greece joined EEC

1980 AD

1987 Single European Act

1986 Spain and Portugal joined

1993 Treaty on European Union came into effect

1990 AD

1991 Maastricht Treaty on European Union

1995 Austria, Finland and Sweden joined

1997 Treaty of Amsterdam

2000 AD

2000 Agreement on European Charter of Fundamental Rights

2004 EU enlarged to 25 countries

2002 Euro introduced

2009 Treaty of Lisbon; legally binding Charter

2007 EU enlarged to 27 countries

2010 AD

2013 EU enlarged to 28 countries (Croatia)

2016 Britain voted for Brexit

2020 AD

2019 Britain to exit the EU – transition phase in place

You will learn to ...

- Evaluate the role of the EU in promoting international co-operation
- Evaluate the role of the EU in promoting justice and human rights
- Analyse the evolution and development of Ireland's links with Europe
- Explore the Nature of History

KEY WORDS

- Co-operation
- Brexit
- Human rights
- Justice
- Enlargement

The Origins of the EU: The Desire for European Unity

Reasons for European unity

The **destruction and suffering** in Europe during World War II led many Europeans to think about the best way to solve Europe's problems and secure peace. For many the solution was greater European unity. *'To build Europe is to build peace,'* said Jean Monnet, who played a very important part in the moves for European unity.

The death and destruction of World War II encouraged European unity

Replace Nationalism with international co-operation

Strengthen Europe to compete against two superpowers, USA and USSR

Nationalism the cause of two world wars

Reasons for European unity

Fear of spread of Communism from the USSR

Encouraged by USA and Britain who did not want to be drawn into further European wars

Revive the economies of Europe after war

Control German aggression

Jean Monnet, who promoted European unity

Steps to the European Union (EU)

After World War II, European unity moved forward in many areas – political, military and economic. But it was mainly through **economic integration** (closer economic co-operation) that progress was made.

This progress led to the establishment of the **European Economic Community** (EEC) in 1958 with the passing of the **Treaty of Rome** (1957). In agreeing to establish the EEC, the six countries concerned – France, West Germany, Belgium, the Netherlands, Luxembourg, and Italy – **handed over some of their power to an outside body**. *'The Treaty of Rome symbolises the triumph of co-operation over national selfishness'*, said Paul-Henri Spaak, regarded as one of the founding fathers of the EEC.

The **aims** of the EEC were to:

- Promote economic activity.
- Raise the living standards of the people.
- Bring the member states closer together.

1. What, do you think, were the two main causes of the movement to European unity after World War II?
2. What Treaty led to the founding of the EEC?
3. Outline one of the aims of the EEC.

How did the enlargement of the EEC promote international co-operation?

The EEC established a **common market** to achieve its goals (aims). All tariffs, or customs duties, and quotas between member states would be abolished. The EEC was based on the **free movement** of goods, persons, services and capital (the Four Freedoms). It was also based on **common policies** in agriculture and transport.

Over the next 30 years, the **EEC expanded** as new countries joined it. These countries included Britain, Ireland and Denmark in 1973. By the 1990s, there were 15 countries in the European Union. The collapse of communism and the Soviet Union in 1990–91 provided the opportunity for many Eastern European countries to join the EU. As a result, ten countries (mostly from Eastern Europe) joined in 2004, with three more by 2013. International co-operation in Europe was improved with this enlargement.

COUNTRIES IN THE EUROPEAN UNION		
1958	6	The original six – France, West Germany, Belgium, the Netherlands, Luxembourg, Italy
1973	9	Britain, Ireland, Denmark
1981	10	Greece
1986	12	Spain, Portugal
1995	15	Austria, Finland, Sweden
2004	25	Hungary, Poland, the Czech Republic, Slovakia, Estonia, Latvia, Lithuania, Slovenia, Malta and Cyprus
2007	27	Romania, Bulgaria
2013	28	Croatia

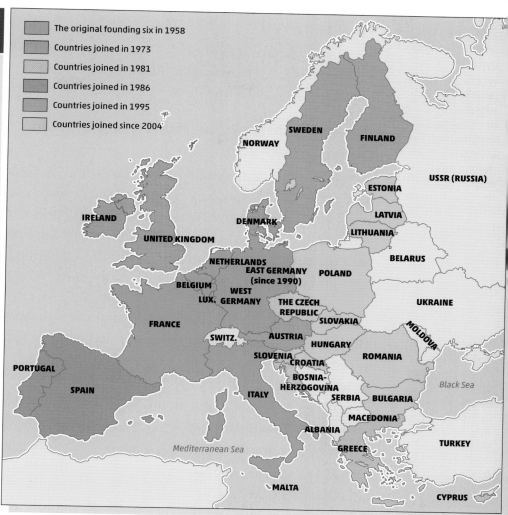

The original founding six in 1958
Countries joined in 1973
Countries joined in 1981
Countries joined in 1986
Countries joined in 1995
Countries joined since 2004

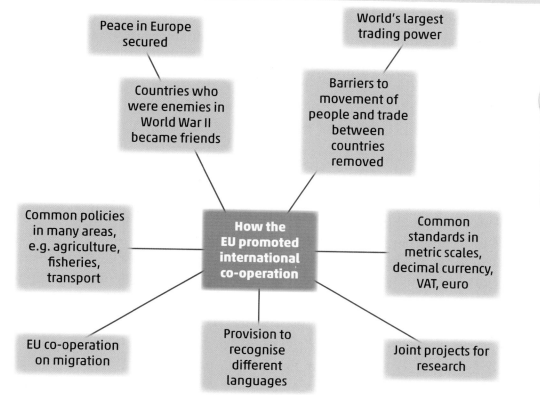

How the EU promoted international co-operation

Peace in Europe secured

World's largest trading power

Countries who were enemies in World War II became friends

Barriers to movement of people and trade between countries removed

Common policies in many areas, e.g. agriculture, fisheries, transport

Common standards in metric scales, decimal currency, VAT, euro

EU co-operation on migration

Provision to recognise different languages

Joint projects for research

What were the most important factors in promoting European co-operation?

1. What is a common market?
2. When did Ireland join the EEC?
3. When was the greatest expansion of the EEC (EU)?
4. Outline three ways in which the EU promoted international co-operation.

From EEC to EU

The name **European Economic Community (EEC)** was used from 1958 onwards. The name was later changed to **European Community** (EC), but since the Maastricht Treaty in 1993, the name **European Union** (EU) has been used.

How did greater powers for the EU promote international co-operation?

As the EEC grew, it also changed its powers, and its name. As the countries of the EEC (later called the European Community (EC)) moved closer together they negotiated the **Single European Act**, the **Treaty on European Union** and the **Treaty of Lisbon**.

The **Single European Act** (1987) formed one large economic unit in Europe by creating a single European market. It did this by eliminating all remaining obstacles (taxes and quotas) to free trade between the member states. It also gave new powers to the European institutions.

A further step in strengthening European unity was the **Treaty on European Union** (1991), or the **Maastricht Treaty**, as it is known. The Treaty:

1. How did the Single European Act promote international co-operation?
2. How did the Maastricht Treaty promote international co-operation?
3. How did the Treaty of Lisbon promote international co-operation?
4. What was the Charter of Fundamental Rights?

- Gave greater power to the European parliament.
- Set out the plans for a single currency, the euro.
- Made each person in the member states a citizen of Europe.
- Stated that member states should co-operate in combating drug trafficking, fraud and other criminal matters.

Overall, the Maastricht Treaty took more power from the national parliaments and gave it to the European Union (EU).

The **Treaty of Lisbon** (2009) changed the balance of power within the EU. It increased the **powers of the European Parliament**, and created a full-time **President** of the European Council. It made the **Charter of Fundamental Rights** legally binding on all states. It also gave states the **right to leave** the EU, and it created the procedures for leaving.

How did the institutions of the EU promote international co-operation?

The institutions of the EU are developed to create a **balance** between national and EU interests, and between big and small states. They work to get **agreement** from all countries on new policies. In deciding on policy and laws, the EU tries to balance the national interest and the EU interest. It also tries to balance the powers between directly elected representatives in the European parliament and ministers representing the individual countries. It brings countries together to **co-operate** in creating laws for the wider European Union.

European Council

- This is composed of the **heads of government** of all EU countries
- It meets at least four times a year
- It decides overall policy or overall guidelines for EU policy

European Parliament

- Members of the European Parliament (MEPs) are directly elected by the people every five years
- They supervise the work of the Council of Ministers and the Commission
- They propose new ideas
- They vote on the budget

European Parliament by Political Groups

Size of the political groups
Number of MEP's in each political group as of 10 September 2015

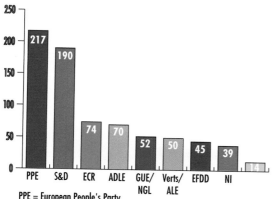

PPE = European People's Party
S&D = Socialists and Democrats
European Conservatives and Reformists
ADLE = Liberals and Democrats
GUE/NGL = Green Party/United Left
Verts/ALE = Greens/European Free Alliance
EFDD = Freedom and Direct Democracy
NI = Nations and Freedom Group

Proportion of members in each political group
Share of each political group in the total 751 seats in the Parliament

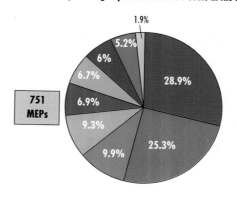

751 MEPs

Total
751 seats

Even though MEPs are elected to represent their own countries, they sit in European-wide political groups. This is balancing the national and EU interest in developing international co-operation.

To which political groupings are Irish political parties attached?

Council of Ministers

- This is one of the main decision-making bodies of the EU: it decides EU laws and budget **together with** the European parliament
- It is composed of **government ministers** from the member states depending on the topics to be decided – one Minister from each EU country – e.g. Agriculture, Education, Industry
- They represent the national interest

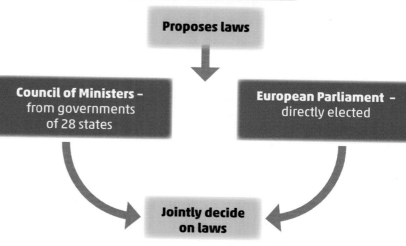

European Commission – civil service of EU, headed by commissioners nominated by EU states

Proposes laws

Council of Ministers – from governments of 28 states

European Parliament – directly elected

Jointly decide on laws

A simplified version of how laws are made in the EU

European Commission

- It is headed by Commissioners nominated from each EU state
- It is composed of the civil servants of the EU, responsible for proposing laws
- Civil servants come from all EU countries
- They carry out EU policy decided by the Council of Ministers, Parliament and European Council
- The Commission operates from Brussels

1. Explain the powers of two of the main European institutions.
2. How are laws made in the EU?

Court of Justice

- 28 Judges, from each EU country, based in Luxembourg
- The Court decides cases based on the European treaties and laws
- It can fine countries that break EU laws

In recent years, the movement for greater co-operation within the EU has encountered difficulties. In a number of countries, anti-EU groups, for example, the National Front in France, have gained popularity. In Britain, anti-EU groups coming mainly from the Conservative Party and UKIP, the United Kingdom Independence Party, won a referendum in 2016 to take the UK out of the EU, or Brexit.

What, do you think, are the most serious factors working against EU cooperation?

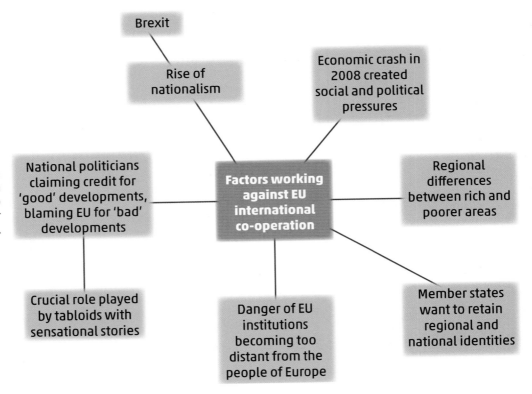

Brexit

Rise of nationalism

Economic crash in 2008 created social and political pressures

National politicians claiming credit for 'good' developments, blaming EU for 'bad' developments

Factors working against EU international co-operation

Regional differences between rich and poorer areas

Crucial role played by tabloids with sensational stories

Danger of EU institutions becoming too distant from the people of Europe

Member states want to retain regional and national identities

Evaluate the role of the EU in promoting justice and human rights

What is the Role of the EU in Promoting Justice and Human Rights?

The **Treaty of Rome** (1957), on which the EEC (EU) was founded, was concerned with **economic matters** such as free trade and the single market. As a result, there was **no reference to human rights** in the Treaty.

It was not until the year 2000 that the **European Charter of Fundamental Rights** was agreed. But that did not become **legally binding** until the **Treaty of Lisbon** came into effect in December 2009.

The Charter of Fundamental Rights outlined the **civil and political rights**, and also the **social and economic rights** of EU citizens. The Charter:

- laid down the fundamental rights that are binding upon the EU institutions and bodies.
- applies to national governments when they are implementing EU law.

People can challenge national laws first through their local courts, and then if that fails, they can appeal to the **Court of Justice of the European Union** (CJEU).

> **DID YOU KNOW?**
> The CJEU is different from the European Court of Human Rights, which judges cases based on the European Convention on Human Rights.

Judges of the Court of Justice of the European Union (CJEU)

The Bosman Case

Jean-Marc Bosman, a Belgian, was a professional footballer who played for RFC Liege, then in the Belgian league. Bosman brought a legal action against the club and the Union of European Football associations (UEFA) because UEFA transfer rules prevented him from moving to a French club.

Jean-Marc Bosman, footballer

He took his case to the Court of Justice of the European Union and won it.

The Court said that the Treaty of Rome guaranteed free movement of people within the Union. It ruled that transfer fees for players were an obstacle to the free movement of workers, and illegal under the Treaty (except when they applied to transfers within a member state). The court also ruled against limiting the number of other EU players in a club team.

Q

1. How has the EU progressed human rights?
2. What did the Bosman case prove?

The EU has set up the **European Union Agency for Fundamental Rights** (FRA) *'to ensure that the fundamental rights of people living in the EU are protected.'* It has also developed an **Action Plan on Human Rights and Democracy**, and each year it reports on progress in achieving the goals of the Action Plan.

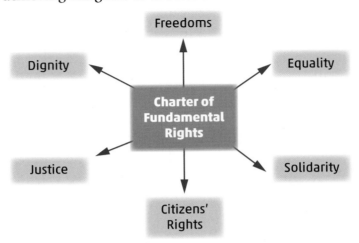

Freedoms

Dignity

Equality

Charter of Fundamental Rights

Justice

Solidarity

Citizens' Rights

Fundamental rights set out minimum standards to ensure that a person is treated with dignity. Whether this is the right to be free from discrimination on the basis of your age, disability or ethnic background, the right to the protection of your personal data, or the right to get access to justice, these rights should all be promoted and protected.

(www.fra.europa.eu)

PROFILE – JACQUES DELORS

Jacques Delors was **President of the European Commission** from **1985 to 1995**. He became President at a time when the movement to European unity was **stagnating**. He used his **leadership skills** and his **powers of persuasion** to get the countries of the EEC (EU) to agree to further steps towards European integration. He developed the European civil service (the Commission) and he co-operated with the European Parliament in furthering European unity. It was during his time in office that the Single European Act, the Maastricht Treaty and the progress towards the Euro were agreed.

The EU has a special representative for Human Rights whose job is to make EU policy on human rights more effective in **non-EU countries**.

The EU policy includes:

- Working to promote the rights of women, children, minorities and displaced persons
- Opposing the death penalty, torture, human trafficking and discrimination
- Defending civil, political, economic, social and cultural rights.

All agreements on trade or co-operation with non-EU countries include a **human rights clause** stating that human rights are central to relations with the EU. The EU has imposed **sanctions** for human rights breaches in a number of instances.

A group of migrants wait on the Macedonian-Greek border near the town of Gevgelija

How did the EU deal with the migrant and refugee crisis in 2015–16?

In 2015–16, Europe experienced the greatest mass movement of people since World War II. More than 1 million refugees and migrants arrived in the EU. Most were escaping war and terror in Syria and other countries in the Middle East.

Many came to the EU to seek **asylum** – international protection given to people fleeing their countries due to the danger of persecution and death. Others left their countries to better their lives as **economic migrants**. Many migrants came **illegally** into the EU.

The EU dealt with the migrant and refugee crisis in a number of ways:

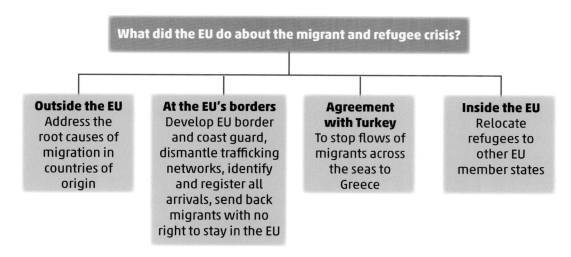

What did the EU do about the migrant and refugee crisis?

Outside the EU	**At the EU's borders**	**Agreement with Turkey**	**Inside the EU**
Address the root causes of migration in countries of origin	Develop EU border and coast guard, dismantle trafficking networks, identify and register all arrivals, send back migrants with no right to stay in the EU	To stop flows of migrants across the seas to Greece	Relocate refugees to other EU member states

Illegal migration to the EU
2014–15

1. What caused the increase in illegal migration in 2014–15?
2. Which EU countries experienced the greatest migration?
3. What problems did the increased migration cause for the EU?

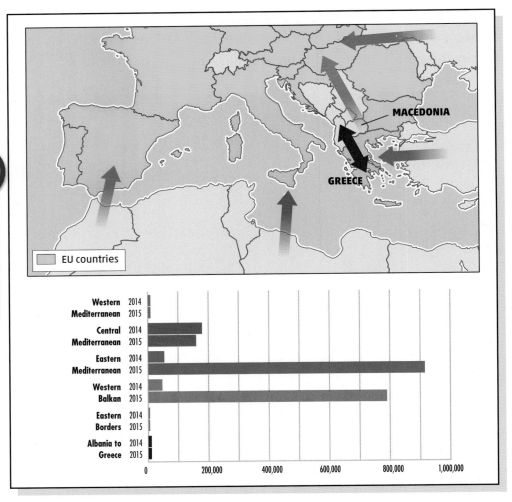

As a result of these actions, the migrant and refugee crisis became **less severe**. However, the crisis itself resulted in **internal political crises** in a number of EU states, including Greece, Italy, Hungary, Germany and Britain.

The flow of migrants from Turkey to Greece, 2015 and 2016

How did EU actions contribute to reducing the daily flow of migrants from Turkey to Greece?

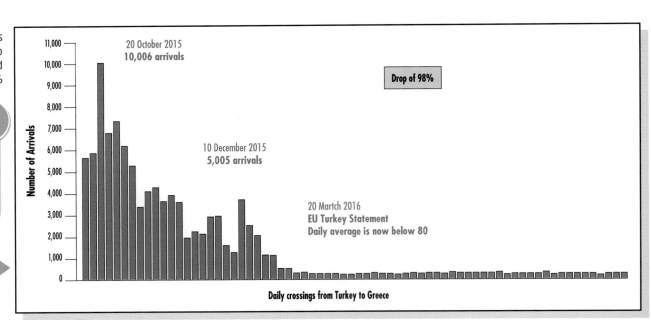

The EU is also concerned with **justice**. It wants a common legal and judicial culture across all the states. The growth of the single market and online sales has inevitably led to greater numbers of cross-border disputes.

In the circumstance, the EU:

- is seeking judicial co-operation to help individuals with cross-border cases
- decides which EU country has jurisdiction to try particular cases involving cross-border matters
- ensures judgements in one country are recognised and enforced in other EU countries.

> The European Parliament's main human rights event is the awarding of the **Sakharov Prize** for Freedom of Thought each December. Past winners of the Sakharov Prize have included famous human rights defenders, such as Nelson Mandela in 1988 who won the first Sakharov Prize, and Malala Yousafzai in 2013.

Ireland's Links with Europe

Early Christian Ireland

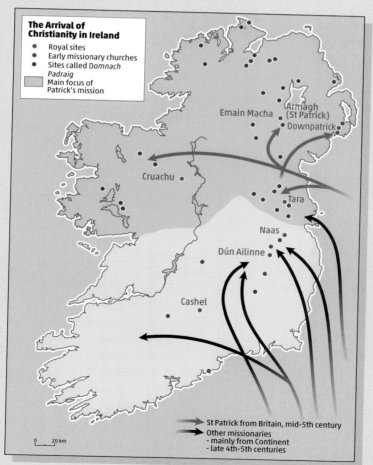

The Arrival of Christianity in Ireland
- Royal sites
- Early missionary churches
- Sites called *Domnach Padraig*
- Main focus of Patrick's mission

Emain Macha · Armagh (St Patrick) · Downpatrick · Cruachu · Tara · Naas · Dún Ailinne · Cashel

St Patrick from Britain, mid-5th century
Other missionaries
- mainly from Continent
- late 4th-5th centuries

0 20 km

> ⊘ Analyse the evolution and development of Ireland's links with Europe

The **pope in Rome** sent missionaries, including St Patrick, to Ireland and these missionaries were mainly responsible for converting the country to Christianity (see p. 46).

In later centuries, **Irish missionaries** were responsible for carrying Christianity into different parts of Europe and founding monasteries there (see p. 49).

The Normans

The Normans invaded Ireland from Britain. Originally from Normandy in France, they brought their land system called **feudalism**, along with castles and stone-walled towns (see Ch. 04). They shaped the **landscape** of Ireland, particularly in the east and south of the country.

The Reformation

The **Protestant Reformation** began in Germany when Martin Luther criticised the Catholic Church. It spread to Ireland in the 16th century through the Tudor kings and queens of England who changed the laws, and who brought Protestant planters to Ireland (see Ch. 07).

Martin Luther

The Nine Years War

Prior to the Ulster Plantation, **Hugh O'Neill** and **Hugh O'Donnell** rebelled against the efforts of Queen Elizabeth to impose English law and the Protestant religion on their territories in Ulster. They got help from **Philip II of Spain**, who sent ships to Kinsale. Even though this ended in defeat for the Ulster chiefs and for the Spanish in Kinsale, it set

The Battle of Kinsale

a **pattern for future rebellions** in Ireland, where help was sought from the enemies of England on the Continent. Soon after their defeat, the Ulster chiefs headed for the Continent in the **Flight of the Earls** (see p. 134).

1798 Rebellion

French revolutionary ideas of Liberty, Equality and Fraternity were popular in Ireland in the 1790s. **Wolfe Tone** and the United Irishmen sought help from France, then at war with England, as they planned the 1798 Rebellion. The French sent ships and soldiers on three occasions – to Bantry Bay, to Killala and to Lough Swilly – but each effort of help failed (see p. 168).

Battle of Killala, Co. Mayo, September 1798

1916 Rising

The leaders of the **1916 Rising** sought arms and ammunition from **Germany**, then fighting Britain in World War I. In the 1916 Proclamation, the leaders said they were supported 'by gallant allies in Europe'. However, the *Aud*, which was bringing the arms and ammunition, was captured off the Kerry coast. This was one reason why the countrywide rising that was planned was confined instead largely to Dublin (see pp. 236–37).

World War II

During World War II, Ireland, which was divided between North and South, played **different parts** in the war. The South stayed **neutral** in the war, while the North as part of the United Kingdom, took an **active part** in the war. However, both parts of the country were bombed, though the North suffered much greater casualties and destruction (see p. 337). The different experiences during the war created **greater differences** between Northern Ireland and the south of Ireland.

Bombing of Belfast

Q What conclusions would you draw about the evolution and development of Ireland's links with Europe from Early Christian Ireland onwards?

⊘ Analyse the evolution and development of Ireland's links with the EU

p. 244 ▶

Ireland and the EEC (EU)

The Republic of Ireland applied to join the **European Economic Community** (EEC) in the early 1960s along with the United Kingdom and Denmark. President de Gaulle of France vetoed the British application so the Irish application fell as well.

However, once de Gaulle left power in France, the three countries applied again. Many people in Ireland wanted to join the EEC. Some believed that Ireland's economy would benefit from membership of the EEC. Those who were against entry said that Ireland would lose some of its independence because the EEC would now make decisions.

A **referendum** (a vote of the people) in 1972 resulted in a huge majority in favour of entering the EEC. Ireland (along with the UK and Denmark) entered on 1 January 1973. Northern Ireland joined the EU as part of the United Kingdom.

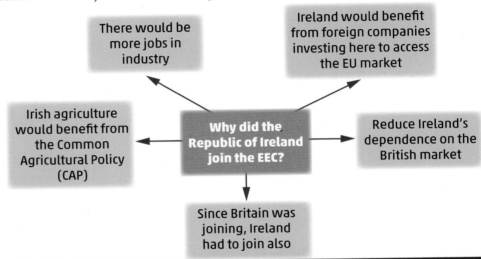

There would be more jobs in industry

Ireland would benefit from foreign companies investing here to access the EU market

Irish agriculture would benefit from the Common Agricultural Policy (CAP)

Why did the Republic of Ireland join the EEC?

Reduce Ireland's dependence on the British market

Since Britain was joining, Ireland had to join also

Analysing Sources

Ireland and the EU

1. This account was written by the European Union (EU). Does that mean it is **biased**?

2. Is it a **primary** or a **secondary** source?

3. List **two facts** from the account.

4. Which of the 'benefits' would you consider the most important?

Q Source 1

Benefits of EU membership to Ireland

Irish businesses have unhindered access to a market of over 510 million people.

An estimated 978,000 jobs have been created in Ireland during the years of membership and trade has increased 150 fold.

Foreign direct investment in to Ireland has increased dramatically from just €16 million in 1972 to more than €30 billion.

Irish citizens have the right to move, work and reside freely within the territory of other member states.

Between 1973 and 2015, Ireland received over €74.3 billion from the EU. During the same time, it contributed approximately €32 billion to the EU budget.

Ireland benefited from **aid** (grants) to provide job training and to improve roads, sewerage and telephone services.

Between 1973 and 2014 Irish farmers received €54 billion from the **Common Agricultural Policy** (CAP).

Irish views and interests are reflected in the policies of the EU towards the rest of the world.

- EU membership has helped bring **peace and political agreement** in **Northern Ireland** through support and investment in cross-border programmes.
- The **Irish language** is an official working language in the EU, which helps to protect the country's native mother tongue for future generations.

(Source: Adapted from https://ec.europa.eu/ireland/about-us/ireland-in-eu_en)

Source 2

After Ireland joined the EEC, the coalition government passed an **Anti-discrimination (Pay) Act** in 1974. But an increase in oil prices in the Middle East caused an economic crisis here so they decided to postpone the expensive business of giving equal pay for equal work, or work of a similar nature, to women and men until 1977. However the EEC compelled the government to grant equal pay in 1976.

Another **Employment Equality Act** was passed in 1977 to deal more effectively with discrimination on grounds of sex or marital status in employment. The **Employment Equality Agency**, chaired by Sylvia Meehan, was set up in the same year to oversee the enforcement of the Act.

Further EEC directives ensured that:

- higher pay scales for married men than for women and single men in the public service were discontinued from 1977.
- women and men received equal access to training, promotion, work conditions, pensions and to social welfare.

(**Source: Discovering Women in Irish History, www.womeninhistory.scoilnet.ie**)

1. Is this a **primary** or a **secondary** source?
2. What points does it make in **favour** of the EEC?
3. Why did the Irish government postpone equal pay for equal work?
4. Are the points made in this source also made in Source 1?
5. What conclusions would you draw about the development of Ireland's links with the EU? Explain your answers by referring to evidence in the sources.

Source 3

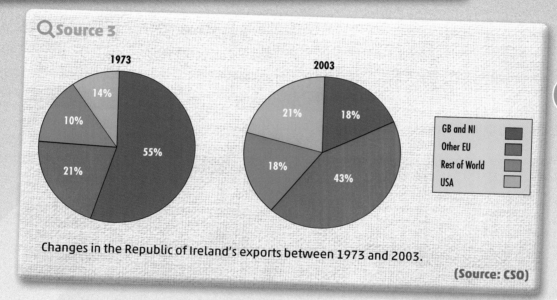

Changes in the Republic of Ireland's exports between 1973 and 2003.

(Source: CSO)

What is the most noticeable change in the pattern of Ireland's exports between 1973, when Ireland joined the EEC, and 2003?

Source 4

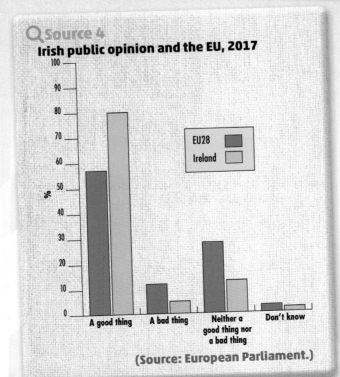

Irish public opinion and the EU, 2017

(Source: European Parliament.)

How do the views of people in the Republic of Ireland compare with the EU in general? How would you explain the difference?

Ireland, Brexit and the EU

Ireland is considered to be the EU member **most affected** by Britain's decision to withdraw from the EU. This is partly because the border between Northern Ireland and the Republic of Ireland would now become an **external border** for the EU. *'There are about 275 land border crossings between Northern Ireland and the Republic of Ireland, compared to 137 crossings on the entirety of the EU's eastern border from Finland to Greece.'* **(European Parliament)** This will make it virtually impossible to monitor trade and people across the border.

A second reason why Ireland will be affected by Brexit concerns the **Good Friday Agreement** and peace in Northern Ireland. There is a strong belief that if a **hard border** (with border controls) was established between North and South that this would lead to an outbreak of violence and a collapse of the peace process in Northern Ireland. These concerns have led the EU to insist that Ireland's 'unique circumstances', including the issue of peace in Northern Ireland, must be addressed in the Brexit negotiations.

Who is the expert on Ireland's links with Europe?

Why is it difficult for historians to make judgments on recent events?

INVESTIGATING A REPOSITORY OF HISTORICAL EVIDENCE FOR THE EU AND IRELAND'S LINKS WITH EUROPE

Europa, Official Website of the European Union, www.europa.eu/european-union

〉 Preparing for CBA1

Your locality can include your county

A project on the life and experiences of a person of historical interest

LOCAL PROJECTS FROM EU AND IRELAND'S LINKS WITH EUROPE

- Your local MEP or past MEPs from your locality
- An election campaign for the European Parliament in your locality
- A large-scale project from your locality that got EU funding

〉 Preparing for CBA2

A project on the life and experience of a person of historical interest

PERSONS OF INTEREST IN THE EU AND IRELAND'S LINKS WITH EUROPE

- Jean Monnet
- Charles de Gaulle
- Máire Geoghegan-Quinn
- Robert Schuman
- Patrick Hillery
- Margaret Thatcher
- Paul-Henri Spaak
- Peter Sutherland

HISTORICAL JUDGEMENT

p. 245 〉
Web Resources and Reading

Focus Task

> Investigate the impact of EU membership on Ireland. On balance, would you say that Ireland has gained more or lost more from membership of the EEC (EU) since 1973? Support your conclusions with evidence from your research.

Glossary

Strand 1

AD	Anno Domini; after the birth of Christ
Archaeology	the study of the past through material remains
Archive	collects and stores mainly written (documentary) sources
Artefact	object made by people e.g. sword, axe; historical sources of evidence
Aural sources	sources that can be heard, such as recordings or videos
Autobiography	story of a person's life, written by that person
BC	before the birth of Christ
Bias	when people deliberately select evidence or sources to support their own case
Big picture	seeing past events within a broad context, national and global
Biography	story of a person's life written by somebody else
Carbon dating	technique used to date ancient objects by measuring the amount of carbon
Cause	actions that result in events happening, actions that bring about effects
Change	how events, issues and people are altered or different from before
Chronological awareness	awareness of historic time, awareness of how events relate to each other in time
Chronology	the study of time and dates, putting events in order of time
Commemoration	a service, monument or celebration that results from some action or event; an act of remembrance of a historically significant event or person
Consequence	something that results from some action or event; an effect
Contentious issue	an issue or topic which causes argument, conflict or controversy
Continuity	the continued existence of something over a long period of time
Controversial issue	an issue or topic which causes argument, conflict (contentious issue)
Cultural inheritance	the objects, traditions and customs which have been handed down from past generations
Dendrochronology	(Tree-ring dating) finding out the age of timber by studying the pattern of rings
Dig	(excavation) digging up the earth in order to look for historical objects (artefacts)
Documents (historical)	written, printed or electronic matter that contains historical information; may be primary or secondary sources
Events	things that happen, especially of historical importance
Evidence	facts or information in support of something happening (events); in support of conclusions
Excavation	(dig) digging up the earth to look for historical objects (artefacts)
Eyewitness account	report by a person who saw events happening
Fact	something known to have happened; something that is known to be true
Geophysical survey	using scientific instruments to find archaeological features under the surface of the ground
Historical consciousness	your understanding of how the past changes, awareness of historical concepts, time and place
Historical context	placing events in a wider development to understand how and what happened
Historical empathy	understanding the motivation, actions, values and beliefs of people in the context of the time in which they lived
Historical enquiry	using the methods of the historian to investigate aspects of the past, of history
Historical era	a period of history with common features
Historical judgement	coming to a conclusion about events, issues and people in history based on the methods of the historian
Historical perspective	being able to place events, issues and people in their historical context; being able to come to conclusions based on understanding how the past changes
Historical significance	events, issues and people, which have an important impact on their time, and on later times; producing historical change (historical importance)
History	the story of the past, using evidence

Interpretations	different historians views about why and how events happened in the past
Issues	topics for debate or discussion
Libraries	for storing books, magazines, reference material for use by the public
Limitations	certain weaknesses relating to sources
Manuscript	a hand-written book
Museum	building for holding and displaying objects (artefacts)
Objective	historical judgement or view not influenced by a person's feelings or opinions in considering what happened
Opinion	a view or judgement formed about what happened; can be objective or subjective
Oral sources	interviews or tape recordings of people's memories of events
Perspective	from a certain viewpoint (different to perspective in art)
Pollen	produced by plants which helps archaeologists to find out what plants were growing, when forests were cleared and when farming spread
Post hole	darkened soil patch where timber post has rotted away
Prehistory	the story of the past before written sources
Primary Sources	sources which come directly from the time that is being studied, e.g. weapons, tools, paintings, letters
Propaganda	use of information to influence opinions of people to ensure power
Radiocarbon dating	technique used to date ancient objects by measuring the amount of carbon
Reliable Sources	sources in which the information can be trusted
Repository of historical evidence	a website, museum, library or archive for storing historical information
Rescue archaeology	archaeological excavation undertaken before new developments (roads, buildings) take place
Secondary Sources	sources which come from after the time which is being studied, e.g. a history book
Source	a document or artefact from which historical information can be obtained; which can be used as evidence in research; can be primary or secondary
Space	the place or area where historical events happened
Stratigraphy	a method of dating objects where the oldest layers are at the bottom and the youngest layers are at the top
Subjective	views influenced by a person's opinions and feelings; opposite to objective
Survey	the examination and recording of an area (place) and its features
Tactile sources	primary or secondary sources, which can be experienced by touch
Time	in history, when events happened
Timeline	usually a line representing an historic period, and on which events can be recorded in the order in which they happened
Tree-ring dating	(Dendrochronology) finding out the age of timber by studying the pattern of rings
Usefulness of sources	how good a source is in providing information on an historic event;
Viewpoint	a person's point of view, can be objective or subjective, biased or not
Visual Sources	photographs, paintings
Wattle and daub walls	interwoven sticks (wattle) and mud (daub) used to build walls in houses from Stone Age to the Middle Ages

Strands 2 and 3

Anaesthetics	a drug that makes a person unable to feel pain
Anglicisation	becoming more English in language and culture
Anti-Semitism	hatred of the Jews
Antiseptics	make clean or free of germs
Appeasement	policy of British government in 1930s which believed that if they gave into Hitler's small demands then they would prevent a world war

Apprentice	a person learning a trade or craft for a number of years
Apprentice Boys	a Protestant society based in Derry/Londonderry, which commemorates the actions of apprentice boys closing the gates of the city during the Siege of Derry in 1689
Aqueduct	bridge for carrying water in Ancient Rome
Arms race	a race between the USA and USSR (Soviet Russia), and their allies to compete for superiority in military arms, often referred to during the Cold War
Artefact	an object made by a person, such as a tool, ornament or weapon, of historical interest
Assassination	a murder for political reasons
Astrolabe	navigation instrument used in the Age of Exploration to find latitude
Atomic bomb	a very destructive bomb based on nuclear energy
Authority	the power or right to give orders and make decisions, usually political power
Auxiliaries	ex-British army officers who were enlisted in the Royal Irish Constabulary during the War of Independence
Battle of Britain	air battle between the Royal Air Force and the German Luftwaffe during the Second World War
Bawn	a fortified or walled enclosure used in the Plantation of Ulster
Beehive hut	stone buildings with a curved shape often used by monks in Early Christian Ireland
Black and Tans	ex-British army soldiers who were enlisted in the Royal Irish Constabulary during the War of Independence
Black Death	plague caused by fleas on rats, which spread in the Middle Ages
Blitz	German bombing of British cities after the Battle of Britain during the Second World War
Blitzkrieg	lightening war tactics used by Germany in the Second World War, using planes, tanks and infantry
Blockade	the sealing off of a place to prevent people or goods from entering or leaving
Bloody Sunday	day in which Collins' Squad killed British spies and Auxiliaries killed spectators in Croke Park in revenge during the War of Independence
Brexit	the UK decision to leave the European Union (EU)
Brownshirts	name given to Hitler's Stormtroopers or SA
Camogie	a game similar to hurling with stick and ball played by girls and women
Capital offence	a crime that is considered so serious that death is a suitable punishment (capital punishment)
Capitalism	an economic and political system in which the country's industry and trade are privately owned, and not by the state
Caravel	ship used by Portuguese and Spanish to explore coasts of Africa and America
Catholic Emancipation	the removing of laws which placed restrictions on Catholics in Britain and Ireland in the 18th and 19th centuries
Chalice	a large cup used in Christian ceremonies
Child mortality	the death of children over one month and under the age of five
Chivalry	the code of behaviour of knights during the Middle Ages or medieval times
Civil rights	the rights of people to fundamental freedoms, irrespective of race, sex or religion
Civilisation	a people or nation (in the past) that was socially and politically developed and organised
Classical	term used for culture, art and architecture of Ancient Greece and Rome
Clinker built	overlapping planks of wood used in building caravels in the Age of Exploration
Co-operation	when people and organisations work together for the same purpose
Coffin ships	name given to badly maintained ships used to transport emigrants to America during the Great Famine
Cold War	period of hostility between the USA and its allies and the Soviet Union and its allies, which lasted from after the Second World War to the collapse of Communism in the early 1990s
Collective	a farm worked as a unit by a community or village under the supervision of the state as in Soviet Russia
Collectivisation	the process of changing privately owned farms into collective farms run by the local community under state control

Colonisation	where a country takes over another country, spreads its culture and settles its people there
Colonist	a person who settles in a colony which is under the control of the mother country
Communism	political belief associated with Soviet Russia that the state (or government) should control industry and agriculture
Concentration camps	camps set up by the Nazis in Germany or Communists in the Soviet Union (gulags) to imprison opponents
Confiscation	the taking over of other people's property
Conquest	where people or a country takes control of another people or country by military force
Conquistadors	Spanish conquerors who defeated native empires in Central and South America
Council of Trent	meeting of cardinals, bishops and Pope to reform the Catholic Church after the Reformation, held in northern Italy
Counter-Reformation	efforts by the Catholic Church to reform itself and stop the spread of Protestantism
Crozier	a hooked staff carried by a bishop as a symbol of his office
Crusade	a military expedition sent from Europe in the Middle Ages/medieval times to recover the Holy Lands from Muslim control
Cult of personality	when propaganda is used to glorify a political leader, to create a god-like image of a political leader
Cultural nationalism	a movement to concentrate on the shared culture of a people to create a national identity as in 19th and 20th century Ireland
Cultural revival	effort to revive/recover the lost or fading culture of a people as in 19th century Ireland
Cultural Revolution	a mass movement in China launched by Mao Zedong in the 1960s, which promoted the application of Mao's teachings on communism
Culture	the language, traditions and customs of a people
D-Day	Operation Overlord – the Allied invasion of Normandy in World War II
Decolonisation	Allied invasion of France on Normandy beaches in the Second World War – code-named Operation Overlord
Democracy	political system, which believes that political power comes from the people who vote for leaders in a general election
Diaspora	where people of an ethnic group (e.g. Irish people) are dispersed around the world through emigration
Dictator	a ruler with full power over a country e.g. Hitler and Stalin
Dictatorship	a country being ruled or governed by a dictator
Discrimination	unjust treatment of different people, usually based on race, religion or sex
Dole	the giving of free grain to the poorer classes in Ancient Rome
Domestic system	the making of goods such as thread and cloth in people's houses before the Industrial Revolution
Dominion status	membership of the British Commonwealth agreed by Ireland in the Anglo-Irish Treaty, similar to Canada and Australia
Domus	the type of house occupied by the upper classes (patricians) in Ancient Rome
Dowry	property or money given by a bride to her husband on marriage
Economic change	a change in the structure of the economy or in the way an economy works
EEC	European Economic Community formed in 1958 by six countries based on the Treaty of Rome, for closer economic and political co-operation
Emergency	name given to time in Ireland during the Second World War
Emigration	movement of people from their own country to settle in another country
Empire	a group of countries ruled by another country
Enabling Act	law passed by Hitler, which gave him power to rule by decree
Enlargement	when a country or state grows larger when more countries join the European Union (EU)
Equal pay	workers doing the same work would get the same pay
European Union (EU)	a union of European countries formed in 1993 with the aim of achieving a closer political and economic union between member states of the European Community (EC)
Evacuation	moving people out of where they live, sometimes for safety

Exploration, Age of	the period in 15th and 16th centuries when European countries explored or searched for other countries in the world
Extermination camps	camps organised by the Nazis in Poland during World War II for killing Jews
Famine	a great shortage of food causing starvation
Fascism	political belief of Mussolini in Italy and Hitler in Germany, which was anti-democratic, anti-communist
Fenians	Irish political group formed in mid-19th century, which believed in the use of physical force to achieve Irish independence, also known as IRB
Feudalism	system of land ownership and government during the Middle Ages
Fief	land given by a king to a lord in the Middle Ages (medieval times)
Filigree	fine gold or silver wire formed into patterns in chalices and other objects
Final Solution	Hitler and the Nazis policy during the Second World War of killing all Jews
Flying column	small units of IRA, which ambushed British forces during the War of Independence
Franchise	the vote or suffrage
Fresco	painting style in Ancient Rome and in the Renaissance where painting is done on damp plaster
Fuhrer	(Leader) title of Hitler after he combined the office of President and Chancellor
GAA	Gaelic Athletic Association formed in 1884 to promote Irish games and athletics
Genocide	the deliberate killing of a large group of people, especially those of a particular nation or ethnic group
Gerrymandering	system of rigging the boundaries of constituencies in Northern Ireland to ensure unionist control
Ghetto	a separate area of a city occupied by people of one particular race or religion
Gothic	style of architecture in the Middle Ages with pointed arches and windows
Guerrilla warfare	military action carried out by small groups of irregular soldiers against usually larger regular forces.
Guild	a trade association in the Middle Ages for craftsmen and merchants
Gulags	prison or concentration camps in Soviet Russia (USSR) under Stalin
High Cross	tall stone cross in monasteries in Early Christian Ireland
Holocaust	the systematic slaughter of European Jews by Nazi Germany during World War II
Home Rule	Irish nationalist policy, which wanted self-government in Ireland with a parliament in Dublin dealing with internal Irish affairs
Human rights	rights that belong to all human beings (people), irrespective of race, colour, religion or sex
Humanism	a Renaissance movement that attached great importance to human affairs as distinct from divine or godly affairs and revived interest in Ancient Greece and Rome
Hunger strike	a refusal to eat for a long time as part of a protest
Identity	the characteristics or features that make a person or people who they are
Impact	the effect or influence of a movement, event or person
Industrial Revolution	rapid industrial growth or change that began in England in the middle of the 18th century and brought about the factory system and the growth of cities
Industrialisation	the development of industries in a country or region
Inoculation	giving a weak form of a disease to a person by injection to protect against that disease (vaccination)
Inquisition	Catholic Church court in Italy and Spain used to try Protestants and Jews
Insula	apartment block in Ancient Rome
International relations	the political relations between two or more countries, based on each country's foreign policy
Internment	the arrest and imprisonment without trial of people suspected of being involved in violence in Northern Ireland during the Troubles
Irish Diaspora	Irish people and their descendants who live outside of Ireland
Irish Republican Army (IRA)	armed movement in Ireland in War of Independence

Irish Republican Brotherhood (IRB)	Irish political group formed in mid-19th century, which believed in the use of physical force to achieve Irish independence, also known as Fenians
Justice	the system of laws that judges people or the administration of laws in a country
Justification by faith	Martin Luther's belief in the Reformation that only faith in God would allow a person to go to heaven
Knight	a mounted soldier in armour trained to fight for his king in the Middle Ages (medieval times)
Lebensraum	Nazi policy of living space, to use Eastern Europe and Russia to provide raw materials and workers for the Nazis
Life expectancy	the average age to which a person might live
Log and line	used in ships of the Age of Exploration to work out the speed of the ship
Loyalist	a supporter of the union between Britain and Northern Ireland or a colonist in 18th century America who favoured or remained loyal to Britain
Luftwaffe	German air force during the Second World War
Manor	a village and the land around it in the Middle Ages
Manuscript	a hand-written book
Master Race	Nazi term for pure and superior white race, who aimed to dominate or rule the world
Medieval society	life in the Middle Ages
Medieval times	centuries during the Middle Ages
Middle Ages	centuries between Ancient Rome and the Renaissance
Migration	the movement of people within or between countries
Modernising	changing to modern ideas and ways
Monastery	building occupied by monks in a religious order (common in medieval times)
Museum	a building to hold and display objects (artefacts) of historical interest or value
Nationalism	political belief that the world is divided into nations and that each nation should have its own government
Nationalist	person who believes in nationalism
Neutrality	policy of Irish government during the Second World War not to take part in the war
Night of the Crystal Glass	('Kristallnacht') night when Hitler's SA attacked Jews, their shops and synagogues after a Polish Jew killed a German diplomat in Paris
Night of the Long Knives	night when Hitler used the SS to arrest and kill leaders of the SA, including Rohm, because they threatened his leadership
North-south relations	relations between Northern Ireland and Éire or the Republic of Ireland in the south
Nuclear war	a war fought with atomic and hydrogen (nuclear) bombs
Nuremberg Laws	Nazi laws against the Jews which deprived them of German citizenship, banned marriages with non-Jews and forced them to wear the Star of David
Operation Barbarossa	German battle plan for the invasion of Soviet Russia during the Second World War
Operation Overlord	code-name for Allied plan to invade France during the Second World War – D-Day
Orator	a public speaker who argues a case
Page	first stage in the training of a boy to be a knight in the Middle Ages (medieval times)
Panzer	German tank during the Second World War
Paramilitary	a group organised like an army but not legal, sometimes supporting the official police or army, sometimes opposing
Parliament	elected group of politicians who make laws for a country
Parliamentary tradition	belief in use of peaceful means to achieve political change, and to achieve Irish independence; opposed to physical force tradition
Passive resistance	non-violent or peaceful opposition to government, not co-operating with government, refusal to obey laws; opposed to physical force
Patrician	noble person or upper class in Ancient Rome
Patron	supporter of the artists during the Renaissance
Peasant	small farmer or farm labourer, who rent land to grow crops or keep animals; often poorer class in the countryside

Peel's Brimstone	name given to maize bought by British government to feed people during the Great Famine, called after Prime Minister, Robert Peel
Penal Laws	laws passed in 17th and 18th century Ireland to control/discriminate against Catholics and Presbyterians
Perspective	technique used by artists in the Renaissance to create illusion of depth (3D effect)
Phoney War	name given to time early in World War II where there were no military operations or fighting on the borders between Germany and France
Physical force	armed uprising
Physical force tradition	belief in use of revolution, armed uprising to achieve Irish independence; opposed to parliamentary tradition
Pillory and stocks	timber frames used in medieval times for punishment when people had their heads locked in place
Plantation	policy of English government to bring in English and Scottish planters to Ireland to establish English authority
Plebeian	commoners in Ancient Rome, not of the patrician class
Pogrom	an organised massacre and persecution of an ethnic or religious group, usually applied to attacks on the Jews in Russia and Nazi Germany
Politics	actions and policies that are used to govern a country, to gain and hold power, also on relations between political parties
Propaganda	use of information to influence opinions of people to ensure power
Provisional IRA	paramilitary nationalist movement in Northern Ireland during the Troubles
Proclamation	document read by Patrick Pearse outside the GPO, Dublin on the first day of the 1916 Rising
Public health	the overall health of the population, as protected and improved by the actions of government
Purges	to remove people by lawful or unlawful means from society in order to eliminate opposition
Quadrant	navigation instrument used in the Age of Exploration to find latitude
Racism	belief that race decides a person's character and that some races are superior to others; prejudice against someone of a different race based on these ideas
Radar	a system for detecting aircraft and ships by using radio waves, which are reflected back from the object
Rationing	use of coupons and ration books to control the amount of food, clothes, footwear and petrol given to each person during the Second World War (the Emergency) in Ireland (also in Britain and Germany)
Rearmament	building up a new stock of military weapons; increasing numbers in the armed forces
Reformation	religious movement in 16th century, which led to the formation of the Protestant churches
Remilitarisation	moving army back into a country or section of country which had been disarmed
Renaissance	time of revival of interest in learning of Ancient Greece and Rome, begun in Italy
Repeal	(of Act of Union) bringing parliament (or Irish members of parliament) back from Westminster to Dublin
Republicanism	political belief in Ireland, which wanted complete independence from Britain and to establish a republic (a government without a monarch), by physical force (rebellion)
Revolution	the overthrow of a government by physical force, to create a new system
Rising	an armed rebellion or uprising
Round Tower	tall tower built in monasteries in Early Christian Ireland as a bell tower
Rule by Decree	where rulers such as Hitler can make laws without the need to pass them in parliament
Scorched earth policy	Russian war tactics during the Second World War to burn crops, destroy bridges and towns as they retreated before the Germans
Scribe	a person (often a monk) who copies documents by hand, such as manuscripts
Scriptorium	the manuscript room in a monastery in Early Christian Ireland or in a medieval monastery
Sectarianism	a form of hatred aimed at opposing (usually) religious groups
Separatist tradition	Irish political tradition to separate Ireland from Britain
Serf	A peasant who worked the land for a lord in the Middle Ages
Sfumato	painting technique associated with Leonardo da Vinci which used blended colours

Shortages	when food or other products cannot be obtained
Show trials	public trials of opposition figures in Soviet Russia organised by Stalin
Slave	a person who is owned by another person and has to obey them
Social change	changes in society, in the way people behave or in culture
Socialism	political belief which favours state (government) control of industry and agriculture
Space Race	competition between the USA and the USSR (Soviet Union) to be better at space exploration
Squad	group of IRA volunteers formed by Michael Collins to kill British spies and others during the War of Independence
Squire	a stage after being a page, in the training for knighthood
Stocks	timber frames used in medieval times for punishment when people had their legs locked in place
Stola	a long robe or garment worn by women in Ancient Rome
Suffragette	woman seeking the right to vote
Superpowers	USA and USSR after World War II, which were the two most powerful countries in the world
Swastika	Nazi symbol of crooked cross
Technology	the practical use or application of methods and machines to produce goods and services
The Troubles	a period of violence and unrest in Northern Ireland beginning in 1968 and continuing until the mid-1990s
Tithe	one tenth of the annual crops given to support the clergy in the Catholic Church or the Church of Ireland
Toga	a long robe for men in Ancient Rome
Tonsure	part of monks head, which was shaved bare, a sign of humility
Turning point	a time when a decisive event occurs, which changes the future
U-boat	German submarine in World War I and World War II
Ulster Solemn League and Covenant	declaration of Ulster unionists to resist Home Rule by all means, signed by over 200,000 men
Undertakers	English planters who got land during the Plantation of Munster, or English and Scottish planters who got land during the Plantation of Ulster
Unemployment	being without a job, or the number of people without jobs
Unionism	political belief, which wanted to maintain the union with Britain, so that parliament in Westminster would continue to make laws for Ireland
Unionist	a supporter in Ireland (and later Northern Ireland) of the union between Ireland (and later Northern Ireland) with Britain
USSR	Union of Soviet Socialist Republics or Soviet Union – union of states under control of Russian Communist Party, established after Russian Revolution in 1917 and lasted until its collapse in 1991
Vassal	person who has been granted land (fief) by a lord in the Middle Ages
Vernacular	the language of the people
Villa	a country house or estate in Ancient Rome
Workhouse	used in Ireland (and England) in the 19th century where poorer people had to live if they wanted to get help
Wattle and daub walls	interwoven sticks (wattle) and mud (daub) used to build walls in houses from Stone Age to the Middle Ages

For permission to reproduce artwork, the author and publisher acknowledge the following copyright holders:
© AKG-IMAGES: 70B, 118TR, 118 (timeline 1517), 121; © Alamy: 1TR, 1BL, 1CL, 3A, 3E, 3G, 3J, 3L, 6 (timeline Bronze Age), 7, 9, 10B, 10D, 14, 16TR, 16CR, 16 (timeline Bronze Age), 20BR, 20CR, 20BL, 21BC, 24, 26, 28TL, 28TR, 32, 33CR, 33BR, 34Bl, 37TR, 38 (timeline Bronze Age), 38TR, 38CR, 42C, 42B, 46, 47BC, 47TR, 47BL, 48CL, 51 (timeline 0), 51TR, 63, 66BL, 83T, 84 (timeline 1472), 86CL, 87CL, 87BR, 87CR, 90CL, 92T, 95TR, 96 (Copernicus), 96 (Kepler), 97, 99CL, 103, 104TL, 104BL, 106TR, 106TL, 106 (timeline 1492), 110, 112, 116CR, 116BL, 118TL, 118 (timeline 1545), 119, 120, 123CRB, 125TR, 125TL, 126CL, 126BL, 127, 128BR, 128, 129CL, 130, 131TR, 142TR, 143TCL, 143CL, 143TR, 145, 150 (timeline 1773), 150 (timeline 1781), 155BL, 155TL, 156, 157, 162TR, 163 (timeline 1782, 1800, 163 (timeline 1829), 1848), 163 (timeline 1867), 163 (timeline 1870, 1893), 165, 166, 167, 168, 172CR, 172TR, 172BL, 174TR, 179BR, 180, 181, 182TL, 186TR, 186 (timeline 1846), 186 (timeline 1845), 189, 191T, 191B, 199, 200 (O'Hara), 200 (Hogan), 200T, 200 (Brady), 200 (McEnroe), 200 (Rice), 200 (Dempsey), 200 (O'Keeffe), 202BR, 202CR, 205CR, 206, 208, 209, 217TL, 221T, 228TL, 229, 230 (timeline 1915), 231CR, 231BR, 232, 234CR, 237, 239, 245TR, 251, 255TL, 255 (timeline 1936), 257 (Goebbels), 257 (Himmler), 257CR, 261CR, 262, 263, 266TR, 272TR, 272TL, 272 (timeline 1917), 274CR, 278BC, 280, 282, 284TR, 288BR, 293, 294TL, 294 (timeline 1944), 298BL, 301CR, 302CL, 305TR, 305, 305B, 306, 308, 313TL, 317, 318, 320TR, 320 (timeline 1942), 320 (timeline 1925), 321CL, 322TL, 326B, 327BL, 331TR, 342TR, 342 (timeline 1953), 344BL, 344CR, 345CR, 345 (timeline 1952), 345 (timeline 1961), 346CR, 349, 351BR, 351BC, 354, 358BR, 362C, 366 (Devlin), 366 (O'Sullivan), 366 (Taylor), 369TR, 370 (timeline 1969), 370 (timeline 1963), 372, 373CR, 373CL, 374, 375, 379T, 380CL, 381TR, 381CR, 382, 385, 386, 389BR, 393TL, 397BL, 397BR, 398BR, 403TR, 403 (timeline 1690), 405, 407B, 407T, 409BR, 413B, 417 (both), 426, 431B; © ASSOCIATED PRESS: 342TL, 355; © BARROW/COAKLEY: 139TR, 146, 149; © BPK IMAGES: 265BR; © BRIDGEMAN IMAGES: Duke William Exhorts his Troops to Prepare Themselves Wisely Like Men for the Battle Against the English Army, detail from the Bayeux Tapestry, before 1082 (wool embroidery on linen)/Musée de la Tapisserie, Bayeux, France/With special authorisation of the city of Bayeux/Bridgeman Images 53T, 430T, Duke William and his fleet cross the Channel to Pevensey, detail from the Bayeux Tapestry, before 1082 (wool embroidery on linen) (see 155377 & 323474 for details)/Musée de la Tapisserie, Bayeux, France/Bridgeman Images 53C, Many fall in battle and King Harold is killed, detail from the Bayeux Tapestry, before 1082 (wool embroidery on linen)/Musée de la Tapisserie, Bayeux, France/Bridgeman Images 53B, Ms 6712 (A.6.89) fol.133r King Stephen (c.1097–1154) miniature from 'Flores Historiarum', by Matthew Paris, 1250–52 (vellum), English School, (13th century)/Chetham's Library, Manchester, UK/Bridgeman Images 66BR, Portrait of Hernan Cortes (1485–1547) (oil on canvas), Spanish School (16th century)/Real Academia de Bellas Artes de San Fernando, Madrid, Spain/Index/Bridgeman Images 111, MS 634 ff1v-2 A General View of the Lands Belonging to the City of London, from 'A Survey of the Estate of the Plantation of the County of Londonderry Taken in 1624 by Sir Thomas Phillips' (vellum), English School, (17th century)/Lambeth Palace Library, London, UK/Bridgeman Images 136TL, Men of the South, 1921, Keating, Sean (1889–1977)/Crawford Art Gallery, Cork, Ireland/ Bridgeman Images 230TL, 243, Photo 12/Alamy Stock Photo 290BR, 350, Cartoon depicting the uneasy alliance between Hitler and Stalin, 1939 (colour litho), Marengo, Kimon Evan (KEM) (1904–88)/Private Collection/ Peter Newark Historical Pictures/Bridgeman Images. Also with kind permission of Richard and Alexander Marengo 291CR, CARTOON: COLD WAR BERLIN, 1948. 'How to Close the Gap?' American cartoon on the Russian attempt to drive the Western powers from Berlin by every possible means short of an outright act of war. Cartoon by D.R. Fitzpatrick, 1948./Granger/Bridgeman Images, Getty Images/Getty Images 425B; © CAIN: 142TL; © COURT OF JUSTICE OF THE EUROPEAN UNION: 425T; © EUROPEAN UNION, 1972/SOURCE: EC – AUDIOVISUAL SERVICE: 419TL, 419 (timeline 1973); © FÁILTE IRELAND: 147; © GETTY IMAGES: Central Press/Getty Images 8, 252, VCG Wilson/Bettmann Archive 19, Bettmann/Contributor 20CL, 272 (timeline 1936), 306, 342 (timeline 1948), 347CR, 397TR, DEA/L. PEDICINI/De Agostini/Getty Images 21CL, DeAgostini/ Getty Images 38TL, 38C, 44, BORIS HORVAT/AFP/Getty Images 66CR, Archiv Gerstenberg/ullstein bild via Getty Images 70TL, Fine Art Images/Heritage Images/Getty Images 87BL, 272BR, David Lees/Corbis/VCG via Getty Images 88, Universal History Archive/UIG via Getty images 113, 202 (timeline 1891), 216, 383B, Popperfoto/ Getty Images 115BL, 380TL, Photo12/UIG via Getty Images 129CR, Hulton-Deutsch Collection/CORBIS/Corbis via Getty Images 174TL, 176, Historical Picture Archive/CORBIS/Corbis via Getty Images 179BL, Universal History Archive/Getty Images 183, 196CR, 302CR, Trevor Humphries/Getty Images 200 (Ali), Ann Ronan Pictures/Print Collector/Getty Images 207, Hulton Archive/Getty Images 214TL, 230TR, 234CR, 241TL, 403 (timeline 1912), Hogan/Hulton Archive/Getty Images 217TR, 222BL, Piaras Ó Mídheach/Sportsfile via Getty Images 222BR, Library of Congress/Corbis/VCG via Getty Images 233TR, Heinrich Hoffmann/ullstein bild via Getty Images 269, Keystone/Getty Images 294TR, 298BR, 330TL, 330 (timeline 1941), 332BR, Fox Photos/ Hulton Archive/Getty Images 298CL, Past Pix/SSPL/Getty Images 298CR, Ozerksy/AFP/Getty Images 301BR, Bentley Archive/Popperfoto/Getty Images 311, 398TL, Carl Mydans/The LIFE Picture Collection/Getty Images 313CR, Anne Frank Fonds – Basel via Getty Images 326TL, Keystone/Hulton Archive/Getty Images 330 (timeline